SHI'ITE LEBANON

HISTORY AND SOCIETY OF THE MODERN MIDDLE EAST

HISTORY AND SOCIETY OF THE MODERN MIDDLE EAST
Leila Fawaz, general editor

Janet Afary
The Iranian Constitutional Revolution, 1906–1911: Grassroots Democracy, Social Democracy, and the Origins of Feminism

Irene L. Gendzier
Notes from the Minefield: United States Intervention in Lebanon and the Middle East, 1945–1958

Andrea B. Rugh
Within the Circle: Parents and Children in an Arab Village

Juan R. I. Cole
Modernity and the Millennium: The Genesis of the Baha'i Faith in the Nineteenth Century

Selma Botman
Engendering Citizenship in Egypt

Elizabeth Thompson
Colonial Citizens: Republican Rights, Paternal Privilege, and Gender in French Syria and Lebanon

Thomas Philipp
Acre: The Rise and Fall of a Palestinian City, 1730–1831

Leila Fawaz and C. A. Bayly
Modernity and Culture: From the Mediterranean to the Indian Ocean

Samir Khalaf
Civil and Uncivil Violence in Lebanon: A History of the Internationalization of Communal Conflict

SHIʻITE LEBANON

*Transnational Religion and the
Making of National Identities*

ROSCHANACK
SHAERY-EISENLOHR

Columbia University Press 〰 *New York*

Columbia University Press
Publishers Since 1893

New York Chichester, West Sussex
Copyright © 2008 Columbia University Press
Paperback edition, 2011

Library of Congress Cataloging-in-Publication Data

Shaery-Eisenlohr, Roschanack.
  Transnational religion and the making of national identities / Roschanack
Shaery-Eisenlohr.
      p. cm.
  Includes bibliographical references and index.
  ISBN 978-0-231-14426-1 (cloth : alk. paper)—ISBN 978-0-231-14427-8 (pbk. : alk.
paper)—ISBN 978-0-231-51313-5 (e-book)
  1. Shi'iah—Lebanon. 2. Shiites—Lebanon—Political activity. 3. Lebanon—Poli-
tics and government—1990– 4. Lebanon—Ethnic relations. I. Title.

  DS80.55.S54S43 2008
  305.6′9782095692—dc22

                                                        2007048438

Printed in the United States of America

c 10 9 8 7 6 5 4 3 2 1
p 10 9 8 7 6 5 4 3 2 1

To my father

Kare ma shayad inast
Ke miyane gole nilufar o qarn
Peye avaze haqiqat bedavim.

—*Sohrab Sepehri*

Contents

CONTENTS

PREFACE

Since the fall of Saddam Husayn in 2003, many have commented on what they see as a rise of Shi'ite power in the Middle East, and some have even speculated about the formation of a putative Shi'ite crescent in the region. This book throws light on a multiplicity of voices, centers, and authorities in the Twelver Shi'ite world by focusing on modern Lebanese Shi'ites in the context of their transnational ties to Iran. It examines the background of the current political crisis in Lebanon, while offering lessons that could provide a different analytical perspective on recent official Iranian activities in Iraq.

I analyze the ideologies, sociopolitical activities, theological-legal doctrinal debates, and popular activities of Lebanese Shi'ites and argue that they are engaged in claiming and reshaping Lebanon by positioning themselves at the center of this nation. This approach implies a break with previously hegemonic images of Lebanon in which Shi'ites have traditionally played only a very marginal role. I show how there is neither a singular conception of what it means to be a Shi'ite in Lebanon nor a singular vision of a Shi'ite Lebanon. Constructions of Shi'ite identity within Lebanon are fluid and contentious and do not constitute a single, united project of creating a Shi'ite-dominated Lebanon with the support of the Iranian government. Using both historical and ethnographic methods, I situate the logic of these ideologies and activities in broader national and transnational contexts since the

1960s—in decades of sociopolitical turbulence both in Lebanon and in the Shi'ite world.

I outline various kinds of Shi'ite-centered Lebanese nationalism by presenting moments of tension that emerge in political and religious debates and in the production of historical memory. In the Lebanese context, nationalism is a necessary practice because engaging in it is a precondition for making claims on citizenship and political power. My use of the term *nationalism* therefore takes into account both analytical and practical dimensions. It is when Lebanese Shi'ites face the other—other Lebanese Shi'ites, Iranian Shi'ites, non-Shi'ite Lebanese—that their vision of themselves and their community is most visible. My approach emphasizes practice and process, as these visions stand in a dialectical relation to each other, which sometimes includes derivative elements.

This nationalism can neither be attributed only to the activism of Shi'ite religious and political leaders—found in the study of elite ideologies, in other words—nor is it formed in isolation from the transnational context or removed from the activities of mid ranking religious scholars, officials, and politicians. While I acknowledge the importance of intellectual history, I view identity production as a more broadly based activity that is grounded in multiple sites. Although this study introduces the ideologies of Lebanese Shi'ite leaders, my main goal is to shift the focus of studies of Lebanon from the ideologies of elites to how nationalism is produced in institutionalized activities and through debates and comments on everyday life among a larger constituency. For example, the debate over which religious textbooks to use in Lebanese Shi'ite-run schools tells us as much about the competing nationalisms of various non-Shi'ite and Shi'ite officials and elite representatives in Lebanon as about how a broader range of Lebanese Shi'ites produce their sense of being Lebanese in a transnational context.

Lebanese Shi'ites, just like Iranian Shi'ites, belong to the Twelver Shi'ite tradition. The so-called Twelvers (*ithna 'ashari*), like other Shi'ite sects, believe that 'Ali was the rightful successor to the leadership of the community of believers after the death of the Prophet Muhammad. But what makes the Twelvers distinct from others is the belief that there were a total of twelve Imams, all descendants of 'Ali and his wife, Fatimah (the daughter of the Prophet), each designated by the previous one, and that the last Imam, the young Imam al-Mahdi, went into occultation and will reappear shortly before Judgment Day. Until the day he reappears, the Shi'ite community will be in need of guidance. The latter point is especially significant because the debate over who should guide them and how is also a key reason for the tensions between various Lebanese Shi'ite groups and the current Iranian government.

Accounts vary on the origins and spread of Twelver Shi'ism to the region known historically as Jabal 'Amil—a major part of this geographic-cultural entity indexing Shi'ite high culture is now South Lebanon, one of the five provinces of modern Lebanon, where a large number of Lebanese Shi'ites live. Yemeni tribes with Shi'ite leanings had settled in Jabal 'Amil before the tenth century and by the time Fatimid rule (969–1174) was extended to Jabal 'Amil, there were already Shi'ite tendencies among the local population. Jabal 'Amil became the principal center of Shi'ite theological and legal learning between the fourteenth and early sixteenth centuries.[1] During Ottoman rule (1516–1918), it was first part of the *vilayet* of Damascus until 1863, and a regional backwater. Through Ottoman administrative reorganization, Jabal 'Amil then became part of the *vilayet* of Beirut in 1864, but remained marginal and in the shadow of Beirut's growing importance. After the collapse of the Ottoman empire in 1918, and the brief period of Faysal's Arab government in Damascus (1918–1920), the French mandate (1920–1943) established control over Syria. Despite some internal and external opposition, such as the Shi'ite elites' equivocal stance toward the mandate's agenda, the Lebanese state was created in September 1920 and was justified in terms of providing a refuge for a minority Christian community, the Maronites, in the Muslim-dominated Arab Middle East. As Greater Lebanon was being created, parts of Jabal 'Amil were annexed to this new entity, which came to be known as South Lebanon. A large number of Shi'ites also lived in the al-Biqa', which was annexed in 1920 as well. A small number have also lived in Kisrawan, north of Beirut. Through the French mandate's official recognition of the Shi'ites as a religious community (*ta' ifa*) in January 1926 and the subsequent creation of some specific Shi'ite institutions, and finally through the colonial census of 1932, the majority of Shi'ites became legal citizens of the new Lebanese state, although they were often seen by others as somewhat extraneous to Lebanon and lacking the sort of full recognition one might call cultural citizenship. Maronites thus became the initial political and cultural producers of Lebanon, positioning other religious sects, especially the Shi'ites, both structurally and symbolically on the margins. There are eighteen registered religious groups in Lebanon, and among the most important religious communities are the Maronites, Sunnis, Shi'ites, and Druze.

The 1943 National Pact, an unwritten agreement between the Christian and Sunni political elite over the political identity of Lebanon, took as its premise a power sharing among all sects. This resulted in the creation of a political structure referred to as political sectarianism (*al-ta'ifiyya al-siyasi-yya*), according to which the supposedly largest religious sect controls the most important position in the state. According to the 1932 colonial census, the last official census taken in Lebanon, the largest religious group was the Maronites. In accordance with this arrangement, the president of the country is a Maronite Christian, the prime minister a Sunni Muslim, and the Speaker of the parliament a Shiʻite Muslim. This arrangement, in fact, created a consociational democracy, in which a simple majority cannot force any decisions. Cabinet posts and positions in the public service were also to be distributed proportionally among all sects. As Article 95 of the 1943 Constitution states, "In keeping with the desire of justice and harmony, the religious communities shall be adequately represented in the civil service and in the cabinet, provided that this does not harm the interests of the state."[2] It is estimated that Twelver Shiʻites comprise about 40 percent of the Lebanese population of about four million. According to Article 95, their sheer numbers should guarantee Shiʻites more powerful political positions as well as seats in the parliament, cabinet, and in the civil service.

Article 9 in the Lebanese Constitution states that all personal status affairs, such as registration of birth, marriage, and divorce, are to be determined by the sectarian communities themselves, according to their religious laws and traditions. Thus, citizenship in Lebanon became mediated through religious identity and membership in a community. Even though this provision appears to remove religious concerns from the business of the state, the purpose of the National Pact and of the discourse of coexistence, defined in terms of a fair distribution of resources and concerned with political power sharing, brought religion to the center of public and political life in Lebanon. Religion thus came to be positioned as the only truly effective discourse to express grievances and resistance to marginalization. Questions such as which community gets how many positions in the cabinet or in the civil service, and how symbolically and materially prestigious these positions are, shape political struggle in Lebanon and are at the center of debates over coexistence, and even over the nature of Christianity and Islam.

These arrangements have to this day shaped nationalist discourses in Lebanon. As I argue throughout this book, competing Shiʻite-centered nationalisms and the boundary making that Lebanese Shiʻites are engaged in vis-à-vis official Iran take the shape of claims to religious authenticity and of debates over normative interpretations of Shiʿism. Doctrinal debates are, therefore, simultaneously debates over Lebanon's identity and its national character. Thus, seemingly internal legal-theological debates within communities are, in fact, very much of concern for a Lebanese national public.

Nationalism altered how many Shiʿites thought of themselves, changing them eventually from Ottoman subjects to members of a larger Arab nation in Syria, and finally to citizens of a new Lebanese nation with overlapping commitments. But activists created a Lebanese Shiʿite-centered national narrative by producing memories of centuries of oppression and interweaving them with specific Shiʿite interpretations of history and conditions in Lebanon. The image of the disadvantaged (*mahrum*) Lebanese Shiʿite thus does not refer solely to their experience with Maronite (and now Sunni) Lebanon but carries with it, according to this national narrative, the memory of centuries of oppression for which Lebanese Shiʿites now seek justice.

After Lebanon's independence in 1943 and up to the arrival of the Iranian-born Shiʿite leader Musa Sadr (born 1928; disappeared August 1978) in Lebanon in 1959, Shiʿite interaction with the Maronite-dominated Lebanese state and nation was mediated mainly through their feudal leaders, the *zuʿama*. However, the many rural and lower-class Shiʿites (but also some ex-students of religion trained in Najaf) were drawn to secular and leftist parties who opposed both the Maronite state as well as the Shiʿite feudal lords. In fact, even in the 1970s, numerically at least, Shiʿites dominated in the Lebanese Communist Party.

The arrival of Sadr did not only, as has often been remarked, politicize Shiʿites along communal lines. Nor can his efforts to create separate Shiʿite institutions solely explain his success. As I show in chapter 1, Sadr was able to create a new discourse of Lebanese Shiʿite identity—one centered on piety and coexistence—the logic of which engaged and partially transformed the image of Lebanon as a nation. This engagement went hand in hand with the communal mobilization Sadr is mainly known for and which set him apart from other older Shiʿite activists. In chapter 2 we see how various Shiʿite groups compete in proving their piety as it consequently expresses also their loyalty to Lebanon.

Sadr also maintained close ties to various Iranians, both to Iranian state representatives and to those opposing the Pahlavi state. As we see in chapter 3, the Iranian-Lebanese Shiʿite network that helped create the Lebanese Shiʿite party of Hizbullah in 1982 did *not* consist of those who maintained close ties to Sadr—in fact, they were his enemies. Nonetheless, the prerevolutionary personal animosity and ideological differences between Sadr and those Iranians who helped create Hizbullah a few years after his disappearance in Libya provided them with the motivation and ideological justification to establish themselves as a rival party to Amal, the first Lebanese Shi'ite militia created by Sadr in 1974. It is also in these prerevolutionary years, characterized by disagreements between Sadr's followers and pro-Khomeini followers, that the Palestinian cause became closely intertwined with a Shi'ite discourse of piety.

This study focuses to a large degree on how the two most dominant parties, Amal and Hizbullah, as well as the prominent religious scholar Sayyid Muhammad Husayn Fadlallah, have built a Lebanese Shi'ite identity in the context of their intensifying ties with Iran and in light of their competition in the Lebanese national arena. I do not wish to imply that Lebanese Shi'ites are fundamentally Iran-oriented. As much as the Iranian ruling religious elite works toward this vision, transnationalism nevertheless becomes entwined with local political and cultural contexts. I argue that such views of Shi'ites as Iran-oriented, or labels like the Lebanonization of Hizbullah, dovetail in fact with strategies of accusation of anti-Hizbullah and anti-Shi'ite groups to marginalize Lebanese Shi'ites. While at one level the term *Lebanonization* refers to Hizbullah's participation in 1992 parliamentary elections, the word used in other contexts takes as its starting point a rather fixed and inflexible notion of Lebanese nationalism to which Hizbullah has to adapt. However, far from submitting to this historically Maronite-dominated national narrative, Shi'ites are engaged in producing competing visions of Lebanon.

The Iranian revolution altered Lebanese Shi'ite identity politics and forced Shi'ites to experiment with new modes of political mobilization and identification. This event also accounts for the relative importance of Iranian-Lebanese Shi'ite ties, instead of, for example, Iraqi-Lebanese Shi'ite relations, to an understanding of Lebanese Shi'ite identity politics since the 1960s. While Iraqi Shi'ite political activism, from communism to Islamism, intellectually inspired many Lebanese Shi'ite students and scholars, the power relations and the political context of this encounter were rather different from postrevolutionary Iranian-Lebanese Shi'ite relations. Lebanese Shi'ites identified with Iraqi Shi'ites at different points as citizens opposed to official state ideologies and sometimes as fellow oppressed Shi'ites in a state that excluded them and against whom they considered political resistance necessary. The Iranian government, on the other hand, is a relatively powerful Shiʻite state with hegemonic interests in Lebanon.

Throughout this book, I often refer to the network of Iranian-Lebanese Shiʻites as transnational. By *transnationalism* I mean an increasing interconnectedness in human relations across national borders. This includes extra-diplomatic relations, ties that are established through individuals, religious establishments (*marjaʻiyya*), NGOs, cultural centers, or student exchanges. These transnational networks are by no means egalitarian, nor do they reproduce themselves simply because those involved share a specific history and common religious tradition. In fact, as is discussed in chapter 4, the very debates about its history, character, and the hierarchical order imagined by Iranian and Lebanese Shiʻites are part of the dimensions of Lebanese Shiʻite competition over claims to being culturally and therefore truly Lebanese. To provide an alternative narrative in which Iran is centrally placed in a Shiʻite world, the Iranian religious elite has used not just diplomatic means or its *marjaʻ* network. As chapter 5 shows, Iranian cultural politics in Lebanon—so far never taken into consideration by other scholars—has provided much of the ideological justification for the Iranian government's involvement in Lebanese Shiʻite affairs.

This book is organized in a thematic rather than a strict chronological order, as I have not aimed to give a comprehensive sociopolitical history of the Lebanese Shiʻite community since the 1960s. In Part I the emphasis is on Lebanese local struggles over the nation and the creation of Shiʻite nationalism as a modular form of Maronite nationalism. It shows the creation of a discourse linking piety to cultural citizenship among Shiʻites. This section is a study of nationalism through ideologies, popular culture, and institutions. It covers the period from 1959 to the present. In Part II, I discuss the transnational dimensions of Lebanese Shiʻite nationalism. Chapter 3 begins with events in 1970 and provides analysis of the history of the formation of yet another central discourse linking Shiʻite piety to the Palestinian cause. Chapter 4 discusses a variety of Lebanese Shiʻite productions of piety in light of their ties to Iran. It covers debates since the early 1980s. Chapter 5 presents Iranian cultural politics in Lebanon starting in the early 1990s and shows how official Iranian institutions support Lebanese Shiʻites in their piety project and ultimately in their reshaping of Lebanon, while at the same time presenting themselves as the most pious Shiʻites. Finally, in the epilogue I offer my interpretation of current Shiʻite politics and events in Lebanon.

Acknowledgments

I would like to thank the following foundations and institutions for supporting my project throughout the process of researching and writing this book: The University of Chicago Council for Advanced Studies in Peace and International Cooperation (CASPIC) awarded me a summer research travel grant, which enabled me to conduct preliminary research in Lebanon in the summer of 2000, and further supported me with a MacArthur Scholars Fellowship in 2001–2002. The Social Science Research Council Program on Global Security and Cooperation provided me with a generous two-year fellowship during field research. I also thank Professor Manfred Kropp at the German Orient Institute in Beirut, where I was a resident scholar during my research, for providing all the facilities I needed to conduct my research.

Parts of chapter 3 appeared in earlier versions in "Post-Revolutionary Iran and Shi'i Lebanon: Contested Histories of Shi'i Transnationalism," *International Journal of Middle East Studies* 39(2): 271–89. Part of chapter 4 appeared in an earlier version in "Imagining Shi'ite Iran: Transnationalism and Religious Authenticity in the Muslim World," *Iranian Studies* 40(1): 17–35, and a small section of chapter 5 appeared in "Iran, the Vatican of Shi'ism?" *Middle East Report* (Winter 2004): 40–43.

My thanks also go to my former advisers, Rashid Khalidi, Rula Jurdi-Abisaab, and Holly Shissler, for their continuous support of my work. Thanks to Nadia Abu el-Haj and Lisa Wedeen for discussing this project in its earlier stages. In addition, I would like to thank Stefan Rosiny for support at the beginning of my research and for generously sharing information and contacts in Lebanon.

In Lebanon I am grateful to the staff at the American University of Beirut for assisting me during library research. Among many persons I came to know in Lebanon, my thanks also to the following who helped at various stages of the research in Lebanon: Ibrahim Shamseddine, Abu Jafar, Haj Faysal, 'Ali Hamdan, Ibrahim Mousawi, Amal Rida, 'Abbas Qabalan, Bernhard Hillekamp, and Katharina Nötzold. Special thanks also to Shaykh Hani Fahs for patiently discussing in many sessions various aspects of Iranian-Lebanese relations. I am also indebted to the Iranian Cultural Center in Beirut, especially Sayyid Hashemi, the Iranian cultural attaché to Lebanon, and his staff.

I am also grateful to several members of the al-Sadr and Charafeddine families: Husayn Charafeddine, Rababa Sadr, and Ra'id Charafeddine discussed with me many aspects of Lebanese Shi'ite life and generously shared documents and contacts. Louay and Farideh opened their house to me, fed me, and provided so much insight both on Iran and on Lebanon. Farideh's love for Iran and Shi'ism was addictive. Their children, Laily and Lina, were always a source of joy.

Special thanks go to my friend Raya Fahs. Her enthusiasm and sense of humor made field research a pleasant experience. I am also grateful for the friendship she and her husband, Muhammad 'Ubayd, offered me. Their daughters, Adan and Dima, entertained us often throughout our discussions and even learned some Persian words to cheer me up. To both of them, *Khoda Bashar*!

Many friends have been supportive throughout graduate school at Chicago: Fred Donner cheered me up with his optimism and was ready to talk to me whenever I needed to. Michael Nijhawan was always ready to listen, and Rochdi Younsi's pragmatism and support saved me days of "unhealthy" worries. My cousin Mohammad Eskandari helped me collect research material in Iran and discussed current political trends there. Kaveh Ehsani and Laurie King-Irani each in their own way listened, encouraged me, and gave much needed advice. And thanks again to Rula Jurdi-Abisaab for patiently writing me long e-mails replying to the stream of questions, ideas, and worries, and for the encouragement to think in so many new ways. I could not have asked for a better friend during this time. Thanks also to Malek Abisaab,

Toufoul Abouhodeib, Akram Khater, Laleh Khalili, and Nadia Sbeiti for each reading earlier versions of a chapter of this book.

At Washington University I would like to thank my friends and colleagues, especially Fatemeh Keshavarz, Ahmet Karamustafa, and Nargis Virani, for their hospitality and readiness to help where they could. Thanks also to Lois Beck, John Bowen, and Jim Wertsch for their suggestions and support at various stages of this project. Many thanks also to Summer Oakes, a former graduate student at Washington University, for reading the entire manuscript with an eye on making the book more accessible to an educated, nonspecialist audience.

I thank my family for never letting me down. My father has insisted, above all, on teaching me the idea of *rahe haq* in whatever I do. My mother came to visit in Lebanon and managed to be proud of me, despite what others around her said about my weird ambitions. My younger sister Yasmin and I have discovered a whole world together through our daily phone conversations. As some Lebanese might say in English, I like her too much. Each of them came to the United States and stayed with us for extended period of times and took care of our daughters, Shirin and Leyli. My older sister Kati made sure I always had enough Persian goodies at home and at least three e-mails a day from Tehran. In its own way, this book is a product of transnational Shi'ite solidarity between Lebanon, Iran, Germany, and the United States. Through this network, pistachios, sweets, rice cookers, books, and ideas about proper family ties and gender roles made their way from Beirut to Tehran to Heidelberg, and finally to St. Louis. At the end of the day, we all agreed that my father can best take care of my daughters and brew tea while I should focus on writing.

Last but not least, I thank my husband, Patrick. He has been a true companion ever since we first met in Heidelberg. Patrick has read many drafts of this book and has ended up being an expert on Shi'ites himself. His love for Lebanon helped me at times to take a step back and become more optimistic about the situation there. He accompanied me to my very first interview meeting in al-Dahiyya on a hot August day in 2000, and in the past two years has spent many Sundays in the zoo with our two daughters so that this book could be completed.

Finally, it is important to note that I alone am responsible for the ideas in this book, as well as any mistakes therein.

NOTE ON TRANSLITERATION

Arabic and Persian words have been transliterated using a simplified version of the system used in the *International Journal of Middle East Studies* (IJMES). All diacritical marks have been omitted, except the 'ayn (') and the hamza ('). I have not changed the transliterations of Persian and Lebanese last names, which are commonly transliterated in either English or French (e.g., Charafeddine instead of Sharaf al-Din, Chamoun instead of Sham'un, and Khomeini instead of Khumayni). In chapter 4, in a section devoted to linguistic performance, ethnographic material is discussed. I have not followed literary transcription conventions but have emphasized a distinction between short *a*, long, backed *A*, short *e*, and long *E*, as it is relevant to the discussion in this section on verbal performance. All Arabic and Persian translations are mine unless otherwise noted.

INTRODUCTION

CLAIMING CULTURAL CITIZENSHIP IN LEBANON,
FROM MARGIN TO CENTER

The citizens of Nabatiyya, a town in South Lebanon with a majority of Shi'ite inhabitants, believe that the Independence Day celebrations of Lebanon, which take place every year on the 22nd of November, are incomplete without honoring the name of Muhammad Bey Fadl, a Shi'ite leader whose family is from Nabatiyya. He was a co-designer of the new Lebanese flag after independence. Fadl's son Ahmad has asked the country's leaders to add Fadl's name to a list of honorees, but so far in vain. Adham Jaber, a Shi'ite and the mayor of Nabatiyya, wonders how "the Lebanese government, since its Independence, has honored independence figures and heroes without considering this city, even for a moment."[1]

An article written in 2004 in the Lebanese *Daily Star* maintained that "sectarianism is eroding Lebanon's identity."[2] The author of the article explained that a minister had granted permission to some public schools to close on Fridays and Sundays instead of the official weekly holidays of Saturday and Sunday. He then argued that, while this decision may not seem important compared with the constitutional amendment extending Emile Lahoud's presidency, it is "a dangerous reflection of the direction our country is taking toward a bigger control of the sectarian over the national." He then describes Lebanon as a parliamentary republic with a centralized, multireligious, and multiparty government, where all religious groups have recognized the power of the

Lebanese constitution, which "guarantees equality in rights and duties." The exception to this rule, the article's author goes on, is that each religious community in Lebanon has a separate personal status court system which accommodates the various religious customs. Yet, in his view, "in all other areas of life there is a full separation of state and religion." Thus, the decision of the minister should be immediately reversed, as it erodes national unity and so "religious interference in civil affairs should be kept at bay."

The article refers to the long-standing struggle of various Lebanese Muslim activists to change the official weekly holiday from Sunday to Friday, because the Sunday holiday is a sign of Christian dominance that places Lebanon at odds with other Arab countries where Friday is the official holiday. In fact, some private Muslim institutions in Lebanon are closed on Fridays as well as on Sundays. Yet, this author, like many other Lebanese as well as some scholars of Lebanon, views such signs of Christian hegemony in Lebanon as part of a natural, civil, and secular order, not as a form of dominance, while any activity directed against this dominance is viewed as sectarianism, which harms national unity.

In this book I show how certain social, political, and religious activities of Lebanese Muslim Shi'ites since the 1960s, though often viewed as promoting so-called sectarianism, are not antagonistic to the discourse of Lebanese nationalism. Far from posing an opposition to the nation, Shi'ite activities have centered on a set of practices and ideologies that seek to break the hegemony of Christian (mainly Maronite) narratives of Lebanon as a nation,[3] to place the historically marginalized Shi'ites in the center of Lebanese national politics and self-imagining, and to change sectarian power relations, granting Shi'ites a more prominent position. These alternative visions of nationhood portray Shi'ites as ideal Lebanese competing for political influence and representation. In this context, transnational Shi'ite relations between Iran and Lebanon have helped articulate new Shi'ite-centered Lebanese national narratives.

My goal in this book is to answer the following questions: Since Shi'ite confessional affiliation in Lebanon serves both as a marker of membership in a transnational network and as an important delineator of group identity and interests within the framework of the nation-state, how is Lebanese Shi'ite nationalism produced in a transnational era? In other words, who produces it? Where is it produced? How is it disseminated and popularized? And, finally, what is the role of transnational ties to Iran, as a major center of Shi'ism, in the production of this nationalism?

By asking these questions, I wish to address two main concerns in modern Middle Eastern studies in light of the growing importance of religion and of globalization in the area. First, I intend to contribute to the study of nationalism in the Middle East. I analyze the nexus of religion and nationalism, showing how religion is in fact an integral part of national imaginations. Shi'ite activism in Lebanon since the 1960s cannot be explained as only instrumentally motivated by a desire for more access to economic and political resources. It needs also to be framed as part of the production of a specific nationalism in which Lebanese Shi'ites break with the dominant national narrative of Maronite Lebanon, with which most of them do not identify, and aim to establish a national narrative dominated by Lebanese Shi'ite visions of morality, themes, and symbolism.

Second, I use my study to throw light on the link between national identity production and transnationalism, especially with regard to Muslim identities in an increasingly globalized world. I do so by arguing that transnationalism always operates locally and that transnational solidarities, as well as boundary making along national lines, both need be studied in their national contexts. It is important to understand the meanings which Lebanese Shi'ites attribute to these twin processes, and how they are deployed in Lebanese politics, a field of competition with others over leadership positions. In fact, as I show, transnational ties can help the production of nationalism and appeals to transnational solidarities are often rooted in nationalist agendas.

Much attention has been paid to Hizbullah's ties to the Iranian religious establishment and government and the consequences of their politics in the Lebanese context, while often ignoring how the two other dominant Shi'ite forces in Lebanon after the civil war, the party of Amal and the prominent and influential Lebanese religious scholar Sayyid Muhammad Husayn Fadlallah, position themselves in a transnational field. This study describes the production of three distinct Shi'ite Lebanese nationalisms backed by Amal, Hizbullah, and Fadlallah in light of their different relationships with the Iranian government. Their nationalism is to a large degree a product of competition among them. As such, their national visions and the logic of their actions come to life when contextualized against a background of this competition. Studying the social and political life of these groups in isolation from each other offers a rather incomplete picture of their identity politics. Each of these Shi'ite visions of the Lebanese nation has different consequences for Lebanese national politics and for the everyday life of Lebanese citizens.

My analysis of Shiʻite politics in Lebanon engages scholarly debates on religion, nationalism, and transnationalism. In Western scholarship on nationalism, the rise of national identifications is often treated as part of the major cultural transformations that have accompanied a process of modernization. For Benedict Anderson and Ernest Gellner, arguably among the most influential scholars on nationalism in the Western world, the development of nationalism is intimately bound up with the transition to a new form of economic organization: the rise of capitalism, especially print capitalism in Anderson's model or industrial civilization in Gellner's approach.[4] For both authors, nationalism as a new form of large-scale identity construction supplants earlier forms of community, transcending face-to-face interaction. The assumption that modernization implies a trend toward secularization is crucial to both Gellner's and Anderson's approaches to nationalism. Anderson makes it clear that he views the new communities of nationalism as replacing waning religious identifications. Both he and Gellner subscribe to the influential account of modernization formulated by Max Weber, according to which the transition to modernity is tied to an overall weakening of the relevance of religion in social life. Other scholars of European nationalism, such as Linda Colley,[5] have argued that the rise of modernity did not necessarily remove religious identifications and discourse from national public spheres and from popular understandings of nationhood. Assigning religious discourses and identifications an even more prominent role in nationalism, Peter van der Veer argues, in his study of nationalism in India,[6] against the idea that nationalism is fundamentally distinct from the formation of religious communities. Van der Veer and Hartmut Lehmann criticize the idea that nations succeed weakened religious forms of community in a transition to modernity and that religion as a political force of community is only relevant in the "backward non-West." Along with Colley, they argue instead that religious thinking and nationalism were eminently compatible in nineteenth-century Europe and elsewhere.[7]

In the Lebanese context, however, scant attention has been devoted to how much religion may be an integral part of national ideology and how religious networks may function partly as mediators of such religiously imagined nationalism.[8] When I refer to religion throughout the book, I draw on Talal Asad's description of it as a set of discursive practices and activities concerned with ultimate truth.[9] From an analytical perspective, Muslim assertions to be authentic in terms of their religious tradition, whether this is voiced as a claim to be traditional or modern or both, need to be historicized and contextualized and cannot be neatly separated from national ideologies. In the context of Lebanese political traditions, visions of the Lebanese nation have often taken the shape of a nationalism highlighting religious belonging. In fact, belonging to a religious community is the only legitimate way of being part of the Lebanese nation.

By interpreting Shi'ite activism as producing religious nationalism, I do not mean that religious nationalism is automatically concerned with the rule of God and with denying popular sovereignty. In my view, it is a way of defining a national public sphere that is in accordance with Shi'ite iconography without necessarily changing the fundamental concepts of territorial integrity and popular sovereignty. Emphasizing a specific reading of history in which Jabal 'Amil (present-day South Lebanon), associated with Shi'ite learning and culture, plays a central role, along with visions of communal and class relations through Shi'ite themes such as images from the battle of Karbala (where the third Shi'ite Imam Husayn was martyred in 680 AD), aims at creating an imagined national community more amenable to Shi'ite concerns and interests.

Much of the scholarship on Lebanon instead follows older paradigms of nationalism studies in which national belonging is conceived as founded on secular values only. Amal Saad-Ghorayeb, for example, suggests that Hizbullah's integration into Lebanese social and political life will be possible once its "political program will be an essentially secular one that will closely correspond to the agendas of leftist and nationalist political forces."[10] Her conclusion is that "judging by the continued subordination of its domestic political role to its geostrategic concerns, it seems as though Hizbullah has evidently chosen to accord its Lebanese identity and role as an influential local political force secondary status to its Islamic identity and role as a revolutionary exemplar for the *umma*."[11]

I recognize the close relationship between the advent of the modern nation-state and the rise of the secular as a hallmark of modernity, which has at the same time created the modern category of religion presupposed by scholarship and liberal political theory as a separate sphere of life distinct from politics, economy, and law.[12] However, I stress that the boundary between the presumably secular nation and religion is often leaking. Even though the modern nation replaces the God-given sovereignty of the dynastic ruler with the exclusive sovereignty of a people over a clearly demarcated territory, it is true that religious language, identifications, and imagery often play a prominent role in how the imagined community of the nation is fashioned and delimited. Nevertheless, studies of Lebanon continue to be informed by a normative dichotomy, in which identification with the nation and religious belonging are at odds with each other. According to this dominant perspective, public expression of religion (often referred to as sectarianism) is imagined as an antithetical force to the nation. In contrast, I treat calls for both secular nationhood and accusations of sectarianism as categories of political practice and as strategies of domination, and argue that nationalism can combine themes described as secular and religious.

Shi'ite Ethnic Entrepreneurs

Shi'ite ethnic entrepreneurs are the main actors at this intersection of the national, the transnational, and the religious. I have taken over the term *ethnic entrepreneurs* from the anthropologist Fredrik Barth,[13] who refers to those people who lead projects that help construct differences to others, be they based on language, race, or religion. Those projects help establish boundaries and consequently create a sense of community. In his context, ethnic does not at all mean one's racial or ethnic identity in a primordial sense, except as it highlights the malleability and shifting quality of whatever counts as an ethnic boundary.

I refer to Lebanese Shi'ite religious and political activists, regardless of their rank and position, whose goal is to break a Christian ideological hegemony over the Lebanese nation, as ethnic entrepreneurs. They seek not only to establish the previously marginalized Shi'ites as part of the Lebanese nation but to claim their central position in it. These activists can be high-ranking religious leaders such as Fadlallah or public intellectuals such as Sayyid Hani Fahs. They may also include less distinguished members of the two Shi'ite political parties, principals and teachers of Shi'ite-run schools, or employees of Shi'ite-run NGOs or cultural centers. In this particular context, the distinction between religious and political, however, is inadequate for explaining the political activities of the *'ulama* or those of nonclerical but religiously inspired political actors. Taking traditional theological and legal studies as a basis for distinguishing between the *'ulama* and other members of society may help address, for example, changes in the nature of religious authority embodied in the shift from an exclusive *'ulama* domination of religious discourse to a more contested and diverse formation of such authority in more recent times. However, this distinction does not do justice to the complex and interdependent activities of Lebanese Shi'ites since the 1960s, nor to how these persons themselves often envision the relationship between religion and politics.

Understanding these persons as Shi'ite ethnic entrepreneurs, whose activities comprise those of the *'ulama* and nonclerics while sharing a self-identification as Lebanese Shi'ites with a mission to change their disadvantaged condition, is more appropriate for an analysis of contemporary Lebanese Shi'ite politics. In present-day Lebanon, the *'ulama* are not the sole decision makers over religious identities, while laypersons also do not have a monopoly over political identities. The blurring of the established religion-politics divide also shows that Lebanese Shi'ite nationalism is a process shaped by a range of actors other than *'ulama* personalities with transnational ties.

In this context it is also important to clarify another issue raised in discussions of the religious identities and motivations of actors in a politics of nationhood. The search for the true inner motives and orientations of Shi'ite ethnic entrepreneurs often becomes an important theme in discourses doubting the supposedly true religiosity or inner piety of religiously motivated participants in Shi'ite politics, suspecting them of a strategic use of Shi'ite symbols and narratives for political gains. Relying on an understanding of political meaning as created through public performance, I suggest that a search for the allegedly true inner motives of Shi'ite ethnic entrepreneurs is not a promising avenue for analyzing contemporary Lebanese Shi'ite politics. In *Shi'ite Lebanon*, their activities, sincere in terms of inner intentions or not, are analyzed as performative practices, establishing notions of Shi'ite authenticity and claims on the Lebanese nation through the creative powers of public performance, irrespective of the ultimately unknowable intentionality of its leading organizers.

For example, Hizbullah and Fadlallah claim to live in an Islamic sphere (*hala al-islamiyya*) and be part of the resistance society (*mujtama' al-muqawam*). They also fashion themselves as truly driven by sincere religious motivations, which they then perform publicly through a set of activities they claim to be normative, *shari'a*-based interpretations of Shi'ism. Such assertions should also be analyzed from the standpoint of performance, as these activities seek to delegitimize potential competitors such as Amal by portraying them as secular and, therefore, as less authentic Shi'ites. I question the comparison often drawn between the degree of the true religiosity of Amal or Hizbullah members. Throughout this book, by giving voice to Amal members, I show that Islamic credentials are also central to Amal politics and that excluding Amal from the Islamic movement is not a useful way to analyze the differences between it and Hizbullah.

Sectarianism Versus Nationalism?

Sectarianism is a key concept in the study of Lebanese identities and politics. It has been identified as Lebanon's central sociopolitical problem, responsible for outbreaks of violence, civil wars, and as a chief obstacle for the creation of a unified nation. Its origins have been traced back to the 1860 Mount Lebanon massacres, but more recent scholarship points to the modernity of sectarianism and its construction at the end of the Ottoman era.[14]

Scholars of Lebanon have often relied on primordialist, functionalist, or Marxist theories to explain the relation between nationalism and sectarianism. The Lebanese sociologist Samir Khalaf defines sectarianism as a public expression of religious identification, a "throw back" form of identity—as a primordial, tribal form of belonging—which stands in opposition to and undermines national identity.[15] Sami Ofeisch explains that it is a tool in the hand of a small political, religious, economic elite who use sectarianism to agitate the masses and to secure its access to vital resources.[16] Marxist intellectuals, such as Mahdi 'Amil, view the sectarian system as a creation of the bourgeoisie to contain and deflect class struggle.[17] Ussama Makdisi shows successfully how the events of 1860 resulted in "a birth of a new culture that singled out religious affiliation as the defining public and political characteristic of a modern subject and citizen."[18] He calls this the culture of sectarianism and argues that sectarianism "was not the failure or corruption of nationalism or the nation-state. . . . Rather . . . it was Lebanese nationalism's specific precursor, a formulation of new public political identities."[19]

I view sectarianism as a category of practice, not of analysis. In doing so I follow Rogers Brubaker and Frederick Cooper's distinction.[20] According to these two scholars, categories of practice, or lay categories, include concepts such as race, identity, and nationalism used by social and political actors to make sense of themselves or to persuade people to think of themselves in a certain way. But their so-called folk usage does not necessarily mean that they are valid analytical concepts as well; researchers, they suggest, should "avoid unintentionally reproducing or reinforcing such reification by uncritically adopting categories of practice as categories of analysis."[21] While the study of sectarianism as a category of practice is important in its own right, as it shows how Lebanese construct differences with each other, how intercommunal relations are organized, how they produce communal identities and maintain a culture of sectarianism, here I am primarily concerned with the analytical perspective on sectarianism and the larger implications of such politics of difference.

In contrast to current assumptions in which sectarianism and nationalism are imagined as standing in an antagonistic zero-sum relationship or in a hierarchy, I argue that what are referred to as sectarian activities should not be understood as opposed to the discourse of nationalism. In modern Lebanon, sectarianism is a set of political, religious, and socioeconomic practices aimed at breaking the hegemonic national claims of other religious communities and of establishing visions of the nation in which the existence of sectarian others is not denied, but in which one's own community is accorded a central place in the nation. Sectarianism is not about the dislike of other religious communities or the unwillingness to coexist, as those practices of boundary making/boundary breaking can be found in many other places. Scholarly works focusing on the Lebanese ability and desire to coexist miss the larger point that the debate over coexistence is not limited to daily practices among citizens but is tightly interwoven with the political setup in Lebanon.[22] Rather, ethnic entrepreneurs are concerned with who will eventually define the terms of this citizenship and coexistence, and which side will be assigned a marginalized position in the newly constructed national narrative. They are constantly engaged in debates over not only their own religious traditions but also about the very notion of religion itself, as well as over images and qualities of other religious traditions. They argue over how to position and present their own religion to members of other religious communities in Lebanon.

Thus, the frequent use of the term *sectarianism* by ethnic leaders, social actors, and even scholars to refer to the political and social conditions in Lebanon does not necessarily mean that the concept is also valid in analyzing what many view as the main obstacle to creating a peaceful and united population in Lebanon. Instead, *sectarianism* is a label used by various ethnic entrepreneurs to undermine political activities connected to the creation of a hegemonic nationalism that is not in line with their own agenda. Finally,

Ussama Makdisi argues that sectarianism is produced and can also be changed. He suggests that in order "to overcome it, if it is at all possible, requires . . . another vision of modernity."[23] In my view, the politics and practices of nationhood in modern Lebanon—the set of ideologies and activities that many label as sectarianism—are about competing visions of modernity, and the way sectarianism is imagined by its practitioners defines these modernities.

Producing Loyal Citizens in a Transnational Era

What is the relationship between transnationalism and nationalism? Where does Iranian government activism in Lebanon fit into this spectrum of Shi'ite nationalism? There is a widely held view that transnational religious ties to the Iranian government potentially detract from Lebanese national unity.[24] However, in this book I stress that transnationalism is always reconfigured in articulation with local sociopolitical and economic realities and interests. Iranian activism among Lebanese Shi'ites has in fact contributed to the production of Shi'ite nationalism and has strengthened Shi'ite claims to this nation. This is because Lebanese Shi'ites have selectively appropriated elements of this transnationalism, such as economic support and some ideologies. They also use these transnational networks to construct images of others whose claims to Shi'ite authenticity are denied in order to position themselves more successfully in the Lebanese national context. In Shi'ite-run institutions such as schools, which have so far been primarily viewed as filling the wide gaps left by the limited social services provided by the Lebanese state, the transnational connections have been locally adapted and reconfigured. I show in chapter 2 how Hizbullah, with Iranian support, has actually promoted itself as the champion of Arab nationalism through their fight against Israel and Zionism and as ideal citizens through their piety in the Lebanese context.

Previous studies on Shi'ism in the Middle East have either explained differences between Shi'ites as the product of national identity or have downplayed the importance of national ideologies by emphasizing transnational solidarity. Raymond Hinnebusch,[25] Graham Fuller and Rend Franke,[26] and Yitzhak Nakash[27] exemplify the former tendency, explaining the differences between Shi'ites in Iran and the Arab world with reference to preexisting ethnic, linguistic, and cultural differences. The historian Juan Cole, on the other hand, inspired by the work of Prasenjit Duara on Chinese history, has issued a call to "rescue Shi'i Islam from the nation."[28] Similarly, Chibli Mallat emphasizes the importance of Najaf theological schools for the creation of "Shi'i international" networks without pointing to the interplay of nationalism and religion or the importance of nonclerics in the production and maintenance of such networks.[29]

The distinction made in both these approaches between national and religious identity is, however, often not useful in explaining transnational Shi'ite activities because religious identities are often constructed and imagined through national ideologies. The activities of the members of transnational Shi'ite networks both construct and reproduce national ideologies. Transnational religious networks then function partly as mediators of these national interests and politics. Perceptions of the differences as well as the similarities between Shi'ites in the Middle East, often described in ethnic, linguistic, or national terms, need to be treated as constructed and as deployed in a shifting manner for a range of sociopolitical reasons. Assumptions that practical categories such as culture, national identity, language, and ethnicity constitute self-evident and self-explanatory barriers separating Shi'ites from each other (such as Arab versus Persian, Farsi versus Arabic), as well as simplistic notions of Shi'ite solidarity across borders are, therefore, questionable.

Scholars of modern Shi'ism in Lebanon addressing postrevolutionary Shi'ite ties to Iran have often given chronological overviews of Shi'ite relations between these two countries reaching back five hundred years without acknowledging the importance of the rise of nationalism, which has motivated new readings of past events.[30] In addition, this history is a contested field intimately connected to questions of religious authenticity and political hegemony among different Shi'ite groups. So far, the extent to which the actors create historical memory to justify claims of religious authenticity and to defend their own political positions and national interest has been largely overlooked.

I seek to show the extent of ideological work needed to both naturalize the operation of such transnational Shi'ite ties across borders as well as to construct differences between Shi'ites separated by national borders. For example, I discuss in chapter 3 the creation of a Shi'ite network between Iranians opposed to the Shah and Amal prior to the Iranian revolution, and the creation of a specific discourse linking the degree of Shi'ite piety to the degree of support of the Palestinian cause. I also show the religious and political struggles of Amal with the religious elite in Iran after the success of the Iranian revolution, as the latter propagated their own vision of Lebanese Shi'ite identity and ultimately helped create Hizbullah as a rival party to Amal in 1985, and then publicized this version of Shi'ite piety in Lebanon.

Within transnational Shi'ite networks, claims of religious authenticity are of great importance as they are intimately connected to power relations and are not limited to debates among religious scholars. Members of such networks establish these claims by constructing hierarchies within sociopolitical and historical contexts. Using ethnographic data collected among Amal members, I show in chapter 4 how they accentuate their differences from the ruling religious elite in Iran through acts of performance, such as linguistic parody in everyday conversation and ritual performance at 'Ashura. I demonstrate how Amal members engage in such performances in order to reject Iranian claims on authentic Shi'ism, which they interpret as attempts to establish hegemony over Lebanese Shi'ites. By claiming to represent the most authentic form of Shi'ism, Amal members draw on a range of narratives, such as Arab nationalism and the importance of the Arabic language. They also emphasize the significance of Jabal 'Amil in southern Lebanon for the origins of Shi'ism in Iran. Amal members deploy these ideologies in order to express the superiority of their Shi'ite traditions over what they refer to as Iranian Shi'ism and to simultaneously position themselves as *the* Shi'ite nationalist party in Lebanon.

In addition, Fadlallah has combined Arabism and a discourse of modernity to justify claims to loyal and committed Lebanese citizenship, while casting himself at the same time as the most suitable candidate for the Shi'ite religious leadership position of *marja'iyya* (the institution of the source of emulation). I explain how religious scholars in their debates and competition over *marja'iyya* also place themselves within contesting Arab and Iranian nationalisms. Competition over notions of Shi'ite authenticity is also intertwined with the reformulation of these nationalisms.

To sustain and legitimize its presence in Lebanon, the Iranian government needs ideological justification, which scholars so far have largely taken for granted based on the assumption that Shi'ite transnationalism reproduces itself when the participants identify themselves as Shi'ites. Interestingly, Jabal 'Amil, the region that plays a key role in Amal's Lebanese Shi'ite identity production, is also the place to which the Iranian government traces its religious genealogy, thus justifying its presence in Lebanon. This is because in the sixteenth century, the rulers of Safavid Persia invited several background also revealed much about issues central to my research. Their positioning of my background helped me to understand the ways in which various Shi'ite groups in Lebanon conceptualize the identities that each claimed for themselves. By positioning me in various ways against the current Iranian government, they revealed much about how they defined their own relations with Iran. Many asked about my views on the Iranian revolution, on the former Iranian president, Muhammad Khatami, and on how I defined my own personal sense of belonging in the context of my multiple backgrounds. When I began answering how I believed that my years in Germany and in the United States had also shaped my identity, I was often interrupted by someone asking, "Why are you ashamed of being a Shi'ite and an Iranian?" These types of questions revealed much about the way Shi'ites were often stigmatized as backward in Lebanon (discussed in chapter 1), which made many of them link the reasons for my lack of identification with my Shi'ite heritage with feelings of shame instead of personal and political convictions.

Perhaps my interlocutors' search for my origin was not entirely unjustified, as I had begun my own research in search of my origins as well. I decided to study Lebanese-Iranian Shi'ite networks while reviewing the scholarship on the Iranian revolution of 1978. The names of Mustafa Chamran and Musa Sadr were occasionally mentioned when referring to protests against the Shah outside of Iran. I became interested in the relationship between Iran and Lebanon while studying the beginnings of this opposition and began researching the secondary material on the Lebanese Shi'ite community. I could find only one article about prerevolutionary Iranian Lebanese ties in the 1970s,[31] while a rather extensive body of scholarship existed on postrevolutionary Iran-Hizbullah ties. This bias in the scholarship motivated me to write a master's thesis on Iranian-Lebanese Shi'ite relations in the 1970s—research and analysis that later informed my doctoral dissertation. A lively picture of interaction and debates between Shi'ites in Lebanon and Iranians in and outside of Iran came to the surface, enabling me to contextualize the postrevolutionary ties and debates. In the summer of 2000 I conducted preliminary research in Lebanon with the goal of finding out more about the types of transnational informal networks since the 1970s. While in Beirut I met with Amal members, Sadr family members, several Shi'ite shaykhs, and two Hizbullah members who all explained their views on prerevolutionary Iranian Lebanese ties. I began to realize that members of these different groups viewed these transnational networks very differently, placing more weight on either prerevolutionary or postrevolutionary ties depending on their political affiliation. Exploring these differences in detail then became the focus of my research in 2002–2003.

My regular trips in shared taxis (*servis*) in Beirut also taught me something about how the Lebanese made sense of my background and their views on Iranian-Lebanese relations. For example, I often visited a Christian friend in a neighborhood of East Beirut, but I lived in West Beirut and worked mainly there and in al-Dahiyya. Although it was not more than a ten-minute drive from my friend's home and Zokak el-Blat, where I frequently worked and which is now a rather poor West Beirut neighborhood with a large Shi'ite population close to the former Green Line dividing the eastern and western parts of the city during the civil war, the psychological barrier for most taxi drivers was great. Many Muslim drivers, most of them Shi'ites from southern Lebanon, would open a conversation by commenting on my Arabic accent; they wanted to know where I came from. When I told them about my Iranian background, they would often turn their face and look at me directly. Then they would continue driving while observing me in the mirror, some remarking that they had never seen an Iranian woman before, still less one without *hijab*. Some assumed that I was an Armenian Iranian because of my accented Arabic. Once I had established that not all Iranian women wear the *hijab* and that I was a Shi'ite nevertheless, some of them, greeting me again and welcoming me to Lebanon, then asked me why I was on my way to (Christian) East Beirut and warned me of the immoral atmosphere they imagined prevailed there.

When I wanted to return to mostly Muslim West Beirut, the fifth or sixth taxi driver who passed me would finally have mercy on me and take me back for twice the price. This time the Christian driver would ask about my background. I would reply that I am an Iranian living in the United States. Once a Christian driver in East Beirut told me that if he knew I was Iranian he would not have let me in! Other East Beiruti drivers were curious about my reasons for staying in Lebanon, while also sharing their stories about how they viewed Lebanese Shi'ites. They would warn me to be careful in West Beirut, and their warnings would be even more intense when I asked them to drive me to al-Dahiyya, the Shi'ite neighborhoods in the southern suburbs of Beirut. Most of them rejected this request immediately, because they did not know their way around there. Even my offer of triple or full price for the *servis* would not persuade them to drive to this unknown, presumably dangerous place. I heard their stories about being in the army with Shi'ites

THE NATION IN THE MAKING

FIGURE 1.1. Amal's folkloristic representation of South Lebanon. *Majlis al-Janub* (2001): 11.

1

TWO NATIONS AND ONE STATE

SHI'ITE AND MARONITE LEBANON

Southern Words

You ask for my name?
My name is The South
My age?
I was born the day freedom lost its way
My identity card?[1]
The identity was lost[2]
And today, my identity
Is a pen, a shovel, a rifle.
I defend the forgotten villages of the south
I defend the holiest of causes
You don't comprehend what a cause is
Your citizenship, a wallet, a beautiful woman, and an American car
They insist on making my cause sectarian
Very well, I will tell you, I am a southern girl
I love creating freedom, and I reject forms of humiliation of slavery
I will revolt against feudalism; I will explode in the face of Zionism,
which made my south a cause.[3]

The inability of the Lebanese state to create and to successfully propagate a
single, minimally coherent national ideology has often been attributed to a

struggle between two opposed visions of the Lebanese nation: Libanism and Arabism. Some scholars argue that the tension between these two political and historical narratives continues to play a significant role in contemporary debates about the Lebanese nation.[4] According to this division, Maronites favor the idea of Libanism,[5] stressing a Lebanese identity apart from the rest of the Arab world, while Arab nationalism, recalling the political context of the 1920s, arises from the desire of a majority of Muslims to integrate Lebanon into Syria. Scholars assessing its status and meaning after the independence of Lebanon in 1943 have associated Arab nationalism with Lebanese Muslims' emphasis on the Arab identity of Lebanon in its domestic and external politics.[6] From their perspective, communal identities have been important mainly because they have played a role in associating specific groups in Lebanese society with one of these two dominant narratives. In this view, sectarianism and political deadlock in Lebanon are linked to the irreconcilability of these two narratives.

I argue, however, while examining the experience of Lebanese Shi'ites since the 1960s, that the construction of a specific Lebanese Shi'ite-centered nationalism has problematized this dichotomy between Arab nationalism and Libanism. I suggest that it has done so in two ways. First, it mingles ideologies of Libanism with Arabism and creates a specifically Lebanese version of Arab nationalism rooted in the sociopolitical context of Lebanon; second, it shows how communal identities, so far viewed as subcategories of these two grand narratives, are themselves part of the construction of this new Lebanese Arab national narrative. Such identities, commonly labeled sectarian, do contribute crucially to a vision of the nation, while not necessarily implying the complete dismissal of older, established pan-Arab ideologies, which are integrated instead into a Shi'ite narrative of the nation. In this context, Lebanese Shi'ite-centered nationalism does not break with other Lebanese national narratives; they are related dialectically.

Lebanon as a Christian and Sunni Nation of Merchants

According to the dominant Christian and Maronite national narrative Lebanon is part of a Mediterranean civilization and its genealogy and history can be traced back to the Phoenician merchant communities who lived in the coastal areas of present-day Lebanon some three to four thousand years ago.

Many Maronites envision the presence of the Arabic language and Islam as alien elements in what they regard as authentic Lebanese culture. In the 1960s, more extreme proponents of the Libanism narrative, such as the Maronite poet Sa'id 'Aql, went so far as to suggest that the Lebanese dialect of Arabic should be adopted as Lebanon's national language and that it was not related to Arabic. He proposed developing a separate writing system for the language used in everyday Lebanese contexts, which he argued was distinctively Lebanese.

Lebanon, as the name suggests, is imagined as a larger version of Mount Lebanon, the historic home of Maronites, thereby marginalizing the other provinces that were annexed to create Lebanon in 1920, such as South Lebanon and al-Biqa', where the majority of Shi'ites live. While Maronites had established official relations based on their religious affinity to Europeans even prior to the French mandate, the creation of Lebanon reinforced their pro-European orientations evident, for example, in the importance many Maronites place on knowledge of French and their selective appropriation of aspects of Western modernity.

Although the regulation of communal relations is defined in Libanism as being based on dialogue (*hiwar*) and coexistence (*ta'ayush*), from the creation of the Lebanese state through French colonial intervention in 1920 and until the beginning of the Lebanese civil war in 1975, Maronites dominated the Lebanese state and nation politically, economically, and culturally and defined Lebanon's identity in terms of their own cultural preferences and class interests, even though they never constituted a numerical majority.

Shi'ites have also aimed at reforming the so-called secular, Sunni-centered Lebanese national narrative in which they are marginal. Sunnis were the leading sectarian community in the coastal towns of Tripoli, Beirut, and Sidon, and members of their elite were partners in the creation of the unwritten National Pact, and in the political and economic development of Lebanon until 1975. This is not to say that there were no economically disadvantaged Sunnis. In fact, Akkar, a predominantly Sunni region in the north, was perhaps as neglected as most of the south. However, throughout the country, Sunni notables had established social and educational institutions, such as the Maqasid society founded in 1878, and their degree of institutionalization and participation in the state could not be compared with that of Shi'ites. Sunni political bosses, most of them merchants of notable background, were interested in maintaining the status quo, as they benefited from the clientelism that was made possible through the political structures. Predictably, they opposed those presidents, such as Fu'ad Shihab, who wanted to limit the power of their political leaders. Michael Johnson argues that Nasserism among the Sunni leaders "provided a political framework for pressing the local demands of different classes within the Sunni community against a Maronite President."[7] This traditional Sunni leadership, in fact, opposed the coalition between the PLO and the Lebanese National Movement (LNM), the so-called Muslim front against the Maronites, at the outset of the civil war. In 1984, the Shi'ite Amal movement (*afwaj al-muqawama al-lubnaniyya*) took over West Beirut, until then the stronghold of the Sunni leadership in Beirut, and Nabih Berri, the leader of Amal, became the master of West Beirut. This changed the Sunni leadership's views of Shi'ites as junior and as peripheral to the Lebanese political scene for good.

After the end of the civil war in 1990, the former prime minister, the since-assassinated Rafiq Hariri, dominated Sunni Lebanese politics. As a Sunni ethnic entrepreneur, he promoted the idea of Lebanon as the nation of a successful, urban-based, secular upper middle class, with strong oligarchic tendencies. Hariri's vision of Lebanon and the type of nationalism he created and supported becomes evident[8] in the pivotal role he played in the postwar reconstruction of Beirut's downtown by leading the firm Solidere, which is in charge of the reconstruction.[9] The downtown area, which was a popular and traditional shopping area before it was destroyed in the civil war, has been transformed to a fancy upscale business district with expensive restaurants and international brand-name stores. In Hariri's view, this new area was supposed to function as a meeting point between Christians and Muslims, a sort of mingling place, a place that should symbolize the potential of the Lebanese for coexistence. In reality, however, few Shi'ites can afford this place of leisure, nor do they agree with this vision of Lebanon. As a result, many among them have created alternative ethnic places for entertainment in their own neighborhoods.

Hariri's nationalism[10] is far from the way many Shi'ites imagine Lebanon's identity. Here, a secular, yet clearly Sunni-centered, oligarchic model with close ties to the West, especially to France, is contrasted with a Shi'ite Islamic subaltern perspective despite a mutual agreement on the Arab identity of Lebanon.[11] For example, the political tensions between Hariri and Hizbullah represented but one dimension of local competition over the national-political space and the envisioned identity of Lebanon.

Struggling Against Marginalization:
Creating Lebanese Shi'ite Nationalisms

Maronite nationalism did not provide a vision of Lebanon in which all of its citizens could recognize a place for themselves. Shi'ite citizens mobilized not only because of economic and political marginalization but because such mobilization was informed by a historical memory that was at odds with the Maronite vision of Lebanon. In Shi'ite Lebanese nationalism, the heavily populated Shi'ite areas took a more central role than Mount Lebanon. By 1943, Jabal 'Amil, as a geographic entity comparable to the symbolic importance of Mount Lebanon, had been successfully incorporated in the collective memory of Shi'ites as a center of culture and historical point of reference.[12]

Although a knowledge of French helped Shi'ites integrate as cultural citizens in Lebanon, this European-oriented cultural capital did not marginalize Arabic. Arabic connected them to the wider Arab and Muslim worlds, whose histories they felt part of, and considered themselves connected to both ethnically and linguistically. The ideals of the Lebanese urban middle class stood in stark contrast to the socioeconomic realities of most Shi'ites, who could not relate to this image of being a Lebanese because few of them were part of that cosmopolitan class.

As for public services and institutions, the state provided few schools or hospitals in the Shi'ite areas, while the contents of history textbooks seemed rather alien because they did not even partially represent Shi'ite aspirations and national narratives. As a result, nation building and disciplining of citizens through schooling failed among Lebanese Shi'ites. Other state institutions, such as the army, also discriminated against Shi'ites, as only they were represented among the lower ranks. This state neglect and discrimination was, of course, limited neither to Shi'ite citizens nor to Shi'ite-inhabited areas. But they were the single largest community in Lebanon with the least political representation and they reacted to this marginalization most severely in the shortest period of time. Since the 1960s, Shi'ite national discourse has become more effective, Shi'ite-run institutions have multiplied, and two dominant political parties have been created (with some other less important movements and parties). Currently, these two parties present the most serious opposition to the mainly Christian, Sunni, and Druze coalition in the government.

Musa Sadr: Jabal 'Amil Challenges Mount Lebanon

Musa Sadr was born into an elite Shiʻite family of religious scholars (*'ulama*) in Qom, Iran, in 1928.[13] His father had been an influential and well-known ayatollah, Sayyid Sadr al-Din Sadr,[14] and his family included figures like Muhammad Baqir al-Sadr, who associated closely with the Daʻwa Party (*hizb al-daʻwa al-islamiyya*) in Iraq in the 1960s.[15] Musa Sadr studied at Tehran University before moving to Najaf for his religious studies. In 1959 he moved to Lebanon where he initially was imam in the mosque in Tyre, in southern Lebanon. He presided over the opening of the Supreme Islamic Shiʻite Council (SISC) in 1967, as the first step to providing Shiʻites with separate institutions. Sadr became the head of SISC until his disappearance in Libya in August 1978. Sadr also organized the Movement of the Deprived (*harakat al-mahrumin*) with a military wing of Amal in 1974, which, since May 1980, shortly after Sadr's disappearance, has been under the de facto leadership of the lawyer Berri, a Lebanese Shiʻite from South Lebanon.[16]

Until the arrival of Sadr in Lebanon in 1959, Shiʻite activism to secure rights from the state took two main forms—working through feudal lords (*zuʻama*) or through communist agitation. The patronage system of Shiʻite *zuʻama* consisted of Shiʻite feudal families, such as the al-Asʻads, Osseyrans, al-Zayns, and al-Khalils. They regulated the relations between the Shiʻite masses and the state, and ideally functioned as intermediaries between the two. Their demands were expressed mainly through writing petitions to state functionaries and meeting with politicians. In reality, while these families provided Shiʻites with some benevolent institutions,[17] they exploited poor Shiʻites and controlled them with a patronage system outside of which few were able to live their lives.[18]

The second group of Shiʻites, principally of working class or from poor agricultural backgrounds, couched their demands to the state in the form of activism in leftist parties such as the Lebanese Communist Party, for example, which demanded a total transformation of state structures and a desectarianization of its institutions. The official position of the Lebanese National Movement (LNM), led by the Druze leader Kamal Jumblat, summarizes secular and left-wing ideologies best, as the LNM represented a coalition of these parties, all of whom demanded a total secularization of the Lebanese state. LNM viewed political sectarianism as a form of undemocratic discrimination and an obstacle in the modernization of the political institutions of the state.[19] In addition, Shi'ite communists believed that, through the abolition of political sectarianism, they could secure more rights for the Shi'ites by breaking the feudal structures of the *zu'ama*.

In the 1960s, amid this Shi'ite activism, the newly arrived Shi'ite leader Sadr also requested from the Lebanese state an improvement in the status of the Shi'ite community. To achieve that, he had to position Shi'ites within the Lebanese national narrative as more than a population on the margins. How did Sadr define Lebanese Shi'ite identity? In an interview in 1969 he was asked, "Is it possible to know who the Shi'ites are? What do they form? And how do they think?" Sadr replied by "summarizing the situation of the Shi'ites at present":

> They are loyal and devoted Lebanese citizens, who believe in the common Arab fate, and consider their first problem that of Zionist greed. As for a quest for their psychological characteristics I will leave it to others to analyze; praising oneself is an ugly thing. Socially, we find them, despite a high level of illiteracy, overwhelmingly geared toward education, and on this path we find them on a quest to improve their social status in different areas.[20]

Elsewhere, scholars have convincingly outlined Sadr's activities to mobilize the Shi'ite community as a coherent political force.[21] Here it will suffice to mention that he viewed the Lebanese Shi'ite community as an oppressed, disadvantaged, and underprivileged community, neglected by the Lebanese state. He united and mobilized a vast range of Shi'ites by drawing on Shi'ite imagery, making parallels between the suffering of Imam Husayn at Karbala and the situation of Lebanese Shi'ites, and representing the situation as a subaltern struggle between an arrogant establishment signifying the state, and an oppressed community.[22]

As other scholars have pointed out, Sadr's efforts to reorganize and unite Shi'ites as one force emphasizing Shi'ite identity encountered resistance from at least two internal forces, the *zu'ama* and the secularists. This resistance to Sadr occurred not only because the *zu'ama* or Shi'ite communists feared their loss of power but also because Sadr imagined and propagated a type of nationalism that competed with the nationalisms of both these groups while it contained elements of both.

Sadr clearly rejected any form of secular state in Lebanon as he argued that religion was the basis of morality for a society. He shared with secularists and communists his concern that the state can continue to exist peacefully only if the political system is transformed into a democratic system, which would allow any person, regardless of religious background, to run for the leading political positions. Sadr was contradictory on this issue. In some of his speeches he affirmed the special position of Maronites in Lebanon, agreeing on their monopoly over the national presidency. Yet, he clearly promoted the abolition of political sectarianism while maintaining religion in the public sphere. Partial secularization of the state meant, for example, that personal status law continued to be the monopoly of religious leaders in the community and that religion continued to be taught at schools. Thus, Sadr resisted the aspirations of the *zu'ama,* who advanced their own interests by cooperating with the state, or the aspirations of the communists of creating a totally secular state, which they believed would also help transform the feudal structures of the *zu'ama.* Sadr agreed with the communists on the need to break feudal structures through abolishing political sectarianism, but he felt that the way to reach these two goals was not through total secularization of the state.[23]

Instead, in Sadr's view:

> Our rejection of political sectarianism does not mean that we are committed to secularization, for there is a third solution that we propose to the Lebanese community that differs from both political sectarianism and secularism. . . . Sectarianism in society is fanaticism for the individual, while secularism in society is atheism for the individual, thus the individual has a third solution left, which is that religion is completely different from fanaticism, therefore the Lebanese society has three solutions:
>
> 1. Political sectarianism is completely unacceptable since it has created for Lebanon problems and difficulties and has not served its purpose.
>
> 2. The second choice is the total secularization of institutions. . . . This is also a solution we reject because of its failure as the international community has suffered from it.
>
> 3. We demand the third solution, which is the *establishment of a state of believers,* in the sense that believing in God and what it entails be the basis of society, and that institutions and systems and the ties that connect the individuals be constructed on the basis of faith. And since believing in God is the common element in Lebanon between the two major religions, I am sure that this solution will be greatly accepted.[24]

The ambiguities present in many of Sadr's speeches were not accidental but were perhaps responsible for his success in breaking the hegemony of the Christian elite. They served to depoliticize the diverse narratives on Lebanese religious nationalism by highlighting shared moral discourses, such as that of faith. In this moral discourse, an opposition is created between the struggles for power as evil, and believing in God as the absolute good. Here he attempts to break the discourse that links coexistence to political sectarianism by claiming that coexistence is better achieved through public piety. In another instance he explained that

> at one point in time political sectarianism was functional for Lebanon and the 5 and 6 formula [referring to the ratio of Muslim-Christian representation in the parliament at the time] was introduced to allow for a fair representation of all communities. But the confessional system did not lead to the desired result and this is why I am convinced that the confessional system is not in the best interest of Lebanon, but actually prevents those who are qualified from reaching suitable posts. I am among those who are convinced that the existence of confessions and sects in Lebanon is great while political sectarianism is without doubt the worst system.[25]

Sadr suggested the creation of religious nationalism in a democratic state. This view differed from those of the traditional opponents of the Maronite state who pushed for a total secularization but was derivative of Lebanese Christian-centered nationalism. In this democratic state, it is through the discourse of religious tradition and values that hegemonies can be established, not through the existing institution of political sectarianism that safeguards the interest of one type of religious nationalism over others. But even within the Shi'ite community, which is viewed as one sect, from a legal point of view, in Lebanon,[26] there has been a lack of consensus on what exactly religion is, and there is no agreement on just how much public performance of religion is appropriate in a multiconfessional society. As the next chapters discuss, the discourse of Shi'ite authenticity also justifies hegemonic claims within the community. In this logic, the most pious should lead the community, serve as its representatives in the state, and work toward advancing Shi'ite interests in the nation. These most pious Shi'ites must demonstrate that their religion is compatible with the concept of coexistence, as it is only through engaging in this discourse successfully that one can become a full citizen.

By engaging in the discourse of coexistence and dialogue, the Maronite-dominated state provided Shi'ites with an effective political vocabulary through which they could express their frustration and demand justice. This discourse then became a category of political practice and a precondition for political participation in the nation. Sadr picked up on the link between the two when he suggested that Lebanon is not a secular state but an assimilation of a variety of religious communities (*al-tawa'if*). In his view it is a unique country where religious coexistence (*ta'ayush*) is practiced and, therefore, it should serve as an example to other countries.[27]

Through partial reproduction of the Christian discourse of coexistence, and the use of keywords and phrases that create intertextual relationships, he managed to position himself (and the Shi'ites) in the intellectual genealogy of those like Michel Chiha, the ideologue of Lebanese Christian nationalism, who stressed that coexistence stands at the core of what defines Lebanon and that the public acknowledgment of religious identities is the only possible and moral way of participation in this nation:

> Lebanon is a country of associated confessional minorities. All these minorities must find a place for themselves and have full rights. This is both the raison d'être of the country and the source of its originality. . . . Since Lebanon is a country made up of many associated confessional, minority communities, it cannot last long, politically speaking, without an assembly which is the meeting-place and the center of unity for these communities.[28]

While many Christians, and especially Maronites, argue that political sectarianism is an institution that secures the concept of coexistence and ultimately Lebanon's existence, Sadr inverted this idea and called the sectarian system evil, an obstacle to true coexistence, and its abolition as the only possible way to Lebanon's further existence. To many Christians, submission to the coexistence formula as secured by political sectarianism is an affirmation of the idea of Lebanon as a multisectarian nation, and a precondition to be full citizens. As Michelle Hartman suggests, "The division of parliament along sectarian lines mirrored the definition of Lebanon as an association of confessional minorities."[29]

During the first phase of the Lebanese civil war, Sadr noted that "the bloody trial [referring to the Lebanese civil war] taught us that the country must remain united, nothing can replace it, and a person's existence is meaningless outside the national context. Dealing with national topics be it social or political should involve *honest and sincere discussion*, removed from *hypocritical political practices*."[30] Here an artificial opposition is created between so-called hypocritical political practices usually conducted by others and "honest and sincere discussions" devoid of such politics obviously assigned to Sadr himself. However, by constructing oppositions within a dualist moral discourse and labeling political struggles as amoral, Sadr casts the Shiʻites (who desire the abolition of political sectarianism) as patriots par excellence, as those who work toward a kind of coexistence that does not need institutions to police and secure it. For example, the following exchange took place in 1976:

> *Interviewer:* Some interpret the revolution of the Shiʻites as a "delayed revolution" against the National Pact established between the Maronites and the Sunnis at the expense of the Shiʻites and the fourteen other sects in 1943. What do you think of this interpretation?
>
> *Sadr:* The Shiʻites' revolution is not for themselves, as their historic revolution was only for their nation. We are now against political sectarianism, *we do not want for the Shiʻites to be a pillar of the sectarian system. We want for ourselves, and for those who have less capacity the same rights as others. We believe in a sufficient amount of resources and rights and demand it.* The Supreme Islamic Shiʻite Council was the first council to demand the abolition of political sectarianism. Again, so that everyone knows, we are not calling for privileges, and we never have during our *political struggle.*[31]

The Shiʻites' political struggle is morally acceptable because it is defined in terms of removing an establishment that harms the national interest of *all* disadvantaged groups and hinders true coexistence by privileging one religious group over the other. However, the notion of coexistence as presented by Sadr has encouraged public performances of piety and, therefore, simultaneously the performance of religious difference.

While competition arises over the public performance of piety, as the second part of this chapter shows, some types of public piety come to be seen as more acceptable than others. These performances become an avenue to simultaneously express the groups' notion of coexistence as well as to claim public space as a community. This explains also, in part, the importance of religious performance among Shi'ites in Lebanon, not because, as some suggest, they are all deeply religious (they might or might not be; that is beside the point), but because religious performance is a type of allegiance to the nation and its fundamental idea. Therefore, as I show throughout the book in discussing the public holding of Shi'ite commemorative gatherings, debates over the content, style, voice, and meaning of the performances are for the participants, at the same time, debates over the nature of the Lebanese nation. In Part II we see, for example, that the question of how loudly piety should be expressed becomes one about conflicting visions of Lebaneseness.

In an interesting parallel, Sandria Freitag, in her study on communal mobilization strategies in colonial India, points out that "the evocation of community . . . has created a special discursive set of idioms that elude the distinctions between the religious and the social. . . . One consequence is that the conflation of religious devotionalism and community activism cries out for individuals to be 'good believers' and 'good citizens' simultaneously. Another consequence is the irrelevance, rhetorically and conceptually, of the Western concept of 'secularism.'"[32] That is, an opposition drawn between religious forms of political mobilization, such as religious communalism in colonial and postcolonial India or so-called sectarianism in Lebanon, and a discourse of the nation inadequately captures the relationship between religious community formation and the politics of modern states.[33]

Sadr and the Maronite State

How did the state react to these Shi'ite demands? Although the state in Lebanon has never been monolithic, with some contradictory policies and state officials often violating state laws,[34] the majority in the government and public service—positions that Maronites and other Christians occupied—were primarily geared toward promoting Christian Lebanon and favoring a small Shi'ite elite group. The state was Sadr's third and main obstacle in putting into practice his religious nationalist project, which he believed would result at least in securing equal rights for Shi'ites and would solve the Lebanese crisis. Sadr's activities certainly built upon existing activities of other Shi'ites in breaking Maronite hegemony over the state and the nation, and the Shihab era (1958–1964), unlike the presidency of Camille Chamoun, provided the fertile ground for such activism. Shihab's policy is perhaps best summarized as *la ghalib wa la maghlub* (literally, neither dominant nor dominated; no winner or loser),[35] by which he meant to create a state of equilibrium in which Muslims and Christians would receive equal shares and rights from the state. Sadr and Shihab's positive cooperation has been described elsewhere; in short, both Sadr and Shihab believed that national unity can be reached through social justice. In practice, social justice meant equal distribution of seats in the parliament between Muslims and Christians, and political and administrative reform to enable both groups equal access to public goods and services.

The 1960s were characterized by the increasing migration of rural Shi'ites to Beirut as a result of changes in state economic policies, which left many without the means to provide for themselves. Shi'ites then constituted almost 30 percent of the population in Beirut, living mainly in the southern suburbs known collectively as al-Dahiyya (literally, suburbs), or the so-called misery belt, as it was often referred to, and many were engaged in manual work. Sadr continued to struggle with state institutions to improve social services in the south, the al-Biqa', and the slums in the southern suburbs of Beirut, and to help break the control of the Shi'ite *zu'ama*.

Conditions in South Lebanon deteriorated increasingly with Israeli bombardments and Palestinian retaliations, so that many Shi'ites lost their homes and became refugees by 1970. Sadr's demands to the state began to take a more concrete form, but this provoked little change in the overall political attitude of the government toward the south.

Up to the formation of the Amal militia in 1974, Sadr continued to express his demands to the state by giving speeches, holding rallies, and organizing strikes. He increasingly and more aggressively demanded the creation of a Lebanon that included Shi'ites. 'Ashura commemorations became a stage to express these demands, but they also served as a hint to the government of the power of the crowd that gathered and occupied public space so ostentatiously to listen to his speeches.

The beginning of the civil war in 1975 opened a new avenue for Shi'ites in accessing the state's economic resources through violent means,[36] helping to strengthen their position. The progressive collapse of state structures, the Syrian support of Amal, and the success of the Iranian revolution, all strengthened the Shi'ite position in Lebanon. In the next chapters I will discuss this period in greater detail, but it suffices to say now that by the end of the civil war the Shi'ite *zu'ama* structures had disintegrated, enabling Berri to become Speaker in the parliamentary elections of 1992, a position he has held to this day. But political sectarianism was not abolished, and Amal began to engage in a similar form of clientelism as had the old Shi'ite *zu'ama* and the leaders of other sectarian communities. But unlike the prewar situation, in which Shi'ite political voices ranged from leftists and secularists to pro-Sadr followers, in the postwar period the dominant voices in the community represented by Amal and Hizbullah (and Sayyid Muhammad Husayn Fadlallah), all claimed to produce loyal citizens within a framework of religious allegiance. In other words, the dominant political discourse in the Shi'ite community became one revolving around the production of religious nationalisms, while secular and leftist voices lost the competition. Religious parties and leaders since have frequently become the central ideologues of such perspectives on the nation, as religious belonging is the precondition to belonging to the Lebanese nation.

Amal: The Bourgeois *Mahrumin*

During the civil war and in postwar Lebanon, Amal sought to break a Maronite dominance over state institutions and national narratives by occupying state positions and through opposition to domestic and external politics. Amal often casts itself as representing the state and its institutions.

The image of Lebanon as presented through the publications of the Council of the South (*majlis al-janub*) exemplifies Amal's nationalism. Following repeated requests from Sadr, the council, under the control of the government, was created in 1970 to help reconstruct the south as a response to the destruction caused by Israeli attacks. In postwar Lebanon, this council is under the control of Berri and is part of Amal's efforts to create relationships of patronage in the south. One instance of the official self-presentation of this institution is through the council's publications, which describe its activities in the south. Published in 1998, "The South, Memory of a Country," a bilingual Arabic and English booklet, describes the south "as the destination of martyrs . . . and the Cradle of Civilizations." This photographic journey through the south shows images of houses destroyed by the Israeli military, the wounded bodies and suffering faces of the people, and the efforts at reconstruction. It shows images of old peasants working, of fishermen, and of girls working in tobacco fields (an essential source of income in the south), of destroyed mosques, of children playing in the rubble of houses and collecting their school books, and the pictures of dead bodies of Christian and Shiʻite children killed by Israeli shelling. It shows Shiʻites returning to their villages despite Israeli attacks, and explains how the south "remained in the hearts and minds of all Lebanese."[37] The efforts of the council in reconstructing buildings and schools and a picture of the Ansar detention camp set up by Israelis in 1982 are shown with the caption "The homeland is there to stay. . . . The occupation will come to an end." Then Berri is pictured laying the foundation stone for the late son of the Syrian leader Hafiz al-Asad at the Basil al-Asad Cultural Center in Tyre; to his right stands Qabalan Qabalan, the head of the Council of the South. The help of Syria in reconstructing the south is acknowledged and pictures of a mosque and a church are placed not far apart from each other with a caption that reads, "Lebanon will always be the country of co-existence."[38]

A second booklet featuring a photographic journey through the south was produced in 2001, a year after the end of the Israeli occupation. While the first section of the booklet remains the same, a new section was added showing UN soldiers helping Shiʻites in the south and old Shiʻite peasants in the field holding a weapon in one hand and an ax in another. A caption reads, "We resist and we plant."[39]

Key themes of Amal's nationalism are manifest in these pictures: the central importance of the south for the nation and of the discourse of coexistence, as evidenced by the picture of a mosque and a church next to each other; pro-Syrian ties; a claim to modernity, as expressed through the construction of new buildings; an interpretation of resistance as the efforts of the people of the south to return to the south despite ongoing destruction; and, finally, Amal's support of the UN soldiers, which positions Amal within an internationally respected framework.

As with the folkloric presentation of Mount Lebanon, South Lebanon is depicted as rural and as the home of peasants, with female tobacco workers in colorful dresses. These pictures convey images of poor but strong-willed Shiʻites, continuing their lives amid the rubble and destruction and acknowledging the help of Syria in rebuilding this nation. They are shown to be ideal citizens, working the land and defending the soil, returning to their villages despite the danger. In chapter 4 we see more specifically how Amal portrays the south as part of historic Jabal ʻAmil, positioning itself as truly Lebanese in the transnational Shiʻite context.

The end of the Israeli occupation is presented as a national effort, even though the main operations against the occupation were carried out by Amal's rival party, Hizbullah. Pictures in the booklet have Lebanese flags dominating the scene and people greeting Lebanese soldiers. A photo journey presented by Hizbullah would certainly carry a different message, one centered on Hizbullah and Lebanese flags, dominated by pictures of Hizbullah martyrs. Just like its strategies in its schools discussed in chapter 2, Amal represents itself as a mainstream party invested in the Lebanese nation, sidelining Hizbullah as a sectarian party. In these pictures, similarly, Amal speaks from the perspective of a nation concerned with the south, although it is performing only its own national narrative, especially since most Lebanese Christians would not interpret the Syrian presence in Lebanon as positive in recent years nor want to represent Lebanon's ties to Syria in the hierarchical order as presented in the booklet.

It was not until the Iranian revolution that Lebanese Shi'ite leaders were forced to explicitly address the question of their people's identity in relation to a wider Shi'ite world, and in particular to clarify their position toward the strong transnational Shi'ite outreach efforts from Iran. As I discuss in chapter 3, Sadr's political involvement in transnational Shi'ite politics was not reflected in his public discourse until 1977. In locating itself in a larger Shi'ite world, Amal tends to publicly follow the ideas of Muhammad Mahdi Shamseddine, the late religious scholar and former representative of SISC (the official organ representing the Shi'ite community), who saw transnational networks, especially with Iran, as harmful to the advancement of Shi'ite interest within the nation.

Muhammad Mahdi Shamseddine: "The Time for Change Has Not Come Yet"

After Sadr's disappearance in Libya in 1978, Shamseddine became the acting representative of SISC until his death in 2001. Shamseddine was born into a Lebanese family in Najaf in 1936 and studied in a theological seminary there, along with Fadlallah and other Shi'ite activists, such as Muhammad Baqir al-Sadr. He was closely associated with the Da'wa Party,[40] one of whose goals was to fight against the growing attraction of many Shi'ites to Communist ideologies.

Upon his return to Lebanon in 1969, Shamseddine opened the charity foundation of *al-jam'iyya al-khayriyya al-thaqafiyya*, first located in mainly Christian-populated East Beirut in al-Nab'a, and later on the southern outskirts of Beirut. (Since his demise it has been taken over by his son, Ibrahim Shamseddine.) In 1975, Shamseddine was nominated to be the representative of the SISC. He joined the Amal party before Sadr's disappearance. In 1983, as a result of his disagreements with Berri on the Shi'ite position toward the Israeli occupation of South Lebanon, Shamseddine formally left Amal,[41] but in later years he reconciled with the party. Although he took part in a conference in 1986 in Tehran which was aimed at drafting an Islamic constitution for Lebanon, in later years he clearly distanced himself from such plans and, after the end of the civil war in 1990, came to be more closely associated with Amal again.[42]

Shamseddine continued to promote coexistence in the tradition of Sadr but did not insist on the abolition of political sectarianism after the end of the civil war. Shamseddine wrote that he reached this solution for Lebanon after "deeply observing Lebanese political dynamics" and concluded that "abolishing political sectarianism in Lebanon might be very hazardous for Lebanon." Yet, this did not mean that abolishing political sectarianism should not be discussed, though it should be regarded as a long-term objective. For the time being, he asked the Shi'ites of Lebanon in particular, and the Lebanese in general, to try to reform the present system without abolishing it. He considered the Ta'if agreement, which put an end to the Lebanese civil war, to be appropriate grounds for such a reform.[43]

In the midst of the civil war in 1985, and at the height of Iranian activities in Lebanon, Shamseddine declared that "the national identity of the Shi'ites is Lebanese, they are Arabs, and their religious identity is Islam, that is common among all Muslims."[44] But at that time he had not made a clear statement about his views on the future Lebanese political system. In his political testament, published in book form and titled *al-Wasaya*,[45] Shamseddine said concerning relations between Shi'ites and the Lebanese state that "Lebanon is the final entity and home to the Lebanese Shi'ites." To emphasize the loyalty of the Shi'ites to Lebanon, he reminded the reader of the statement Sadr had issued in 1977, the *Sigha*, which was meant as a reaffirmation of the loyalty of Muslims to the idea of Lebanon as their homeland in the face of growing accusations of many Lebanese Maronites regarding this issue, as they believed many Muslims to closely associate with their enemy, the PLO.

Shamseddine called on "all Twelver Shi'ites in all their nations and societies to merge in those nations and societies and not to distinguish themselves in any particular way from others, because the main principle is that of

Islam and the unity of the *umma*."[46] He further advised the Shi'ites not to be influenced by any suggestions to distinguish themselves from others as a minority for, according to him, the Shi'ites do not constitute a minority in any Arab land.[47] In the last part of the book, Shamseddine warns the Arab Shi'ites not to fall into the trap of the games great powers have often played with minorities, using them to maintain instability in the region and to incorporate Israel within it.[48] Shi'ites should refrain from any claims as a minority, even if they are subject to some injustice and grievances, he wrote, and Shamseddine refused any organizations that were concerned with the rights of Shi'ites and such claims.[49] He considered the Shi'ite experience in Lebanon the only successful one in rectifying the status of the Shi'ites in a pluralist society, and he believed that this success was due to Sadr's activities.[50] Shamseddine repeatedly called for Shi'ites to merge into their nations and respective societies and to refrain from what he believed to be separatist activities, resulting in suspicion and fear among other Muslims.[51] He did not refer directly to Arab Shi'ite ties to Iran, but clearly pointed out that his suggestions were addressed to the non-Iranian (both Arab and non-Arab) Shi'ite communities all over the world, because Iran is an independent state and represents a case in itself.[52] But it is not difficult to read between the lines of his suggestions that he warned Arab Shi'ites not to associate too closely with Iran, a state believed to encourage minority politics in Arab countries.

In short then, Amal continues to refer to Sadr's and Shamseddine's vision of Lebanon and relies for its political orientation on the charter of the Movement of the Deprived formulated in 1974. Its members view Lebanon as part of the Arab world, with Arabic as its national language. Amal desires the abolition of political sectarianism while it argues for keeping religion in the public sphere, as religion in the view of its leading members serves as a moral guidance for society. It considers Shi'ites the most loyal citizens of Lebanon and the most disadvantaged. As the booklets show, its national identity is based on the figure of the disadvantaged *mahrum* Shi'ite from the south. In practice, its members are actively involved in changing this subaltern image and seek upward mobility to meet the ideals of an urban Sunni and Christian bourgeoisie. Shi'ites, as Lebanese citizens who suffered most from Israeli attacks and thus deserve a more privileged position in the state and in the national narrative, are also central to Amal's identity. Its members argue that they follow the example of Sadr, who viewed Islam and Christianity as two equal world religions, and suggest that coexistence is therefore guaranteed through their interpretation of their own religion and that it does not need institutions to safeguard it.

Hizbullah: "The Most Loyal Citizens" with Intense Transnational Ties

In 1982, some members split from Amal and created Amal al-Islami, the Islamic Amal. Merging with some other Shi'ite groups, they became officially known by 1985 as Hizbullah. Amal al-Islami parted from Amal over Berri's stance regarding Amal's relations to postrevolutionary Iran, as well as the modalities of resistance against the Israelis in South Lebanon. It was created in 1982 with the support of members of the religious elite in Iran, and many have questioned its loyalty to the Lebanese nation because of the dense transnational ties on various levels that it maintains with Iran.

Hizbullah's ideologies and institutions are the most researched among scholars of Lebanon. Here I will highlight only some of its ideologies and visions as they relate to the arguments of the book. In chapter 2, I examine one of the schools that are closely affiliated with Hizbullah and show how the party envisions a Shi'ite-centered Lebanon. In chapter 3 I discuss the formation of the party in its transnational context. I then discuss in chapters 4 and 5 Hizbullah's strategies to position itself in the Lebanese national context.

Hizbullah, like other Islamist groups, has an elaborate and detailed vision of the society and the production of its citizens based on its interpretation of Islamic law (*shari'a*) as provided by its *marja'*. The interpretation of the concepts of *jihad* as a religious, personal, and political struggle, and of martyrdom (*istishhad*), has been central to the production of the selfhood of Hizbullah members. Hizbullah's ideologues regard the successful resistance against Israeli occupation in South Lebanon, their well-organized and effective social institutions, and their involvement in Lebanon's political life, which they see as positive, as the result of religious practice and strong faith.[53] To them, the virtuous citizen is the one "whose behavior is reflected in his approach to society, for he is required to be reliable; impartial; honest; sincere; a working contributor to society whose religion deters him from committing the prohibited due to a strong faith in God Almighty's wakeful supervision, judgment and the Day of Resurrection."[54]

The main difference between Amal and Hizbullah can be found in the way each claims citizenship in Lebanon: Amal engages in a discourse of origins; that is, it seeks to position itself through a variety of strategies as culturally Lebanese, discussed in detail in chapter 4, while Hizbullah seeks the transformation of the society which it believes to be successful only when a personal transformation has taken place. In addition, the elaborate culture of martyrdom and jihad as an absolute fight against Zionism is absent from Amal's nationalism. Resistance is not taken to mean active fighting against Israel but is interpreted as the will of the Shi'ites in the south to keep rebuilding and starting their lives again. So both Hizbullah and Amal claim to be part of a resistance society, while their notion of resistance differs greatly.

In the next chapters I show the differences between Amal and Hizbullah's Shi'ite Lebanon in more detail. On the surface, Hizbullah's vision of Lebanon's political identity overlaps with that of Amal on some levels, such as in the emphasis on the Arab and Islamic identity of Lebanon, using Arabic as its national language, and secularizing its political institutions, without secularizing the personal status law. The insistence on keeping this area of law under the control of religiously organized personal affairs courts illustrates the party's desire to monopolize the shaping of citizen's identities and to spread its vision of Lebanon.

Just like their Maronite counterparts but with very different goals, Hizbullah insists on defining Lebanon through the lens of religion, as it argues for only a partial secularization of the system. According to this camp, a totally secularized Lebanon would lose its meaning. Hizbullah also emphasizes that the establishment of an Islamic state does not contradict the multiconfessional identity of Lebanon, as Islam does not stand in any contradiction to Christianity, but rather completes it. Hizbullah is unlike Amal, whose way of breaking the Maronite dominance is mainly through increasing its control of state institutions and which engages in a discourse of viewing these two religions as equal while presenting Lebanon as their crossroads. Hizbullah does not step back from arguing that Islam is superior to Christianity because of what its members consider its comprehensiveness as a social order and form of governance.[55] However, as the people of the book (ahl al-kitab), Christians of Lebanon will not be forced to conversion and will be protected under shari'a. While de facto in both Amal's and Hizbullah's Shi'ite Lebanon other religious sects will be politically and socially marginalized, each party defines sectarian relations differently. For example, 'Ammar Musawi, one of the eight representatives of Hizbullah in parliament,[56] argues that the party's desire to abolish political sectarianism should not be misunderstood as its desire to wipe out other sects, nor to ruin the multiconfessional culture in Lebanon.[57] But if Christians' rights as citizens in Lebanon are defined through Hizbullah's interpretation of *shari'a*, they will certainly be at the margins of Lebanon's political and social life, while Amal would sideline them politically and socially without judicial justification.

Hizbullah emphasizes that its identity comes from representing the disempowered (*mustad'afun*),[58] and it takes pride in this subaltern identity, as it generates a sense of moral superiority toward the immoral rich. In other words, it does not seek to be part of the bourgeoisie and it argues that the welfare of the community goes above personal welfare. In this discourse, developed by Sadr and Khomeini based on a specifically Shi'ite interpretation of the Quran and Islamic history, the arrogant and powerful elite (*mustakbirun*) are identified as the corrupt and immoral while the oppressed (*mustad'afun*) are associated with the hardworking and the faithful. Hizbullah's Shi'ite Lebanon is a nation of this faithful, subaltern, disempowered population which abides by Hizbullah's vision of social justice (*al-'adala al-ijtima'iyya*). Breaking Maronite and Sunni hegemony over the nation is then justified in this moral discourse, as they are imagined as corrupt, weak in faith (that is, secular, in Hizbullah's interpretation), and oppressive, while Hizbullah members are the most loyal citizens through their resistance to Israel and by providing social services to Lebanese citizens, that is through defending the land and creating social justice. This same discourse is applied to Hizbullah's approach to foreign policy. The Maronite/Sunni hegemony over the nation is resisted by opposing close relations with some European governments and especially with the United States, which are viewed as oppressive world powers, and instead by maintaining close ties with Iran and Syria.

Shaping Lebanese Shi'ite Citizens

Apart from its ability to propagate a holistic vision of social justice and a moral society through personal status courts, informal networks, and other institutions,[59] Hizbullah's elaborate process of recruiting and training its members is another avenue to shape citizens and disseminate its vision of Shi'ite Lebanon. Recruits undergo intense two-year training before being admitted as members of the party. A one-year training, called reinforcement (*taba'a*) consists of the teaching of Hizbullah ideology as well as proper understanding of Shi'ism, according to the teaching of their *marja'*, 'Ali Khamenei. The second year of training, called ordered discipline (*intizam*), consists of teaching party discipline and physical and military training.[60]

According to Shaykh Na'im Qasim, Hizbullah's secretary-general deputy and one of its main ideologues, political parties are joined in Lebanon for confessional or doctrinal reasons. To him, a confessional person is one who joins a religious party because of his birth into that community, rather than out of a conscious decision and knowledge of the party's doctrinal conviction. He argues, however, that most of Hizbullah's followers join the party based on their conscious choice, a "free-will allegiance to an all-embracing vision of the world, humankind, and life," because of doctrinal allegiance, and not solely because Hizbullah is a Shi'ite party.[61] According to this logic, a conscious decision to belong to a religious community and a total commitment to its religious teachings makes one a nationalist rather than a sectarian person.

When many Lebanese imagine the activities of some communally marked parties, especially Hizbullah, in opposition to the national interest (although most of the parties in postwar Lebanon are organized along communal lines), Hizbullah ideologues position themselves as part of a national doctrinal party that stresses public performance and a conscious enacting of religious identity. This interpretation of the relationship between religion and nation is a continuation and expansion of Sadr's argument that piety and citizenship go hand in hand in Lebanon. Hizbullah members emphasize that the most committed citizens are those most committed to publicly act upon and perform their faithfulness.

Whose Lebanon? The Politics of *Mahrumin* and the Peripheralization of Shi'ites

My Lebanese Arabic tutor, Rima, expected every morning that I report to her in Lebanese Arabic what I had done the previous day. So I began to tell her that I had gone to al-Dahiyya visiting a Shi'ite family, or that I had visited a Shi'ite-run school, or had participated in an event. She would then ask me questions: How clean was the house? How many children did the family have? Were you scared when you went to their home? One day during the break she told me: "I have lived in Dubai and know many Iranians. I know Iranian Shi'ites are not like Lebanese Shi'ites. But in Lebanon it doesn't matter how rich and educated Shi'ites become, they will always remain uncultured." Rima was a Sunni (middle-class) woman from Beirut or a normal/average ('aadi) Lebanese, as she described herself.

—FIELDNOTES, BEIRUT, JULY 2002

In the introduction I argued that sectarianism, viewed from an analytical perspective, is a set of activities concerned with positioning one's own community as consisting of exemplary citizens in the Lebanese national context, thereby justifying claims to hegemony. Sectarianism and nationalism do not have different genealogies, nor do they stand in a dialectic relation or are opposed.

However, sectarianism as a category of practice is very much alive and well in Lebanon. Ussama Makdisi discusses the production of a "culture of sectarianism" at the end of the Ottoman era in Mount Lebanon, and Max Weiss shows, for example, how between 1920 and 1947 the identity of Shi'ites as a sectarian community (ta'ifa) in Lebanon was produced through a variety of institutional and cultural practices.[62] One avenue of understanding Shi'ite public identity and politics is through analyzing the social context in which Lebanese Shi'ites have to define themselves. Sectarian practices, among many of their other functions, are forms of essentializing the other and attributing characteristics to them believed to be inherent in their religion, language, or even race; one's self supposedly emerges on the more moral side of this construction. My main concern is to explain the larger political implications of this particular form of difference making called sectarianism.

In Lebanon, religious identities and class construct each other rather than being reducible to each other. Sectarian practices are not hidden forms of class struggle, nor are class struggles subordinate to the construction of religious difference. Class is, at one level, about access to material resources, but this access is also a matter of cultural performance. Not only is it visible, it is reproduced through a set of practices and activities that hierarchically distinguish citizens from each other. As the examples below show, many Lebanese do not clearly distinguish between class and religious identity; for them, both overlap. Public religious performance becomes part of this cultural production of class, and as I show in chapter 4, Fadlallah's interpretations of religious ritual also involve an uplifting of the lower-class image of Shi'ites, informed by what are considered middle-class norms of religious practice.

For Rima, being Sunni is an index for being secular (although privately pious), cosmopolitan, modern, sober, rational, urban, middle class, educated, clean, not sexually driven, and nationalist. In other words, all the characteristics she believes are moral and make an exemplary citizen, and which she imagines Shi'ites to lack.[63] Being Sunni then provides one vision of the

Lebanese nation in which Shi'ites are both politically and culturally peripheral at best. Rima justifies assigning Shi'ites this peripheral position *because* to her they are morally corrupt.

So the question remains, is Lebanon the middle-class merchant nation or the subaltern society? Non-Shi'ite Lebanese express in the form of jokes, anecdotes, and discussions their resistance to the image of the *mahrum* and *mustad'af* as a suitable candidate for citizenship, and express that Shi'ites do not deserve to play any significant role in the Lebanese nation. There is a constant negotiation of power positions through the telling of these anecdotes and gendered jokes and the presentations of them, through the classification of people according to religious identity, and through discussions of Lebanese history and politics, all of which result in speakers positioning their own community as the most appropriate model for the Lebanese national image.[64] These situated comments and discourses elucidate an ironic critique of a dominant Shi'ite national narrative.

I have chosen popularly circulated jokes as examples of how Shi'ite stereotypes are constructed, since for jokes to be understood and considered funny, they must draw on shared knowledge and, in this case, shared negative stereotypes about a certain group. Gestures and body language are also important parts of the performance in telling such jokes or anecdotes. Everyone I met during my fieldwork knew about my research project in broad terms; that is, they knew that I was researching the Shi'ite community in Lebanon since the 1960s for a PhD based in the United States. They also knew that I was Shi'ite myself. One of the first reactions of non-Shi'ites when I approached them explaining my research project was to start with small personal stories and impressions of the situation of Shi'ites. Then jokes and personal anecdotes were told about Shi'ites they knew from the army, from the university, or from daily encounters, while people listening all shook their heads in a sort of disbelief. This body language and the order of the conversations, replicated by numerous acquaintances, led me to think about the larger political implications of these jokes.

While jokes revolving around stereotypes are an integral part of Iranian conversations in which I have participated throughout my life, the gestures of the persons performing the telling of a joke or acting as an audience were rather different among my Lebanese interlocutors. While stereotypical representations of people from Azerbaijan in western Iran as dull and simple-minded often make Persian Iranians laugh, they are never linked to suspicions that Azeris might one day take over power in the centralized government in Tehran. This is because Iranian nationalism has constructed them as a minority and marginalized them politically without portraying them as a threat to mainstream Persian Iranian nationalism. But my Lebanese interlocutors who shake their heads in disbelief illustrate a rather different constellation of ethnic stereotyping and politics, one that suggests that culturally marginalized Shi'ites are a serious political threat.

These jokes have to be interpreted against the actual political power of Shi'ites in post–civil war Lebanon. While jokes and anecdotes as ways of boundary making are certainly not unique to Lebanon, in this case these stereotypes are expressions of a struggle to ideologically marginalize Shi'ites as unsuitable candidates for the category of the exemplary national. Most of these jokes are about Lebanese from the south, while jokes about Shi'ites from al-Biqa' describe them as noble savages. Through this jocular talk about the nation the al-Biqa'i Shi'ites are excluded immediately by both Shi'ites from the south and by non-Shi'ite Lebanese.

Gendered Lebanon; or, Sexy Shi'ites

A number of stereotypes are frequently invoked in imagining the Shi'ite community as an underclass. Among the most popular of these are the high birthrates of Shi'ites in Lebanon. These are viewed not only in terms of the number of children involved but also as evidence of the supposedly high degree of sexual desire that gives both Shi'ite men and women an almost animal character. Shi'ite relations between man and woman and between parents and children are envisioned as lacking so-called true love. The partners' motivation for sex seems to be rooted neither in love for each other nor for their many children. In these stereotypes, these children then are imagined as posing a burden to the Lebanese state, as the parents cannot afford to take care of them. The balance of coexistence is offset, so they imagine, not only by the obvious change of demography in the long term but because Shi'ites do not take their responsibility as citizens seriously, as they lack rationality and act out of passion.

Consider the following jokes related to high Shi'ite birthrates:

> "Once upon a time there was a Shi'ite man and a Shi'ite woman. Now there are millions."

"A Shi'ite family is driving in a BMW 316 when the door suddenly opens and 'Ali, one of the five sons, falls out of the car. The mother starts screaming and tells the husband to stop the car. He looks at her in surprise and tells her not to worry because they will just get another 'Ali soon."

In another joke I heard both from Shi'ites and non-Shi'ites, and which pointed to the supposed difference in degree of Shi'ite sexual abilities and desires, Shi'ite men are referred to as 220 (volts) while Sunni men are referred to as 110. While in Lebanon until recently, Sunni/Shi'ite relations were often imagined as between an older and a younger brother. Shi'ites reject this inferiorization and point to their maturity and independence as full men. For non-Shi'ites, however, this overt sexuality is not a sign of maturity but rather a lack of morality and a sign of irresponsibility.

One sunny day when I was sitting in a taxi—a private taxi, not a shared *servis*—the driver, who turned out to be a Maronite, began to ask me where I came from and what I was doing in Lebanon. When I responded that I was doing research on the Lebanese Shi'ite community, he sighed and said:

> You know, I am not a sectarian person, I am a Maronite and believe in God. I have friends from all sects. Especially in the army, I was close to a Shi'ite, his name was 'Ali. You know how it is in Lebanon, once you get out of the army people don't interact with each other anymore. We live here and they live in their own area. I just know that he has ten children now. Can you imagine ten? I have two and I don't know how to feed them. I mean, Lebanon is such a small country, how are we all going to live if the Shi'ites keep having children? So how many children do you have? What is it in your religion that tells you to keep having children?

I had heard such stories too many times at that stage and was tired of getting into arguments. I turned the stereotype around and said that Catholics keep having children, too, and they don't seem to stop. He just gave me an angry look through the front mirror and said, "We feed our children with our own hard work at least!"

A Shi'ite Taste?

The second stereotype is about Shi'ites' supposed lack of taste. While the word *metwali* refers to the 'Amili Shi'ites and means "followers of 'Ali," it is a term used in a derogatory way by non-Shi'ites in Lebanon to refer to low-class behavior and taste.[65] Shi'ite taste is considered to be bad taste or a lack of good taste. What does this presumed lack of taste mean? Pierre Bourdieu has pointed out that the construction of taste and its relation to class in a system of differences indicate the unequal distribution of symbolic capital, social taste being one of its key modes.[66] According to Bourdieu, the symbolic capital of taste is misrecognized as an essential attribute of a person, when it actually is the product of complex processes of transformation of economic capital into symbolic capital and vice versa, as determined by a person's position in a class structure based on unequal access to resources. Taste is thus a component of wider systems of symbolic distinction, in which hierarchical relationships are constructed. Having no taste signifies a lack of command over legitimate symbolic forms and is held to justify a person's inferior status in a class structure.

In the Lebanese context, one way of pointing to this supposed lack of taste is by establishing links between brand names (types of cars, for example) and social stereotypes. The BMW 316 (the same car the Shi'ite man was driving in the joke above) is considered by many the Shi'ite car par excellence. I was driving with a non-Shi'ite friend in Beirut, and as we saw a black BMW 316 pass us, my friend turned to me, chuckling, and said, "Don't you study these people? Here, this is what they drive." He was amused to find his stereotype reconfirmed as a poster of Sadr was glued to the rear window of the car. BMW, he then told me smilingly, stands for *Bani Metwali* Warriors (the Shi'ite warriors). The BMW 316, a symbol of upward mobility for many Shi'ites, is associated clearly with a lack of taste and a lower-class background by many Lebanese non-Shi'ites, even if Shi'ites purchase luxury automobiles.

This supposed lack of Shi'ite taste was evident in perceptions of the so-called typical Shi'ite household, where African art, associated with a nouveau riche, kitsch taste by non-Shi'ites, was believed to be in abundance. African art symbolizes the Shi'ite migration to West Africa, whence many Shi'ites returned relatively wealthy and built mansions in the south or bought houses in Beirut. The central point of the jokes and anecdotes is that Shi'ite wealth does not change their underclass status, as Shi'ites would spend large sums to buy bright shiny colors considered tasteless by the majority society to decorate their homes. This became clear to me in a conversation with a group of AUB students regarding an exhibition of handmade vases in Nabatiyya, a city mainly inhabited by Shi'ites. One of the men present began to tell how his friend who was responsible for selling the vases in

Nabatiyya already knew to stockpile them in bright colors, as such vases would sell well there. The crowd immediately began to laugh.

Another anecdote that one of my non-Shiʻite male friends remembered in talking about the color of the vases was how, as a child in the early 1970s, he had once dressed quickly in his room with whatever he had found in his dresser, not paying attention to matching the colors, to go out to play, when his mother started yelling at him that he looked like a *metwali* and forced him to change his clothes. He recalls how the word *metwali* was used to refer to everything that was considered low-class, tasteless, and vulgar.

The Subaltern Screams: Shiʻism as a Loud Religion

To many Lebanese, the elaborate Shiʻite ritual practices during ʻAshura express their seemingly excessive religiosity, another prevalent stereotype. Now that Shiʻites reside all over the West Beirut area, lower-class Shiʻite men—that is how other Shiʻites classified them in conversations with me—among them janitors, clerks, and mechanics, often set up provisionary black tents for commemorations during the month of Muharram. I have observed a number of such gatherings in different parts of the city and have listened to descriptions of many more of them by Shiʻite and non-Shiʻite interlocutors. For example, in March 2003, a group of about ten young and middle-aged Shiʻite men (mostly associated with Amal) dressed in black, either in black T-shirts or in black shirts with some of the top buttons open, unshaven, gathered in a small parking lot in the middle-class West Beirut neighborhood of Clemenceau, where the great majority of inhabitants are not Shiʻites. There were some white plastic chairs outside the tent. Loudspeakers were hanging on each side of it, and the group was listening to a taped sermon turned up too loud for the loudspeakers' capacity. The men listened to the taped sermons and intermittently cried and beat their chests, and the gathering was evidently also a form of informal socializing. After the sermons the men continued to sit outside the tent, talk, and smoke water pipes. While the number of participants at that particular occasion was rather small, probably because few Shiʻites live in the immediate vicinity, gatherings in other mixed neighborhoods can be substantially larger, and of course in predominantly Shiʻite areas in the city those attending often number in the hundreds.

This occupation of public space with gatherings and speeches over loudspeakers has reinforced the stereotype of Shiʻites as religious fanatics. The presumed low-class qualities of Shi'ites become most obvious during these periods for several reasons. First, they set up tents where they are not supposed to, according to many of their neighbors, as in garages or on neighborhood corners. Second, they are represented as not showing any consideration for their neighbors. During Muharram, one of the main complaints of non-Shi'ite friends was the constant noise they had to endure and the dramatic speeches they were forced to listen to, which depressed them. At my workplace, two Sunni women would spend the weekends during Muharram at friends' houses because Shi'ites had set up tents in the parking lot below their house where the gathering was large. Third, the degree of Shi'ites' religiosity was not viewed as appropriate for a multisectarian setting, where religion is not supposed to be expressed so publicly. The rural background of these Shi'ites was taken as an explanation for such behavior in urban cosmopolitan places. Thus, implicitly, the rural areas were imagined to be more religiously homogeneous than urban centers of Lebanon, and as poor and lower class.

The popular movie *West Beirut,* directed by Ziad Doueiri and released in 1998, provides perhaps some of the clearest evidence for the functioning of such stereotyping of Shi'ites in the Lebanese nationalist project. The story concerns two young Sunni boys, Omar and Tarek, who experience the civil war of 1975–1990 and who learn the deadly importance of having the correct religious identity while under the harassment of militias during the war. There is also a story about innocent love between two teenagers—May, a Christian girl, and Tarek, a Sunni boy in the same neighborhood. May plays the piano, and Tarek's father, an intellectual and an Arab nationalist, plays the 'oud. Tarek's mother is a lawyer who works in East Beirut.

West Beirut presents a Sunni-Christian space with shared notions of bourgeois respectability in a cosmopolitan city, and with many markers of high urban culture. But this ideal world of West Beirut is frequently disturbed by the presence of a loud, vulgar, and fat Shi'ite woman living in the same building, yelling at chickens and neighbors at the same time in her (supposedly) thick southern accent. She represents the antithesis to this world of West Beiruti middle class. Everything about her is supposed to represent her low-class status. She is loud, violent, she uses vulgar language, and she is sexual in a cheap and unappealing manner, as opposed to the true love and friendship portrayed between Tarek's parents.

Her way of claiming space, and the way one of the neighbors reacts to her presence in the neighborhood finds parallels in everyday settings in Beirut. When the Shi'ite woman yells at the chickens early in the morning, one of the neighbors opens her window and yells, "Refugee, you don't belong here, pack your shit and go home." Upon which the Shi'ite woman replies, "Perfume your month before talking about the south." After Tarek has angered the Shi'ite woman, she comes up to his apartment, where Tarek's mother protects her son from being beaten up by this woman and tells the Shi'ite woman, "If you touch my son I will drag your ass to the south myself." Upon which the Shi'ite lady screams, "You and your son are lower than the garbage in the south."

West Beirut presents a vision of an ideal Lebanese national identity. It rejects Phoenicianism, a tendency to link Lebanese national identity to the ancient Phoenicians that is widespread mainly among Lebanese Maronites, as represented in a long conversation Tarek's father has with his son, during which Tarek obviously repeats the official history of Lebanon he had been taught at his school that traces the genealogy of Lebanese to the Phoenicians instead of emphasizing their Arab identity. It also rejects the excessive religiosity of Omar's father, who forces him to attend the mosque. Both Tarek and Omar know passages from the Quran, which shows they are to a certain degree pious, but both believe that Omar's father is becoming somewhat abnormal as a result of the civil war by sending Omar to a mosque. The moral of the story is that the friendship between these three teenagers continues despite war propaganda that attempts to divide Lebanese along religious lines. All three are to some extent pious, but their piety is something of a private matter, a natural part of who they are, which they do not need to publicly perform on and develop further, as Omar's father for example wishes to. The message therefore also pertains to the ideal Lebanese national identity as embodied by the middle-class, urban-based, cosmopolitan elite, represented for a long time by the Sunni and the Christians in West Beirut. Shi'ites and the south, as signified through the vulgar woman (but also Palestinians, as presented through the militia), find no place in this national imagery.

One group attempting to break the hegemony of this Beirut-centered, Christian-Sunni cosmopolitan version of Lebanon's national identity in popular culture and literary narratives has been the Shi'ite poets calling themselves the Poets of the South (*shu'ara al-janub*). They emerged after the Israeli invasion in 1982 and brought through their poems the plight of the south to the very center of national talk. Similar to the picture series of the Council of the South discussed above, the poets described the oppression, alienation, and despair of the rural Lebanese in the south, often combining the poems with Karbala imagery. These poems also stood in stark contrast to the popular poems of Khalil Gibran, for example, with his idealized notion of Lebanon as a larger version of a tranquil Christian village.[67]

Shi'ite activism from the 1960s, often depicted as sectarian activities at odds with a commitment to the nation, is an effort to break the Maronite-centered national narrative and to create an alternative nationalism in which Shi'ites inhabit a central position. The "third path" suggested by Sadr, that is, the production of religious visions of the nation, has become the dominant force in the construction of Shi'ite narratives of the nation since the 1970s. Sadr was successful in breaking the Maronite hegemony exactly because his nationalism stood in dialogue with Maronite nationalism and was to a certain extent a derivative form of it. He emphasized the importance of religious identity as a necessity to maintain morality in society. His attempt to decouple the ideology of coexistence from the institutional setup of political sectarianism, while still stressing the unique position of Lebanon as a place of Muslim-Christian coexistence, has been among the most successful ways for Shi'ite leaders to break a Maronite monopoly over such discursive themes.

By analyzing gendered jokes and anecdotes about Shi'ites in which they are identified as an underclass marked by their high birthrates, their rural identity, their supposed lack of taste, and their presumably excessive religious practices, I have pointed to the diverse ways of imagining Lebanese national identities. There, piety, while important, was often presented as a personal and private matter. However, in the view of Sadr and Hizbullah ideologues, Shi'ites' subaltern status, and their embrace of publicly staged piety, make them the most loyal citizens. These ideologues have mingled Maronite discourses of the nation with Shi'ite themes and inverted the labels given to Shi'ites to create Shi'ite nationalism. But Shi'ite activism to break away from these stereotypes, to advance their interests in Lebanon, and to ultimately transform the Lebanese nation has not been limited on a discursive level but has been accompanied by institution building. It is to one such institution, the Shi'ite-run schools, that we turn in the next chapter.

2

Schooling and the Creation of Lebanese Shi'ite Public Identity

In the opening scenes of the movie *West Beirut*, Tarek, a local Sunni boy, attends a French school in East Beirut where the teacher makes all students, standing in orderly rows in the schoolyard, sing the French national anthem. Tarek sneaks away and, appearing on a balcony, interrupts "La Marseillaise" by singing the Lebanese national anthem through a megaphone, as all the students enthusiastically join in. When the French teacher tries to discipline Tarek later in class, he mocks her, then is thrown out of the class. The teacher launches into a lecture, saying "Let us not forget that France has created your country, gave you your borders, and has taught you peace. France has provided the base for your civilization, and has prepared your constitution. You should know that education, particularly French education, is the only way for you to leave behind your barbarian customs." This scene takes place on April 13, 1975, the day the civil war began in Lebanon.

—FIELDNOTES, BEIRUT, 2003

Schools are sites of the production of nationalism and effective grounds for propagating visions of a moral society and public ethics. But what happens when a state fails to monopolize and disseminate one coherent national narrative and one vision of morality to its citizens? In Lebanon, because of constitutional definitions and its weak public infrastructure, religious communities often take over school education for the citizens. The Lebanese

Constitution defines its citizens—regardless of self-identification—as subjects belonging to religious communities. These communities are accorded "unequal access to political power and public office."[1] As a result of this political structure, community leaders and their institutions often mediate between citizen and state.

Weak public infrastructure accounts for the existence of a variety of community-organized schools. But it is this condition of unequal access to political power and public services based on the subject's religious identity that accounts for competition among these schools to promote their own national narrative, notions of social justice, and visions of ideal Lebanese citizens framed in religious discourse. This link between the degree of political power and religious identity explains the constant evaluation by Lebanese citizens of their religion compared with others. Debates over ideal citizenship carried through religious discourse are then intimately related to disputes over the political structure of the Lebanese state: either justifying the status quo or urging its modification.

The dramatic rise in the number of Shi'ite-run educational centers during and after the civil war demonstrates the awareness of Shi'ite ethnic entrepreneurs that education is one important avenue to change their image in Lebanon as backward and that such institutions are important in producing and popularizing their ideologies, national and otherwise.

Statistics from the United Nations Development Program (UNDP) reflect both the state's failure to invest in public schools and the cacophony of education in Lebanon. For instance, UNDP statistics for the academic year 1995–1996 show only 16.2 percent of students attending public schools in Beirut, whereas 74.4 percent went to fee-charging private schools which are often operated by the community. This is because only 28 percent of the schools in Beirut are public compared with the 60 percent that are fee-charging and private. In the suburbs of Beirut (where the majority of inhabitants are Shi'ites), only 13.5 percent of students go to public schools,[2] compared with 75.1 percent who attend fee-charging private schools. Only 22 percent of the suburban schools are public; 61 percent are fee-charging private schools.[3] Therefore, in Beirut and its southern suburbs, of all 95,920 students, about 20.26 percent attend public schools, while the remaining 79.74 percent attend private schools (both free and fee-charging).[4] This represents one of the weaknesses of the public education sector,[5] which provides Shi'ite-run schools with vast opportunities to create a *"homo nationalis"*[6] in line with their own religious and political vision. But despite the diversity of political and religious ideals in the Lebanese Shi'ite community, is there nonetheless consensus among Shi'ites as to who this ideal citizen is? This chapter throws light on some fierce competition among parties and factions in the Shi'ite community as they each claim to create those exemplary citizens in their schools.

Shi'ite-run Schools

Meeting with Ibrahim Shamseddine, the son of the late Shi'ite scholar and vice-president of the SISC, in his office in the Islamic Technical Institute (*al-ma'had al-fanni al-islami*) in the southern suburbs of Beirut, I asked how he compares his Shi'ite school (*al-madrasa al-shi'iyya*) to others, translating "Shi'ite school" from Arabic into English. He immediately noted that "we are not a religious school here. To me a Shi'ite school would mean something like a *hawza*, a school where you learn about Shi'ite theology. That is not what we do here, our school is open to all religious groups; it happens that it is run by a Shi'ite."

I encountered similar resistance to the term "Shi'ite schools," although the Arabic expression used in informal settings always referred to them as such or would include the names of the party or the religious leaders who run them. Lebanese referred to these schools as Hizbullah schools (*madaris hizbullah*), Amal schools (*madaris al-haraka*), or Fadlallah's charity organization (*mabarrat fadlallah*). The official names of these schools would also indicate their Shi'ite identity: Al-'Amiliyya, for example, refers to the Jabal 'Amil, now South Lebanon, as it is associated as a center with religious and intellectual tradition among Shi'ites. Hizbullah-run schools are called *Madaris al-Mahdi*, referring to the vanished Twelfth Shi'ite Imam. The schools of *Mu'assasat Amal al-Tarbawiyya* are named after a series of Shi'ite martyrs associated with Amal.[7] The names of other Shi'ite-run schools follow the same pattern. And in fact, despite the insistence of their leaders, few non-Shi'ites attended these schools. But how I referred to the schools mattered to school directors who did not want to imply that they serve only their own community or that education in religion is the main goal in these schools. So I came up with the term "Shi'ite-run schools" to denote schools mainly funded and operated by Shi'ites, usually located in Shi'ite neighborhoods, with almost all Shi'ite staff and students.

These schools, which are still in their early stages, attract mainly students from weaker economic backgrounds (although al-Mustafa schools are much more expensive compared with other Shi'ite-run schools, and they try to train elite Shi'ite students). In fact, many well-off Shi'ites, and the majority of Shi'ite ethnic entrepreneurs, do not send their own children to these schools. Most senior Amal members I knew, and many members of the Sadr family, send their children to international schools, as Shi'ite-run schools do not have the same academic prestige as Christian or internationally run schools in Lebanon and are assumed not to provide the same cultural capital as the older, established schools.

Filling Gaps and/or Giving Meaning to Life?

Scholars have pointed to the relative delay in the creation of Shi'ite-run schools compared with those in other communities in Lebanon.[8] They have also discussed the relative discrepancy between the high number of Shi'ites in Lebanon and the lower number of Shi'ite students in schools,[9] and the wide range of Shi'ite educational centers for addressing the internal diversity of the Lebanese Shi'ite community and its institutions.[10] Scholarship on the al-'Amiliyya school and other minor Shi'ite-run schools in Nabatiyya,[11] together with brief discussions of Hizbullah's educational centers,[12] has so far dominated the studies on Shi'ite-run schools in Lebanon.

Much attention has been paid to history books rather than to other techniques that form national identities in Lebanon. However, the geographic location of these schools, the layout, extracurricular activities, and their choice of religion textbooks also need to be taken into consideration when studying how schools produce nationalism and how they create a sense of locality. By analyzing the educational goals, the choices of religious teaching material, and the extracurricular activities (*nashatat*) of three Shi'ite-run schools, I explore various types of Shi'ite nationalism. I show the competition among them in claiming to represent the most authentic Shi'ites and the most loyal citizens in Lebanon. The three types of schools are the al-'Amiliyya; the al-Mustafa schools belonging to the Islamic Religious Education Council (*jam'iyyat al-ta'lim al-dini al-islami*, hereafter referred to as JTDI); and the Amal Educational Centers (*mu'assasat amal al-tarbawiyya*). While these last two also operate schools outside of Beirut, I focus on their branches within the city. I present these three distinct religious nationalist narratives as constructing Lebanese Shiʿite identities in light of their transnational ties to Iran.[13]

Al-ʿAmiliyya was the first Shiʿite-run school in Beirut and was founded in 1929, well before Lebanon gained its independence in 1943. It operated at the height of secular Arab nationalism and maintained ties to Iran long before 1979. JTDI, on the other hand, began its activities in 1974, opened its first school in 1983 in al-Dahiyya (*harat hurayk*),[14] and has maintained close ties to Iran ever since the success of its Islamic revolution. Amal educational centers began operating only after the end of the Lebanese civil war in 1990, and their activities so far do not reflect important ties to Iran. Thus, these three schools constitute an interesting range of comparison in terms of the particular political atmosphere in which each began to operate, their political and educational ideologies, and the types of transnational networks they maintain.

However, these schools also exhibit some similarities:

1. Each is part of a larger institution, either a benevolent society or a political party.
2. They do not state publicly that they are institutions only for Shiʿites and emphasize their openness to other religious communities, when in fact almost all of their students are Shiʿites associated with the school's respective institution or political party.
3. They are part of the fee-paying private school system. In other words, they rely on student fees, and religious charity donations (*zakat*), in addition to some state subsidies.
4. In Lebanon, where religious education in schools is often viewed as the promotion of sectarianism, the continuing existence of religious education at these schools is legitimized in terms of its goal of raising moral standards in society.
5. The existence of all these schools is justified in terms of filling a gap caused by the shortcomings of public schools in Lebanon.

Unify the Schools, Unify the Nation?

A widely held assumption in Lebanon, as among some scholars,[15] is that there is an inherent link between secularism and the successful production of democracy and of loyal national subjects. Accordingly, religion in what is seen as the public sphere is imagined to be the main force dividing the people and the most persistent obstacle for successful national coexistence. Following this perspective, a unified education system, in particular one with standardized history books[16] and a unified policy regarding the language of instruction as well as the elimination of religion (or at least the option of doing so) from the curriculum, will produce students more committed to the Lebanese nation and less prone to engage in sectarian violence. This reasoning about nationality and schools also is often linked to the idea that transnational forces are harmful to the production of loyal citizens. According to that point of view, the maintenance of certain types of transnational networks is equated with disloyalty to the idea of Lebanon.

In public discourse, the lack of a clear national educational policy[17] has been considered one of the reasons for the continuing strength of so-called sectarianism in Lebanon; it has consequently been held responsible for the perceived failure in creating national subjects.[18] Public debates, conferences, and newspapers serve as forums for voicing such concerns, while religious scholars and ethnic leaders associated with the schools have sought to dispel such suspicions.[19] There have been protracted experiments regarding standardizing textbooks,[20] introducing civic education textbooks,[21] and making religious education optional[22] or limiting the number of hours devoted to it, all in the belief that a secular, unified education system produces national homogeneity and helps to eliminate what is thought of as sectarianism. But a considerable part of the production of Shiʻite citizens, as in the production of other communal national identities, takes place in extracurricular activities and in the wider environment within which the school operates, with almost entirely Shiʻite staff and students, and in Shiʻite neighborhoods. In addition, in most of these debates, religion is viewed as operating outside a historical and sociopolitical context where, in fact, religion as structured through political sectarianism creates obstacles for politics of solidarity rather than what these policymakers believe to be the characteristics of religion itself.

In the debates on creating a unified education system, one can discern three different themes.[23] First and most important, discussions revolve around the issue of what a unified history textbook should contain.[24] Second, there is a disagreement about teaching religion and the actual content of civic-education textbooks.[25] Promoters of the total secularization of the state, unlike those who advocate only the secularization of the political system, see teaching religion as an obstacle to the creation of a *homo nationalis*, while religious leaders from all communities urge the continued presence of religion in public institutions[26] and teaching religion in schools. They suggest that only religion can be the basis for producing a truly moral society. More important, religious leaders consider the presence of religious instruction and symbols in the public institutions, such as education, a necessity for the creation of loyal citizens and patriots.[27]

Third, there is the question of the language of instruction: Arabic, French, and English are all possible candidates. With three types of school systems[28] operating parallel to each other—public schools, free-of-charge (*majjani*) private schools, and fee-charging (*ghayr majjani*) private schools—choices among school subjects and methods are often politicized. Does teaching Arabic emphasize a specific group as exemplary nationals? Should omitting religion from schools be read as a sign of commitment to the idea of Lebanon? This chapter analyzes how three Shi'ite-run schools oriented toward different ideologies claim to produce authentic Lebanese nationals, while being clearly faith-based.

Working Within the System: Al-'Amiliyya Islamic Charity Organization (*al-jam'iyya al-khayriyya al-islamiyya al-'amiliyya*)

Al-'Amiliyya is considered the first Shi'ite-run school in Beirut; it remained the only regular school until 1983. Established in 1929 when Lebanon was under the French mandate, this school was created because of the discrimination and socioeconomic difficulties confronting rural and poor Shi'ite migrants to Beirut.[29] The goal of establishing this school—according to its founder, the late Rashid Baydun,[30] a Shi'ite leader from South Lebanon—where the curriculum included secular subjects and knowledge associated with the West, was to combat "ignorance and poverty." Al-'Amiliyya was financed with the help of private contributions, student fees, state subsidies, foreign government donations, and contributions from religious endowments (*awqaf*).[31] In its early years, al-'Amiliyya filled a void, by not only providing schooling for Shi'ite children but also becoming a socioreligious center for many Shi'ite residents in Beirut. For example, 'Ashura commemorations took place in the al-'Amiliyya, and after such meetings donations were collected for the school.

By 1937, al-'Amiliyya planned to expand from one to forty-seven schools as public schools were rare in Shi'ite-inhabited areas and Shi'ite religious leaders had issued a fatwa to ban Shi'ites from missionary schools. However, due to financial constraints, all forty-seven schools were closed down by 1944.[32] Until 1954, the activity of al-'Amiliyya was limited to providing secondary education for boys[33] in Beirut, but with the increasing migration of rural Shi'ites to Beirut by the end of the 1960s and early 1970s, both as a result of unemployment and because of Israeli attacks in South Lebanon, in 1970–1971 a total of 2,030 were registered in the various schools of al-'Amiliyya.[34] Besides Arabic, French and, later, English were taught at these secondary schools.[35]

Above the entrance to the al-'Amiliyya school is carved the sword of Imam 'Ali, a clear public sign of the school's Shi'ite identity. The teaching of the Quran as well as religious instruction were part of the curriculum and, depending on the grade, Shi'ite shaykhs taught an hour of Quran recitation in addition to an hour of religious instruction. Younger students had to pray at noon. Al-'Amiliyya was a faith-based school.

How did Rashid Baydun justify the creation of al-'Amiliyya? How did he reconcile the production of faith-based and nationalizing identities? How did he formulate and integrate the school's religious activities in national terms? In his view, the structure of the Lebanese state is based on sectarianism, as groups are forced to provide public services for their own communities. Nevertheless, he often expressed a wish to abolish the sectarian system, which he believed hindered the creation of a unified nation.[36] But given these structural limitations, he argued that supporting one's own religious community and loyalty to the nation were not mutually exclusive. For example, in 1939, on celebrating the acquisition of land he had purchased with funds contributed by the Shi'ite diaspora,[37] he expressed how such financial support for education helps free Lebanon from the French, since knowledge is very important for reaching independence. Similarly, in laying the foundation stones for the al-'Amiliyya Technical School in 1957, he stressed the importance of education, which would make students "feel they are from Lebanon, the country of knowledge and light."[38]

On various occasions, Baydun affirmed the Lebanese patriotism he considered characteristic of his school. For example, the religious activities of al-'Amiliyya, such as the commemoration of 'Ashura, were attended also by non-Shi'ite religious leaders and sometimes by provincial leaders of the government. 'Ashura had not become overtly politicized in Lebanon in the 1940s and 1950s and the commemorations did not yet represent a platform by which Shi'ites expressed political demands and voiced ideas about an alternative Lebanese national identity. Still, these gatherings offered an opportunity to pledge loyalty to Lebanon in a direct way and to place political demands on many non-Shi'ite leaders attending. On the occasion of 'Ashura in 1965, he appealed to those present to support al-'Amiliyya because, as he said, "When one trusts that the national cause becomes the cause of all its communities . . . then the citizens become all [loyal to] the country and the country becomes a state for all."[39] Sports activities by students of al-'Amiliyya were also an occasion for bringing members of various religious groups together. The publicity for such occasions was portrayed as evidence of the commitment of both leader and school to the Lebanese nation.[40]

A Failed Project: Teaching Farsi to Shi'ites in Lebanon

From its beginning, al-'Amiliyya depended heavily on funds from outside Lebanon for its continued existence. Egyptian President Gamal 'Abdel Nasser donated to al-'Amiliyya.[41] Rashid Baydun took many trips to countries in Africa to collect funds from the Lebanese Shi'ite diaspora to continue and to improve the school. In 1959, members of al-'Amiliyya also established contacts with the Iranian education ministry for support of their schools.[42] In exchange for support from Iran, which provided money as well as equipment for chemistry and biology labs, al-'Amiliyya agreed to teach Farsi to the students as a foreign language. A training class was organized in which Lebanese teachers were taught Farsi with the aim of being able to teach it to students in the future.[43] Two Iranian teachers also began teaching two hours of Farsi per week at the school, and the Iranian government made some scholarships available for graduates of al-'Amiliyya to study at universities in Iran. The first group of al-'Amiliyya graduates left for Iran in 1960, and in November 1962 Rashid Baydun took an official one-month trip to Iran, where he visited Lebanese graduate students at Tehran University.[44]

But the teaching of Farsi did not last long. Husayn Yatim, a former teacher at al-'Amiliyya and also the head of the Arab Institute (*al-ma'had al-'arabi*) in Beirut, where Farsi was also taught,[45] argues that the project failed for two main reasons. The first was the irrelevance of Farsi in the Lebanese context. Due to its colonial presence in Lebanon, French had been the most important foreign language taught at most Lebanese public and private schools until political ties to the United States were strengthened and the international importance of English was acknowledged in Lebanon. French was taught from the establishment of al-'Amiliyya, while English was introduced only in 1962.[46] Farsi was not considered an internationally important language, and it was difficult to motivate students to pursue it.

The failure of Farsi teaching in the 1960s was also directly related to the political atmosphere of Lebanon in that decade. Many Shi'ites in the 1960s were sympathizers or members of leftist and Arab nationalist parties (*al-ahzab al-qawmiyya*). During an interview, Yatim described for me the political mood of the time:

> Lebanese Shi'ites were among the most committed supporters of Nasser, the political mood among Shi'ites in that period was [secular] nationalist, nationalist, nationalist (*qawmi, qawmi, qawmi*), in all its forms. There was no room, no interest in a connection to a Shi'ite person called Reza Pahlavi with good relations with Israel and America. The Lebanese Shi'ites were not Iranian Shi'ites. I don't mean to say that the Iranians liked the Shah, but he was the government and we didn't like his style and his politics. Liking the language and culture of a country depends on the political stance between the two countries. If you like the politics, you want to learn their language. The Islamic position/mood (*al-mawqif al-islami*) was not the dominant political force at that time and that's why the Shi'ite connection did not work back then.

But Lebanon was divided on Nasser's aims. Camille Chamoun, the president of Lebanon until 1958, feared the emergence of a strong Muslim unity, which might have endangered Christian power in Lebanon, while many Lebanese Muslims were strong supporters of Nasser. The Shah of Iran maintained close ties to Chamoun, who saw in the Shah a power capable of countering Nasser. Iran also maintained ties to Israel[47] until the Iranian revolution, and many Arab nationalists viewed the Shah as a stooge of the Americans. One can imagine how in such a political atmosphere the teaching of Farsi would have been evaluated in any Arab Muslim institution at the time. To demonstrate their disagreement with the Shah's politics, students would regularly boycott classes. Yatim remembers the students getting into ideological discussions with their teacher of Farsi, whom they saw as a representative of the Iranian government. In one case, some students even physically attacked the Iranian teacher. The situation deteriorated to such an extent that Farsi classes had to be canceled altogether. Ties between al-'Amiliyya members and the Iranian embassy were not broken because of these cancellations, but continued on an informal level until the success of the Iranian revolution.[48]

The only other attempt at teaching Farsi to Lebanese Shi'ites at school occurred almost forty years later in a more favorable political atmosphere—
one dominated by what Yatim referred to as the "Islamic mood." The Wit-
ness schools (al-shaahid) are connected to the Martyrs Foundation (mu'assasat
al-shahid), which is a branch of the Iranian Martyrs Foundation.[49] Opened
in 1998, the al-Shaahid schools are mainly designed to educate students not
only from families who lost a member fighting the Israelis but also from
other disadvantaged Shi'ite families affiliated with Hizbullah. Until the academic year of 2002–2003, the school operated classes from preschool
through the secondary level. Of about four thousand students enrolled in
these schools, a quarter comes from families in which someone had been
martyred.[50]

In the view of the director of the Martyrs Foundation, al-Haj Qasim 'Aliq,
the goals of the schools are

> to build a faithful, authentic (asila), balanced, open-minded, Muslim identity.
> . . . The school also aims to sow the seeds of commitment, trust, and con-
> sciousness about the religion and the true message of Islam, as exemplified by
> Imam al-Khomeini and those who walked in his path afterwards [referring to
> Khamenei].[51]

Perhaps al-Shaahid schools can be viewed as one of the most visible of
the transnational Shi'ite networks that now operate between Iran and Lebanon. In the academic year 2002–2003, al-Shaahid schools introduced Farsi
as the third foreign language after English and French in the tenth-grade
curriculum. Some of these students grew up in Iran. Their fathers were either studying in Qom or were part of the Hizbullah-Iranian military, and
they had a basic knowledge of the language. Although these students are
devoted to the leader of the Islamic Republic of Iran and define their relations to Iran to be on a religious level, language does not seem to be the medium through which these ties are expressed. Students at the al-Shaahid
school are not interested in learning Farsi, since they regard it as a "useless
language." Parents complain about the overload in the school's curriculum
and how learning Farsi as the third foreign language diminishes the chances
that the students will improve in both English and French, which the parents consider highly relevant for their children's future. The director of the
school decided to introduce Farsi as part of the curriculum because, in his

opinion, most graduates will eventually leave with stipends provided from the Iranian government to attend higher education in Iran. In his view, having learned Farsi at school will make this transition easier for students.

Muna Mu'ayyad, daughter of an Iranian shaykh, teaches Farsi at one of these schools. She believes that the teaching has not been successful, not only because the language is largely irrelevant to the immediate needs of the students but also because of a lack of a clear curriculum.[52] She suggests a more interactive approach that would attract students; for example, in her two-hour class she often shows Iranian movies to the students so that they can "find out what Iranian culture (farhang-i irani) is about." She also likes the idea of rewarding successful students with gifts and travel to Iran, which she believes would raise the motivation of the students. In her opinion, the teaching of Farsi at the school should result in developing connections to Iran, thereby stimulating students' interest in the language, rather than focusing on the direct, technical acquisition of Farsi:

> I work only on the psychological level with them this year (faqat az lahaz-i ra-
> vani bahashun kar mikonam), but I think teaching Farsi is really good and nec-
> essary to familiarize students with Persian culture. Even knowing a few words
> will help them understand the culture better. Farsi needs to become part of the
> curriculum of this school as it is connected to the Shahid schools in Iran. But
> as long as there is no clear planning on how to teach it and on how to reward
> the students, the project will fail.

In the 1960s, Farsi was perceived as an index of the Shah's anti-Nasser, anti-Arabist, and pro-Israeli policies and was thus rejected by schools, teachers, and the students. In 2003, the teaching of Farsi as a medium to intensify transnational Shi'ite ties turned out to be a failure in one of the schools most closely associated with postrevolutionary official Iran. In the 1960s the teaching of Farsi was also associated with the Shi'ite Shah in a surge of secular Arab nationalism in which many Lebanese Shi'ites took part.

As the failed experience of teaching Farsi in 2002–2003 shows, a generation ago the Persian language was often negatively associated with Shi'ism, but now many Lebanese Shi'ites simply do not view it as a key dimension of transnational Shi'ite networks. Considering the importance of Farsi in the construction of secular Iranian nationalist ideologies,[53] the Shah's decision to encourage the teaching of it in return for his financial support came from such a perspective, while the postrevolutionary effort to introduce Farsi was meant to tighten transnational religious ties. In both instances Lebanese Shi'ites perceived it as indicative of intentions inverse to their actual goals. The Shah's policy was taken as intending to strengthen Shi'ite ties, while postrevolutionary plans to introduce Farsi were not so interpreted but were seen as an example of Iranian nationalism not based on affiliation with Shi'ism.

Lebanese domestication of transnational Shi'ite support also becomes clear in this context. While the financial support of the Iranian government and foundations has been welcomed at these schools both prior and after the success of the Iranian revolution, Lebanese Shi'ites are really striving to gain the cultural capital associated with a knowledge of French and English, and a high score in the final national exams, which is most valued in the Lebanese context. By improving the educational level of Shi'ites, who lag behind other communities in this regard, transnational Shi'ite ties are viewed as supportive on two interrelated levels. By raising the educational level of a larger number of Shi'ites, it is hoped that their chances of entering Lebanese governmental jobs are enhanced. At the same time, through transnational support, these schools can more successfully engage in the creation of certain types of Shi'ite-centered Lebanese national identities in line with the larger parties they are affiliated with. Transnational Shi'ite forces from Iran do not have the vast power many Western observers and Lebanese alike often assume, as Lebanese Hizbullah decides how to channel transnational support to enhance its own position in Lebanon. In this respect, transnationalism provides resources needed to place credible claims on the Lebanese nation.

Producing Textbooks, Producing Nationalism: The Foundation for Islamic Religious Education (jam'iyyat al-ta'lim al-dini al-islami)

Created in 1974, this foundation intended "to fill the gap that existed in Shi'ite religious education in Lebanese schools."[54] Its establishment was part of a range of Shi'ite efforts to institutionalize their existence as a community in Lebanon. Prior to 1974, several shaykhs had compiled their own religion textbooks, which they used as teaching material in schools located in Shi'ite neighborhoods. Musa Sadr's al-Islam: Din wa Hayat[55] as well as

Hidayat al-Muta'allimin,[56] and *Rub' Yasin* were among these.[57] Although a legal commission had existed since 1967, according to SISC's internal law number 28, to supervise the production of Shi'ite religion textbooks,[58] by 1974 it had not yet succeeded in getting any such books published.

Among the founding members of JTDI was Shaykh Na'im Qasim, currently Hizbullah's secretary-general deputy. These members had two goals in mind in creating JTDI: training Shi'ite religion teachers and publishing religion textbooks specifically designed for Shi'ites.[59] In the first year after the establishment of the foundation, they produced handwritten textbooks and gave copies to the religion teachers, who at that time did not exceed ten in number, while preparing the contents of their religion books called *al-Islam Risalatuna*.

JTDI feared the loss of Shi'ite students to Christian missionary schools and felt the need to open specifically Shi'ite-run educational institutions as a countermeasure. In their view, the majority of Shi'ite students who attended Christian schools had become attracted to the strong Catholic missionary activities of such schools. Those Shi'ites going to public schools did not receive any instruction in religion at all since it was not part of the public school curriculum. In the view of JTDI's director of research, "The social atmosphere of Lebanon required that Muslims would need to establish their own schools in order to compete with the high level of education offered in other schools, and to teach the proper way of Islam."[60]

With that in mind, the founding members asked a number of high-ranking Shi'ite shaykhs in Lebanon, such as Muhammad Husayn Fadlallah, Shaykh 'Ali Kurani, Shaykh Muhammad Mahdi Shamseddine, and Sadr, to support their undertaking.[61] Since SISC had failed to produce adequate religion textbooks, Sadr, then head of the organization, welcomed this suggestion and offered financial support to the group, but after he disappeared on his trip in Libya in 1978, the founding members were left with a funding gap. They decided to travel to Arab countries in the gulf to collect money for the production of the books and the training of teachers until financial support became available through Iran after the success of the Islamic revolution. These funds, which led to the opening of JTDI's first school in 1983, came either directly from the Iranian government or through the religious offices of Iranian *maraji'* such as Khomeini and, later, Khamenei. Since JTDI members acknowledge the latter two as their "source of emulation," these religious leaders issued special permission clearly stating how religious taxes should be spent. Khamenei, for example, gave written permission for JTDI members to spend religious tax money on expanding and maintaining the schools.[62]

Another important transnational Shi'ite component played a role in developing JTDI in its earlier stages. While many Shi'ite-run schools more recently have used JTDI-produced religion textbooks, and JTDI has also provided these schools with its own trained Lebanese teachers of religion, initially the teaching of the Shi'ite religion in Lebanon became more organized through JTDI's cooperation with Shi'ite shaykhs from Iraq. Some Iraqi shaykhs, mainly students of the Shi'ite scholar Sayyid Muhammad Baqir al-Sadr (d. 1980),[63] who were fleeing the Iraqi Ba'ath regime in the 1970s and 1980s, took refuge in Lebanon. As the teaching of their religion became an increasingly sensitive topic among Lebanese Shi'ites, these Iraqi shaykhs found a niche in the Lebanese school system.[64] By 1978, Iraqi shaykhs were teaching at schools in southern suburbs of Beirut, in Ba'albak, and in some Shi'ite neighborhoods in East Beirut. Al-Haj Husayn Diab, one of the founding members of JTDI, recalls that their teaching was satisfactory, but when one of them asked to become the director of the foundation, the idea that an Iraqi should lead a Lebanese institution, despite his Shi'ite ties, was considered unacceptable by the leaders of the foundation. This incident led the members to appoint Na'im Qasim the director of JTDI. Tensions along perceived national lines have also existed in this transnational Iraqi-Lebanese Shi'ite network, even though what is understood to be Iraqi Shi'ism represents the most authentic form of Shi'ism for many Lebanese Shi'ites.[65]

Teaching Religion

Religion in schools is vital for JTDI, but it is not meant to be only a subject in class; in fact, the main part of religious education takes place in extracurricular activities. The overall goal is the shaping of a Muslim subject:[66] "The most seamless way to build a strong open religious character, calling for Islam, and thus representing what Islam is to us: the air we breathe, the water we drink and a heart beating with life."[67] Religion is viewed as a total way of life, an essential part of producing a comprehensive identity, rather than an objectified Islam taught like other subjects in class.[68]

Al-Mustafa schools *(madaris al-mustafa)* are directly under the supervision of JTDI. Branches of the schools exist in Beirut, Nabatiyya, Tyre, and other areas in Lebanon. There were 8,091 students enrolled in the academic year 2001–2002.[69] More recently, in public schools located in Shi'ite neighborhoods, the government has allowed one hour per week of religious instruction. JTDI provides these public schools with teachers and with appropriate religion textbooks. In 2001–2002 there were three hundred JTDI-trained teachers active in 492 schools (238 private and 254 public schools) all over Lebanon, teaching 126,000 students.[70] These religion teachers, even if they are graduates of Shi'ite theological seminaries (*hawzat*), need to undergo six hundred hours (about a year) of training at JTDI before they receive permission to teach at any school.

Religious education in these schools is divided into three parts. The first is the in-class teaching of religion, which consists of two one-hour sessions per week, the first of which is the actual teaching of the Quran. The second part also takes place in class and is referred to as the educational considerations of religion. Students' behavior indicating a commitment to religious duties such as prayer is observed by teachers; if a need for improvement is perceived, it is talked about during a "free discussion" class. The third part of religious education in al-Mustafa schools is a combination of additional in-class and extracurricular activities. In-class activities include commemorating important religious occasions such as 'Ashura, while extracurricular activities include taking part in religious occasions outside the school.[71] Extracurricular activities undertaken in the academic year 2000–2001 included the following:[72]

1. organizing three *iftar* dinners in Beirut, in the south, and in the al-Biqa';
2. organizing processions for 'Ashura and for the *hajj*, as well as some processions during Ramadan;
3. celebrating the *'id al-adha* for orphans;
4. organizing celebrations for female students who have reached the age of nine and are to begin wearing the *hijab*;
5. organizing two nationwide academic competitions, in which 2,355 students took part;
6. celebrating the birth of Imam 'Ali by organizing various school competitions such as Quran readings;
7. celebrating the birth of Imam Mahdi (the twelfth and last Shi'ite Imam, who is believed to have disappeared at a young age);
8. organizing pilgrimages for students, teachers, and employees to Shi'ite holy sites;

9. organizing courses for students to memorize the Quran;
10. commemorating the death of the third Shi'ite Imam, Husayn.

Like representatives of other faith-based schools, JTDI leaders argue that the importance of keeping religious education in schools and in a wider public sphere is connected to raising moral values of the society.[73] If religion is considered the main source for moral values, it is directly connected to the creation of patriots and loyal citizens. With this logic, JTDI claims to produce the most loyal citizens, since in the view of its leaders it practices religion in its most authentic and most complete form. Sayyid Ibrahim Amin al-Sayyid, a leading ideologue of Hizbullah, and a former member of the Lebanese parliament, explains that before "the revolution of Imam Khomeini" there was "a cultural problem between Islam and national movements," so that religious education in schools was viewed as a school subject only. But "after the success of the Revolution the whole issue changed completely . . . as religious education became a culmination of modernization, of development, of success . . . of jihad and blood."[74] JTDI members, who are most often affiliated with Hizbullah, present themselves as strongly committed to the idea of Lebanon as a place of coexistence. As proof of their loyalty to Lebanon and of their nationalism, they emphasize the resistance activities in South Lebanon. A Week of Resistance in schools is celebrated with special programs for the students.[75] JTDI schools also have programs to celebrate the Independence Day of Lebanon, as do other schools all over Lebanon.

Hizbullah's Lebanon

While scholars have discussed Hizbullah's political convictions, its intellectual commitments, and its religious vision of the society, the practical dimension and the reception of this vision remain rather unexplored. An exception is Lara Deeb's *An Enchanted Modern*, in which she discusses the lived experiences of Hizbullah and Fadlallah followers, especially their gendered notions of piety and public morality.[76] Here, I am specifically concerned with the dialogic relation between Hizbullah's central pillars of identity—the concept of martyrdom, the creation of the resistance society, and its subaltern identity—and its national vision of Lebanon. This new nation is imagined and explained through religious imagery, while at the same time these seemingly religious pillars win meaning in the Lebanese context.

Ajyal al-Mustafa, a widely circulated journal published by the JTDI since 1995, provides both an illustration for processes of Shiʿite national identity construction as well as the perception of such identity politics in these schools. This journal includes descriptions of school activities, interviews with religious leaders, texts and poems written by students of these schools, as well as paintings and discussions on topics such as health and the environment.

A student's poem called "My Beirut" is an example of how Hizbullah's Shiʿite identity is experienced as a subaltern in Lebanon. It describes an underclass which yet claims its share of Beirut, a Beirut that is fully authentic *when* it represents mainly this disempowered group:[77]

My Beirut

You have your Beirut and I have my Beirut
Your Beirut is high buildings smeared with black, and pocked with
    snipers and bombers where warplanes shatter the sky's silence.
Your Beirut is alleys in which fire is exchanged and shops blown up.
And my Beirut is a small brick house on whose walls children draw
    pictures under the shadow of what they feel and what they think.
And my Beirut is an angel crowned a queen by the whole universe.
Your Beirut is an old portrait hung on the walls of each house.
And my Beirut is a young girl who doesn't know but the silver touch of
    moon and golden glim of the sun.
Your Beirut is a repeated poem by a very known poet who speaks to
    himself in a mirror.
And my Beirut is a poem that is every day changing read by the sky and
    written on the golden rocks of the seas.
Your Beirut is dinner parties full of most delicious food and my Beirut is
    a piece of bread in a hand of hungry kid and a doll in the hand of a
    poor girl.
Your Beirut is sandcastles against the storms.
And my Beirut is a tough rock that waves could not and will never
erode.

Or consider this poem, written by another student,[78] as an example of religious nationalist practice and imagination:

I am a child from Lebanon
Like a flower in a garden
I walk over sadness
I face the injustice of time
I carry in my palm a flower, I learn from it a lesson
I love all people, I respect all feelings
I am like my country Lebanon
Want the best for the people
I carry the torch of my belief
In Islam and in the Quran.

Students also submit drawings to the journal. Some of these have religious themes, such as scenes of Karbala, or they convey the idea of martyrdom through flowers with drops of blood. Others are scenes of nature or ordinary life. Some have the Lebanese flag integrated into them.

FIGURE 2.1. (A) Modified versions of the Lebanese flag drawn by students of the al-Mustafa school. *Ajyal-al-Mustafa* 18 (June 2001), back cover.

FIGURE 2.1. (B)

FIGURE 2.1. (C)

The cover of one of the issues of *Ajyal-al-Mustafa*, published after the liberation of South Lebanon from Israeli occupation in 2000, shows modified
versions of the Lebanese flag. Written on the flag are *kulluna lil-watan* ("All
of us for the country") and *kulluna muqawama* ("All of us are part of the resistance"), the latter phrase clearly associated with Hizbullah's resistance
activities but also with its vision of a moral society that resists material and
other types of corruption.[79] On the last page of the journal, where children's
drawings are usually presented, is a picture by a third-grade student of Israelis fighting in South Lebanon and Hizbullah members defeating them. The

Israeli flag has been thrown to the ground, while the Lebanese flag has been raised. On the Lebanese flag has been written *kulluna muqawama.*

JTDI is also promoting its own vision of Lebanon while constructing Muslim citizens using proper ways of greeting. A teacher discusses the merits of French versus Arabic greetings in an article called "Between al-Bonjour and al-Salam 'alaykum" *(bayn al-bonjour wa al-salam 'alaykum)*.[80] The Arabic greeting, often associated with practicing Muslims, is interpreted as promoting Arab identity, while the French greeting, often used in Lebanon by a wider range of people, but associated with Lebanese Christians, is frowned upon. While both JTDI and Amal openly promote an Arab identity for Lebanon, many Amal members use the term *marhaba* to greet one another, as *al-Salam wa'alaykum* is regarded as a religious salutation improper for everyday usage. I never heard any member of Hizbullah or JTDI use any other greeting but *al-Salam wa'alaykum.* The Westernized greeting indexes an imagined anti-Arab stance of many Lebanese Christians; the superiority of the Arabic greeting as a form of native and therefore culturally authentic Lebanese is affirmed. By promoting the idea that the term *al-Salam 'alaykum* emphasizes *Arab* identity as compared with the Westernized *bonjour*, JTDI members are promoting at once their own notion of Islam, of piety, and of an Arab identity as central to the Lebanese nation.

These articles, poems, and drawings clearly express, in a multilayered way, the promotion of a specific Lebanese national project embedded in a particular Shi'ite reading of Islamic values. The centrality of the Shi'ite *mustad'af* in an alternatively envisioned Lebanon—as expressed in the poems—is one component in the creation of an authentic new Lebanese nation. The new Lebanon shifts away from the image of belonging to and representing a Christian and Sunni bourgeoisie to that of a revolution of the subaltern, underclass Shi'ites. In chapter 1 I discussed some of these class struggles—referred to as the politics of *mahrumin*—and their implications for claiming the Lebanese nation. Another component is the importance of the resistance society embedded in the self-image of Hizbullah—which views itself as the revolutionary Shi'ites—for the creation of an authentic Lebanon, a new Lebanon with a new flag whose national image embodies an uncompromising resistance to Israel and to the injustice of both foreign invaders and domestic oppressors. As the first poem suggests, Hizbullah also spreads humanism—unlike a self-centered Christian bourgeois national project of state domination and exclusion—and equality among all citizens. Greetings have also become politicized, especially in the Shi'ite community, as ways to produce claims of religious authenticity and to resist dominance.

Ties to the Ruling Religious Elite in Iran

The development of JTDI is perhaps the best example of how its transnational ties to official Iran have influenced the lives of Shi'ites in Lebanon on a practical level. Founding members of JTDI became key members in the organization of Hizbullah and have maintained close ties to postrevolutionary Iranian leadership since 1982. Through the financial support it has received, JTDI has been able to succeed in its original goal of producing Shi'ite religion textbooks and attracting Shi'ite students away from what it perceives as Christian missionary activities. It was even able to open its own schools. Appropriating and adapting the discourse of the revolution in Iran, it has been able to express its own needs and struggles more quickly and more precisely.

JTDI's ties to the Iranian government and the Shi'ite religious elite become evident on various levels. The death of Khomeini was commemorated, for example, in its journal by publishing his pictures, poems on his personality and his contribution to Islam, and short articles by students.[81] On other occasions, gifts have been made to members of the Iranian embassy in Beirut who have either just taken up their posts or finished their tenure in Beirut and are returning to Iran.[82] The majority of the articles and pictures reflect the hierarchical nature of this particular transnational Shi'ite relationship. Official visitors from Iran, such as 'Ali Akbar Natiq Nuri, the advisor to the supreme leader 'Ali Khamenei, are shown being greeted by students gathered in the streets.[83] The victory anniversary of the Iranian revolution (dahe-i fajr), which is celebrated throughout schools in Iran by organizing special programs, is similarly commemorated at JTDI schools. Documentary films on the Iranian revolution as well as speeches of Khomeini are shown to students during these festive days.[84] Perhaps the article that best summarizes the nature of this transnational link is one written by a secondary school student from Nabatiyya:

> Conserving the Islamic republic is everyone's duty and one of the most important ones. It is even more important than keeping prayers, because it is about conserving Islam and prayers are a part of Islam. Conserving religion is a global obligation, and should therefore come before any other obligation [referring to religious obligations such as prayers].[85]

In this text, Iran as a country is certainly less the subject of interest than is the Islamic republic—a country imagined without its people—which indexes authentic Shi'ite Islam.

Reading the journal *Ajyal al-Mustafa* as an Iranian who was directly exposed to the practical implications of the ideological shift from pre- to post- revolutionary educational policy in Iran, I was at first struck by the apparent parallels between these two policies and the rhetoric used for the Islamic revolution. But a more careful reading suggests that, in fact, these discourses and images are significantly altered in their meaning and message to match a specifically Lebanese Shi'ite context characterized by the immediate experience of displacement and political frustration. Against that background the Iranian discourses and images are transformed and domesticated. For example, while during my own schooling in Iran the metaphor of the Yazid as the enemy at the battle of Karbala was used to describe the war between Iran and Iraq in the 1980s and the unjust Iraqi aggression, the Karbala motif has been transformed in Lebanon to mobilize resistance against unjust acts of Israel. The Yazid in the battle of Karbala, as depicted by Hizbullah, is Israel, while in the Iran of the 1980s Yazid represented Saddam Husayn (*saddam yazid-i kafir*) during the Iran-Iraq War.

The discourse on the importance of creating good Muslims in Iran was mainly justified in terms of the perceived lack of moral values in Iranian society prior to the revolution. In contrast, in the Lebanese context the importance of religious education, while also rhetorically connected to raising moral standards in society, is often justified in terms of defending the right of people to practice their own religion in the multiconfessional society of Lebanon. This was not an issue for the postrevolutionary Iranian government, given the overwhelming Shi'ite majority and the very small number of non-Muslims in Iran. The oppressors and the arrogant *mustakbirun* (*mustakberin*) in Iran were identified with the associates of the Shah prior to the revolution, while the *mustakbirun* of Lebanon in the view of Hizbullah have been the Christian-dominated state and the predominantly amoral Christian and Sunni bourgeoisie that have oppressed the Lebanese Shi'ites and still do not provide them with an adequate share of wealth and power.

There are ideological connections between JTDI members and the Iranian government and religious personalities in Iran, but only a few student exchanges have taken place between the two countries. For example, since 1992, nine hundred students have graduated from JTDI schools, but only twenty-three of them have left for Iran to study, compared with 142 who left for universities in the West. According to their director, problems of language acquisition, as well as the complex bureaucratic process of gaining admission to Iranian universities discourage many Lebanese Shi'ite students from applying to Iranian universities. Furthermore, Iranian scholarships do not cover the cost of living in Iran.[86] Thus, although the ideology of the Islamic republic dominates JTDI activities, recontextualized and fitted to the Lebanese setting, the actual exchange of students is rare, which shows how the transnational networks with Iran have been adapted to local needs, as locals' assessments of needed cultural capital informed by European standards have not changed. Despite strong ties to the clerical establishment in Iran and despite praise for the Islamic revolution, studies at European and American universities are much preferred to attending Iranian universities. The failed attempts to teach Farsi at the al-Shaahid schools also show that the domestication of transnational funds to achieve cultural capital in the Lebanese context is what is most important to these Lebanese Shi'ites.

Thus, the cultivation of intense transnational ties does not necessarily imply that national identities become irrelevant. On the contrary, they often contribute to the emergence of nationality by providing discourse and imagery to be reworked into national narratives. Transnational ties also strengthen claims on the nation by supporting the establishment of local institutions dedicated to this task.

The Islamic Bloc Fragments: Mabarrat Charity Foundation (jam'iyyat al-mabarrat al-khayriyya)

Musa Sadr's contemporary, Sayyid Muhammad Husayn Fadlallah,[87] was born into a southern Lebanese family with a strong theological background in Najaf in 1936.[88] He had studied with Ayatollah 'Abul al-Qasim Kho'i, became closely associated with Baqir al-Sadr, and joined the Iraqi Islamist Da'wa Party. Upon Fadlallah's return to Lebanon in 1966, he supervised the Society of the Family Brethren (jam'iyyat usrat al-takhi) in Nab'a, a poor, Shi'ite neighborhood in East Beirut. In 1977, with the support of Kho'i, he opened a series of social institutions called jam'iyyat al-mabarrat al-khayriyya, the goal of which was initially to provide schooling for orphaned children who had lost their parents during the civil war in Lebanon. Since 1977, six such schools for orphans have been built, two in Beirut, two in the al-

Biqa', and two in South Lebanon.[89] In 2002, about thirty-three hundred students were enrolled in these schools.

With the progressive deterioration of public order and state institutions in Lebanon in the 1980s and the poor quality of public school education, Fadlallah and his associates decided to expand their project and open schools for all Shi'ites. Despite the ongoing civil war, many Shi'ite students still attended Christian-run schools, which did not offer them religious education. This led to the opening of the first Mabarrat school for all Shi'ites called the Imam Baqir School in al-Hirmil, a region with a dense Shi'ite population, in 1988.[90] By 2000 the foundation had established twelve schools, located in Beirut, al-Biqa', and the south, with a total of 14,300 students.[91] For example, al-Kawthar all-girls' high school in Beirut opened in 1996 as a kindergarten but soon expanded to offer all levels of school education. In 2002 there were 1,850 students enrolled in this school. Although Rana Isma'il, the director of this high school, affirms that the school is open to all other religions, in 2002 only one Christian, two Druze, and a few Sunni students attended. She blames the small number of non-Shi'ite students on the decision of parents not to send their children to al-Kawthar, even though it is in fact open to other religious communities.

The *hijab* is obligatory for female students at Mabarrat schools and is part of the school uniform. Beside the one hour of religion and one hour of Quran study every week for students, the director points out that the main work of instilling Islamic values and principles takes place in the "hidden curriculum."[92] The extracurricular (so-called hidden curriculum) activities of the students at Mabarrat fall into five categories: physical activities, religious and national events, cultural clubs, intellectual meetings and dialogues, and field activities.

The Mabarrat schools initially used the teaching materials provided by JTDI but then began to produce their own religion textbooks, arguing that JTDI books are outdated because of the overall changes in education in Lebanon since the mid-1990s. Isma'il argues that the new religion textbooks are "only about one-third theoretical and two-thirds based on *scientific facts*; the books are more attractive to students that way."[93] Teachers of religion and the Quran at Fadlallah schools are graduates of the Mabarrat *hawza*, which are part of the larger Mabarrat Foundation. These teachers are followers of Fadlallah, whom they acknowledge as their source of emulation and whose vision of Shi'ite religion they propagate in the schools.

Fadlallah promotes his Lebanese Shi'ite nationalism in an institutionalized form by emphasizing that this more scientific approach to the teaching
of religion would make the boundaries between religious groups in Lebanon more permeable, as it does away with fanaticism and the promotion of

sectarianism often associated with the teaching of religion at schools in Lebanon. Interestingly enough, non-Shi'ite Lebanese, and even other Shi'ites,
often refer to Fadlallah schools as *al-madaris al-islamiyya* or Islamic schools,
referring to the emphasis on religious instruction in these schools, which
often take the school's style of *hijab* as their indicator for their degree of religiosity. For many Lebanese, this equals what they believe to be the creation
of sectarian identities as opposed to Lebanese national identity.

Finally, the creation of these new religion books has a transnational dimension as well. Fadlallah is setting himself apart from Hizbullah and ultimately from the Iranian religious elite who provide funds for JTDI. Despite
the lip service he pays to the legacy of Khomeini and the public display of
solidarity between the Iranian ruling elite and Fadlallah since the success of
the revolution (with a break of a few years in between in the early 1990s that
I will discuss in chapter 4), he is in practice creating boundaries between his
followers in Lebanon and those of Hizbullah. Fadlallah argues for an approach to religious tradition and history based on what he refers to as scientific and rational methods. The production of new religion textbooks under
the banner of promoting a more "scientific approach to religion" is part of
the practical implementation of Fadlallah's reputation as a modern theolo-
gian as opposed to what his followers have come to identify as traditional
Iranian scholarship, lacking scientific approaches to religion. This is a clear
sign of the further fragmentation of the Islamic Shi'ite bloc in Lebanon and
the differences in their vision of Lebanon and of the Islamic condition (*hala
al-islamiyya*) there.

Ethnic Entrepreneurs in State Institutions: Amal Educational Centers
(*mu'assasat amal al-tarbawiyya*)

The competition between Amal and Hizbullah in presenting themselves as
the most suitable leaders of the Shi'ite community, along with Hizbullah's
success in attracting large numbers of Shi'ites and establishing social institutions during the 1980s, was one of the reasons Amal opened a series
of schools in post–civil war Lebanon. But wider Lebanese intra-communal

competition also motivated the establishment of these schools. In postwar Lebanon, when it finally succeeded in becoming part of the state and to ensure its continued presence in the state apparatus, Amal needed to create a generation of loyal, educated ethnic entrepreneurs who would take up the positions the party created for these pro-Amal Shi'ites in the state.

Between 1990 and 2002, the Amal party opened a total of seven schools in heavily Shi'ite areas. Four schools are in South Lebanon, two in the al-Biqa', and one in Beirut.[94] A total of 9,176 studied in these schools in 2002–2003.[95] At the end of the Lebanese civil war in 1990, Amal opened its first school, the Bilal Fahs Institute, in South Lebanon in the town of Tul. In the 2002–2003 academic year, 3,005 students were enrolled at various levels of this school. According to the director of this school,

> much of the financial support for Amal was solicited during the war, especially between 1985 and 1991. This was a period when the influence of Amal as a militia was at its height and when it was able to collect funds from numerous sources. Besides receiving substantial contributions from wealthy immigrants, Amal militiamen exploited the Ouzai Port, taking a tax on all the imports. This form of extortion was widespread during the war. . . . Amal also monopolized the oil refineries in the south.[96]

Amal schools are fee-paying private schools; so after the Tul school began generating income, it supported the establishment of further institutions. This might explain the gradual development of Amal schools, spread over more than a decade, as compared with the JTDI or Mabarrat, which received a major part of their funding from the offices of their *maraji'*.

Among the stated goals of Amal educational centers is the "promotion and solidification of belief in God (*tanmiya wa tarsikh al-iman bi allah*)," "the promotion of the idea of national belonging," and the "promotion of the idea of belonging to the soil of a Lebanon that is united and independent, while understanding its history and geography within the context of its Arab identity." The importance of learning Arabic is also emphasized because it is the "mother tongue" and because "the knowledge of it opens a gate to Arab civilization."[97]

Abu Jafar (Muhammad Nasrallah), the director of Martyrs Hasan Qasir School in Beirut, so far the only Beirut-based school under the supervision of the Amal educational centers, described the overall policy of the schools and their goal to me in the following terms: "Our schools have no political coloring (*bidun ay lawn siyasi*), and no sectarian tone; it is an ordinary school (*madrasa 'aadiyya*), our only goal is education (*hadaf al-ta'lim faqat*)."[98] In his view, community-based schools are gap fillers for the state's shortcomings. Ideally the state should take over the education of all students in Lebanon for two central reasons. First, community-based schools (*madaris 'ala asas al-ta'ifa*) inevitably produce "sons of the community" (*abna' al-ta'ifa*) and not "sons of the nation" (*abna' al-watan*). He sees great danger for the future of the country in the diversity of schools and schoolbooks produced by community leaders: "The existence of unified books results in the creation of a unified culture and [consequently results in the creation of a] unified nation (*tawhid al-kitab ya'ni tawhid al-thaqafa ya'ni tawhid al-watan*)." There is also the question of financing these community-based schools. In his view, it is the duty of the state to provide all its students with equal opportunities to attend state schools, as it is a burden for the political parties and private persons to finance such costly projects.

Cleary Abu Jafar's claim that Amal-run schools will submit to decisions of the state is, in fact, problematic. Abu Jafar mentions the state as if Amal party leaders did not occupy central positions in the government and would not influence any decisions regarding public school policy. In other words, Amal and the state cannot be separated in the manner Abu Jafar suggests. He expresses a claim to neutrality and a desire for a unified culture and nation as if the decision about practicing such an approach did not involve Amal as a political force entrenched in the state apparatus. In other words, the creation of this unified culture and nation is not outside Amal's control.

Amal includes among its educational goals the creation of faithful persons (*mu'minun*), and it engages both students and teachers in some specifically Shi'ite religious activities. Amal's avoidance of clearly spelled out school policies regarding religion is not coincidental, since this is part of its larger effort to present itself as the suitable candidate to ideally establish a hegemony over the entire Lebanese Shi'ite community—and many of these Shi'ites are secularists. Yet, many Shi'ites also believe that teaching of religion, for example, should not be left to individual decision. Amal claims to be the most suitable political force to represent Shi'ite interests in Lebanon. It says it is "not too religious" but not "too secular"; in other words, Amal's official self-representation and its practice in education or 'Ashura rituals leaves open a wide range of interpretations.

The diversity in the ideological commitments of Amal members prior to their joining Amal, as well as the more loosely structured party organization as compared to Hizbullah can also be counted as responsible for a relative lack of standardization among its educational institutions. This diversity, when coupled with the frequent differences between the ideas of urban and rural Shi'ites regarding the place of religion in their lives, leaves individual Amal leaders some leeway in introducing their own ideas about the place of religion in education and about the practical implications of such decisions in the daily lives of their followers.

For example, discussions about proper Islamic dress codes for men and women, and especially the degrees of *hijab* to be worn by women, are obvious areas of struggle over the relative authenticity of the Shi'ite identity of groups in Lebanon. At Amal schools, wearing the *hijab* is obligatory for female teachers but not for female students, while at JTDI schools *hijab* is obligatory for both female students and teachers.[99] At Amal schools one can observe that in Beirut fewer students wear the *hijab* than in their other schools in the south. This can be explained in terms of the school directors' personal visions of the role of religion in the society as well as in the students' family preferences. At one level, Amal school policy indicates that, at least with respect to students, religious symbols are a matter of the so-called private sphere since parents are responsible for such decisions. Yet the decision that teachers, as direct employees under Amal supervision, should wear *hijab* is one of the ways Amal clearly claims a public Muslim Shi'ite identity.

The Religion Textbook Debate; or, Who Is More Lebanese?

When asked about the number of hours reserved for teaching religion at his school, Abu Jafar, the general director of Amal educational centers, as well as of their branch in Beirut, smiled at me and said, "Only one hour. We are not a *hawza 'ilmiyya* [a theological school] in Qom here. This is a [secular] school."[100] Religion, he went on to say, is important in schools because "without religion we turn into animals." He views religion as enhancing the morality of society; thus, it is a medium for something else, not an end in itself.

JTDI used to provide textbooks to schools with Shi'ite students until Amal opened its own educational institutions in the 1990s. Now Amal uses religion textbooks produced by the Supreme Islamic Shi'ite Council (SISC) known as *al-Tarbiyya al-Diniyya*. SISC is the sole representative of Shi'ite affairs recognized by the Lebanese state, and is de facto under the control of Amal. In fact, Amal pushed SISC representatives to produce separate religion textbooks for their schools. In Shi'ite-run schools, the choice between the religion textbooks produced by SISC and those produced by JTDI is crucial because of the political orientation of the producers of these books, and not so much because of their content.[101]

Muhammad Nasrallah suggests that the reason books produced by SISC are used in Amal schools and not those published by JTDI is that "we [the school] are part of the Shi'ite community and SISC is the official organ for representing Lebanese Shi'ite affairs, so we use their books." But it was clear from the conversation that he presented his own political beliefs as well as the Amal choice of the SISC religion textbook as "more Lebanese," since Amal uses the religion textbooks published by an official Lebanese institution claiming to be the highest authority among Shi'ites. Muhammad Nasrallah said that the practices of JTDI, which produces and uses its own books, were a breaking away from the national laws governing religious affairs in Lebanon, where religious councils such as SISC are supposed to be coordinating religious affairs; publishing religion textbooks is part of its duties. He portrays this difference as indicative of the two organizations' different political ties to Iran and what he sees as JTDI's state-in-a-state existence. He draws attention away from Amal's de facto hegemony over SISC and presents its own school (and ultimately its own party) as more committed to the Lebanese nation than its competitors in Hizbullah and other JTDI organizations. As SISC is closely associated with Amal, Hizbullah does not entertain links with the council, in the belief that the foundation does not really represent all Shi'ites.[102]

He adds that "the majority of our students are Shi'ites; we operate in a Shi'ite neighborhood; there is no unified textbook; all these factors make us obliged (*yujib 'alayna*) to use Shi'ite textbooks." From his argument and the impersonal verb he uses, it becomes clear that he does not present the Amal party as an active agent, but attributes responsibility for these choices to structural problems such as the lack of unified religion textbooks, or the predominance of Shi'ite students in its schools.

By this logic, claims by Amal representatives to fully support a policy of nationalizing schools have to be placed in a certain context. Amal exercises control over some state institutions that would be in charge of such a policy, providing Amal with unique opportunities to influence what is promoted as the national religion. This is the background for Muhammad Nasrallah's insistence on a state-sponsored, unified religion textbook, which all students, regardless of their religious backgrounds, would use.[103]

The production of religious identities at Amal schools takes place mainly through extracurricular activities and often in their scout activities. Amal's Islamic Scout Society (*jamʿiyyat kashshafat al-risala al-islamiyya*) was established in 1977 and is currently headed by Nabih Berri. The political party of Amal has about ten thousand scouts,[104] many of them students. Their activities are framed as being in the national interest. In Berri's view, "developing the nation" takes place "through securing the strength of the youth."[105] Activities of these students vary from organized marches in commemorating Sadr on August 31 each year[106] to fundraising. Scouts also participate in organizing some religious events in the schools or in planning outings.[107] For example, religious activities at the Amal-run school in Tul included an *iftar* dinner, and on the *ʿId al-Ghadir*, the day on which Shiʿites believe that the Prophet Muhammad publicly announced Imam ʿAli to succeed him after his death, the school had a special program for female students who had reached the age of nine and were to begin wearing the *hijab*. During Muharram, the directing board at the Bilal Fahs Institute in Tul also organized a trip to the shrine of Sayyida Zaynab, the sister of Imam Husayn, in Damascus.[108]

Boy Scouts has a tradition in Europe going back to the turn of the twentieth century. The British founder of the Boy Scout movement, Lord Baden-Powell, while not "militaristically nationalist" in his ideas, imagined the Boy Scouts as a "character factory," encouraging "patriotism," belief in the existing social order, and respect for Christian religious values.[109] These character traits he believed would create good citizens serving British interests in the colonies.[110] Other countries appropriated the idea of youth organizations modeled on the Boy Scouts, but each adapted the innovation to local circumstances. For example, while what the Russian Poteshney established in 1908–1909 was oriented toward the British Boy Scout model, it had a more militarist character, and its leaders placed central importance on training for future army service.[111] The most dramatically militant nationalist youth movement, the Hitler Jugend (HJ), was established during the national-socialist period in Germany. Organized hikes, camping trips, and youth orchestra were among the many activities of this movement, which was intended to popularize Nazi ideology and shape the German youth into committed nationalists. Inspired by the discipline and the type of nationalism

HJ promoted, the Maronite Pierre Jumayil created the Kata'ib political party in November 1936 with similar activities.[112] Many of its members joined the militia during the Lebanese civil war.

Not infrequently in Lebanon, one comes across a group of Amal students holding up Amal flags during fundraising activities on the streets only a few meters away from Hizbullah scouts engaged in the same activity. Fights between these two scout groups are common, and they often revolve around specific spots and places on which each group desires to put up flags or posters of their leaders. These small fights are representative of the larger battles both Shi'ite parties are involved in; they are about claiming public space and proving strength to lead the Shi'ite community in the larger national arena. More than just school-related practices, these scout activities are also thought of as recruiting future activists for their political parties.

While the Amal scouts do not engage in organized military training as does the Hizbullah Imam al-Mahdi Scout Society (jam'iyyat kashshafat al-imam al-mahdi), the Amal scout activities, just like those of Maronite scouts in Lebanon, certainly help create a setting in which young Shi'ites establish personal and ideological ties and can then be turned into militia fighters in case of an outbreak of civil war in Lebanon. Despite Berri's presentation of the idea that Amal scout activities take place within a national frame and that strengthening the youth strengthens the nation, Amal scout activities in Lebanon are one of the avenues for Amal to create specifically Shi'ite national citizens according to its party ideology. The nation Berri refers to is the nation he hopes to shape, and certainly not the nation non-Amal and non-Shi'ite communities envision.

Amal educational centers can claim that their school policy does not encourage the teaching of religion per se nor involve students in specifically Shi'ite activities (as compared to JTDI) because scout groups organize and take part in such out-of-school activities. But since Amal schools cannot be viewed separately from the Amal political party, this move can be interpreted as one of their strategies for keeping both Shi'ites and non-Shi'ites satisfied, as well as for positioning themselves within Lebanese nation building. To use their own wording, "the school activities are not overtly religious"; thus, in a political atmosphere where emphasis on religious education is interpreted as sectarian, they pass as being more compatible with intersectarian coexistence than those of JTDI, for example. Religious activities of Amal scouts can find support among a wide array of Shi'ites who either want to emphasize their religious identity and so send their children to the scouts or who do not take any particular interest in this aspect and benefit from Amal educational centers.

Ties to Iran

Improving relations between Amal and the Iranian government after the election of Muhammad Khatami as Iranian president in 1997 and the subsequent reopening of the Amal political office in Tehran in 2001 led the government to give financial support for Amal's construction of a new school in the previously Israeli-occupied south (in al-Shayt).

Amal has a quota of fifty students to send annually to Iranian universities with Iranian government funding.[113] Muhammad Nasrallah makes a point of explaining that Iran's financial support to Amal in assisting school construction does not mean that the new school will in any way be connected to the Iranian government as it will be completely under the supervision of the Amal educational centers. The Iranian government, according to the director, "decided to build a school for the disadvantaged; the goal was not domination." As the general director of Amal educational centers, Muhammad Nasrallah had also expressed his wish to open a branch of its center in Qom for the children of the Lebanese students of religion (*tullab*) who pursue studies at the theological-legal schools (*hawzat*) there. A branch of *Madaris al-Mahdi*, under the supervision of Hizbullah, was at that point the only Lebanese school operating in Qom, and JTDI provided the school textbooks. Prior to its opening, children of Lebanese *tullab* attended either Iranian schools or an Iraqi-operated school in Qom. Upon their return to Lebanon, many students lagged behind in Arabic if they were enrolled in Iranian schools or lagged behind in English and French if they were part of the Iraqi school, since neither the Iraqi nor the Iranian schools place great emphasis on teaching foreign languages. The Iranian embassy in Beirut had, by the time of my stay in 2003, rejected the idea of Amal's opening a school in Qom. This issue can be viewed as another indicator of the future development of Iranian-Amal relations. As a gesture for improving relations, perhaps Amal will be permitted to open a school in Qom. It will be interesting to see whether the school will have to compromise on its choices of its overall educational policy and religion textbooks in Qom.

One way of breaking Christian ideological hegemony is by competing in the educational sphere with their institutions in a way not limited to the creation of better-educated Lebanese Shi'ites but also focusing on the creation of a specifically Lebanese Shi'ite citizen, the Shi'ite *homo nationalis,* with icons and symbols representing a Shi'ite identity. This particular mode of claiming national space through education also results in competition with Sunni institutions in Lebanon and their long-standing efforts to promote a version of Arabism as an alternative to the Maronite national narrative, in both of which the presence of Shi'ites is ignored. At the same time, the competing approaches that characterize such redefinition of the Lebanese nation are shaped by the different positions Shi'ite political leaders take in the encounter with other communities in Lebanon, in the Lebanese government, and in the Lebanese Shi'ite community.

But Lebanese Shi'ite community leaders—although agreeing that a new vision of the Lebanese nation should represent Shi'ites in a way that it did not in prewar Lebanon—do not agree on how exactly this new Lebanese nation should be shaped nor on what type of Shi'ite identity should constitute the centerpiece of a national imagination appropriate for multisectarian Lebanon. This chapter has focused on a range of Shi'ite-run schools to show the multiplicity of Shi'ite voices, all claiming to produce in their schools the most authentic Shi'ite citizens loyal to the Lebanese nation.

Both Amal and JTDI are engaged in the creation of Lebanese nationalisms, but with different logics, producing contrasting claims for their Lebaneseness. These contrasting claims are related to ways each of these groups imagines the category of religion and its role in the everyday life of the citizens. While JTDI views religion as a total way of life in which Islam touches every aspect of human activity and directs its actions, for Amal religion is more of an objectified subject. This allows Amal members to suggest that their schools have a secular character, with religious education being just one subject among others, all the while carrying out part of their religious nationalist projects in their scout activities.

In addition, Amal claims to run the more authentically national schools compared with those of JTDI. Amal representatives suggest that their schools use religion textbooks produced by a local foundation, SISC, which is also the official state-recognized representative for Shi'ites in Lebanon, downplaying the fact that Amal controls SISC. Amal representatives thus question JTDI's loyalty to Lebanon, suggesting that JTDI schools and their curriculum and activities are not as oriented to Lebanon as a nation as are Amal's. JTDI produces its own textbooks and maintains strong transnational ties with the Iranian government. In this context, Amal plays on

Christian fears that maintenance of intense transnational ties to Iran indicates weak loyalty to the Lebanese nation (although Amal itself maintains very close ties to Syria), thus constructing the image of Amal as a local and reliably national party as opposed to the supposedly internationalist orientation of Hizbullah.

Amal educational centers also try to meet the ideologies of the Christian bourgeoisie halfway by downplaying their Muslim Shi'ite identity, such as by not insisting on visible icons of identity, like the wearing of the *hijab*. Thus Amal-run schools do not enforce a strict Islamic dress code for students, while not being lenient in the requirement of *hijab* for female teachers, as this would negatively affect their standing among many Shi'ites. JTDI, on the other hand, enforces strict dress codes and religious training for its students and teachers alike by arguing that only a totally committed religious person can be the most loyal citizen and JTDI schools produce a resistance society fighting foreign oppression such as that by Israel; after all, the martyrs who die to free their land are the most loyal and exemplary of all citizens. JTDI also points to the existence of numerous Christian-run schools and to the fact that religion is extensively taught in those schools to produce Christian citizens. In this way, it clearly seeks to appeal to a section of the Christian community that also supports the idea of keeping religion centrally placed in the Lebanese public sphere.

Connected as it is to Hizbullah, JTDI maintains Boy Scout groups with military training, whereas Amal scouts do not have the same overtly military character and seem on the surface to be more engaged in "harmless" activities such as excursions, orchestra practice, parades, and so forth. Again, Amal seeks to position itself in a more national frame than does JTDI and points to the military character of JTDI scouts, suggesting that these compete with state authority and thus are less loyal to the Lebanese nation. Yet, Amal and JTDI Boy Scout activities, regardless of their particular forms, produce Shi'ite-centered nationalism because their goal is to organize a homogeneous, like-minded group regardless of differences in styles.

Amal also points to the fact that its schools do not emphasize religion in their curriculum and activities to the extent that JTDI does. Yet, Amal scout activities engage in similar religious activities that do not take place in Amal-run schools. Because the Amal scout groups were created several years before Amal-run schools were set up, a large part of the ideological work and religious activities of the Amal party were done by Amal's scout organizations. JTDI and Hizbullah scouts, on the other hand, came into existence with the schools, and the scout activities can be viewed as the practical continuation of the school ideology of creating a resistance society.

Finally, Amal school directors can claim that their expressed wish for unified, state-produced religion textbooks and curricula, and for the eventual

merging of all schools into a public school system, is evidence of their commitment to the Lebanese nation-state. After all, their leaders already occupy key positions in the state apparatus and would certainly want to safeguard Amal interests and power. On the other hand, Hizbullah and JTDI leaders cannot with the same ease agree to an eventual integration of their schools into a public school system, because they do not have the same representation in the government to ensure protection of their interests.

Amal and Hizbullah activists, as evident in their debates about schooling as well as their schooling practices, are trying to outdo each other in proving their embeddedness in the nation. To understand the logic of Amal and Hizbullah's competing nationalisms, we need to examine the Lebanese Shi'ite world of the 1970s and the early 1980s in its transnational context, and historicize the development of this competition. During that period, both Iranian and Lebanese Shi'ite ethnic entrepreneurs debated and fought over the meaning of a Lebanese Shi'ite identity, and constantly negotiated and readjusted the boundaries between the local and the foreign, and between the supposedly Lebanese and Iranian characteristics of people and practices. The next chapter discusses the formation of some of the key discourses dominating Amal and Hizbullah's national identity politics since the early 1980s.

Transnational Debates
and Local Struggles

3

SHI'ITE PIETY AND THE PALESTINIAN CAUSE

THE HISTORY OF A DISCOURSE

Iranian-Lebanese Shi'ite relations are like those of an old married couple: they can neither live together nor live apart.

—SAYYID HANI FAHS, A LEBANESE SHI'ITE INTELLECTUAL AND SCHOLAR

Iran is the kind mother (*al-umm al-hanun*) of the Shi'ites in Lebanon, just like France is to the Maronites. It should not expect something in return for the favors it does.

—AN AMAL MEMBER

The relation between Iran and Lebanese Shi'ites is that of a father to his sons. Iran should act like a just father. How could it prefer one son [Hizbullah] over another son [Amal]?

—A LEBANESE SHI'ITE INTERN AT *AL-MAJLIS AL-THAQAFI LI LUBNAN AL-JANUBI* IN BEIRUT

Since the early 1970s, the attitude of Shi'ites toward the Palestinian cause has increasingly shaped debates over Lebanese Shi'ite public identity. In this context, the term *Palestinian cause* has incorporated at least two meanings: the subaltern struggle against imperialism in general (third worldism) as well as the specific Lebanese configuration of this cause, i.e., the question regarding the presence of Palestinian refugees as well as their battles against Israel from southern Lebanon. When the Iranian revolution succeeded in 1979, a discourse had already been formed in the transnational Shi'ite world that linked Shi'ite piety to the support of these two aspects of the Palestinian cause. By 1982, advocates of this discourse had established themselves as the ruling elite in Iran.

This chapter examines the Lebanese-Iranian dimension of the history of this discourse as it continues to shape Amal's and Hizbullah's politics of national identity. It introduces the main actors and their personal animosities and ideological differences. I discuss their debates beginning in the 1970s and show how some Iranian activists in the Shi'ite transnational network, whose interactions I trace, derived justification from these debates for supporting the formation of Hizbullah. I also describe how the same debates helped some disaffected Amal members, who constituted the initial ranks of Hizbullah, to articulate their dissatisfaction with Amal leadership in a discourse of (the lack of) awareness of Shi'ite beliefs. Those who saw themselves as aware (*agah* in Persian-language sources) Shi'ites disassociated themselves from their political past, which they came to consider a time of stagnation with a lack of conscious leadership. For them, awareness thus became associated with a sense of the empowerment of Shi'ites that would eventually result in fighting Zionism successfully.

In other words, by 1982 some Lebanese Shi'ites created a discourse that built on the prerevolutionary, transnational Shi'ite debates but added to them a progressivist temporality that fit those 1970s debates into the specific Lebanese Shi'ite context of the early 1980s. Accordingly, those lacking such awareness were supposedly ignorant of true Shi'ism, as manifest in their insufficient support of the Palestinian cause, their lack of commitment to fight Zionists who had occupied Shi'ite-inhabited Lebanese land, and, ultimately, their lack of courage for martyrdom. As I will show, the activism of the representatives of the postrevolutionary Iranian government in Lebanon not only split the Lebanese Shi'ite community along the lines of two political parties and further encouraged it to articulate Lebanese nationalism within a discourse of Shi'ite authenticity, but the community was also led to rally around two distinct modes of linking Shi'ite tradition to the political horizon of the present.

The creation of Hizbullah, as this chapter shows, was not about exporting the revolution by a group unfamiliar to Lebanon. It provided an opportunity for the ruling elite in Iran to settle accounts, declare themselves winners of the debate, and, so they thought, end that 1970s debate with force. Support for Hizbullah was in part a response to their failed attempts to shape Amal's Shi'ite Lebanon between 1974 and 1982.

Here I do not want to simply fill a historical gap by showing the dynamics of transnational Shi'ite ties between Iran and Lebanon prior to the creation of Hizbullah. Rather, I seek to contextualize and historicize Shi'ite piety politics, a key discourse in competing visions of Shi'ite Lebanon. This chapter discusses the context for the formation of centrally important components of Hizbullah's project, such as the fight against Zionism, martyrdom, and jihad as both personal and political struggles, and as they become linked to a discourse of Shi'ite authenticity that identifies the authentic with supposedly aware Shi'ites.

Shi'ites had a stake in membership in Lebanon, a nation in which claims to a hegemonic position were often framed in discourses of progressivist modernity, and in which the Shi'ites were frequently labeled as traditional and backward and therefore unfit for full citizenship. This aspect of the Lebanese national context was of key importance in the debates about Shi'ite piety and authenticity. In this chapter I discuss the formation of a Shi'ite discourse of piety in its transnational context; in the next, I offer insights on how Lebanese Shi'ites negotiate national identities in light of such transnational debates.

Friends of Maronite Lebanon: The Pahlavi Government

From the 1950s to the success of the Iranian revolution in 1979, relations between governments, states, and parties in most Middle Eastern countries were defined according to cold war dynamics, their attitudes toward the Palestinian cause, and subsequently their relations with the state of Israel.

During the height of Arab nationalism in the Middle East as led by Gamal 'Abdel Nasser in the 1950s, which culminated in the creation of the United Arab Republic (UAR) in February 1958, the Shah of Iran and Camille Chamoun, the president of Lebanon from 1952 to 1958, were close friends and allies, and both feared the impact of Arab nationalist ideologies in the region. The Shah supported Chamoun's national vision of a Christian-dominated Lebanon which marginalized Muslims and in which Lebanon was neither ideologically nor culturally part of the Arab world as it was imagined by contemporary Arab nationalists, some of whom demanded that Lebanon join the UAR.[1] Both the Lebanese state and the Iranian government, which also recognized Israel as a state in 1950, viewed Nasser's Arab nationalism and his emphasis on the significance of the Palestinian cause as a threat to their pro-Western orientation.[2]

Yet, the Shah's policy toward Lebanon had contradictory aspects, as he to a certain degree also supported the Muslim Shiʻites, most of whom were part of the opposition to the Lebanese state. In the 1960s, while the Shah and Ahmad Atabaki, the Iranian ambassador to Lebanon at the time, were still close allies of Chamoun, the Shah also provided the Shiʻite community of Lebanon with some financial assistance.[3] Aid to the Shiʻite community in Lebanon was often given on the request of Musa Sadr and was channeled through the religious establishment in Qom, which the Savak (the Iranian security and intelligence agency under the Shah) monitored closely.[4]

In 1970, two important events caused the Iranian government to pay special attention to Lebanon in general, as it had become a haven for anti-Shah opposition activities, and to the person of Sadr in particular. Until then, Sadr had not been viewed as a threat to the Iranian government.[5] The first event was the relocation of another large number of PLO fighters to Lebanon after their expulsion from Jordan in September 1970 (which became known as Black September), and the second was the arrival in Lebanon of Mustafa Chamran, who was opposed to the Shah. As soon as diplomatic relations between Iran and Lebanon resumed, after a two-year hiatus, in 1971,[6] the Iranian embassy in Beirut focused its attention on the activities of various anti-Shah movements, the members of some of which had received military training at PLO camps. These activities played a major part in defining Iranian-Lebanese diplomatic relations from 1971 until the success of the Iranian revolution. The Iranian government requested from the Lebanese government strict control over these anti-Shah activities and the extradition of opposition members, but the Lebanese government was unable to oblige due to its weakness and limited control of the country.

Savak material published after the Iranian revolution[7] reveals how concerned the Iranian embassy in Beirut was about anti-Shah activities in Lebanon in the 1970s.[8] These documents help reconstruct Iranian-Lebanese official relations and those between Sadr and the Iranian government, while showing how Iranian state officials assessed (often wrongly) anti-Shah activities in Lebanon. They can also be used to understand the tensions and disjunctures between Sadr's vision of the Lebanese nation, with the position of Shiʻites in it, on one hand, with the dominant voice in the Maronite community, represented by Chamoun and the state on the other. For example, the burial ceremony of Dr. 'Ali Shari'ati in Damascus and the fortieth-day mourning ceremony held in his honor in 1977 illustrate these diverging visions.

Shari'ati, one of the most important ideologues of the Iranian revolution, some of whose thoughts were appropriated by Ruhollah Khomeini, was an active member of the Liberation Movement of Iran (abroad)—LMI(a)—an Iranian anti-Shah movement, some of whose members were close to Sadr and stationed in Lebanon. Shari'ati was responsible for the European branch of the opposition movement in Paris. When he died of a heart attack in London shortly before the Iranian revolution in June 1977, his body was taken to Damascus where, thanks to Sadr's widespread connections, Shari'ati was buried near the Shi'ite shrine of Sayyida Zaynab. The fortieth-day commemoration of his death took place in Beirut and at the Technical School in Tyre, a school for Shi'ites under the supervision of Chamran and Sadr. Arafat and Sadiq Qutbzadeh, another founding member of LMI(a), were present at the event, delivering speeches attacking the Shah and the Iranian government, but also renewing oaths of allegiance between Amal and the PLO despite the increasing tensions between the two groups in southern Lebanon. Through Savak, the Iranian government had detailed information on this commemoration. It complained to the Lebanese authorities,[9] who then apologized, stating that

> even though the Lebanese government tries with all its power to forbid such roguish activities *(afsaar gosikhtegi-ha)* opposing the Lebanese state interests . . . the government of Iran should understand the difficult situation of Lebanon. . . . None of the important Lebanese figures took part in the [fortieth] anniversary . . . only some students from the Technical School and members of Amal. Musa Sadr had promised our security police that the ceremony will not have a political coloring *(rang-i siyasi)*.[10]

In 1977, the gap between how Sadr envisioned Lebanon's relation to Iran and the Maronite perspective becomes even more obvious. According to a report to Savak by Mansur Qadar, the Iranian ambassador to Lebanon, Chamoun sent Victor Musa, the president of his political office, to the Iranian embassy in Beirut to express the friendship and the loyalty of the "true citizens of Lebanon *(atba'-i haqiqi-i in keshvar)*, the Christians of Lebanon, to the Iranian government," pledging that the "Christian leaders are sincere friends *(iradatmand va mokhlis)* of the great Iranian Shah, a great leader and a supporter of the free countries *(keshvarha-i azad)* in this region."[11] Further-more, Chamoun described Sadr's involvement in holding the fortieth-day mourning ceremony for Shari'ati in Lebanon as yet "another attempt of Sadr to darken the relations of Lebanon with the brother government of Iran *(dawlat-i baradar-i iran)*."[12]

Clearly, amid the ongoing civil war, Chamoun imagined the role of the Shi'ites in the Lebanese nation as peripheral, since he refers to the Christians as the true citizens of Lebanon and draws an image of Sadr as an undesirable element creating problems for the Lebanese state through his actions. In addition, the statement by Chamoun's attaché that no important political figure took part in the ceremony is also indicative of how marginal the Shi'ites and Sadr were regarded officially in the Lebanese context and how dismissive these officials were of Sadr's views of Lebanon's position toward the Palestinian cause. As much as Sadr's stance appeared pro-Palestinian and antinational to the Maronite leaders however in the transnational Shi'ite context, Sadr seemed insufficiently pro-Palestinian to many. This was a major reason for others to dismiss and to resist his vision of Lebanese Shi'ite identity.

Friends of Shi'ite Lebanon: The Anti-Shah Opposition Movement of LMI

"Shemiran [as Lebanese Shi'ites pronounce the name Chamran] was an exceptional man," Khalil Hamdan, who was a young Amal member in the 1970s when Chamran was supervising the Technical School in Tyre, remembers nostalgically: I went to visit him in his home, it wasn't a home really, one simple room where he had put blankets on the floor to sleep, nothing else. While we were talking, a mouse ran over the room and I tried to kill it. Chamran got upset and told me that the mouse is his best friend, a good friend in lonely nights when Israelis were bombing South Lebanon. He was not like the Iranians now; if he was alive the Iranians would not have dared treating us like this.

—FIELDNOTES, BEIRUT, JUNE 2002

The most important transnational network between Iranian and Lebanese Shi'ites in the 1970s was the close relation between the members of the Iranian Liberation Movement (LMI) *(nehzat-i azadi-i iran)*, an anti-Shah movement, and Sadr and Amal.[13] LMI members included activists outside of Iran, and perhaps one of the best known among those was Chamran, residing in Lebanon. Born in 1933 into a religious family in Tehran, he pursued studies in electrical engineering at the technical college of the University of Tehran, where he became politically active in the National Resistance Movement, which came into existence shortly after the fall of Muhammad Mussadiq in 1953 and whose members were mostly from a religious *bazaari* background.[14] Chamran left Iran on a scholarship in 1959 to continue his studies in the United States, receiving his PhD in electrical engineering from the University of California at Berkeley. He later moved to the East Coast to be closer to the anti-Shah activities of his friends Qutbzadeh (d. 1982), and Ibrahim Yazdi, both prominent in the Islamic Student Organization. In late 1963, Chamran made his first trip to Egypt because the representatives of LMI(a), mainly he, Qutbzadeh, and Yazdi, hoped to find backing for a military wing to fight the Shah in Iran. However, Egyptian President Nasser had other ideas about how to oppose the Shah's influence. Chamran left Egypt for the United States in 1966 and returned to the Middle East only in 1970, when he went to Lebanon, as he knew Sadr from his university days in Tehran. Chamran stayed there until the success of the Iranian revolution, when he returned to Iran.[15] In his memoirs, titled *Lobnan*,[16] he wrote:

> I spent eight years in Lebanon, a hard and dangerous period in the midst of death and life and martyrdom. I am proud to have been the organizer of the largest ideological movement in Lebanon: *harakat al-mahrumin* and Amal [the military wing of *harakat al-mahrumin*], which was established by Imam Musa Sadr. The organization of Amal was my responsibility. I have been in the midst of political and revolutionary currents in Lebanon and other Middle Eastern countries and I know more than anyone else about the issues in this region and I have been more than anyone else involved in the destiny of the Shi'ites.[17]

Chamran's undertakings in Lebanon were thus not confined to anti-Shah activities; he was also deeply involved in Lebanese Shi'ite affairs associated with Sadr. As a result of this close cooperation and friendship, several other anti-Shah groups began to associate LMI(a) members and their ideologies with Sadr and his activism and outlook in Lebanon. This association became an important ideological tool in the hands of the LMI(a) opponents who helped establish Islamic Amal as a rival party to Amal in 1982.

The LMI(a) with Chamran as its representative was not the only anti-Shah activist group based in Lebanon in the 1970s claiming an Islamic orientation. Muhammad Montazeri,[18] Jalal al-Din Farsi[19] and 'Ali Akbar Mohtashami,[20] then close associates of Khomeini and often referred to as the founding figures of Hizbullah in Lebanon in the early 1980s, also mention in their memoirs their stays in and regular visits to Lebanon in the 1970s.

In looking at the debates between these two camps, between Chamran's LMI and several activists who later became members of the Iranian government, I suggest that we distinguish between two different transnational Shi'ite anti-Shah networks with ties to Lebanon operating in the 1970s.[21] These two networks, at times fluid and overlapping, were neither officially separated nor were all Islamist opposition members involved in them. Chamran, for example, considered himself closely associated with both Sadr and Khomeini, but Farsi and Mohtashami claimed that commitments to these two figures were mutually exclusive. Their debates, as we will see, illuminate to some degree the conflicts that have arisen between the Iranian ruling religious elite's vision of Iranian-Lebanese Shi'ite relations after the revolution (and ultimately of Lebanese Shi'ite identity) and that of Amal, the first major Lebanese Shi'ite movement.

Montazeri, Farsi, and Mohtashami turned into opponents of LMI(a) activism, which they equated with Amal politics, because they disagreed with the focus of Sadr's activism for several reasons. They criticized what they saw as Sadr's lack of cooperation with the PLO in Lebanon and believed his first priority should have been to serve as a spokesperson for Palestinian interests there. Based on this position, these key figures accused LMI leaders of a lack of enthusiasm in putting the Palestinian cause at the center of their politics. When Chamran gave a speech in Hamburg to a crowd of Iranian students, according to the source published by these students, he talked about clashes between Palestinians and Lebanese Shi'ites in South Lebanon and how, in his view, many of the latter desired to get rid of the Palestinians. He supposedly said, "The Shi'ites beg us to give them weapons so they can kill the Palestinians." Some students in the audience accused Chamran and Sadr of covering their own crimes committed against the Palestinian refugees in the south and of having incited Lebanese Shi'ites against Palestinians to the extent that they would favor "such illogical actions."[22] After the success of the Iranian revolution, Sayyid Hamid Rawhani, a close companion of Khomeini from his Najaf days, even went so far as to call the party of Amal the "first security belt of the Israelis in South Lebanon."[23]

Another reason Khomeini's inner circle opposed Sadr and Chamran was that Sadr maintained relations with the Iranian embassy in Beirut, where the Shah's anti-Palestinian attitude was represented. In addition, Iranian embassies worked closely with Savak, the Iranian secret service, in monitoring the political activities of Iranians residing outside Iran. They accused Sadr of being nonrevolutionary and an agent of the Shah's regime, even though Sadr's contact with the Iranian embassy was limited and related to securing money from the Shah for Lebanese Shi'ites.[24] He did not cooperate with the Iranian embassy. In Savak documents one can read how officials often complained about Sadr's lack of cooperation with the Iranian embassy in turning in Iranian anti-Shah activists based in Lebanon.[25]

Nonetheless, in this context, the anti-Sadr group also accused Chamran and other members of the LMI of cooperating with Savak.[26] Meantime, the Iranian embassy in Beirut had classified Chamran as a leftist (a common label given to opposition groups of all ideological walks) and was not aware of the extent of the ties between him and Sadr.[27] Despite these accusations, Sadr was unwilling to subordinate the interests and aspirations of Lebanese Shi'ites to those of Khomeini, and he did not take a public anti-Shah position until 1977, shortly before his disappearance and probable death. Because both the Lebanese Maronites and the Shah of Iran were not invested in the Palestinian cause in the discourse created by Khomeini followers, any association with these two governments meant that these people were automatically anti-Palestinian and pro-imperialist.

For all of these reasons, Sadr was accused of standing for an inauthentic Shi'ite Islam. In the words of his opponents, "How can the LMI leaders present Sadr as the leader of the Shi'ites in Lebanon and of the Lebanese Muslims? Muslims and Shi'ites hate the deeds and stance of Musa Sadr and the leaders of the Movement of the Deprived, and the Lebanese Shi'ites have expressed their hatred for their treacherous deeds (*khiyanatha va mozduriha*)."[28]

In fact, Sadr's standing and popularity were a potential threat to Khomeini's claims to leadership, despite the fact that Khomeini was clearly senior in his theological-legal training to Sadr. He did not want the Lebanese Shi'ites to be subordinated to Khomeini, whose interest lay principally in the Iranian context of opposing the Shah.[29] Followers of Khomeini had begun to view him as their source of emulation (*marja'*), whereas Sadr and

Lebanese Shi'ites followed the teachings of the *marja'*, Ayatollah Abul al-Qasim Kho'i (d. 1992), whom Khomeini viewed as his rival. Kho'i, unlike Khomeini, did not believe religious scholars should be involved in politics and, until 1975, did not participate with Khomeini followers in criticizing the Shah. Instead, Kho'i argued that the religious establishment should concentrate on its theological duties, such as preaching and training students of religion.[30] On some level then, the debates in Lebanon between Khomeini's followers and Sadr reflected the ongoing disagreements between the theological establishments in Najaf and Qom prior to the Iranian revolution as to the degree of the religious scholars' involvement in politics and the modalities of resistance to oppressive states.[31] In Khomeini's Manichaean worldview, reflected in his public statements and writings, one was a supporter of the Palestinian cause only when *publicly* taking a stance against the Shah of Iran.

These questions of leadership were not always directly debated. Instead, they were often framed as a competition over who had the most impeccable credentials in supporting the Palestinian cause and the Palestinians in Lebanon, and ultimately in fighting those who favored Israel, i.e., the Shah of Iran and the Maronite state. Sadr clearly was not willing to support Palestinian militias in South Lebanon to the extent that it would harm Lebanese Shi'ites more than the Palestinian-Israeli clashes in the south already had, no matter how intensely other members of the Iranian opposition movement criticized him for this position, accusing him of disregarding and even attempting to change the fundamental pillars of Shi'ism to please the Maronites.[32]

Mohtashami, for example, claims that on one of his visits to Tyre, Sadr gave a speech blaming the Palestinian presence in South Lebanon for Israeli military attacks there. Mohtashami reveals how this incident caused him to worry and how he began "to feel the danger for the future of the Palestinians" because what he saw "would sour the minds of the people of the south and [would] create a situation where the Palestinians would not be able to attack Israel from South Lebanon." Thus, he decided to meet with "the imam [Khomeini]" as soon as he returned to Iraq to "explain the various dimensions of this matter."[33] Mohtashami wanted to leave Lebanon as soon as possible, for "the undesirable political situation in Lebanon was not in accordance with political inclinations of people like me." In addition, he noted how disappointed he was with the "political line" and "the so-called nonrevolutionary encounters and attitudes of Mr. Sadr (*barkhordhay-i be istelah ghayr-i inqilabi-i aqay-i sadr*)."[34] It is highly unlikely, however, that Sadr had ever given such a speech, as he did support the Palestinian cause and his anti-Israeli stance was well known.

Shi'ite-Palestinian Relations in South Lebanon

The relations between Shi'ites and Palestinians in South Lebanon were, in fact, more complex on the ground than these Iranian anti-Sadr opposition members reported in their memoirs. For example, before the founding of the Amal movement in 1974, many Lebanese Shi'ites were active in Palestinian organizations, from which they received military training. Arafat regularly visited these training camps, often located in villages around Ba'albak (Yamunah and 'Ayn al-Boniyyeh), and gave speeches during their graduation ceremonies.[35] Even after the creation of Amal, for the first few years many of the Amal military trainers remained Palestinians, and Chamran would accompany his students from the Technical School in Tyre to these training camps. Many of the Fatah fighters were also Shi'ite. One gets the picture that Shi'ites closely identified the Palestinian plight with their own disadvantaged situation in Lebanon, and both cooperated with each other in the early 1970s.

The PLO in Lebanon consisted of two wings. One was Fatah, with Arafat as its principal leader, which coordinated activities with the Lebanese National Movement (LNM), a coalition of mainly Muslim and leftist groups in Lebanon led by the Druze leader Kamal Jumblat, whose secularist politics were opposed to Sadr's vision of a nonsecular Lebanon. The Syrians backed this coalition until January 1976, and that probably explains why at the outset of the civil war in 1975, Amal informally associated with the LNM. The second Palestinian wing, with which Amal and Syria associated afterward, included the Palestinian National Salvation Front organizations and the Democratic Front for the Liberation of Palestine.[36]

In the view of Chamran, the most important problem some South Lebanese Shi'ites faced was Arafat's lack of discipline in exercising his power among his fighters in Lebanon, as some Palestinian guerrillas had already split off from Fatah and were acting on their own in the south, often harassing Shi'ite inhabitants in the Fatah-controlled region. Sadr grew increasingly impatient with Fatah's loose organization in the south, with Israeli retaliation attacks that killed mainly Shi'ites, and with Arafat's cooperation with the LNM, which competed with Amal to win Shi'ite members. By 1976, the clashes between Palestinian militias in the south and Shi'ites had also increased, giving Sadr the justification to disassociate from LNM and side with the Syrians, who had in May 1976 invaded Lebanon under the pretext of supporting the Christian Lebanese Front and limiting Arafat's activities in Lebanon.[37] The Syrian role was crucial in mobilizing Amal against Fatah and the LNM, and was congruent with their strategy of divide and rule to control Lebanon, especially to weaken the LNM-PLO coalition. Amal was a major part of the alliance that the Syrians forged against the LNM-PLO coalition, and Amal did not take part in the fighting that erupted between the leftist PLO and the right-wing Lebanese forces.

Despite these clashes and their ideological differences, according to Chamran, on the fortieth-day commemoration of the death of Shari'ati in 1977, Arafat proclaimed in Beirut that "Amal is Fatah and Fatah is Amal; if Amal does not support Fatah there would be no Fatah."[38] In fact, Sadr had mediated between Hafiz al-Asad and Arafat and had organized many meetings between them. As a result of what he saw as a lack of discipline and an incoherent ideological stance, Chamran noted that despite Arafat's claim of close relations between Amal and Fatah, clashes between Shi'ites and Palestinian militias were increasing, with the latter still exercising their power on a daily basis over Shi'ites in the south. These frequent clashes increased resentment among some Shi'ites toward Palestinian refugees in general, whom they had come to view as responsible for their plight by drawing Israeli attacks in the region. South Lebanon, in fact, was often called Fatahland, the name implying total Palestinian militia control.

To the close followers of Khomeini, who mainly heard about these events rather than witnessing them, these incidents were rare and most instigated by Amal members and leaders, who—these followers of Khomeini argued—viewed Palestinians as unwelcome guests.[39] Although Chamran remained faithful to the fight against Israel, he became increasingly suspicious about Fatah's attitude in South Lebanon. Arafat also became closer to Iranian opposition members like Farsi, who supported Fatah's military activities against Israel on Lebanese territory without paying attention to Lebanese Shi'ite interests and local politics.

Inspired by the distinction Shari'ati made between authentic 'Ali's Shi'ism and the inauthentic Safavid Shi'ism, opponents of Sadr, taking Shari'ati's ideas out of context, accused Sadr of creating a specific type of presumably impure Shi'ite Islam or a "Shi'ite-Crusader sect" (firqi-i shi'i-salibi),[40] based on his supposedly political decision to cooperate with the Syrian-backed Maronites against the Palestinians. These Iranians opposed to Sadr's activism in Lebanon in the 1970s did not share his outlook and politics vis-à-vis the multireligious composition of Lebanese society. According to their logic, Sadr sought to advance his *own* personal interests rather than that of the Lebanese Shi'ite community. He was criticized for praying in a church or for inviting non-Muslims to lead the Friday prayers, the very people these Iranians held accountable to fight Palestinians in Lebanon.[41]

The clashes between Amal and various Palestinian factions in the south were most intense from 1978 until 1982, especially between 1980 and 1982, and it was amid this fighting that Sadr disappeared and the Iranian revolution succeeded. On February 17, 1979, a plane took off from Damascus to carry Arafat and Farsi to Tehran to congratulate Khomeini on the success of the revolution. Arafat was the first official visitor to postrevolutionary Iran, landing just days after the arrival of Khomeini himself. Farsi, who became the spokesman for Fatah in Iran, was by then an open enemy of Sadr. On February 24, Chamran and a delegation of Amal leaders—Husayn Husayni and Nabih Berri, as well as the Lebanese Shi'ite religious scholar then associated with Amal, the late Shaykh Muhammad Mahdi Shamseddine—also left Beirut for Tehran. They considered themselves to be as much a part of the success of the Iranian revolution as did Arafat and his associates.

From Inauthentic to Authentic Shi'ites and Back in Three Years: The Iranian Government and Amal, 1979–1982

Iranian-Amal relations were multilayered and contradictory between 1979 and 1982. The Iranian government was fragmented, being composed of those who associated with Amal as well as those who despised Sadr and Amal. LMI(a) members and Amal continued their close ties both on a personal and political level after the success of the Iranian revolution. Prior to their loss of power in 1982, LMI members occupied political posts in the newly formed Iranian government. Mehdi Bazargan assumed the post of prime minister in February 1979, Chamran became Iranian minister of defense, and Qutbzadeh became director of national Iranian radio and television.

Amal demonstrated its enthusiasm for the newly formed government in Iran in multiple ways. It hosted groups of Iranians who came to visit Shi'ite regions in Lebanon to assess the degree of damage inflicted by the Israeli military. One such person was the daughter of Navab Safavi,[42] who came along with Ghada Jaber, the Lebanese wife of Chamran and herself a member of Amal, to visit a village in al-Biqa' (Yammuneh), where Chamran had trained Amal members, to make a report for an Iranian television program.[43]

In addition, Amal expressed solidarity with Iran by commemorating the death of Iranian leaders in Lebanon. While Amal considers Chamran one of its own leaders and has commemorated his demise every year, it also commemorated the deaths of seventy-five[44] members of the Iranian parliament in a bomb attack on June 28, 1981, that was attributed to the Mojahedin-i Khalq. Commemorations took place in various Shi'ite regions in Lebanon, and telegrams were sent to Khomeini and Iranian officials in the government to express Amal's grief.[45]

Amal, the official weekly newsletter of the party, also featured an extraordinary amount of coverage of events in Iran during that period. The Iraqi invasion of Iran is discussed at length in the newsletter, positioning Amal on the side of the Iranians despite the Arab identity of Iraq.[46] The deaths of Sayyid Muhammad Baqir al-Sadr and his sister, Bint al-Huda,[47] who were assassinated by Saddam Husayn's regime on April 8, 1980, contributed to Iranian efforts to win the sympathy of Amal officials, who saw Iran as yet another victim of Iraqi Ba'ath aggression. In fact, roughly six hundred Amal members left Lebanon and accompanied Chamran to Iran to fight on the front near the Iran-Iraq border.[48]

Hasan Shaqra, a Shi'ite from the south now in his midforties, says it was his admiration for and friendship with Chamran that led him to go to Iran and fight against the Iraqi invasion. He had been so impressed with Chamran's activism for the Lebanese Shi'ite cause in the south that he was convinced that Chamran would not fight against an enemy if it were not for a just cause. As Shaqra explained the importance of Chamran, "We respected the Iranian revolution and Imam Khomeini; we didn't know Iran would turn against us. At any rate, once Chamran was martyred [in June 1981] we all returned to Lebanon; our connection to Iran was through Chamran."[49]

For Abu Kharif it was a similar story. He had been close to Chamran during the formative years of Amal, and there was no question of leaving Chamran alone in this fight, as in his view Chamran had not left them alone in theirs against the Israelis since 1970. He joined other Amal members to accompany Chamran to Iran and recalled that "the question was not about Arabism. Saddam was against the Shi'ites and he had killed Shi'ite leaders;

we hated him." When I interviewed him, he took an envelope out of his pocket and showed me pictures from his time in Iran. One showed him close to Chamran in Kurdistan, the other was a scene of him kissing the hand of Ayatollah Taleqani. At the end of our conversation, he sighed, shaking his head and telling me, "Now it is all about politics, there is no genuine belief anymore, all party politics and money, it wasn't always like this."[50]

A Disappointed Amal

Despite close ties with Iran, three interrelated issues—the Iranian government's lack of interest in finding Sadr, the question of sending Iranian volunteers to South Lebanon, and Amal's resistance to becoming subordinate to the concept of *vilayat-i faqih*—alarmed Amal members about the future of their relations with that government as well as their plans for Shi'ites in Lebanon.

Amal delegations regularly visited Iran to form networks on all levels up to 1982, but their main concern was to gain information about the fate of

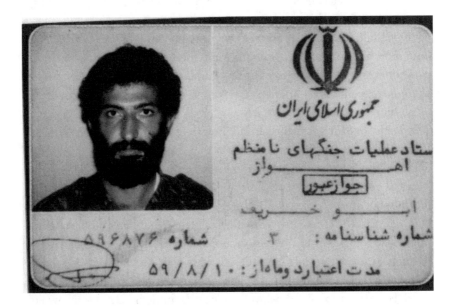

FIGURE 3.1. The Iranian-issued military identity card of an Amal member who fought for Iran during the Iran-Iraq war. *From the personal collection of the author.*

Sadr, who had disappeared in Libya[51] in August 1978. They saw in the success of the revolution a key chance to rally international support and to find him. These delegations would meet with Iranian officials and Khomeini in order to ask for the latter's support in finding Sadr or in clarifying his fate.[52]

Every attempt to gain more information about Sadr through Iranian channels was unsuccessful, however. Despite the lip service they paid to the cause, the postrevolutionary Iranian leadership lacked interest in Sadr's whereabouts, for reasons already cited but which were not known to all Amal members. Although LMI members can be assumed to have genuinely desired to find Sadr, despite publicly distancing themselves from others who openly maintained relations with Mu'ammar Qaddafi in Libya,[53] they did not have the power to terminate or even interfere with them. Sadiq Khalkhali,[54] Montazeri, and Farsi continued to entertain Qaddafi, whom Lebanese Shi'ites have considered responsible for Sadr's disappearance. Also, Khomeini, as the leader of the Iranian revolution, apparently did not make use of his powers to find Sadr. Although he did not agree to meet with a Libyan delegation that had come to Iran, he also did not attempt to stop radicals in his entourage from continuing to maintain contacts with Qaddafi. The lack of any serious initiative by religious and political leaders in Iran to find Sadr—whom Amal members considered one of the most important Shi'ite figures in the world—made the members wonder about postrevolutionary Iranian claims to be a pan-Islamic and pan-Shi'ite revolution.

Apart from Sadr's fate, the second important debate that informed Amal-Iranian relations from 1979 to 1982 was that about sending Iranian Revolutionary Guards to South Lebanon to form a resistance against Israeli invasion and occupation. Such deliberations date back to January 1980,[55] only a few months after the success of the revolution, contrary to the commonly held view that the Israeli invasion of Lebanon in June 1982 and the appointment of Mohtashami to the post of ambassador to Damascus in that year promoted the idea. In fact, to settle accounts with Amal, which was siding with the Syrians against Fatah, the new religious elite suggested this plan in 1980. For reasons outlined below the idea was immediately rejected by Husayni, the first Amal leader, and then by Berri, his successor in 1980. Amal's refusal to accept the volunteers and its resistance to the vilayat-i faqih only added more to the list of grievances of Khomeini followers who, now being in a position of power, waited for the right moment to strike back.

Labeling Amal as a Secular Party

In the context of increasing suspicion among Lebanese Christians about an export of the Islamic revolution to Lebanon through Lebanese Shi'ites, Amal leaders and Shamseddine repeatedly engaged in discourses which Sadr was known for in order to define Amal's position within the Lebanese context. These statements set the terms for how Amal has ever since represented itself as a national party, and how often others have portrayed it as a *secular* national party. Addressing the possibility of sending Iranian troops to Lebanon, Husayni defined the relations between Amal and postrevolutionary Iran quite clearly:

> We view the Iranian revolution from two perspectives. The first perspective is our common religious identity, the fact that we are also Shi'ites. Although that Shi'ite identity has given us a lot—our patriotism and our nationalism—some have doubted our patriotism for a simple reason that the majority of the Iranians are Shi'ites, too. During the Pahlavi regime, Iran was still a Shi'ite country, but since the policies of the Shah were against our national and patriotic interests, mainly the Shah's relations to Israel, we did not maintain contacts. But after the success of the revolution Imam Khomeini's policies of breaking contact with Israel and his ideas of freeing Palestine . . . have not been contradictory to our patriotic and national interests. The second perspective from which we appreciate the Iranian revolution is that as Arabs we know that Israel with its intentions . . . is against Arabs and Israel's policies have resulted in the occupation of Jerusalem and of Arab lands. The success of the Iranian revolution with its anti-Israeli policy can help us free our Lebanese land in South Lebanon. Thus it is from these two perspectives that we consider the Iranian revolution an event that is to our advantage and not to our disadvantage, and in accordance to our national interests. As for the sending of Iranian troops to South Lebanon, this is the idea of Muhammad Montazeri . . . who is not part of the mainstream in the current Iranian politics. We do not interfere in internal Iranian affairs and do not want Iran to interfere in our internal affairs.[56]

In a similar vein, as Berri explained in June 1980:

> Amal is not a fanatic/dogmatic movement (*amal laysat haraka madhhabiyya*). We consider the resistance a noble necessity. Amal is neither fanatic nor

sectarian (*amal laysat madhhabiyya wa la ta'ifiyya*). Amal is a national movement (*hiya haraka wataniyya*). . . . Amal is against fanaticism and sectarianism (*amal didda al-madhhabiyya wa al-ta'ifiyya*), Amal is a movement of the believers (*hiya haraka mu'mina*), Amal is a Lebanese national movement (*haraka wataniyya lubnaniyya*).[57]

With the intensification of Shi'ite ties to postrevolutionary official Iran Amal was forced to define the categories of foreign, local, and religion in new terms. Husayni and Berri, although rivals, both decided that, while what they called religion binds Lebanese Shi'ites to Iran, Amal is a national movement emphatically distinct from Iranian political influence in Lebanon. They thus created for Amal a Lebanese national identity in which submission to the concept of *vilayat-i faqih* and the acceptance of Iranian citizens (the volunteers) on Lebanese soil came to mean opposition to a national movement (*haraka wataniyya*). In this discourse maintaining transnational Shi'ite networks to Iran, through which people, ideas, money, and ideologies moved, then came to be portrayed as opposed to Amal's professed Lebanese nationalism. The constructedness of such commonsensical boundaries becomes obvious only if one considers how a decade earlier these boundaries were set differently. Sadr and Chamran, the two men responsible for creating Amal in 1974, were products of these transnational Shi'ite ties, in fact holding Iranian citizenship. In 1982, a clear shift in Amal's nationalism was evident, not, as many have observed, because it was becoming a secular party, but because it reconfigured the categories of local and foreign, of internal and external, and how religion related to these categories.

Actually, Amal never claimed to be a secular party, and the fact that the party which split from Amal called itself Islamic Amal did not necessarily imply that Amal's political project was in any way less concerned with identifying itself as a pious Shi'ite party. The politics of such self-prescribed categories need to be analyzed within the competing nationalist projects of these two parties and not taken at face value. As I mentioned in the previous chapter on Amal's educational politics, the party is far from a monolithic entity. Class, urban-rural divisions, and the ideological orientations some of its members had developed before joining Amal have resulted in the emergence of factions. But to my best knowledge most Amal members actually reject a secular image, and they often blame Hizbullah for creating it in order to strengthen Hizbullah's position and prove its superiority in Shi'ite authenticity and piety. Secularism in this context clearly comes to mean godlessness, lack of piety, and a disloyalty to the idea of Lebanon. Besides, secularism in Lebanon was associated with a specific ideological trend that sought to secularize all public institutions in Lebanon, and not just to abolish political sectarianism. These were represented by the Lebanese Communist Party and the Progressive Socialist Party (PSP), later forming a coalition known as the Lebanese National Movement (LNM) which Amal opposed, as I have stated.

Nevertheless, national movement as Amal called itself came to be understood as a secular national movement by many scholars, for two reasons. First, Lebanese nationalism was primarily associated with Maronites and their nationalism. As explained in the introduction, this brand of nationalism was often viewed as secular and civil. Amal's intermittent association with Maronite projects such as Berri's participation in the 1982 Salvation Committee to cut a deal with Israel for withdrawal from its territories after the invasion, in which the leftist Walid Jumblat also participated, was partly responsible for creating this idea.

The second reason Amal was labeled a secular party was the European-derived assumption that nationalisms are based on secularism, superseding an earlier world of dynastic polities and religious solidarities and orientations. In the early 1980s, when the Iranian revolution propagated pan-Islamic solidarity, recalling ideas about the artificial nature of national boundaries that separate the Islamic *umma*, Amal's decision not to submit to the official Iran-propagated concept of *vilayat-i faqih* was reason enough to view it as a national and secular party.

For example, Andreas Rieck explains the split between Amal and Islamic Amal (whose members merged with some other groups to form Hizbullah in the early 1980s) in terms of the latter's desire to emphasize the religious identity of Amal and to distance itself from the secular trends of Amal leaders.[58] Here, the distinction between secular and religious party orientation is probably based on the fact that Berri was not a cleric himself. But, as discussed in the introduction, such distinctions based on the legal-theological training of the ethnic entrepreneurs do not reflect the complexity of the dialectics of politics and religion in Lebanon, or elsewhere.

Stefan Rosiny also describes the religious attitude of Amal as "close to folk-religious practices, syncretistic with functionalist usage of religious symbolism," and the Islamists' religious attitude as a "legally-based ethical understanding of Islam (*gesetzesethisches Islamverständnis*)."[59] However, claims that Islamists (*al-islamiyyun*) practice a legally based form of Islam should be partially interpreted in the context of the exclusion of other Shi'ite groups in the Lebanese national context. As chapter 1 illustrates, the discourse, as promoted by Sadr, that links piety with membership in the nation came to dominate nationalist rhetoric among Shi'ites in Lebanon. Islamist statements about practicing authentic religion and representing the true Shi'ites therefore facilitate the establishment of hegemony and leadership over the Shi'ite community in Lebanon. They also convince many Shi'ites that Hizbullah will also adequately represent them.

The disagreements between Amal, Islamic Amal, and the Iranian religious elite were about accepting a hierarchical order in the Shi'ite world as envisioned by the Iranian clerics. This center-periphery struggle was expressed in a discourse of Shi'ite authenticity, one that engaged the members in debating the supposed degree of Shi'ite religiosity, which was often imagined to be measurable by how much the party expresses its wish to establish a *shari'a*-based Islamic government modeled after the Islamic Republic of Iran. In particular, they were related to how religiosity was to be articulated, namely in the ways Amal defined its relation to the Islamic Republic of Iran, this powerful force that claimed to represent the most pious Shi'ite government, and consequently to how Amal defined its position toward the Palestinians in South Lebanon. Amal rejected the political principle of *vilayat-i faqih* (rule of the jurisprudent), the official political theory of the Islamic Republic of Iran, which also assigned to Khomeini his role as both the temporal and spiritual head of Iran and the grand-*marja'* of Shi'ites in the world (*marja' al-taqlid al-a'zam*). Most Amal members continued to follow the teachings of Kho'i, as had their leader, Sadr. Ever since Kho'i's death in 1992, they have considered Ayatollah 'Ali Sistani their leading *marja'*. Once Amal refused to include the version of Shi'ite piety that linked the degree of piety to the degree of commitment to the Palestinian cause and to the acceptance of the *vilayat-i faqih,* Amal's Shi'ite authenticity came under attack from within and without. This in turn justified the Iranian government's overt support of Hizbullah.

As Ibrahim Shamseddine (son of the late Muhammad Mahdi Shamseddine), who is affiliated neither with Amal nor Hizbullah, noted in one of our conversations about Iranian-Lebanese Shi'ite relations, the attitude of the Iranian government was that "you are either with us or against us. Iran did not leave a third choice. By 'with us' it meant being completely subordinated to Iranian rules, and by 'against us' it meant that you are a nonbeliever (*kafir*) and it was thus their duty to destroy you."[60] In my view, his statement quite clearly explains the attitude of the Iranian clerical circles toward Lebanese Shi'ites in the 1980s. Yet, the end of the Lebanese civil war in 1990, the election of Ayatollah Hashemi Rafsanjani in 1989 and Muhammad Khatami to the presidency in 1997, and the growing independence of Hizbullah from these clerical circles in Iran, as well as the growing power of Amal in the state apparatus, have forced these circles associated with Lebanese politics to readjust their either-or categorization and to encourage Hizbullah's cooperation with Amal, the erstwhile nonbelievers.

Oranges from Gaza and the Creation of Conscious Shi'ites, 1982

In a conversation with Bazargan, Farsi urged him to import oranges from Gaza to support the Palestinian economy (and implicitly the Palestinian cause). Presumably, Bazargan looked at Farsi in surprise and said, "We did not import oranges from Gaza during the Pahlavi regime. It will harm our own farmers if we do so. Why then should we import them now?" From this episode, Farsi concluded that the Palestinian cause was not at the top agenda of the LMI members.[61]

Other scholars have convincingly laid out Hizbullah's ideologies and its subordination to the concept of *vilayat-i faqih*, as well as the meaning Hizbullah generates from it.[62] My goal here is to do two things. First, I give voice to those who participated in performing these ideologies—the Iranian volunteers in 1982. While on their journey from Iran to Lebanon, these volunteers, who were simple militia members, midranking officials, and religious leaders, offered interpretations of what it meant to be a true Shi'ite—sometimes channeling Khomeini's ideas of authentic Shi'ism—and acted upon them. Second, I show how this new vision of Shi'ite identity played in the Lebanese context. This volunteer movement, symbolic as the act was since they did not actually fight Israel, supported the emergence of a new Lebanese Shi'ite nationalism that would be centered on the absolute fight against Zionism as well as the public performance of religious identity (*iltizam*)—themes which were much more pronounced than Sadr's vision of Shi'ite Lebanon. To make this new nationalism, part of the past, that is, of Sadr's activism and prerevolutionary Iranian-Lebanese Shi'ite ties, needed to be narrated in a new light.

While in Iran, the LMI members succeeded in blocking the plan of sending Iranian fighters to Lebanon until 1982, but by June of that year most of them had been either killed or politically muted. Finally, the Israeli invasion in June 1982 made it possible for Mohtashami and his entourage to send some troops to Lebanon only a few days after the invasion.[63] It was the beginning of the promotion of a new vision of Shi'ite identity in Lebanon. A lengthy article in Omid-i Inqilab (The Hope of the Revolution)[64] describes step by step the activities of the Iranian Revolutionary Guards (Pasdaran) from the time they are set to leave Iran until they arrive in Ba'albak via Syria. The tone of the article is full of enthusiasm; euphoric attitudes to martyrdom are reported to have prevailed among the almost one thousand Pasdaran members, as they are aware of their "historic" mission to fight the Israeli invasion in Lebanon. Many of the Pasdaran are physically challenged and some clearly too old to fight, provoking astonishment among observing Syrian soldiers.[65] In Damascus, regular visits to the shrine of Sayyida Zaynab, communal prayers, and Quran readings dominated daily activities apart from military preparations. Mohtashami, then the Iranian ambassador to Syria, as well as Hujjat al-Islam Sadiq Musavi, then the director of the Office of Islamic Propaganda in Iran (daftar-i tablighat-i islami), both gave talks in honor of the Pasdaran at the shrine of Sayyida Zaynab. 'Ali Akbar Velayati, then the Iranian foreign minister, spoke of "creating a spark which would serve as the introduction to a holy flame . . . to rid the holy land of our ancestors and Prophets of the dirty bodies of the occupiers."[66] In the same context, Mansur, the head of the military commando unit of the Pasdaran called the Forces of Muhammad, the Prophet of God (qova-i muhammad rasul-allah), proclaimed in his speech to these Pasdaran members:

> All Lebanese see you [Iranians] as their refuge (or source of comfort) and source of emulation (malja' va marja') and as their representative. . . . We fight with our belief, let them say we have come to commit suicide . . . we will make the day come when the Israelis will be so frightened of our guns because they would think, instead of bullets, Pasdars will come out of them . . . we are to start a war against Israel, whoever is with us, bismillah [i.e., welcome], and whoever is not with us [then let's say] goodbye [to them].[67]

The mission was less to literally fight against the Israelis, since the main activity of the Iranian Pasdaran was providing military training to Lebanese Shi'ites in Ba'albak; rather, in the words of Mansur, it was to "to propagate the idea that Israel is defeatable (tude'-i kardan-i ide'-i isra'il shekast pazir ast)."[68] Most noteworthy is the visit of the group to the Umayyad Mosque in Damascus prior to their departure to Lebanon, to which the journalist, by drawing parallels between the event of Karbala and the Pasdaran's mission to Lebanon, is giving historic importance:

> History was repeating itself, the followers of Husayn were on their way to the Umayyad Mosque again, but with the difference that in the year 61 *hijra* [i.e., after the battle of Karbala] they were captured by Yazid and this time they were successful conquerors and with weapons in their hands.[69]

What becomes clear from all this is that the role of the Pasdaran is to embody a new prototype of a Shi'ite person that envisions itself to be radically different from past Shi'ite identities. This new Shi'ite person is one who despite physical challenges, and despite the knowledge that death might await him, is ready to fight for an Islamic cause. He is so powerful as to even change the course of the battle of Karbala with a positive outcome. The Pasdaran are not simply providing interpretations of the battle of Karbala, of its characters, and of their motivations for participating in this battle, but are radically breaking with the paradigm altogether as Husayn's followers are presented as the winners of the battle, not just in symbolic and moral terms but literally—they are envisioned with weapons in their hands in Damascus, defeating Yazid.

In other words, we see the performance of the central components of Hizbullah's identity: *jihad* as a personal and political struggle, the celebration of martyrdom, and a total commitment to fight Zionism. Through Shi'ite activism in the present and the creation of a new Shi'ite person, this battle can be relived and its course can even be changed.

Producing Memories; or, Lebanese Shi'ites' Second Awakening?

But what exactly are the characteristics of this authentic Shi'ite person? As Sayyid Muhammad Husayn Fadlallah pointed out in an interview while attending the Week of Islamic Unity (*hafti'-i vahdat-i islami*) in Tehran in August 1982:

> Prior to the Iranian revolution the intellectuals, the religious, and the fighters were each embodied in a different person, but when I came to Iran I saw that a new Muslim generation is created, one who reflects the kind of Islam we are thinking about. Now the Iranian Muslim prototype is a fighter, a religious person, a pious (*'abid*), an ascetic, an intellectual, and a political person, all

FIGURE 3.2. A page from a children's storybook published by an independent Shi'ite publishing house after the Israeli withdrawal from South Lebanon in 2000. *Qissat al-intisar* (Beirut: Dar al-Hadi, 2000), 18–19. This publishing house is not affiliated with Hizbullah but, in this book, has appropriated Hizbullah's rhetoric and national vision. It offers an interesting perspective of how non-Hizbullah Shi'ites envision Hizbullah's identity and try to imitate its rhetoric. The caption next to the picture depicts the conversation of these three young boys and reads: At the Lebanese-Palestinian border three boys had gathered: Ahmad, Husayn, and Yusuf.

AHMAD: Look at the horizon over there.

HUSAYN: It is our honored *al-Quds*.

YUSUF: Today South Lebanon [was freed].

AHMAD: And tomorrow Palestine, *inshaallah*.

HUSAYN: Then from today on let's help to accomplish this goal.

incorporated in one person. What I saw in the Muslim Iranian youth, especially about the Pasdaran [is that] they are politically aware, and they have a religious dimension, they are pious believers, courageous, and active in social welfare.[70]

Fadlallah is clearly alluding to Sadr. The creation of this new, authentic Shi'ite identity needed to be accompanied by the denunciation of older Lebanese Shi'ite identities promoted by Amal and its leader Sadr. Reflected in Fadlallah's writings in 1980, right after the success of the revolution, is the idea that the Iranian revolution triggered a dynamism that transformed Muslims from a state of resignation and liberated their will to implement Islamic law in its various dimensions.[71]

Similarly, the Lebanese Sayyid 'Abbas Musawi, then a member of the religious seminary in Ba'albak who was elected in 1991 to be Hizbullah's general secretary and had volunteered to take part in one of the Iranian military training camps in Ba'albak, described the need to follow the Iranian model because in his view the Lebanese Shi'ite community lacked an aware leader (rahbari agah), one who would stand against Israel's aggressions in Lebanon. He referred to the animosity between "some Shi'ite groups in the south" and the Palestinians, and stated that the "believers" (mu'minun) among the Shi'ites in the south wanted to cooperate with the Palestinians but because of the lack of a "pious leader" this cooperation failed, until "these believers found their voice in Imam Khomeini."[72] This critique was directed at the organization of Amal. Sayyid Sadiq Musavi,[73] the head of the Office of Islamic Propaganda in Iran, characterized Amal and its ties to the Iranian ruling circles after the revolution up to 1982 as follows:

Mr. Sadr wanted to enter the Lebanese parliament, thus he decided to put all various influential Shi'ite groups under Amal, without any prior consideration of their ideological background. He believed that once they are in Amal, slowly they themselves will find their religious and ideological orientation. . . . In this process the Iranian revolution was on its way to success, and since most of these people were Shi'ites and the Iranian revolution was under the guardianship of Imam Khomeini, so it had a Shi'ite dimension. The Lebanese Shi'ites felt an unconscious bond (vabastegi-i nakhodagah) with the Islamic revolution, but the revolution was at the beginning not yet in the right hands and it was following a liberal line [referring to LMI members], and these liberals, based on a series of their own ideas, had put all their efforts in supporting one specific group in

Lebanon [i.e., Amal] instead of trying to attract a large number of followers. . . .
It was as if the line of the revolution had been defined by Bazargan, Yazdi, and
Qutbzadeh, but as the Iranian people never agreed on having them represent

the line of the revolution, here [in Lebanon] many didn't accept it either. Since
the line of the revolution was to incorporate all under its wings, despite the
weaknesses of this group [i.e., Amal], the revolution reacted positively toward
them. But with the last Israeli attack, fights broke out among the Amal members and the party split. But this is natural, once the basis and skeleton of something is not exact and proper, this is what will happen to it. . . . There are leaders
in the Amal who wanted to make peace with Israel, also those who, based on
their belief in Islam, wanted to fight Israel, and those who due to their weakness
of belief (za'fi imani) [i.e., Amal] didn't resist Israel and surrendered.[74]

To present Hizbullah as an authentic Shi'ite party—that is conscious and
strong in belief—and to justify its creation, Musavi portrays Sadr as a cynical
opportunist whose lack of religious vision led to the situation in which Amal
found itself in 1982. Sadr is presented as having gathered Amal members
around himself, hoping they would gradually find their way to a more authentic Shi'ism by themselves. But according to Musavi's logic, Sadr's lack of leadership results in "weakness of belief" among his Amal followers, and therefore a weakness in resisting Israel. He defines these characteristics in
opposition to those following the "line of the Imam (Khomeini)." In the 1980s
Hizbullah's identity then became shaped in the belief that it was in fundamental opposition to Amal's, and not as a group that split off from it with
some common goals and a common genealogy. The period of Sadr is regarded
as a time before true awareness, making a radical break necessary.

This description is also perhaps the more illustrative account in which
we can discern the creation of a new narrative describing the early phases of
Iran-Amal relations. Musavi then has to explain why Amal-Iranian ties were
close just shortly before the creation of Hizbullah. If Amal has been weak all
throughout, what required such a radical break with them in 1982 and not
right after the success of the revolution in 1979? He emphasizes Amal-LMI
ties to deflect any responsibility for maintaining such ties with the new enemy. Statements such as "Amal's martyrs are martyrs of the Iranian revolution and vice versa," made only one and a half years earlier by the representative of Khomeini's office in Beirut, had to be explained in a way that would
not place the new ruling elite in Iran in a questionable light. Musavi does so
by pointing to the supposedly generous policy of the post-LMI leaders of the

new Iranian government, who "while being aware of the weakness of Amal tried to incorporate them into the system" to "help" them. Musavi is clearly creating a narration in order to explain the support of Hizbullah as a logical correction of pre- and postrevolutionary miscalculations.

Evidently, many Amal members do not share this assessment of their supposedly misguided beliefs and orientations, and they have offered a different narrative of the events, one that represents Sadr and Amal members as pious Shi'ites who granted refuge to anti-Shah activists in Lebanon and supported the spread of Khomeini's messages in the Western media. All of these factors, Amal members argue, led to the success of the Iranian revolution.

As both remembering and forgetting historical events are related dialectically to current political context, memory often becomes a category of political practice and as such can be used to establish differences among Shi'ites as well as to create Shi'ite solidarities across borders. Memory, as all these examples show, is not simply the mental ability to retrieve past events.

Improved Relations and Enduring Tensions

Since the split in the Amal party in 1982 and the creation of Hizbullah, fully encouraged and supported as it was by the Iranian government, Amal-Iranian political relations have undergone many changes. Hizbullah, financially and ideologically backed by the religious elite in Iran, has become a full-fledged rival party to Amal, competing for resources, members, and political power in Lebanon. To Amal members, the outbreak of fighting between them and Hizbullah in 1988–1990, which cost the lives of at least three thousand Lebanese Shi'ites, was a direct consequence of Iranian meddling in Lebanese politics. Yet, both the death of Khomeini and the Ta'if Accord in 1989 (which put an end to the Lebanese civil war) opened a new page in Amal-Iranian relations. In 1996, an official Amal delegation visited Iran for the first time, during the presidency of Rafsanjani (1989–1997). In the same year, Muhammad Khatami, then acting as the minister of culture, visited Lebanon to give a series of lectures on civil society and democracy. Amal members regard Khatami with favor, often noting how his views on Lebanon reminded them of Sadr. In this, Amal positions itself as the Shi'ite party that favors a multisectarian Lebanon and as a party that encourages coexistence, while casting Hizbullah and the ruling clerics in Iran as being those in favor of an Islamic republic in Lebanon, whose form of government in Amal's view discourages coexistence.

It was no surprise, then, that the 1997 election of Khatami to the Iranian presidency was a milestone in improving relations between the Iranian government and Amal. To recover relations with Amal, the director of Khatami's presidential office, Sayyid Muhammad 'Ali Abtahi, had several informal visits with Muhammad 'Ubayd, then a high-ranking Amal member and former director of the ministry of media. Abtahi's personal friendships with some high-ranking Amal members, and the more official negotiations, resulted in Amal reopening its political office in Tehran in 2001, where the government allowed Amal to commemorate the disappearance of Sadr in an official manner for the first time since the revolution. As another gesture of improving relations, such as was discussed in chapter 2, the Iranian government provided funds for Amal educational facilities and helped build a new school in the former occupied territories in South Lebanon.

On his three-day visit to Lebanon in May 2003, Khatami stated clearly that "our support is a support for all Lebanon; it is not a support for a particular sect or a particular group."[75] Khatami's comments stand for the so-called Iranian reformists' views on how deeply Iran should be involved in Lebanese Shi'ite affairs. Although the special relationship between Iran and Lebanese Shi'ite is not denied,[76] these self-styled reformists, who feature members such as Mohtashami, now prefer to use official state channels to shape Iranian-Lebanese relations.

Still More Memory Production: Commemorating Chamran in 2002

Despite political rapprochement, the commemoration in 2002 of Chamran, which I attended, in Chiyah, a southern suburb of Beirut, twenty years after the split in Amal, was illustrative of the continuing disagreements and debates between Amal and the Iranian government. This commemoration is of special interest because it occurred in the first year after official relations between Amal and the Iranian government had resumed; Amal had inaugurated its political office in Tehran in 2001. As a result, the Iranian ambassador to Lebanon, Muhammad 'Ali Sobhani, was invited to give a speech at an Amal-organized commemoration of Chamran.

In this speech Sobhani describes Chamran's character as exemplary (*shakhsiyat-i nimunih*) and educated; he was an innocent mystic (*'arifi pak*). Sobhani then adds that "in order to understand the unique characters of such persons, one needs to speak of the movement of Imam Khomeini," which he does for most of the rest of his speech. He compares Khomeini's and Chamran's levels of mysticism and suggests that the success of the revolution was in large part due to the level of postnationalism that they had reached. He then moves on to stress that next to Sadr, Chamran also played a large role in the renewal of Lebanese Shi'ite identity (*tajdid-i huwiyyat-i shi'i*). He mentions that when he met members of the resistance (*guruh-i muqawami*, here referring to Hizbullah members), they told him that they were either students or friends of Chamran in the 1970s.

Sobhani clearly connects Chamran to the postrevolutionary Iranian government and justifies Iran's political involvement in Lebanon by emphasizing that Hizbullah members knew this prominent Iranian prior to the revolution. To underscore this, he further points out that when Chamran came back to Iran in 1979, he introduced himself to Iranians by saying, "I have come from Jabal 'Amil, the land of Abu Dharr [al-Ghifari]. I am the representative of the people of South Lebanon." Sobhani concludes from this statement that, because of Chamran's unique position in South Lebanon, "Chamran was able to bring dialogue and unity between the people of South Lebanon and Iran." Sobhani says a prayer at the end of his speech. He prays, "Let us maintain this strong bridge that Chamran has created with his blood and the blood of young Lebanese and Iranian fighters between the people of Iran and Lebanon, especially between Iran and the people of South Lebanon."

Sobhani was evidently presenting the prerevolutionary networks that linked the LMI and Sadr as a preparatory step for the relations between Iran and Hizbullah now. By reminding attendees—who were mainly Amal affiliates—of Chamran's statement that he had come from Jabal 'Amil, in South Lebanon, supposedly the place where Abu Dharr al-Ghifari, the companion of the Prophet Muhammad, introduced Shi'ite tradition to Jabal 'Amil, Sobhani justified and in a certain way naturalized the current official Iranian presence in Lebanon, above all in the south. Chamran was obviously of Iranian origin, and active in South Lebanon prior to the revolution. According to Sobhani, Chamran helped renew Lebanese Shi'ite identity and legitimized Sobhani's presence in Lebanon some twenty years later.

After Sobhani's speech, Amal deputy 'Ali Kharis began his commemorative speech on Chamran. Although he praised Chamran's unique character in a way similar to Sobhani's, his vision differed greatly. Kharis situated Chamran in a different Shi'ite network of the 1970s. His speech stressed the importance of Sadr to the success of the Iranian revolution by suggesting how "Musa Sadr and Chamran were the backbone (*jism al-asaasi*) of the Iranian Revolution and how one cannot speak of the Iranian revolution without mentioning these two people." Kharis does not subordinate Sadr and Chamran's activism to that of Khomeini. Instead, he reverses the hierarchical order evident in Sobhani's speech. In Sobhani's speech Sadr's activism is peripheral to Khomeini's. Kharis suggests a reversal of this order as he speaks at length about Sadr's activism in Lebanon and what he considers Sadr's fundamental role in the success of the Iranian revolution.

Competition between Amal and the Iranian religious elite over a central position in the Shi'ite world and their claims to Shi'ite authenticity have not been limited to military combat, diplomatic negotiations, and political statements and speeches. In chapter 4 we will see how Amal members construct differences to the Iranian religious elite through ritual and parodic performances and discourses that enable them at the same time to firmly establish themselves in the Lebanese national context. As will be discussed in chapter 5, the Iranian government in Lebanon is not only engaged in religious and political activities to change Lebanese Shi'ite identities; it hopes to promote a Lebanese Shi'ite-centered nationalism more attuned to its own interests through its nuanced cultural politics in Lebanon.

4

THE POLITICS OF SHI'ITE
AUTHENTICITY SINCE 1982

Lebanese Shi'ites are the showcase for Arab Shi'ism. Iranian Shi'ism is something totally different. Lebanese Shi'ites are the gate to the heart of Arab Shi'ites.[1]

— 'ALI HAMDAN, AMAL'S HEAD OF THE FOREIGN AFFAIRS BUREAU

As Islam does not recognize the concept of nationality, leading to the foundation of a pan-Islamic ideology, it was natural that most senior clergy and their disciples in Najaf and Karbala forged close and personal friendships [in the 1960s] regardless of nationality.[2]

— MAGNUS RANSTORP, A SCHOLAR OF INTERNATIONAL RELATIONS

Nationalism does not contradict Islam. Nationalism is to assert your rights in your country and regime as a member of the country.[3]

— SAYYID MUHAMMAD HUSAYN FADLALLAH,

A PROMINENT LEBANESE SHI'ITE MARJA'

When the Iranian government sent volunteers to Lebanon to fight against the Israeli invasion in 1982 despite Amal's disapproval, many Amal members began to resist Iranian hegemonic claims. This resistance was multilayered and its overarching theme was to locate Iranian Shi'ites on the less authentic side of Shi'ism. In this chapter, I focus on some of these boundary-making processes as they unfold in everyday life, in religious ritual, and in theological-legal debates. The performance of parodies of Iranians, for example, is one component of a broader production of narratives and stereotypes about a presumably distinct Iranian form of Shi'ism, which many Amal associates believe to involve Shi'ite practices that are less authentic than Arab Shi'ism. In these narratives and stereotypes, Iranian history, a presumed Iranian national character, and the Persian language account for the emergence of this supposedly inauthentic form of Shi'ism.

Amal's Shi'ite Lebanon is most conspicuous when it positions itself against a powerful transnational force. Since 1982, Amal members have produced images of piety for themselves by drawing on the value of Arabic, on the central importance of Jabal 'Amil as a site of authentic Shi'ism, and on the claim to be locally and culturally rooted in Lebanon through performances of some ritual practices during 'Ashura. The official ideologies of their leaders, but especially their own interpretations of language, history, and tradition, come to be mobilized in the everyday lives of Amal members and to generate meaning for them as Shi'ites in Lebanon, as members or associates of the main Shi'ite party in competition with Hizbullah, and as members of the larger Shi'ite world. The first of two parts of this chapter attempts to show how Amal does that.

In the second part I discuss yet another Lebanese Shi'ite group who also set themselves apart from the Iranian ruling religious elite and question their Shi'ite authority—the followers of the Lebanese Shi'ite religious scholar Sayyid Muhammad Husayn Fadlallah. While there are considerable differences between Fadlallah's and Amal's politics in Lebanon, because Fadlallah considers himself part of an Islamist bloc (al-islamiyyun) along with Hizbullah and to which he does not consider Amal belonging, both Amal and Fadlallah have placed great emphasis on building ethnic boundaries against the Iranian leadership. Fadlallah constructs his Shi'ite Lebanon by cultivating an Arab nationalist discourse, which he links to narratives about the renewal and modernization of Shi'ite traditions. By engaging in a discourse of modernity and establishing a reputation as a specifically Arab marja' whose up-to-date and progressive interpretations of Shi'ism center Shi'ites in Lebanon and support the Shi'ite community in establishing a prominent position in the Lebanese nation, he de facto breaks away from Hizbullah, too.

In the previous chapter we saw how the new, authentic Shi'ism claimed by Hizbullah presented the past as being characterized by a lack of leadership and the Iranian revolution as bringing about an awakening and a coming to awareness, justifying a radical break with Amal. The first part of this chapter discusses Amal's strategies to counter this discourse by presenting itself as imbued with religious authenticity. Amal members make broad use of a discourse of origins. Accordingly, being Arab and speaking Arabic brings them closer to authentic Islam, and claiming Jabal ʻAmil as part of their history positions them as senior in Shiʻite tradition. This discourse of authentic origins is also combined with the Western notion presupposing religion and politics as two distinct categories under conditions of modernity. Official Iran and Hizbullah emerge as inauthentic because their focus on conscious awareness in their piety makes them politically tainted and, therefore, hypocritical. Here Amal members seek to emphasize that piety and religious practice are most authentic when not connected to calculating awareness, but when habitually emerging from a putative, locally grounded tradition.

For the followers of Amal and of Fadlallah, piety forms the centerpiece of imagining differences among competing Shiʻite groups. But why should piety define loyalty and allow membership in the nation? As discussed in chapter 1, coexistence forms the core of what defines Lebanon. Coexistence acknowledges difference and encourages its public performance. While some Lebanese wish to protect political sectarianism as a guarantee of coexistence, Shiʻites push for the abolition of the political system while also pledging allegiance to the concept of coexistence. Whatever their differences, they all engage in the discourse of coexistence. In the view of Musa Sadr—whose ideas continue to shape Amal's public identity—as well as of Fadlallah (and Hizbullah), the most pious Shiʻite is most capable of coexisting with other religious groups. Piety defines loyalty to the Lebanese nation and creates access to its symbolic and material resources. But who is the most pious among the Shiʻites and who can lead the Lebanese Shiʻite community and help those within it become full cultural citizens? This chapter tells the story of a competition for this role as it is carried out in conversations, theological-legal debates, and rituals.

AMAL'S SHIʻITE LEBANON

Arabic as the Language of Authentic Shiʻites

The discourse of language superiority is one way Amal members express their claim of authority and authenticity in the Shiʻite world vis-à-vis the

Shi'ite religious elite of Iran. In their view, Arabic, as the language of the Quran (and as their native language), is superior to Persian. In the examples discussed below, Amal members systematically create a link between the degree of religious authenticity and the degree of what they would recognize as correct pronunciation of Arabic words. Amal members often label Iranians' pronunciation of Arabic words ridiculous (*maschara*), and therefore disqualify Iranians from laying claims on Islam and Shi'ism, not to speak of Iranians' hegemonic claims among Lebanese Shi'ites. Since the early 1980s, Amal members sometimes enact this claim of authenticity by parodying the Persian language—which contains many Arabic loanwords—and what they see as Persian-accented Arabic.

On the International Day of Jerusalem, a day that Khomeini dedicated to remember the Israeli occupation of Jerusalem, a conference was held in Tehran in 2001 which a group of Amal members attended. One of the attendees thought it would be nice to surprise me, and so he called me at my home in the United States to tell me that he was in Tehran. I picked up the phone and, after a minute, asked him what he was doing in Tehran. He muttered in parodied Persian, "*rUz-E jahAni-E ghods*" (i.e., World Jerusalem Day), burst into laughter, and handed over the phone to one of his friends, who told me they had left the conference early that day because they felt it was like a comedy and were now meeting with some other friends to eat dinner.

The parody centers on this phrase on several levels. First, the speaker lengthened the *U* in an exaggerated way, saying *rUz*. Then he put major emphasis on the genitive case marker after *rUz* by excessively lengthening the *E*. He then stylized the long *A* in *jahani* by pronouncing it in an extremely backed manner, resulting almost in an *O*. Finally, he pronounced the word *al-Quds* as Persian speakers would pronounce it, not making the distinction between the *q* and *qh*, which is characteristic of the Arabic sound system. To him, the Persian-accented pronunciation of *al-Quds* (*Ghods*) was a sign of the spurious nature of the Iranian government's involvement with Jerusalem. In the view of these Amal members, if the Iranian ruling elite cannot even properly pronounce the Arabic name of Jerusalem, *al-Quds*, which is *the* symbol of the Palestinian cause, how can they even begin to claim to represent themselves as the champions of the Palestinian cause? This parody was intended to invalidate the discourse linking Shi'ite piety and the support of the Palestinian cause, as discussed in chapter 3, which is so central to official Iranian and Hizbullah identity and to their vision of Lebanon.

On several other occasions, Amal associates drew a link between stylizing the letter A (from Arabic loanwords in Persian), by pronouncing it in a backed manner, and Iranians' presumed lack of religious authenticity. Once, as we were about to go out for lunch, an Amal official whom I call Husayn was sitting across from me in my office in Beirut and was talking about his latest visit to the Iranian embassy. He was angry because, as he explained to me, the employees at the Iranian embassy had treated him and his friends "like little children who needed guidance." To illustrate his point, Husayn started parodying the Iranian official with whom they had had a meeting at the embassy. Husayn rubbed his hands together, looked toward the floor, and began whispering slowly "*besmellAh-E rahmAn-E rahIm*" (i.e., in the name of God, the merciful) in caricaturized Arabic with a Persian accent to signal the beginning of their conversation at the embassy. After that he kept silent for a bit and looked at me peacefully. Then he shook his head in disgust at this attitude of the Iranian government official toward his group. "You Iranians think you are God, Allah himself," he said, "sent to us to teach us real Islam, as if we didn't know we were Shi'ites before; oh no, as if we didn't bring Shi'ism to Iran. Iran would be following bin-Laden now if it wasn't for us!"

These performances of the Iranian other are meaningful on various levels. First, as mentioned above, ideas about language purity and the authenticity of religious practices prevail among many Amal members, constituting a linguistic ideology[4] and drawing systematic links between the perceived purity of Arabic usage and authentic religious practice. Conversely, the parody of the Iranian official and Husayn's later comments on Iranian characters in performance connect an assumed deficiency in Arabic usage (perceived as an accent) with a lack of religious authority.[5] Body language, such as folding the hands while looking down with the head slightly tilted and beginning utterances by invoking the name of God by whispering "*besmEllAh*," as if only speaking to oneself, followed by silence before continuing any everyday conversation, have all been considered symbols of modesty and piety not only in the Iranian religious establishment but also among pious Iranian Shi'ites more generally, and should be viewed as part of the local Iranian construction of pious personhood.

Husayn's parody of this body language and the slow pronunciation of *besmEllAh* in a Persian accent are meant to emphasize the slickness of the Iranian official who was only *pretending* to be a pious religious man. Here the question of intention becomes central. The Iranian official is not really pious, but just pretending to be. The Amal member accuses Iranians of lacking religious authenticity by drawing on Western notions of modernity that presuppose the existence of religion and politics as two distinct spheres that should not be mixed. Engaging in this discourse that equates pure intentions with authentic piety is a recurring theme among Amal members. Similar to the folklorist presentation discussed in chapter 1, and as we see throughout this chapter, Amal members present themselves as nativist, deeply embedded in Lebanon, and as culturally Lebanese.

Q, a Shi'ite in his early forties, once had intended to study in Iran, but he returned after a few months. As he remembered it, "Every day there was something going on in Iran. It was like a film, the characters like caricatures. I thought I was in a comic film when I was in Iran." He started describing the scene in Arabic, parodying the characters and their spoken Farsi. He said that one day in Qasvin, at the local university, all the students had gathered to listen to a talk by a man named Abu Turab (probably referring to Abu Turabi), who had been a detainee in Iraq for ten years. Abu Turab came up to the podium and was silent for a full ten minutes. Everybody was waiting, but he didn't say anything and played with his prayer beads. Then suddenly he started talking in a mixture of Arabic and Persian for one or two minutes. Q began imitating this Abu Turab, who seems to have repeated only the following two phrases interchangeably: "*kAfErin va mOslemin, mOslemin va kAfErin*" (i.e., unbelievers and Muslims, Muslims and unbelievers). After this nonsense speech, everybody applauded and Abu Turab left. Q, stunned that the talk was so strange, with no apparent meaning, turned around and saw students screaming, "*marg bar AmrikA*" (i.e., Death to America), which is also considered typical of the repertoire of political slogans in postrevolutionary Iran.

The long, strongly backed Persian *alif* vowel, as in *kAferin* (which I have marked with an *A*), indicates that while the words are in Arabic, their pronunciation by a speaker of Farsi makes them inauthentic and indicative of the strangeness of the entire situation that Q describes. In addition, the letter *wa* in Arabic is usually strongly voiced, while the Persian rendering of it, *va*, is voiceless. Furthermore, Arabic loanwords in Persian are often taken over in the accusative (unlike Arabic, Persian nouns do not exhibit case marking). For example, in the context that Q describes, the correct Arabic form would be *kafirun wa muslimun*, since Abu Turab seems to have used these nouns in a way that would require use only of the nominative case. Q was amused that, instead, both the grammatical form of the words Abu

Turab used as well as his pronunciation of the words with the long *A* and the *w*, were supposedly wrong.

In another interesting example, Q links the sounds of Persian, especially the long, backed *A* vowel, to a situation in which Iranians are described as hypocritical. During his stay in Iran, Q was invited to the house of Iranian acquaintances. Describing how they open the door, he launched into parody again: "*salAm, befarmAyEd, befarmAyEd*" (i.e., Hello, please enter, please enter). Q mimics the hand movements of the host for entering. Discovering that the wife is angry at the husband because he has invited someone in, he concluded that Iranians were not genuinely hospitable, but only performed *tarof* (a ritual of politeness)[6] and never seriously meant to invite anyone. But as he was unfamiliar with the concept of *tarof*, he had entered the house with the man.

These linguistic stereotypes of Persian speakers' use of Arabic become loaded with symbolic value when Lebanese parody the Iranians they have encountered. They come to stand for the perceived slickness and untrustworthiness of Iranians, according to these Amal members who have spent time in Iran.

The novelty of this linguistic ideology became clear during interviews with members of Amal who referred nostalgically to the sweetness of the Persian accent of their religious leader, Musa Sadr. Born and raised in Iran, although living eventually in Lebanon, he still spoke a heavy Arabic, which was considered sweet and pleasant, whereas the same accent used by other Iranians now is interpreted negatively.

One Amal member recalled a rally in the 1970s in the middle of summer at which Sadr gave a speech. He was standing under a roofed podium, but his audience was out in the sun. Sadr decided to come down to join the crowd because he thought it was unfair for him to be in a shaded place. The Amal member repeated what Sadr had said at the time in accented Arabic, as he remembered it: "*ana fi al-zill va* (instead of the Arabic *wa*) *antum fi al-shams*" (i.e., I am in the shadow and you are under the sun). The Amal member recalled how sweet his accent was when he said that sentence and said that he will never forget the sound of it in his ears.

This demonstrates the power of linguistic ideologies in making ethnic and political differences: how in different political contexts the same accent is evaluated as having different characteristics. To contextualize these parodies, the construction of the other must be seen against the background of power struggles that also historicizes Amal's identity politics and the ruptures within it. Prior to the Iranian revolution, the emphasis on Arabic instead of French as the dominant language of Lebanon was a way for Shi'ite leaders to position Lebanese Shi'ites in the mainstream Arab Muslim world (however Sunni dominated). In the 1980s, this emphasis on Arabic as a marker of Amal's identity took a specifically Shi'ite Arab twist.

Sacred Jabal 'Amil: Creating a Discourse of Origins

If this world is what you seek,
Then leave to India
If the hereafter is what you desire,
Then you must come to Bahrain
But if you seek neither this world nor the next,
Then reside in Persia.[7]

—'AMILI SCHOLAR HUSAYN IBN 'ABD AL-SAMAD (D. AD 1576)

TO HIS SON BAHA'I IN A LETTER

Shi'ites refer to Jabal 'Amil as a geographic and cultural entity with religious significance that roughly corresponds to the present-day province of South Lebanon, though parts of historic Jabal 'Amil are now in northern Palestine and in western Syria. By the tenth century, some Yemeni tribes with Shi'ite leanings, among them the 'Amila tribe, had settled in the region. However, embedded in 'Amili oral history and later in 'Amili writings has been the view that a close companion of the Prophet Abu Dharr al-Ghifari (d. AD 651) introduced Shi'ism to the region. 'Amilis then "prided themselves on being among the earliest if not the first converts to Twelver Shi'ism."[8] They also claim Jabal 'Amil as the foremost center of Shi'ite scholastic leadership, sidelining historical evidence that points to Hilla in present-day Iraq as a prestigious center of religious learning where, during the twelfth to the fourteenth centuries, many leading Jabal 'Amili scholars received their training. It was only during the fourteenth century that 'Amili scholars established centers of learning throughout Jabal 'Amil and that the number of 'Amili scholars increased. By the late fifteenth and early sixteenth centuries, Jabal 'Amil became the most accredited center of Shi'ite learning, with an emphasis on linguistic, legalistic, and doctrinal disciplines, and a clear shift occurred from Hilla to various villages in Jabal 'Amil, such as Inatha, Jizzine, Mays al-Jabal, and Juba'. However, due to a range of economic and political reasons, by the first decade of the sixteenth century the religious schools in Jabal 'Amil began to decline, and a large-scale migration of these scholars that lasted for about two centuries took place. A total of 159 of these 'Amili scholars left for the Safavid empire, whose rulers were eager to spread the Twelver Shi'ite tradition quickly and effectively. In the sixteenth century these 'Amilis held lucrative posts at the court and enjoyed great respect due to the reputation of the Jabal 'Amili scholars as representatives of Shi'ite legalistic tradition.[9] Nevertheless, by the mid-seventeenth century, due to the political changes in the Safavid court and its religious taste and inclinations, the interest in 'Amilis' version of Shi'ism waned and the migration of 'Amili scholars decreased significantly.[10]

Amal members emphasize Jabal 'Amil as part of their national narrative. They remember in a particular way the migration of these 'Amili scholars to Persia. They claim that it was Lebanese religious scholars from South Lebanon who introduced Shi'ism to Iran. They nationalize the social memory of a historical process—the sixteenth-century migration of Shi'ite *'ulama* from Syrian Jabal 'Amil to Safavid Persia—as evidence of their superior position in the wider Shi'ite tradition and history. Many Amal members and affiliates bring up the issue of the senior and thus more authentic position of Lebanese Shi'ites because of the good reputation of 'Amili scholars and the significance of Jabal 'Amil.[11] Hasan, an Amal member who had gone to Iran in 1981 to accompany Mustafa Chamran to fight against the Iraqi invasion, spoke at length about Chamran and the Iran-Iraq war. But when he analyzed Amal-Iranian relations in the 1980s, which he characterized as the phase of Iranian support for Hizbullah against Amal, he became upset. "After all," he said, "the Lebanese Shi'ites were from Jabal 'Amil, and the 'Amili scholars had brought Shi'ism to Iran, so is it then right for Iran to fight us [i.e., Amal] like this?"

In a conversation in Beirut with Abu Kharif, another Amal member, who had also accompanied Chamran to Iran on several trips from 1979 to 1981, he remembered how the people he had met in Iran had been so welcoming to him and his Lebanese friends even though neither side spoke the language of the other. In his view, the Iranians were so hospitable because they identified Lebanese Shi'ites with Jabal 'Amil. When he mentioned his Lebanese identity, Iranians would call him 'Amili and point to a mosque. Abu Kharif concluded that the people in Iran held no grudge against Lebanese Shi'ites[12] or against Amal, but that it was the Iranian government that was at odds with Amal.

It should be remembered that although Shi'ite traditions were indeed introduced to Safavid Persia by Jabal 'Amili scholars, postrevolutionary Iran is not Safavid Persia and Jabal 'Amili scholars in the sixteenth century were not Amal members. Furthermore, the interaction of Safavid Persia and Jabal 'Amili scholars was a complex process that certainly cannot be reduced to "exporting Shi'ism from Jabal 'Amil to Safavid Persia,"[13] just as the postrevolutionary Iranian-Lebanese Shi'ite relations in the 1980s and the creation of Hizbullah cannot be reduced to the narrative of an export of the revolution. Amal members whose sense of Shi'ite ancestry and authenticity is very much linked to the idea of Jabal 'Amil thus project the contemporary national categories of Iran and Lebanon onto a reading of the past, identifying the people of sixteenth-century Jabal 'Amil with the modern nation-state of Lebanon, and the empire of the Safavids with the Islamic Republic of Iran. As a consequence of this ideological move, Amal members emerge on the more authentic side of this opposition of modern categories which a modern reading of the distant past makes relevant.

Was Musa Sadr Iranian or Lebanese? Accent Versus Genealogy

Whenever I pointed out to Amal members that the accent now regarded negatively is the same Persian accent Sadr and Chamran, leaders and organizers of Amal, were also known for, their response shifted in the case of Sadr to an assessment of family origins (*asl*). Seeking to reconcile the status of a revered leader with his accent now read as a sign of foreignness, religious inauthenticity, and character deficiencies, my interlocutors emphasized that Sadr was actually from Jabal 'Amil, that he was only born in Iran, and that his family was Lebanese.

During the course of my research, many asked me about Sadr's origins. Among them was a policymaker at the German embassy in Beirut who asked, "So tell me, who was Musa Sadr? Was he really Iranian or was he actually Lebanese?" When I began to explain that in my view defining his identity was related to the interpretation of a number of sociopolitical events and that, depending on one's political stance, one could argue either way, I noticed a clear sign of disappointment on his face. It suggested to me that I had not done my homework well enough to find the truth, just as I did not have any answers to the questions about the whereabouts of Sadr or even whether he was still alive.

To many of Sadr's political opponents, among them many of the Shi'ite *zu'ama*, Sadr was born in Qom, Iran, and he held an Iranian passport—although he did receive Lebanese nationality before his disappearance—and he spoke Arabic with a Persian accent. These were reasons enough to label Sadr an Iranian in order to marginalize him politically. Yet, postrevolutionary official Iran never showed any interest in claiming him, partly because of certain religious and political disagreements and rivalries, some of which I discussed in the previous chapter. To his followers in Lebanon who agreed with Sadr's activism he was clearly a Lebanese. To Amal members, his speeches given in Arabic with a Persian accent were simply part of his charm and charisma, and the memory of that accent brings smiles to their faces and prompts the telling of sympathetic anecdotes. Sadr's accent for them was merely a *historical coincidence* without deeper implications, which led this 'Amili to speak Arabic with a Persian accent even though the same accent later became a reason to deny current Iranian claims to piety. At any rate, supporters as well as opponents of Sadr engaged in a discourse of origins to decide his identity. Some traced his genealogy as far back as the nineteenth century to include him in the Lebanese context; others took his birthplace as a starting point from which to exclude him from Lebanese political life.

But Sadr, who actively positioned himself in the Lebanese context and in particular in South Lebanon and who traced his genealogy to Jabal 'Amil, contributed to this particular narrative conforming his Lebanese identity. He introduced himself in the following way, only two years after his arrival in Lebanon in 1961, using his Persian-accented Arabic:

> *Interviewer:* I know your origins are Lebanese (*min asl lubnani*), but when did your family emigrate, and why?
>
> *Sadr:* My origins can be traced back to Sayyid Salih Charafeddine, who emigrated with his son Sadr al-Din to Iraq 150 years ago as a result of the well-known attacks of al-Jazzar. . . . Ever since, a large family section, which took the name Sadr, has lived in Iran and Iraq.[14]

By 1966, when his activities in Lebanon to bring the south to the attention of the Lebanese state had slowly begun to take off, and the need to clarify his position toward the Shi'ite feudal lords in the south and the larger public became more pressing, Sadr changed his position slightly. To the question "Is it right what some say that you are a descendant of a Persian family?" he responded:

> I am from a Lebanese religious family who used to live in the *south*, my grandfather Sayyid Salih had emigrated from the village of Ma'rake, *in the vicinity of Tyre* during the Turkish period. . . . We used to live in Iraq where my grandfather established a family known as the *bayt al-Sadr*. Then his son Sayyid Sadr al-Din traveled to Iran to visit the tomb of Imam al-Rida. When passing through Isfahan his relatives urged him to stay, due to their custom of respecting Lebanese 'Amili *'ulama*, so he stayed and established a large family. . . . Both families in Iran and Iraq have kept their title of *al-'Amiliyyin*.[15]

Here we see a shift in Sadr's interpretation of his identity. The emphasis on tracing his genealogy to the south and Jabal 'Amil becomes central, as does the emphasis on how the Sadr family in the so called Iranian diaspora kept its 'Amili title (and implicitly its heritage).[16]

But Amal's explaining away a Persian accent as an unimportant historical coincidence is more difficult to apply to Chamran, an Iranian who was neither a religious scholar nor could be easily connected to 'Amili tradition by ancestry like Sadr. His accent also reportedly sounded sweet, and many Amal members were fond of telling stories about his mistakes in spoken Arabic. They said "he was an exception," "a real phenomenon," "a true Shi'ite (*shi'i haqiqi*)." In other words, while to them there is no questioning of Sadr's Lebanese identity because of his 'Amili origins, Chamran is appropriated by Amal claiming that he was an *exception*, certainly unlike the other Iranians they have encountered since the success of the Iranian revolution.

To summarize, by successfully incorporating Sadr into a Lebanese narrative by focusing on his family's links with Jabal 'Amil and playing down his accent and his birth of place as a matter of mere historical coincidence, it became possible to use the linguistic ideology of exclusion based on politically and morally loaded evaluations of accent as a strategy of national authentication.

'Ashura in Nabatiyya, or When the Local Is the Authentic

On the tenth day of Muharram (*yawm 'ashura*), Shi'ites engage in three different types of activities in Nabatiyya, one of the chief cities of South

Lebanon, to mourn the death of Imam Husayn (d. 680), the grandson of Prophet Muhammad, who had fought the Umayyads (661–750) and considered himself the rightful leader of the Muslim community. In what came to be known as the battle of Karbala, Husayn, along with seventy-two others, was martyred.

Commemorations often take place simultaneously in the downtown area of the city. First among them is the reenacting of the battle of Karbala (*shabih/tamthil al-husayn*);[17] second is the processions (*masiraat*), which often involve various styles of self-flagellation by participants; third is the mourning ceremonies (*majalis ta'ziyya*) where (professional) reciter/performers (*qurra'*) and prominent religious scholars give speeches about the meaning and the relevance of the Karbala event.

While 'Ashura was publicly commemorated by Persian residents of Istanbul during most of Ottoman rule,[18] for Ottoman Shi'ite subjects like the Shi'ites in Jabal 'Amil such commemorations were restricted to their homes. Beginning in 1895, Iranian merchant residents, holding special permission from the *vilayet* of Beirut, held yearly commemorations in front of their homes in Nabatiyya in which local Shi'ites participated even though they

FIGURE 4.1. 'Ashura, Nabatiyya, March 2003. A group of middle-aged local merchants prepare to hit *haydar*, with some having hit already. *Photograph taken by the author.*

FIGURE 4.2. 'Ashura, Nabatiyya, March 2003. Amal sympathizer wearing a T-shirt with an Amal emblem, his clothes stained with blood after having hit *haydar*. *Photograph taken by the author.*

were not legally permitted to. By 1921, after the collapse of the Ottoman empire and the creation of Lebanon, Mirza Ibrahim, an Iranian merchant in Nabatiyya whose son Behjat was a student of medicine at the American University of Beirut (AUB), was engaged in promoting and spreading the practice of *haydar*. Commemoration rituals have become more elaborate since the initial phase, against the background of their increasing popularity and growing economic importance.

The ritual practice of *haydar* involves cutting the skin of the forehead of participants with knives or swords and then continuously and rhythmically beating the wound until it bleeds severely, while crying out *haydar, haydar,* it being one of the names of Imam 'Ali, the father of Imam Husayn. To commemorate the martyrdom of Imam Husayn, participants in the ritual usually wear white shrouds (the *kafan*), which quickly become stained with blood.

Sayyid Muhsin al-Amin, a well-known Shi'ite religious scholar from Jabal 'Amil active in Damascus in the 1920s, was among the fierce opponents of this practice, which he thought gave a bad image to Islam, while also pointing to the Iranian influence behind the spread of the practice and its

FIGURE 4.3. 'Ashura, Nabatiyya, March 2003. Lebanese Red Cross members running to their tents to provide for a man who has lost too much blood after hitting *haydar*. *Photograph taken by the author.*

supposedly alien status in Jabal 'Amil. The practice of *haydar* continued to thrive despite such opposition from the 1930s to the present. The yearly commemorations held in Nabatiyya resulted in the rise of an "'Ashura economy" for the locals, and soon the gathering also served as an occasion on which new social links, such as through the arrangement of marriages, were established and reinforced. In other words, the 'Ashura event in Nabatiyya with *haydar* as its trademark—just like other major public performances— is a multifaceted event.

Nevertheless, frequently since the 1960s, Shi'ite leaders such as Sadr, Fadlallah, as well as two SISC representatives, the late Shaykh Muhammad Mahdi Shamseddine and Shaykh 'Abd al-Amir Qabalan, have discouraged Lebanese Shi'ites from engaging in this practice for two reasons. First, it allegedly damages the reputation of Islam and specifically of Shi'ites around the world. Second, theological debates have revolved around the meaning of Imam Husayn's death in the battle of Karbala, in which some have questioned whether crying and self-flagellation correspond to the way he would have liked his martyrdom remembered, and whether these modes of commemoration are really an effective practice of spiritual intercession.[19]

Despite these calls to cease performing *haydar*, the practice continued in Nabatiyya throughout the 1970s. A main force behind this persistence at the time was the Imam of Nabatiyya, Shaykh al-Sadiq. He was responsible for the organization of the Muharram commemorations and was a close ally of Kamil al-As'ad, a Shi'ite *za'im* and sponsor of the commemorations, who was opposed to Sadr and his growing popularity among Lebanese Shi'ites.[20]

In the 1980s,[21] after the success of the Iranian revolution and the creation of Hizbullah in 1982, the ritual practice of *haydar* became a stage for Hizbullah to attract followers and to publicly demonstrate how the number of its adherents grew from year to year. The clashes between Israeli soldiers and Shi'ite commemorators during 'Ashura in Nabatiyya in 1983 helped to politicize the practice and helped 'Ashura become an occasion for the expression of resistance to Israeli attacks and occupation in Lebanon. In 1983 about 150,000 people took part in the Muharram programs, and the number of self-flagellants grew to five thousand. By 1985, Amal and Hizbullah had begun to stage separate processions, and in 1986 about eight hundred Hizbullah members disturbed an Amal-organized 'Ashura procession in Nabatiyya. Amal members have ever since engaged in a competition with Hizbullah and have held a separate procession in Nabatiyya. The number of Amal self-flagellants, who are mainly from the lower and lower-middle-class background, in 1987 increased to about three thousand.²² Participants showed their affiliation to each political party by wearing headbands or T-shirts or by tying scarves and flags around their necks with an emblem of the Amal or Hizbullah Party.

The 1994 Fatwa; or, Is Blood Donation Antinational?

In 1994, the Iranian supreme spiritual leader, Ayatollah 'Ali Khamenei, issued a fatwa in which he demanded a stop to violent self-flagellation among Shi'ites in the world and encouraged the participants to donate blood instead.²³ Although similar fatwas had been issued in the past, Hizbullah members who consider Khamenei their *marja'* stopped the practice of *haydar* and soon began to hold processions without it.²⁴

Because Khomeini had issued a similar opinion (but not a fatwa) before his death in 1989 to refrain from the practice of *haydar*, the success of Khamenei's fatwa is certainly due to the improved formal and informal networks of Hizbullah throughout Lebanon since the early 1990s.²⁵ For example, on Hizbullah's television station, al-Manar, as well as on its radio station, al-Nur, discussions about proper forms of holding commemorations are often repeated throughout the month of Muharram. Hizbullah-run schools and public religious education in Shi'ite neighborhoods—which are under the supervision of the *jam'iyyat al-ta'lim al-dini al-islami*—also engage students in 'Ashura processions and teach them "correct and authentic" forms of commemorating Imam Husayn.

Hizbullah began to transform 'Ashura processions after the fatwa and to spread the new interpretations of the event through various media by promoting the idea that instead of shedding blood committed Shi'ites should donate blood. Amal sympathizers, however, continued the practice of *haydar*. They do not consider Khamenei their *marja'* nor his fatwa authoritative. The practice of *haydar* thus came to be associated with Amal, whose leaders silently saw in the continuation of the practice a demonstration of their independence from Iranian dominance over Shi'ite affairs in Lebanon. 'Ashura commemorations in Nabatiyya continued to be a stage for violent clashes between Amal and Hizbullah members every year until 2001, with leaders and members of both parties being well aware of the interconnectedness between ritual processions, the claiming of public space, and political power.

Amal members presented Hizbullah's submission to the fatwa as additional proof of its close ties to Iran, as several fatwas from Lebanese shaykhs had not moved it to such a decision. Amal members constructed an opposition to Hizbullah by relying again on a discourse of origins, thereby positioning themselves as the bearers of a local tradition that is culturally Lebanese,[26] while positioning Hizbullah as foreign-oriented because it practices a new form of ritual that is outside authentic Lebanese traditions. In this context, blood donation as practiced and propagated by Hizbullah on 'Ashura,[27] in lieu of practicing *haydar,* came to be viewed as antipatriotic by Amal members because the motivation for such a practice had come from abroad.

Nevertheless, blood donation was certainly welcomed by the Red Cross and the hospitals in the south and in Beirut. Many hospitals in Beirut shut their doors to patients suffering from wounds and loss of blood due to the practice of *haydar,* and view it as irresponsible to use scarce blood reserves for those who harm themselves deliberately. Red Cross members, alongside Amal scouts, frantically try to control the crowds during 'Ashura in Nabatiyya and treat those who fall down unconscious after losing too much blood in tents specifically set up for this purpose. All in all, there is little doubt that blood donation is viewed as preferable to *haydar* by many non-Shi'ites[28] to whom the images of Shi'ites covered in their own blood with swords drawn are hardly comprehensible, represent signs of exaggerated religiosity and backwardness,[29] and reinforce the kind of stereotypes I discussed in chapter 1.

On the other hand, the bombastic, military-style processions Hizbullah organizes during 'Ashura are certainly a message to other Lebanese and to the wider world of their existence and their degree of organization, two factors that often worry other Lebanese citizens. Nasrallah, for example, usually delivers programmatic speeches to a crowd of approximately one hundred thousand, discussing current political events while outlining how Lebanon as a state should act in the regional and international political context.[30]

The Iran-Amal Rapprochement: Reversing Labels,
or When the Local Tradition Becomes Foreign

With the continuous improvement in Amal-Iranian relations after the election of the Iranian president Khatami in 1997, Nabih Berri has again encouraged Amal sympathizers to refrain from the practice of *haydar,* since one of the principal tenets of recent Iranian policy in Lebanon has been a rapprochement between Amal and Hizbullah. This has become the case since Iranian government actors realized the key importance of Amal in their desire to influence Lebanese government decision making. Both Berri and Nasrallah explicitly called upon the participants to refrain from visibly identifying themselves with any party flags during the 'Ashura commemorations in 2001, and by 2004 they had planned to hold jointly organized commemorations in Nabatiyya. With this move, Berri disassociates Amal *officially* from the practice of *haydar*, deflecting any responsibility for those who pretend to be part of the party. But how do Amal leaders persuade the participants to refrain from the practice without appearing to submit to the Iranian *marja'* Khamenei? Amal members again mobilize a discourse of origins, but this time move back further in history to sixteenth-century Safavid Persia to point to the supposedly foreign origin of *haydar*.

Sayyid Hani Fahs, a Shi'ite intellectual who has recently become an Amal sympathizer, places the origins of *haydar* within the history of Iran. According to Fahs, the violence was adopted from an Iranian tradition used to convert the masses to Shi'ism in the Safavid period. He points out that the violence of *haydar* should be contextualized with respect to that historical period and its purpose clarified.[31] *Haydar*, he continues, is not a Lebanese practice because the violent aspects of 'Ashura commemoration, such as flagellation, were introduced to South Lebanon by an Iranian immigrant named Doctor Mirza. Like others before him, Fahs has chosen to emphasize the foreign origin of the practice in order to discourage Lebanese Shi'ites from engaging in it. However, this argument has remained an intellectual exercise, as the practice of *haydar* is tightly connected to the local economy and is popular among many lower-class and lower-middle-class merchant families from the south, some of whom consider themselves Amal sympathizers.

Reducing the question of *haydar* to a simple Amal-Hizbullah political antagonism, or to theological-legal differences within the community, would understate the complexity of the issue. This ritual performance, based on the memory of a historical event, is intimately related to interpretations of Lebanese nationalism. A dichotomizing discourse of local tradition versus inauthentic innovation imposed by foreigners seizes debates about this ritual practice to create a presumably authentic, locally rooted, Lebanese Shi'ite heritage in light of Lebanese Christians' fear of the increasing dominance of Iran.

While processions with the practice of *haydar* served as a stage for Hizbullah members to attract followers ever since Khamenei's fatwa in 1994, Hizbullah members have refrained from the practice, instead holding processions in Nabatiyya without this kind of self-flagellation, while rhythmically beating their chests during the processions and donating blood. Hizbullah members and sympathizers watch the performance of *ta'ziyya* and attend their own mourning ceremonies, often in tents set up in Nabatiyya.[32] They argue that *haydar* is an exaggerated form of grieving during 'Ashura that reinforces the image of Shi'ites as backward in Lebanon. Instead, the organized performances and the speeches of Nasrallah,[33] Hizbullah's secretary general, can be viewed as a departure from older visions of Shi'ite identity and of Lebanon. These new practices are part of the construction of a specific Lebanese Shi'ite nationalism rooted in Hizbullah's vision of a future Lebanon. In fact, refraining from a practice that causes such an outcry among many non-Shi'ites in Lebanon can be viewed as one of the most successful strategies of Hizbullah positioning itself as respectable, organized, rational, and thus capable of participation in and, in the view of Hizbullah members, of eventually leading the Lebanese nation.

Amal sympathizers have engaged in another strategy to prove their Lebanese identity. By continuing the practice of *haydar*, they create a discourse linking piety to local tradition. They would often refer to it as a practice that is originally and authentically Lebanese (*min asl lubnani*) and not from Iran (*min iran* or *irani*). Most pious is the one practicing a local form of tradition as opposed to what Hizbullah's practices are thought to be, namely foreign-imported tradition (despite the fact that *haydar* was spread in South Lebanon through Iranian merchant families in the 1920s). According to this logic, so-called traditional practices, those believed to be local and those who engage in them without consciously choosing to do so, emerge as more authentic. Traditional practices are believed to be habitual and genuine (coming from the heart), almost folkloristic, without any political calculations. Amal positions new commemorative practices as signs of Hizbullah's submission to a foreign power and as politically motivated acts. In their logic, these practices are not expressions of genuine piety but are about pure politics. The reverse discourse is true among Hizbullah members, as the most pious is the one who is conscious and aware about the meaning and reasons for every ritual.[34]

Producing Ethnicity, Performing the Other; or, "Why Do Iranians Cry So Much for Husayn?"

The idea that the difference between Shi'ism in Iran and Lebanese Arab Shi'ism is based on several psychological and historical factors in the Iranian experience provides ample material for many Amal members to perform parodies of Iranians. Unlike *haydar*, which pertains to the specific context of an annual ritual of commemoration, parodies of Iranians are more a feature of everyday life for many Amal members.

One evening at T's place, when two friends of the family arrived who had not met me before, one such parody performance took place. The Ts have been associated with Amal in postwar Lebanon, and their friends had visited and traveled to Iran for study, staying there for longer periods. As usual, I was introduced as *bahitha iraniyya* (a female Iranian researcher), and eyebrows were raised in surprise to see an Iranian woman without a *hijab* in Lebanon. Conversation followed the usual path. They asked if I was married or had children, how I liked Lebanon, and what I thought about President Khatami. Usually after the last question it would be my turn to ask about their experiences in Iran, what they did, and so forth. This time, A started off immediately with a story about his experiences in Iran, and in no time all five people at the table were parodying Iranian accents when speaking Arabic and were mimicking the Iranian system of manners known as *tarof* and laughing—performances I had gotten used to by that time. But then suddenly one of the women in the group who was associated with Amal (I will call her S) and who had spent some time in Iran as her father had studied in the seminaries in Qom in the 1980s, began to perform the following scene: She is in the shrine of Sayyida Zaynab in Damascus during the month of Muharram, and Iranian women on pilgrimage are commemorating Imam Husayn and his sister Zaynab. She performs a parody of how the Iranian women were crying in a dramatic way. She acts out one dialogue between Zaynab and Imam Husayn as performed presumably by the Iranian women S had seen in Damascus, then another imitating how the Iranian women interpreted Zaynab's condition in Karbala.

S raises her voice and animates the Iranian women's voices with great drama (in Persian).

Soon the groups at the table have tears in their eyes from laughter, so she stops, turns to us at the table, and says, *"an jad ma'uleh?"* (Seriously, is this normal/possible?) Everybody nodded in agreement that Iranians are melodramatic, just as she had parodied them, and that they knew exactly what she was talking about.

Another Lebanese woman (I will call her M) then began performing a similar narrative about her experiences in a *hawza* for women in Qom during her youth. M had moved to Iran because her husband had studied at one of the

TABLE 4.1

Ya Husayn, chera mano tanha gozashti?	1 Oh Husayn, why did you leave me alone?
(S's voice is raised even louder and she almost screams in an angry tone.)	
CHERA?	WHY?
Bebin chi shod ba man?	See what happened to me?
Uhuhuh, ahhhhh	5 Uhuhuh, ahhhhh
(She is imitating the crying of the women and continues in a lower voice.)	
Zaynab-i bichare'	Poor Zaynab
(Begins to slap her own face and breasts)	
bedun-i ab tu sahra!	10 Without water in the desert!

theological seminaries in Qom, and she herself decided to join a *hawza*, as such an establishment did not exist in Lebanon for women at that time. Both became disillusioned, as they saw how the ideals of the Iranian revolution were not practiced in Iran. They decided to return to Lebanon in the middle of the civil war and began identifying themselves more with Amal.

Her narrative goes like this: M is in the *hawza* in Qom; it is her first day of classes. Like all the women, she is wrapped in chador down to the toes; she shows how only half an eye was visible. Then the shaykh comes in and sits on the floor with his back to the women, even though all of them are covered completely. M imitates the voice of the shaykh when he begins asking the women in a frightening and suspicious tone, "What will you do if Imam Mahdi comes now? RIGHT NOW!" M raises her voice and continues to parody the shaykh in a suspicious tone: "WHAT WILL YOU TELL HIM?" M actually says these two sentences in English; she switches to Arabic when describing the atmosphere of the next scene. She tells us that at this point all the women in the room began to cry and she imitates them by putting her scarf over her face and switching to Persian: "Uhuhhh, ya imam mahdi, koja'i?" (i.e., Uhuhhh, oh Imam Mahdi, where are you?) Following this episode, she decided to leave the *hawza* and, shaking her head, turns to us at the table and says, "*khalas*, Iranians love *majlis 'aza'* (a commemoration service); after every class or anything you need to have a *majlis 'aza'*."

While analyzing these performances and the way they contribute to the construction of ethnic stereotypes and boundaries, it is useful to draw on the concept of voicing developed by Mikhail Bakhtin, the Russian literary critic and philosopher of language. According to Bakhtin, utterances always constitute a "social voice"; that is, they represent subjects who inhabit particular social and historical positions and speak from a particular ideological position. Bakhtin applied these ideas to the analysis of literary language, in particular the novel, which is inhabited by a diversity of characters whose social voices are represented and juxtaposed by the writer.[35] Bakhtin paid particular attention to the way reported speech, the use of other peoples' words in order to present a viewpoint of one's own, often results in a certain double-voicedness or "heteroglossia"[36] of the utterance. Reported speech is heteroglossic because it is often impossible to completely suppress awareness of the prior uses, meanings, and intentions associated with the words reported. The narrated voice and the narrator's voice coexist in such forms of speech, and may even enter into conflict with one another. Parody, or the animation of other people's words in a manner that is usually critical of the narrated voice, is an important stylistic strategy in literature as well as in social life that makes use of the double-voicedness of reported speech. Linguistic anthropologists, for example, have been inspired by Bakhtin's insights and have applied them to the analysis of social conflict and interaction in a range of cultural contexts.[37] I suggest that the performative animation of voices of Iranian Shiʻites by Lebanese Shiʻites, as in the examples above, represents the similar use of such voices against the intentions of the original speakers.

In another important dimension of hierarchical difference-making, the Lebanese narrators position themselves against Iranian Shiʻites according to a logic of ethnic and moral difference, which delegitimizes Iranian claims of authority and leadership and to authentic and correct Shiʻite practice. Iranian Shiʻite men and women are not only stereotypically represented as excessively emotional and as exhibiting theatrical behavior, which is somewhat hysterical and lacking in sobriety and self-control, but also as having an amusing and deficient accent while speaking Arabic, the language of original Islam. By skillfully stereotyping Iranian Shiʻites, Amal members also tend to claim an image of themselves as Shiʻites oriented toward more appropriate expressions of piety. They construct an image of themselves as legitimate, mainstream Shiʻites whose comportment more closely corresponds to the ideal of Muslim piety that is centered on sobriety, self-control, and proper gender behavior.

In this section, the institution of *marja'iyya* will be introduced and Fadlallah's interpretation of Arab nationalism will be shown to be an ideology that gives meaning to the everyday life of his followers. I then focus on his vision of the modernity of Islam and outline his views on how a so-called rational and modern religion can solve Lebanon's political tensions, which he refers to as sectarianism. Finally, Fadlallah's theological ruling in the al-Zahra controversy and his interpretation of 'Ashura rituals serve as examples of how theological debates do not happen in a vacuum but are created and are in dialogue with their political and socioeconomic context. By constructing an identity as a *modern* Arab *marja'*, Fadlallah claims to present the most authentic vision of Shi'ism that is truly compatible with coexistence in Lebanon. As such, Fadlallah's notion of a modern Shi'ite is embedded in a specifically Lebanese context.

Marja'iyya, an Introduction

During the late eighteenth and early nineteenth centuries, *marja'iyya*, the institution that organizes the relations between believers and their leaders, was established to coordinate Shi'ite responses to world affairs in the absence of the Twelfth Imam as well as to organize the religious leadership of the entire Shi'ite community and create lines of authority.[38]

The highest rank in Shi'ite learning is to reach the level of a *mujtahid*. From among these *mujtahids*, few emerge as a source of emulation, the *marja'*. These scholars attain a position that allows them to issue opinions (fatwas) based on sources of theological-legal rulings produced by themselves and by other credited Shi'ite religious scholars and supported by the Quran and chains of transmissions (*asnad*) of the sayings of the Prophet Muhammad (*ahadith*) and his family.

Ideally based on the superiority of his knowledge—as reflected in his writings, such as in the level of sophistication of his collection of legal opinion (*risala 'amaliyya*)—and on his piety, a *mujtahid* would be appointed a *marja'*, or even a *marja' al-taqlid al-tamm*, the single religious leader of the Shi'ites. The *marja'*, this source of emulation, is a temporary representative of the Twelfth Shi'ite Imam, *Imam al-mahdi*, who according to Twelver Shi'ite tradition went into occultation at a young age in AD 874 and whose return pious Shi'ites await. Followers of a *marja'* are called *muqallids*, literally "those who imitate," and they ideally follow his decisions regarding religious, social, and political conduct.

The position of the *marja'* has always been intertwined with politics. The Iranian revolution has simply institutionalized this political activism in the doctrine of the *vilayat-i faqih*, the rule of the jurisprudent, and done away with the constant tension that existed between religious scholars and the state rulers as these scholars now represent the state themselves in Iran. Khomeini, who is associated with the doctrine of *vilayat-i faqih*, claimed to be a leader and guide, a *vali*, until his death in 1989.

Khomeini was the first person to argue that in the absence of the Twelfth Imam, the religious scholars, but mainly the jurists (*fuqaha*) among them, should not only provide religious guidance but should also serve as the political leaders of the community, positions associated until then with the Prophet and the twelve Imams only. Leadership could be limited to one religious scholar or consist of a council (*shura*) of several. In fact, in Khomeini's opinion, the distinction between religion and politics did not exist in Islam. The distinction was a Western concept imported to Islamic countries to divide and weaken Muslims. To Khomeini, the clerical rule in an Islamic state, in which *shari'a* regulates all aspects of life, would be the only acceptable form of political life for Muslims and should serve as an example for other Muslim countries as well.

His followers had claimed Khomeini to be a *marja'* even prior to the revolution, although he was an unknown figure in the Arab Shi'ite world. Many in Iran knew of him as a religious figure and anti-Shah activist, especially with respect to the 1963 uprising against the Shah in Qom, but did not consider him a particularly high-ranking Shi'ite scholar. When followers of Khomeini declared him a *marja'*, his rival, Ayatollah Abul Qasim Kho'i, was already an established *marja'* with widespread social institutions and many followers in both Iran and the Arab world in the mid-1970s. He was chosen by the previous senior *marja'*, Ayatollah Muhsin al-Hakim, before his death in June 1970, as the tradition of passing on the position required.

In Lebanon, both Fadlallah and Sadr were followers of Kho'i. Despite his close ties to the Iranian religious elite and his acceptance of the concept of *vilayat-i faqih*, Fadlallah served as the representative (*vakil*) of Kho'i in Lebanon until Kho'i's death in 1992. Shortly after his death, the prominent religious scholar Ayatollah 'Ali Sistani, who rejects the notion of *vilayat*, became a leading *marja'* in the Shi'ite world, having been appointed by Kho'i. By

1995, Fadlallah claimed to be a *marja'* himself, distancing himself both from Sistani, who was an Iranian-born *marja'* residing in Najaf, as well as from Khamenei, whom Khomeini had appointed prior to his death as a *vali*, and who claimed to be the *marja'* for Shi'ites outside of Iran and whom Hizbullah members have acknowledged as their religious leader ever since the death of Khomeini.

Fadlallah's decision in 1995 to declare himself a *marja'* met with resistance both inside and outside Lebanon. In Lebanon, the late Shamseddine, then vice president of the Supreme Islamic Shi'ite Council, the official organ of coordinating Shi'ite affairs in Lebanon, publicly denounced Fadlallah's claims to credentials as a *marja'*, arguing that "Fadlallah lacked the basic requirements of *ijtihad*, since he had no proof of it other than his own claims."[39] The Iranian religious ruling elite saw him as a rival in Lebanon.

Arabs and Islam: The Old Center-Periphery Debate Revisited in the Shi'ite World

Fadlallah claims the senior position of Arabs in Islam as a way to disqualify, as authentic leaders, those powerful factions and rivals who are often of Iranian background, although often not of ethnic Persian background. Engaging in an ethnonationalist reading of the history of Islam, he notes that Iranians have been monopolizing the institution of *marja'iyya* for too long and suggests that *vilayat-i faqih* should not be tied to one nationality or one location but should rotate among the most learned of the Shi'ites, regardless of their ethnic background: "The Iranian theologians believe that Iran is the only Shi'ite Islamic authority, because they consider Iran as the headquarters of Shi'ite influence. The Iranians believe that all decisions regarding Shi'ite Islam must come from Iran."[40]

Reflections on his statement regarding the alleged Iranian monopolization of Shi'ite power have appeared in Lebanese Shi'ite journals and newspapers:

> Sayyid Fadlallah does not openly suggest, but still realizes, that the Iranians fight him because he is an Arab and they do not want an Arab authority. Does he respond by embracing the "authority" of Khamenei, which no one recognizes, even though he is the most powerful in Iran, giving him the right of custody over the followers and "friends" of Iran in Lebanon and elsewhere?[41]

According to Fadlallah:

Arabism (al-'uruba) is a human condition, just as Persian nationalism (al-farisiyya) and Turkism (al-turkiyya). Islam was able to give the Arabs their history . . . and [by this statement] we don't want to be dismissive about Arabs' pre-Islamic history. But Islam gave them their history, their culture, and connected them to the world, just as the Arabs gave Islam a lot through their efforts. That is why nobody can criticize the Islamists about their Arabism. We are intertwined with Arabic, our Prophet was Arab, our language is Arabic, and for this reason Islam has been able to expand in the Arab circle through its language and culture, and [that is how] many non-Arabs entered Arab history.[42]

Fadlallah argues that Islamists have a self-evident right to be Arab nationalists[43] by pointing to their central role in Islamic history. He connects several ideological positions rarely expressed by contemporary Arab Islamists with unprecedented clarity. First is the idea that Arabs[44] and Islam are intimately linked, giving Arabs more right to claim Islam than any other ethnic group. Fadlallah connects Arabism to Islamism by projecting modern nationalist categories on early Islamic history.[45] By making this connection, he also offers an alternative meaning to this secular yet, until recently, clearly Sunni-dominated ideology.

Second, he argues that the cultural achievements in Islamic civilization are primarily those of the Arabs. Third, and related to the second point, is the idea that Islam was subsequently exported, so to speak, to non-Arab parts of the world. Clearly, Fadlallah is inventing a tradition of Arab Islamism by projecting current political debates and concerns onto his reading of the past and selecting elements of the past to support his argument. It is beyond the scope of this book to discuss the diversity of contributions in creating what is thought of as an Islamic civilization. Suffice it to say that prominent scholars of early Islamic history, such as Fred Donner, have convincingly shown how the Muslims as a community, and Islam as an institutionalized religion, were not established until some time after the death of the Prophet Muhammad, the time when Arabic speakers delivered Muhammad's message far beyond their original domain into other territories.[46] That accounts for why the exclusive achievements of Arabs in Islamic history and culture are as much a part of recent Arab nationalist ideology as are the claims by Iranian officials, discussed in chapter 5, about the specifically *Iranian* contribution to Islamic history.

Rational Arabs and Emotional Iranians

Once, on a Sunday afternoon, I was sipping tea with Fadlallah's son-in-law in his home in Jibsheet, a small town in South Lebanon. He had lived in Qom for eight years from 1979 as a student of religion (*talib*), returning to Lebanon in 1987. Fluent in Persian, he began our discussion in classical Arabic, adding Persian words or half sentences here and there. "You know," he asked me, "why Iranian men like the idea of martyrdom? It is because they have an inferiority complex toward the Iranian women." I began to smile. I thought he was joking and telling me this to tease me a little, as we had exchanged some amusing stories before the interview. But far from that, he continued in his serious tone:

> It is not normal that we interpret the love of martyrdom among Iranians as their love for the Imam Husayn's revolution (*thawrat al-imam al-husayn*). No, I believe that even if the idea of the Imam Husayn revolution did not exist, the Iranians would go for revolutions. The Iranian man loves to undertake a revolution (*huwa 'indahu hubb an yaqum bi thawra*) . . . the revolution of Imam Husayn only provides Iranians with justifications for their revolutionary attitude.[47]

Speaking as someone who had lived in Iran for an extended period of time, the son-in-law arrived at the conclusion that Iranians are "emotional people leading a life of Sufis" and that this "tradition of a Sufi mentality goes back to pre-Islamic times." Iranians converted to Shi'ism at some point in history, but they continued to practice and understand the new religion with this Sufi mentality. In his view, that explains also the love of the Iranians for martyrdom, for death, for believing "in the sacrificial figure of the Imam Husayn as an oppressed, imprisoned, and underprivileged person." Iranians gave these Sufi mentalities a lawful religious dimension (*bu'd dini shar'i*), and they cry over the death of Imam Husayn. But then he asked me again, "Why? Why cry about his death? It would only imply that he was weak if we cry."

To him, Islam legalized the desire of Iranians for expressing sad feelings, and it provided a religious legal framework for their alleged Sufi mentality.

It became obvious that the perceived emotional attachment of Iranians to the *ahl al-bayt*, and to the revolution of Imam Husayn and Karbala really surprised him. He explained that this emotionalism was something he could not relate to as an Arab Shi'ite.

Many scholars of Shi'ism continue to distinguish between Iranian Shi'ism and Arab Shi'ism in similar ways. Yitzhak Nakash, for example, points to the "down-to-earth" quality of Iraqi Shi'ite religious practices compared with Iranian ritual practices,[48] while Frank Korom, relying on Peter Chelkowski's interpretation of the meaning of *ta'ziyya*, links the genealogy of Indian Shi'ism to Iran by tracing the origins of Muharram in Iran to pre-Islamic beliefs there:[49]

> Veneration of deceased heroes had long been an important part of Persian culture; the theme of redemption through sacrifice found parallels in such pre-Islamic legends as the death of Siyavush . . . and in the ancient Mesopotamian rituals of renewal for Tammuz and Adonis. . . . Perhaps because of their system of hereditary kingship and strong nationalist sentiment, the people of the Iranian plateau were particularly hospitable to the Shi'i form of Islam.[50]

Korom goes on to explain that, during the Safavid period, Shi'ite symbols and narratives were used to unify the country against Sunnis: "It was at this time that the Karbala narrative was used to bolster a strong sense of national unity [among Iranians.] . . . Commemoration of Husayn's martyrdom increasingly became a vehicle for patriotic sentiment even as it retained its soteriological function as a ritualistic act."[51] He writes that the "invocation of the Husayn myth ever since has served, *inter alia*, to separate Shi'i from Sunni and Iranian from Arab."[52] Korom's interpretation regarding the particularity of Iranian Shi'ism as a "creolized" religious form removed from an ideal-typical, legally-based Shi'ism is a case in point.

The views of Fadlallah's son-in-law about emotionality in commemorating Imam Husayn and the alleged Sufi mentality of Iranians need to be contextualized in wider disagreement and competition between Fadlallah and Khamenei. But the son-in-law's distancing from Iranian Shi'ite traditions, which he views as irrational and theatrical, is also telling about how he and other followers of Fadlallah position themselves in the modern Lebanese nation. Relying on a discourse of origins, he draws a link between purity of religious practice, sobriety in conduct, and Arab identity.

To Fadlallah, modernity in Shi'ism entails both spiritual and material progress. To emphasize its material progress, he proposes for example the use of a telescope to determine the exact time for the beginning and end of Ramadan. As the *marja'* first sights the moon, he declares the beginning of the month of fasting, and Ramadan begins. Heretofore, most religious scholars have decided this by simply looking to the sky with the naked eye, but Fadlallah's usage of a telescope makes determining the exact beginning and end of Ramadan supposedly more accurate.

Those who admire Fadlallah's recourse to science (but also his rulings on women's issues) approve, saying "He is so modern," "he is so cultured," "he is so civilized," or "he is so progressive."[53] Fadlallah's drawing on other emblems of technical modernity and progress is also evident in brochures promoting his social institutions by providing pictures of new school buildings and explaining up-to-date methods of teaching usually indexed by the number of computers available in the classrooms. The spiritual progress accomplished by these institutions is given at least as much importance because both ultimately increase modernity.[54]

Fadlallah is presented as explaining Islam in a language that the modern person (*al-insan al-mu'asir*) can understand, and he speaks to various sections of society.[55] He places importance on introducing Islam to non-Muslims in Lebanon in a "civilized manner" (*bi tariqa hadariyya*)

> because we do not present Islam as trying to cause fanaticism and difference. Islam invites to common terms in every matter. Some people, when talking to the other (*al-akharin*), withdraw from their Islamic identity, worrying at being accused of sectarianism. We say to them: The person who withdraws from his Islam vis-à-vis the other does not make those people trust him. That is because if this person doesn't stand up for his own religion and his stance and position how can he win the trust of the other?[56]

In this interpretation, public piety provides a solution to sectarianism as lack of trust among communities is viewed as one of the main reasons for outbreaks of violence. Implicit in this argument is the adoption of a modern notion of subjectivity based on a distinction between interior intentionality and affect and outward behavior. The ideal aimed at is an overlap of so-called

148

interior feelings and intentions with behavior, a view privileging subjective sincerity often associated with modern Protestants. According to Fadlallah's adoption of this modern model of subjectivity, such transparency helps to build up trust among communities and enables coexistence.

And why is it important to be a conscious and aware Shi'ite person in the Lebanese context? In other words, why engage in a discourse of modernity and not one of tradition, for example, to present the same arguments? How does this claim to modernity influence relations between Shi'ites and the state? Fadlallah seeks to project an image of Lebanese Shi'ites to other Lebanese that breaks with stereotypes of them as a backward, extremist, and irrational underclass driven by their religious (but also sexual) passions. Narratives of classical Western modernity associate all these aspects with the "traditional." Instead, he presents Shi'ism as a rational religion able to participate in dialogue, thus legitimizing a central position for Shi'ites in the Lebanese nation. Accordingly, rationality and sincerity is a precondition for citizenship in Lebanon, since Lebaneseness is about continuous dialogue with other communities. Meaningful dialogue is possible between people recognized as rational and sincere by the other. To be recognized as rational, Fadlallah argues for the importance of public piety, the very (engineered and controlled) act of the visibility of piety that brings Shi'ites' internal and external faces together. By being "themselves," Shi'ites can acknowledge the other. In Fadlallah's view, once the boundaries between communities are set, the other is recognized and respected fully through dialogue.

In the view of some scholars, in a multiconfessional society such as Lebanon, Fadlallah's presumably modern approach to religion avoids "the provocative distinctiveness of Shiite mythology."[57] Fadlallah's engaging in the discourse of modernity enables him to present his other Shi'ite competitors as following rigid sectarianism through what he defines as their emphasis on a distinct Shi'ite identity. This assessment of Fadlallah as a renewer and reformer of a religious sect that in Lebanon is often associated with rigid sectarianism and even backwardness is also shared among diverse Lebanese constituencies, even those suspicious of Islamism, implying an acceptance of pluralism as a way of becoming part of a Lebanese nation.

Fadlallah's notion of modernity therefore is also deeply connected to the politics of coexistence in Lebanon. What kind of Shi'ism can coexist with others, according to Fadlallah? A *modern* Shi'ism, one that acknowledges difference while it does not define its own identity as in opposition to other communities in Lebanon but just as different from them. But what are those negative and distinct characteristics that create obstacles to coexistence and why would *modernity* remove that distinctiveness?

The Islamist claim to modernity has often been explained as the promotion of alternative modernities. Considering it as such, however, implies that modernity is already represented as an accomplished reality by the West, and that alternative modernities are modular forms of it. Lara Deeb shows in her work on Shi'ite Islamists in Beirut, among them many Fadlallah followers, that they view Islam as modern and that they engage in the discourse of Western modernity as well as in those discourses "rooted in their own emphasis on pious or enchanted ways of being modern."[58] I treat all these statements as engaging in the discourse of modernity in some way or other, and view this engagement not only as strategies to catch up with other communities in Lebanon but also enabling these community leaders to position themselves in national leadership roles and to redefine the powers behind the politics of coexistence.

In the Lebanese context, narratives of modernity empower Shi'ite leaders to counter the hegemonic discourse of modernity brought forward by other communities. For instance, Fadlallah declares membership in the Lebanese nation and aims at its reconfiguration without agreeing to the notions of modernity forwarded by representatives of other Lebanese communities, such as the connection between it and secularism and the maintenance of close political and cultural ties to the West.

But, as the next section shows, Fadlallah's claim on modernity also has a transnational dimension, and this image embeds him as an ideal Lebanese citizen both against his Shi'ite competitors in Lebanon as well as in the transnational Shi'ite world. As the examples of the al-Zahra controversy and 'Ashura rituals show, the question of which elements of Shi'ite practice and dogma are to be considered excessively distinct is itself embedded in both national and transnational contexts.

The al-Zahra Controversy

Relations between Fadlallah and the Iranian religious elite darkened especially when disagreements emerged between Fadlallah and Shaykh Ja'far Murtada 'Amili (b. 1945), a Lebanese Shi'ite scholar who lived in Qom and entertains close relationships to the Iranian official religious establishment, over interpretations of an event that took place shortly after the death of the

Prophet Muhammad and which is known as the tragedy/sufferings of al-Zahra' (*m'aasat al-zahra/ranjha-i hazrat-i zahra*). The controversy, which began in 1993, has mainly taken place in the form of successive written attacks and counterattacks between the two Shi'ite scholars, a customary mode in which debates are carried out among scholars of religion in Islam.

'Amili positions himself within the historical school of Shi'ism (*al-madrasa al-tarikhiyya*), which believes in preserving what he views as Shi'ite tradition, thus presenting him as a fierce defender of Shi'ism. Fadlallah considers himself part of a rationalist school (*al-madrasa al-'aqliyya*) and believes that his understanding of Shi'ite history is innovative and in accordance with modern needs and times.

According to 'Amili's interpretation of the sufferings of al-Zahra, Fatimah al-Zahra, the daughter of Prophet Muhammad and an icon in Shi'ite tradition, lost her unborn child, Muhsin, because of the aggressive behavior of Omar, a figure associated in Shi'ite tradition with Sunni oppression. According to 'Amili, these events unfolded in the following way: Since Imam 'Ali rejected the legitimacy of Abu Bakr as a successor to the Prophet Muhammad and considered himself to be the rightful Khalif, Omar and his followers came to the house of 'Ali to force him to go to the mosque to give his oath of allegiance to Abu Bakr. Fatimah, the wife of Imam 'Ali, was standing behind the door when Omar pushed it open forcefully, breaking her ribs and striking Fatimah's pregnant belly. She fell and lost the baby.[59]

Fadlallah believes that this incident accounts for one of the grudges Shi'ites hold against Sunnis. Presenting himself as promoter of the idea of *taqrib*, the process of rapprochement between Shi'ites and Sunnis, Fadlallah argues against emphasizing that such an incident is relevant when the Muslim world is facing more pressing issues. Instead, while not denying that the event took place, he argues that the story has been exaggerated, stirring and deepening sectarian differences among Muslims. He wonders whether Fatimah could also have lost her child due to a natural event; whether doors in that period were built in the same way as today, so that Omar could have pushed it open suddenly, and why Fatimah opened the door if traditionally a man (in this case 'Ali) was supposed to open the front door to his house.

In his study called the "Sufferings of al-Zahra," 'Amili provides ample evidence, ranging from Arabic poems in which this event was mentioned to collections of *ahadith* by the *ahl al-bayt* members, to an in-depth study of the types of doors in that period to disprove Fadlallah's claim about the exaggerated rendering of the event.[60] Throughout his study, 'Amili criticizes

Fadlallah's arguments, and ultimately Fadlallah himself, for presumably destroying Shi'ism from within, and for not protecting the Shi'ite community. According to 'Amili, "a *real Shia* should not weaken but defend his community."[61] Many Iranian religious students in Qom, as well as Iranian religious scholars, have shared this view with 'Amili, which was one reason Fadlallah's relations with Iranian ruling circles deteriorated.

The historian Stefan Rosiny, who has also followed these debates, describes how "the causes of the controversy were some interpretations offered by Fadlallah *who aims at reaching a modern, reasonable understanding even of the metaphysical aspects of his religion.*"[62] Rosiny goes on to write that "Ja'far Murtada tries to escape into the obscurantist dogmatism of the myths and the cordoning off of his own community, whereas Fadlallah endeavors to *formulate a rational and more up-to-date interpretation of religion,* which he wants to open up for a dialogue with members of other faiths and even with unbelievers."[63] Rather than viewing these debates as part of a discursive tradition and highlighting the strategic uses of tradition and modernity, Rosiny replicates the image Fadlallah seeks to promote of himself; that is, aiming to arrive at a more "correct version of religion" through "objective knowledge" and "rational reasoning."[64]

This controversy between Fadlallah and 'Amili shows how the official voices of state-sponsored religion in Iran base their claims of truth on different rhetorical approaches. While 'Amili relies on claims of tradition in the form of particular representations of past events, Fadlallah couches his position in the language of rationalism and renewal. In the context of the controversy, Fadlallah deemphasizes the particularity of Shi'ism by creating a narrative in which the so-called Sunni leadership did not harm the Shi'ites. By providing an alternative narrative to the one 'Amili presents, Fadlallah also implies different power relations between Sunnis and Shi'ites, and moves away from the image of Shi'ites as perpetually oppressed and disadvantaged. Fadlallah's arguments in the al-Zahra debate are an example of how his self-styling as a Shi'ite modernist is rooted in a particularly Lebanese context. They enhance his position there by promoting the concept of *taqrib,* which reduces what he refers to as sectarianism. Whether Sunni Lebanese desire rapprochement and understand such interpretations of past events as supporting rapprochement between Shi'ites and Sunnis is a question that Fadlallah admirers and scholars such as Rosiny do not pose.

Finally, the al-Zahra controversy has a transnational dimension not because, as Rosiny points out, "It *coincides* with a religious and political power struggle over *marja'iyya* and over the control of the Lebanese Shiite community,"[65] but because this controversy *is* about this very power struggle. Rosiny believes that Iranian animosity toward Fadlallah strengthens his reputation among Arabs "who prefer to see one of their own in the position of *marja'iyya*."[66] Contrary to this view, Fadlallah has been actively involved in playing up ethnic sentiments to promote his own position as the Arab *marja'*, as I discussed above.

There is no inherent logic to the idea that Arabs prefer to see one of their own in such a position, as shown by the central position in current Iraqi politics of Sistani, an Iranian *marja'* who supposedly has a heavy Persian accent. The construction of differences along imagined ethnic lines is not a new phenomenon in the history of Arabs and Iranians. Fadlallah's own close ties to postrevolutionary Iran just a decade ago, as discussed in chapter 3, exemplify the constructedness and shifting qualities in the context of power struggles.

Measuring Emotions Scientifically; or,
How Much Is a Lebanese Allowed to Cry?

Fadlallah also establishes his position as a modern religious scholar through a reinterpretation of the event of Karbala and through propagating new forms of commemoration. I suggested in chapter 1 that many Lebanese do not make a clear distinction between class and religious identity in Lebanon, and that to them both overlap. I also suggested that, according to this logic, religious performance constitutes one aspect of the performative dimensions of class. The questions then became: Which religious performances are supposedly lower class? Which ones are respectable, considering that Shi'ites are often imagined (among non-Shi'ites) to be simultaneously lower class and excessively religious? What type of Shi'ism can turn the Lebanese Shi'ites into cultural citizens? The discussion here is by no means meant to be exhaustive, but I want to offer a perspective on the embeddedness of religious rulings in national and transnational political contexts and contests.

In Fadlallah's view, processions are an unnecessary part of the 'Ashura commemorations, and attending commemorative gatherings (*majalis*) should form the core activity during these days. But even in the *majlis*, one should deemphasize crying for the sake of Imam Husayn as, in his view, the sad texts of 'Ashura were produced to attract followers: "Crying is a natural result of feelings, but the goal of crying should not be to receive spiritual benefits (*hasanat*) as this type of crying is not natural crying, natural crying is spontaneous crying."[67] Fadlallah further suggests that the texts of 'Ashura sermons (which are about narratives of Imam Husayn's martyrdom), just like any other historical text, need to be criticized and reviewed in an objective, scientific manner (*al-naqd al-'ilmi al-mawdu'i*), as many myths and untrue stories have been mixed into the 'Ashura narrative that are responsible for stirring emotions.[68] Instead, by scrutinizing the text, one would arrive at a more balanced view on the life and biography of Imam Husayn. In his annual sermons during 'Ashura, he focuses on themes of moral guidance and admonition, among them propagating a conscious form of 'Ashura instead of a passive form (*'ashura al-wa'i la al-infi'al*).[69]

In presenting these arguments, Fadlallah links himself to the well-known Shi'ite scholar Muhsin al-Amin (1867–1952), who had "sought to reform and standardize both the texts and rituals associated with communal mourning ceremonies during 'Ashura."[70] Al-Amin had suggested *majalis* be held instead of the practice of self-flagellation (*latam*, especially *haydar*), which he deemed as a foreign, Iranian-imported practice and unsuitable in the local, multiconfessional context. As part of his concept of *taqrib* (Sunni-Shi'ite rapprochement), any form of public procession and public sermon would harm this rapprochement and focus unnecessary attention on Sunni-Shi'ite differences. In the 1950s and 1960s, according to al-Amin's line of interpreting the 'Ashura commemorations, Rashid Baydun, a former student of al-Amin and the head of the al-'Amiliyya, the only Shi'ite-run school in Beirut then, organized yearly 'Ashura commemorations in his school.[71] Later on, Sadr, Shamseddine, and Qabalan gave speeches there every year and many Lebanese Christian and Sunni personalities attended.

By creating an intellectual genealogy to al-Amin, Fadlallah produces a sense of rootedness in Lebanon, whose prominent leaders have continuously emphasized rational Shi'ism. Fadlallah is also well aware of the importance of processions as a way of claiming public space, as exemplified by Hizbullah's practice. Yet, with new interpretations of 'Ashura based on supposedly critical and objective reasoning, he believes he offers a partial solution to Lebanese sectarianism by downplaying Shi'ite practices that take place in public. While he emphasizes public piety on other issues, especially in such gendered themes as women's *hijab*, he does not view public processions and public rituals during 'Ashura to be the best avenue to express such piety. In this he distances himself from Hizbullah with their extensive parades, whose members believe that participating in 'Ashura rituals is one of the key opportunities to express piety.

Various Lebanese Shi'ite scholars have drawn parallels between the situation of Lebanese Shi'ites and the battle of Karbala. Sadr referred to Shi'ites as *mahrum*, the disadvantaged, and offered new interpretations of the battle of Karbala by drawing parallels between the Maronite state and the oppressive Umayyads. However, Fadlallah's labeling of crying as a sign of weakness is aimed at reformulating the idea that Lebanese Shi'ites are *mahrum*, a disadvantaged community that cannot improve its plight. By emphasizing that crying would imply that Imam Husayn was weak, he and his associates aim at transforming the image of Lebanese Shi'ites. As in the gendered imagery used for Iranian Shi'ite men as deployed by some Lebanese Shi'ites cited earlier in this chapter, the transformation is ultimately from the passive and feminized to an active man leading a community whose fate is not dictated by history, but which can change its course. This man is not the Shi'ite man imagined by non-Shi'ite Lebanese, who is presumably sexually driven (a sign of his lack of consciousness) and irrational (hurting himself by hitting *haydar*), but one fully in control of his feelings and conscious in his actions.

Fadlallah's wish to eliminate processions as part of 'Ashura commemorations expresses neither his lack of interest in Shi'ite eventual dominance nor a claiming of public space in Lebanon. Rather, he relies on different strategies to break the hegemony of other groups. For example, by suggesting elimination of what he considers the emotional part of the commemorations, such as crying and the *haydar*, Fadlallah presents himself as the only modern Shi'ite leader capable of leading the community into dialogue with other sects in Lebanon. But his rulings are not aimed only at supporting the coexistence concept in Lebanon by "overcoming the provocative aspects of Shia dogmas."[72] They are also meant to define the very terms of coexistence by reconfiguring the meaning of Shi'ism and its relation to other religions. What is provocative in religious dogma is assessed through standards of respectability that are, in turn, part of a nexus of class and politics. Both middle-class respectability and the political discourse of coexistence are social dimensions from which Shi'ites have traditionally considered themselves marginalized. Fadlallah's project aims to break the hegemony and ownership other sectarian groups, in particular Christians and Sunnis, have held over these two central modes of fully participating in the nation.

The Emerging Discourse on Gender in the Transnational Shi'ite World

Amid this politics of piety, gender emerges as one site of structuring identities, political relations, and of defining authority and religious hierarchy in the Shi'ite world. Since the early twentieth century, interpretations of proper 'Ashura commemorative practices, and ultimately the meaning of the battle of Karbala, have expressed a variety of concepts among Shi'ites in Lebanon. Proper conduct as well as women's participation in public life are but two of these issues that are renegotiated through meanings attributed to the event.[73] Recently, discussions about proper Shi'ite commemorative practices in the transnational Shi'ite world have not only drawn on gendered imagery but have shaped understandings of what constitute proper gender roles. These debates offer insights on Amal's and Fadlallah's strategies to break the hegemonic claims of official Iran. At the same time, gendered stereotyping offers another site to study contemporary Lebanese Shi'ite identity production.

I have presented the political context and offered some ethnographic material to show how Amal and Fadlallah associates perform their gendered visions of proper and improper conduct. In these performances and conversations, Iranian men and women are depicted as excessively emotional in their performance of 'Ashura rituals, while extreme crying becomes associated with what is portrayed as the typical behavior of Iranian women. But Iranian men are also presented as weak because they excessively cry for the death of Imam Husayn just as Iranian women do.

In the gendered symbolism of narrative commemorations of Karbala, men are associated with martyrdom, women mainly with mourning.[74] In the eyes of some Amal and Fadlallah associates, Iranian men, however, are weak because they mourn like women and because their intentions for martyrdom are not pure. Accordingly, Iranian men do not choose martyrdom out of free choice, but only out of fear of their women. They are thus stereotyped as doubly inauthentic, being weak in two dimensions: excessively crying like a woman and fearing women at the same time. In this vision, Iranian men do not act out of free will as self-determined subjects.

In the analysis of both Amal and Fadlallah's followers, the Lebanese Shi'ites, both men and women, emerge on the more authentic side because they appear to be sober, rational, and modern—as having qualities they imagine to both ideally describe pious Shi'ites and as preconditions for full membership in the Lebanese nation. However, as demonstrated in chapter

1, the labels of traditional, irrational, passionate, and passive are exactly what non-Shi'ite Lebanese frequently attribute to Lebanese Shi'ites to deny their position as full cultural citizens of Lebanon. By creating an Iranian Shi'ite other who corresponds to these negative images, some Amal and Fadlallah associates deflect such stereotyping, claiming a mainstream Lebanese identity instead. By doing so, they simultaneously position themselves as superior to Hizbullah followers, whom they portray as dominated by weak, effeminate Iranian men.

As I have shown, neither Amal, Hizbullah, nor Fadlallah agree on the interpretation of the events of Karbala or on its ritual commemoration. Both Hizbullah and Fadlallah label Amal's ritual practices traditional in the sense that they do it out of habit, and see a lack of reflection as evidence of their backwardness, and therefore of their lack of authenticity. Amal in turn emphasizes that in fact it is the traditional aspect of these ritual practices that makes them authentic, because the intentions of their practitioners are pure, that is, without any political calculations, and because these rituals are Lebanese local traditions, not foreign dictated and newly imported. The Iranian religious elite fight these marginalization attempts by de-territorializing Shi'ite identities in Lebanon, promoting themselves as the most pious Shi'ites. But this is the story of the next chapter.

5

IRANIAN CULTURAL POLITICS IN LEBANON

Culture has an important role in developing the society and its advancement . . . with culture the society matures and progresses. Culture includes thoughts, languages, universities, books, theater, films, music, habits, traditions, and literature (*al-taqalid wa al-sunan wa al-adab*), all of these are categories given under the banner of culture. This collection is the backbone of any society or any civilization. And it is natural that each nation has its culture and its specific way to frame this culture and this tradition, [the nation has] its own thoughts, its own intellectual scientific cultural preference. . . . And we [the Iranian government] believe that respecting the cultural identity of people is a very important matter.[1]

—SAYYID MUHAMMAD HUSAYN HASHEMI,
IRANIAN CULTURAL ATTACHÉ TO BEIRUT (2001–2004)

DE- AND RETERRITORIALIZING LEBANESE SHI'ITE IDENTITIES

By the end of the Lebanese civil war in 1990, the Iranian government realized that its long-term presence in Lebanon depended on more refined strategies than direct military, economic, and ideological support of Hizbullah that drew on pan-Islamic and pan-Shi'ite discourses and practices. To advance their postwar projects and interests, the Iranian government and the ruling religious elite were in need of appropriate cultural politics in Lebanon. To claim what they thought was their share they had to adjust, adapt, and propagate their strategies in discourses that shape Lebanon and to participate in some of the ongoing public debates there.

At the same time, as the previous chapter indicates, they also needed to find nonmilitary means of countering those Lebanese Shi'ite voices, such as Amal, who rejected the Iranian government's implicit claims of seniority and authority in Shi'ism. Iranian cultural politics in Lebanon has set in motion certain ideologies and practices justifying Iran's official presence there, among both Shi'ites and non-Shi'ites. Its activities have been aimed at deterritorializing Lebanese Shi'ite identities by emphasizing themes specifically important to the Lebanese Shi'ite experience, such as being historically rooted in Lebanon, modernity, piety, and a commitment to coexistence. Lebanese have been encouraged to listen to certain types of poetry, to read certain books, and to visit Iran. This cultural politics attempts to reverse all the characteristics that followers of Amal and Sayyid Muhammad Husayn Fadlallah have assigned to Iranians to counter their hegemonic claims in Lebanon.

A History of Iranian Cultural Activities in Lebanon

In 1958, Iranian students at the American University of Beirut (AUB) elected an eight-person committee to supervise and organize Iranian cultural programs at the university. In 1967 this committee expanded, as the members decided to coordinate their activities with those of Iranian students at other Lebanese universities, such as Université St. Joseph, Middle East College, and Haigazian College. On May 20, 1967, the Iranian Students' Association was founded as a cultural and educational club. Its goals were to organize cultural and artistic programs as well as ancient and national rituals for students and for the Iranian residents in Lebanon and to introduce Iranian culture and art to the university community in Beirut.

To this end, every year Iranian students on the AUB campus celebrated *Chahar Shanbe' Suri*, a pre-Islamic Persian ritual of jumping over fire on the last Tuesday night before *Nowruz*, the Persian New Year. For months, Iranian students would plan celebrations of *Nowruz*, with Iranian musicians playing traditional Persian music and with beautifully arranged Persian food being served. The Iranian embassy in Beirut supported these student-organized programs and occasionally staged some for the Lebanese public, even flying in performers of traditional Persian music and arts from Iran.[2]

But against a politically sensitive background, the Iranian embassy sometimes took the initiative directly to promote an image of Iran as both a center of civilization and as a secular government that is nevertheless committed to Shi'ite tradition and beliefs. Upon the invitation of the Iranian embassy in Beirut in 1962, the Lebanese intellectual Nizar al-Zayn, then chief editor of the Shi'ite-run journal *al-'Irfan*, visited some Iranian cities and the shrine of Imam Reza in Mashhad. He praised the efforts of the Pahlavi government in taking care of the shrine and, in a series of illustrated, sequential reportages, described in detail the number and types of books in the libraries and the contents of the museum adjacent to the shrine.[3] In the context of the tensions between the Arab nationalist and anti-Israel stances prevalent among Arab Muslims in the 1960s and the pro-American and pro-Israel policy of the Pahlavi regime, the Iranian ambassador had invited Zayn to Iran and shown him the Astane complex in Mashhad as a way of improving the image of the Iranian government as a guardian of Shi'ism (and implicitly of Islam).

Upon his return, Zayn (and his entourage) published long articles about it in *al-'Irfan*, which enjoyed a large Shi'ite readership. While Zayn could not ignore the Arab nationalist orientation of the readers and their disapproval of the Shah's foreign policy, he justified his trip by comparing the bond between Shi'ites outside of and in Iran to that of children and their parents.[4] He was able to present their relations as something natural, despite the Shah's unfavorable policies, as similar to the way in which children are exhorted to forgive parents for their mistakes because filial bonds are supposed to override any other commitments.

In the 1960s and 1970s, as discussed in chapter 2, the Iranian embassy was also promoting the Persian language at some Shi'ite-run schools in Beirut and Tyre in southern Lebanon as part of the financial support the Iranian government offered to these schools. This project failed because many Lebanese Shi'ites, associating strongly with Arab nationalism, saw it as an attempt by the Shah to intensify Shi'ite transnational bonds and to draw Lebanese Shi'ites to his pro-American policies.

However, besides attending to some Lebanese Shi'ite elite visitors to Iran and providing sporadic financial support to Lebanese Shi'ite institutions upon request, the Pahlavi regime was not particularly invested in intensifying its ties with Lebanese Shi'ites, many of whom were supporters of Nasser's brand of Arab nationalism.

A New Era, a New Cultural Policy

The success of the Iranian revolution brought with it a new interest in Lebanon by the Iranian government, an interest which eventually required an elaborate cultural politics for its support.[5] Until 1987, the cultural section of the Iranian embassy in Beirut coordinated activities considered cultural (*barnameha-i farhangi*), which the Ministry of Foreign Affairs in Iran monitored. With the creation of the Ministry of Culture and Islamic Guidance in Iran, in 1987, the government decided to separate the cultural section from some Iranian embassies located in strategically important countries, and to trust its cultural politics to the newly established ministry.

The Cultural Center of the Islamic Republic of Iran in Beirut (ICC) (*al-mustashariyya al-thaqafiyya liljumhuriyya al-islamiyya al-iraniyya fi bayrut*), opened its first independent branch in Beirut under the umbrella of this ministry. In 2003 a total of twenty-three employees worked at the ICC; seventeen of them were of Lebanese origin, and the rest were sent from Iran by the Iranian Ministry of Culture and Islamic Guidance. Because of the need to establish itself and because of the ongoing Lebanese civil war, which ended in 1990, the ICC initially had limited activities. In postwar Lebanon its responsibility was to "coordinate the official cultural relations"[6] between Iran and Lebanon. Its official purpose has been to "deepen cultural, scientific, and intellectual [relations], as well as to deepen scientific academic relations through universities and professors and through cultural centers and [organized group] activities (*nashatat*) and artistic and scientific activities."[7]

In effect, most of these activities are organized around two main themes: the propagation of a narrative of Iranian-Lebanese Shi'ite history that justifies Iran's current official presence in Lebanon and the dissemination of the idea that Iran stands at the center of Islamic civilization, and has contributed to its flourishing at least as much as have the Arabs.

The ICC focuses on three periods to emphasize a sense of shared and continuous history with Lebanese Shi'ites. The first is the sixteenth century, when some Syrian Jabal 'Amili scholars moved to Safavid Persia; the second is the 1950s, when the Pahlavi government opened a Persian language center at Lebanese University; the third is the Iranian anti-Shah opposition activism in the 1970s in Lebanon. The ICC disseminates these visions of shared history by holding conferences and inviting Lebanese personalities from all religious communities. Evident in all these activities is the traditional telescoping of time, as the vast differences between the past and the current horizon of political, religious, and cultural relations between modern Lebanon and Iran are minimized. By suggesting continuity, or even equivalence, between these events selected for the production of historical memory and the present, ICC staff casts the current activities of official Iran in Lebanon as the self-evident continuation of a deep tradition, while momentarily suspending the temporal distance and marked social and political dissimilarities between past events and the shifting outlook of the present. To propagate the idea that Iran has greatly contributed to the flourishing of an Islamic civilization, with the goal of presenting it as the most pious and modern Shi'ite government, the ICC also screens films and exhibits art.

From Jabal 'Amil to Safavid Persia—from Iran to Lebanon

The ICC uses the sixteenth-century Shi'ite interactions between Jabal 'Amil, which had just fallen under Ottoman rule, and Safavid Persia as a key theme in making the current intensity of Shi'ite networks between Iran and Lebanon self-evident. Through a narrative reorganization of historical memory, Safavid Persia is identified with present-day Iran, and Jabal 'Amil with South Lebanon and ultimately with Lebanon as a whole.

Perhaps the best description illustrating this narrative is in a report prepared for the ICC by Dr. Muhammad Charafeddine, a highly respected person among both Lebanese and Iranian Shi'ites in Lebanon.[8] In his view,

> Iran and Lebanon have had close relations during three historical periods: during the Achaemenid, during the Safavid period, and with the beginning of the success of the glorious Islamic revolution in Iran. Of course, relations [between Iran and Lebanon] have never been cut off between these periods and connections and mutual social political and cultural influences have existed throughout. . . . *Lebanon, from 538 to 331 BC was part of the fifth province of the Achaemenid Empire, which means that for 207 years Lebanon was Iranian-governed.* . . . During the 'Abbasid and Fatimid period, *the Muslim inhabitants of Kisrawan and Tyre, who were originally Iranians (iraniyyu al-asl)* became Shi'ites. . . . From the Safavid period onwards, mutual migrations between

Iranians and Lebanese Shi'ites increased to such an extent that in Iran tens of last names such as Jabal 'Amili, 'Amili, and Sur [Tyre] 'Amili exist. Let us mention one example of the migration of Lebanese families to Iran. In 1784, Ahmad Pasha Jazzar, the vali of 'Akkar, attacked Jabal 'Amil and defeated the 'Amili military . . . destroying villages, burning all libraries, and killing most of Jabal 'Amili elites and *turning the 'ulama into refugees.*[9]

The author then describes how these *'ulama* fled to Iraq and then eventually settled in Iran. After covering the "historical relations between Iran and Lebanon," the author provides a nine-page list of approximately 162 last names of Lebanese families, both Christian and Muslim, and traces their origins to Iran (*iraniyyu al-asl*) by tracing the linguistic root of the last names to Persian. The report also points to the influence of the Persian language in Lebanese Arabic and the spread of an Iranian-style 'Ashura commemoration, known as *ta'ziyya-khani*, in South Lebanon.

Similarly, when asked to evaluate the cultural activities of the ICC in Lebanon, Sayyid Muhammad Husayn Hashemi, the previous Iranian cultural attaché to Beirut, began by pointing out that

the cultural relations between Iran and Lebanon are not new, they are really old relations dating back to a long history. They have continued on a scientific and intellectual level. As you know, Jabal 'Amil played a large role in [the production] of knowledge, culture, thoughts, and sciences. Jabal 'Amil in Lebanon produced a large number of well-known scholars, some of whom moved to Iran. . . . There are good relations between the Iranian government and the Lebanese government as well as between the people of Iran and the people of Lebanon, continuous relations; and based on these continuous relations there is a humble cultural exchange between Iran and Lebanon, and our role and the role of the Lebanese in charge in the fields of culture is really important, based on our presence here and our interaction with the Lebanese officials in fields of science, culture, and art, we try to deepen this interaction and deepen these relations.[10]

Perceptions of the relative closeness or distance between Lebanese Shi'ites and Iranian Shi'ites are flexible and shifting, based on varying political ties, and consequently on the interpretations of the historical Shi'ite religious ties between Lebanon and Iran and of Iran's contribution to Islamic civilization, which are crucially informed by narratives of Iranian and Lebanese Shi'ite nationalism. Unlike institutions of the Islamic Republic, the Pahlavi regime did not emphasize such intense Shi'ite religious ties to Lebanon.

Nevertheless, there has been a tendency in the scholarship on Lebanon to portray the significance of Shi'ite links between Iran and Lebanon as commonsensical. Does the fact that both Lebanese Shi'ites and those who stand for an official Shi'ism in the Iranian government, and are active in maintaining these transnational ties, identify themselves as Shi'ites justify the view that the existence of such networks is self-evident? Several scholarly works see current Iranian-Lebanese Shi'ite relations as building upon and as representing a continuation of the religious networks existing since the sixteenth century, sidelining the dramatic impact that the rise of nationalism has had on interpretations of the past.[11]

While this view of the past is certainly the one that the current Iranian government hopes to establish because it suits its political agenda in Lebanon, scholars should be cautious in reproducing such perspectives. While 'Amili-Safavid Shi'ite networks played important roles in the sixteenth century, current Iranian-Lebanese Shi'ite relations are not simply a continuation of these ties. In particular, the memory of these interactions five hundred years ago has, in the meantime, become refracted in different ways through Arab and Iranian nationalist ideologies. The memory of this event is a contested field among members of the Shi'ite transnational network, and interpretations such as the reasons for the migration of these scholars from Jabal 'Amil, their mission in Safavid Persia, and the type of identity these migrants formed there are all intimately connected to present-day politics. For Amal members this 'Amili migration to Persia justifies their superior claim on authenticity in Shi'ism over Iranians, as discussed in chapter 4, while the ICC's activities aim at presenting this migration as a sign of the historical closeness between Iran and Lebanon and undoing the hierarchical order imagined by them.

Reopening the Center for Persian Language: Persian and Arabic as "Twin Languages"

Offering Persian language classes to Lebanese at the ICC and promoting the teaching of Persian at the Lebanese University have been one of the main concerns of Iranian cultural attachés in Lebanon since the 1990s. Persian courses are offered on three levels on a regular basis at the ICC, although they are not very popular and few Lebanese attend them. In addition, due to the efforts of one of the former Iranian cultural attachés, Shaykh Muhammad Taskhiri, the ICC reopened the Center for Persian Language at Lebanese University (*markaz-i tadris-i zaban-i farsi dar daneshgah-i lobnan*) in June 1999 after more than twenty years of interruption due to the Lebanese civil war and the Iranian revolution.

Originally, the Center for Persian Language and Its Literature (*qism al-lugha al-farisiyya wa adabiha*) was created at the Lebanese University (LU) in Beirut in 1956. Dr. Muhammad Muhammadi, who was a professor of Arabic at Tehran University, became the chair of the center at LU. The majority of those who studied Persian were students of literature, history, and Islamic philosophy. Persian was an optional subject of study in LU's Department of Literature and Human Sciences, along with Hebrew and Turkish.

Because the Lebanese civil war destroyed much of the archival material at the center, I have been unable to collect complete data on the numbers of students prior to the revolution. But the material still available[12] suggests that while the long-term ratio between the number of Lebanese Shi'ite students at LU and the number of other religious group members is unclear, as is the number registered for Persian, there is a clear indication that there was no connection between the choice of language learning and the religious background of the students. In the academic year 1970–1971, the number of Muslim and Christian students registered for Persian classes at LU was approximately equal.[13]

In the 1960s, students were to fill out a form and state their reasons for taking Persian. If they did indeed fill it out, the students, regardless of their religious background, made comments about a perceived linguistic similarity between Arabic and Persian. In the academic year 1965–1966, one-third of the students filled out the section, and the majority of the comments were based on their belief that there is a linguistic connection between the two languages, that "Persian resembles Arabic a lot," or that there is a "direct connection to Arabic," or that Persian is the "sister of the Arabic language." In none of the students' files was there any specific mention of Persian as a language of Islam, or any indication that Shi'ite students in particular viewed Persian as being connected to Islam or Shi'ism. Students at LU viewed Persian differently compared with those at the al-'Amiliyya, discussed in chapter 2, in the 1950s and 1960s. Students at al-'Amiliyya were forced to take Persian classes, associated Persian with Shi'ism, and believed the Shah wanted to strengthen Shi'ite ties to combat what they viewed as the secular Arab nationalism of Nasser. Students at LU who decided on their own to study Persian did not associate Persian with Shi'ism and stressed what they considered similarities between Persian and Arabic. These examples illustrate the malleable nature of transnational Shi'ism and the existence of different perspectives in such networks.

In 1959, the center launched its first bilingual Arabic-Persian journal called *al-Dirasat al-Adabiyya*. This journal, as its name suggested, contained articles on the analysis of Persian poetry and the works of Arab literary figures. The publication of this journal was discontinued in 1967 for thirty-three years; in 1978, due to the intensification of the war in Lebanon and the political upheavals in Iran, the center in Beirut closed.

The Center for Persian Language Turns Shi'ite

In 1999 the ICC reopened the center, and the journal resumed publication in spring 2000. The center and the journal kept their old names, and the 1956 agreement between the governments of Iran and Lebanon to open the center at LU was renewed in 1997.[14] But ideas about the importance of Persian language teaching in Lebanon and on the relationship between Iran and Lebanon had changed dramatically. First, the meaning of teaching Persian at LU had changed from "teaching Persian in an Arabic-speaking country" to teaching Persian specifically in Lebanon. Reestablishing the teaching of Persian at LU was taken as yet another example of long-standing Iranian-Lebanese Shi'ite relations. Second, there was a new and striking interest in proving the specific Shi'ite connection between Iran and Lebanese Shi'ites through linguistic research, which was entirely absent prior to the Iranian revolution. Third, both Arabic and Persian were Islamicized. Prior to the revolution, both languages were viewed as an index of Arab and Persian civilizations and not framed in a specifically Islamic context.

These changes express the ideologies of the ICC in trying to deterritorialize Lebanese Shi'ite identities, as is evident in comparing opening speeches at the center delivered in 1956 to those in 1999, along with the changing content of some of the journals and with my interviews with Hashemi and the Persian language teacher at the ICC. A close look at the way the ICC contextualizes Persian language teaching at Lebanese University reveals much about the postrevolutionary Iranian government's attempts to construct and to highlight an age-old Iranian-Lebanese bond. In the words of Hashemi,

> One needs to frame Persian language teaching in the age-old history of Lebanese-Iranian relations (*ravabet-i dirine*) that date back to what Lebanese refer to as *al-hijra al-'amiliyya* ['Amili migration to Safavid Persia]. These ties were certainly not limited to religious relations; there were also cultural exchanges, and the teaching of Persian language in Lebanon needs to be viewed in this context, and the arrival of Professor Muhammadi [the first Persian teacher at LU] in the 1950s should be understood as taking up these relations.[15]

Yet this was certainly not the context in which Muhammadi explained the purpose of Persian teaching in Lebanon in the 1950s. In laying out the goals of the journal, Muhammadi made not a single specific reference in the entire text of his speech to Iranian-Lebanese relations, but rather explained the goals of the journal and of Persian language teaching as "a bridge to connect the two cultures, Arab and Persian."[16]

The contemporary construction of these seemingly age-old relations is taking place on two levels. First, Persian language teaching at LU is currently viewed as a continuation of pre revolutionary ties, even though the government of the Islamic Republic otherwise distances itself clearly from Pahlavi politics in Lebanon. In addition, prior to the revolution the Pahlavi regime did not maintain a separate cultural center in Lebanon,[17] as cultural activities were carried out through the cultural section of the Iranian embassy. Cultural activities and exchanges between Iran and Lebanon were mainly limited to the activities of Iranian students at Lebanese universities and to the scholarly exchanges between Tehran University and the LU, of which the creation of the center there had been a part. When pointing to long-standing relations between Iran and Lebanon, the ICC clearly selects which parts of the past are important and in which context they should be interpreted. For example, in the context of ICC activities, the role of Musa Sadr in facilitating the military training of hundreds of Iranians active in the anti-Shah movement in the 1970s in Lebanon is not mentioned. This is because the ruling religious elite in Iran claims the success of the revolution to be entirely due to their own efforts, strategically sidelining those of other persons and parties.

Second, the contrast between pre- and postrevolutionary ideas about the relationship between Persian and Arabic language and civilization reveals much about how the ICC conceives of Iranian-Lebanese relations and Lebanese Shi'ite identity. For example, prior to the Iranian revolution, the goal of the journal *al-Dirasat al-Adabiyya* had been defined as "making the Iranians aware of the events and transformations in the Arab culture, language, and society, and Arabs aware of the cultural pieces and literary richness and current social transformation in Iran."[18] Yet, in 1999, at the reopening ceremony of the center, Victor el-Kek, the head of the center, pointed out how it expressed the long-standing cultural relations between Iran and Lebanon. He stressed that the connections between these two countries go far back in history and that they were especially intensified during the Safavid period in the sixteenth century, when Lebanese from Jabal 'Amil played an extraordinary role in spreading Shi'ism in Iran. He maintained that relations between Iran and Lebanon are not confined to the Shi'ite community and that the influence of the Persian language is felt in all Lebanese communities. To support his argument, Kek mentioned the al-Hikma School in Beirut, where a Christian bishop used to teach Firdawsi's *Shahnameh*, the most famous work of this tenth-century Persian poet, in the 1870s.[19]

Prior to the revolution, Muhammadi and others had spoken of the mutual influence of Persian and Arab cultures (*nofuz-i do farhang-i irani va 'arabi*) on each other and how these influences could be studied in the literatures of both languages.[20] Speeches delivered after the revolution at the reopening session of the center clearly aimed to connect Iran to Lebanon as countries, so that the fact that the center was located *in* Lebanon became the focus of attention. In the 1950s, the opening of the center at LU did not in any way imply that this project was meant to strengthen Iranian-Lebanese relations based on 'Amili migration to Safavid Persia, nor was Arabic taken as an index to signify Lebanese civilization. Lebanon was simply recognized as an Arabic-speaking country with a flourishing cultural environment, and as such, considering the close political friendship between Lebanese President Camille Chamoun and the Shah, the decision was made to open the center in Lebanon.

The difference between the pre- and postrevolutionary ideologies prevalent in Iranian government institutions, and the implications for relations with Lebanon, becomes even clearer in two articles that appeared in the second quarterly edition of *al-Dirasat al-Adabiyya*.[21] These articles dealt specifically with Iranian-Jabal 'Amil relations. In the first article, "Persian Words in Vernacular Jabal 'Amili" (*al-alfaz al-farisiyya fi 'ammiyyat jabal 'amil*), the author seeks to explain in general terms the mutual influence of Persian and

Arabic, a topic that the ICC and its associates (Kek and other Persian teachers at LU) also constantly emphasize in their speeches, papers, and interviews.[22] A link between language mixing and the social and political closeness of people is, thereby, often presupposed. The author of "Persian Words" comments on the influence of Persian in Lebanon by pointing to the ancient Achaemenid presence there. Finally, he explains the reason for the existence of Persian words in Jabal 'Amil by pointing to the 'Amili scholars' migration to Iran, while sidestepping the fact that there are many Persian loanwords in Arabic in general and many more Arabic loanwords in Persian. After this so-called historical overview, he provides twenty-four pages of Persian words presumably common in the Jabal 'Amil region.

In the Arab nationalist context of the 1920s and 1930s in the Arab East, Lebanese Shiʻite scholars, such as Muhsin al-Amin, emphasized the Arabness of Jabal 'Amil Shiʻites, trying to counter the claims of Orientalists who connected Shiʻite practices, believed to be less monotheistic, to the mental and cultural attitude of the Aryan race, opposing them to Semitic mental attitudes they believed were the reason for the existence of a Sunni tradition among Arabs. Based on this logic, the Belgian Orientalist Henri Lammens traced the racial origins of these 'Amili Shiʻites to Iran.[23] The ICC has been ignoring the pro-Arab argument of these Lebanese scholars, who deflected any linguistic and racial commonalities with Iranians, to stress what it considers to be deeply rooted ties between Iran and Jabal 'Amil using linguistic evidence.

The second article is about the role of the 'Amili scholars in building the Safavid state. The author refers to Jabal 'Amil as Lebanon and to Safavid Persia as Iran and creates a narrative of a continuously shared history right up to present-day Iran and Lebanon. These attempts minimize the differences between Iranian and Lebanese Shiʻites based on a particular linguistic ideology,[24] according to which perceived linguistic closeness and mixing of vocabulary is held to be indicative of social and political proximity. This assumed proximity of languages is drawn upon as evidence of cultural, historical, and ideological commonalities.

Islamicization of Languages; or, Who Contributed Most to Islamic Civilization?

In the speech Hashemi delivered on the first day of resuming Persian classes at the ICC in 2002, he stressed the importance of Persian by pointing out that "if Arabic was the language of the Quran, which we in Iran consider the gate to our knowledge of Islam and its eminent teachings, then Farsi is the language of the Islamic revolution and it is also the language of high culture (*adab*), poetry, and a language of interaction between religions and civilizations for all of its history."[25] He added that "many of the great scholars well-known in the Arab world were from Iran (*hum min bilad faris*), such as al-Razi, al-Farabi, al-Kharazmi, Ibn Sina, Ibn al-Muqaffa', and three imams of the Islamic sects (*a'immat al-madahib al-islamiyya*),[26] and many other scholarly characters."[27]

While the goal of introducing Persian at LU before the revolution had been for Arab students "to inform themselves about Persian culture and social transformations in Iran," afterward the ICC tried to promote Persian as the language of the Islamic revolution by placing almost the same emphasis on the revolution as on the rise of Islam itself. Hashemi argues that many well-known scholars, as well as some members of the Prophet's family, came from Iran. In this way he suggests that Persian and Iran have contributed centrally to Islamic civilization. At the same time, he presents a picture of the past in which those settled in the region called Iran today also spoke Farsi, although they wrote in Arabic. In short, while he characterizes Islamic civilization as not having been solely an Arab achievement (countering, for example, Arab Islamists' claims, such as those presented by Fadlallah), he reterritorializes this Islamic civilization, while assigning present-day Iran a central position in it.

Indeed, Persian language classes offered at LU since 2001 have attracted many Lebanese students, which seems to attest at first glance to the possibility that this new ideology is not alienating students. In 2002, fifty registered for Persian at the branch of the LU in Zahle, a mainly Christian-populated town in the al-Biqa'. Six had registered for Turkish and four for Hebrew.[28] How can we interpret these numbers? Did Hashemi's words convince the Lebanese students of the importance of the Persian language for Islamic civilization? Enrollment would have not been as high without two special incentives from the ICC. First, it organized a competition among students of Persian at LU and decided to nominate the twelve best, two from each of the five branches of LU throughout Lebanon and two from the ICC Persian classes, for a two-week sightseeing trip to Iran. According to Muna Mu'ayyad, the ICC's Persian teacher, this project was so successful that in the next academic year Persian classes at LU were packed with students. Second, students who registered for Persian did not have to pay the approximately $50 registration fee usually required for such classes, nor were they required to attend classes regularly to receive the equivalent of an A, as is the rule in other courses. The ICC also provided the books free of charge. Mu'ayyad argues that many Lebanese students also find Persian an easy language, as many words seem to be the same in both Arabic and Persian. But clearly this was not as much of a motivating factor as the competition.

Mustafa Chamran and the 1970s

The prerevolutionary ties between Sadr and Iranian anti-Shah members also provide material for the ICC to create a narrative of continuous relations between Iran and Lebanese Shi'ites. In 2002 the ICC invited Mehdi Chamran to visit Lebanon. Chamran's late brother, Mustafa, was a member of an anti-Pahlavi opposition movement with bases in Lebanon from 1970 to 1979, whose activities were discussed in chapter 3. During his visit, Chamran was to meet several Lebanese Shi'ite personalities and to visit Shi'ite-run institutions in South Lebanon, including those affiliated with Amal, which is headed by the current speaker of the Lebanese Parliament, Nabih Berri, to speak about his late brother. In fact, many of the Lebanese Shi'ites attending the speech had personally known Mustafa. He had, after all, offered military training to many active in Lebanon's first Shi'ite militia, which subsequently became the Amal movement.

On February 15, at the Nabih Berri Cultural Complex in a town near Nabatiyya, in South Lebanon, Chamran began a speech by reading passages from his brother's letters and notes from 1973 that described the political atmosphere in South Lebanon amid Israeli military attacks. For example, Mehdi read sections from his brother's book, *Lobnan*,[29] where Mustafa had described fighting in those specific regions in detail. When he was later taken to visit the Jabal 'Amil Technical Institute in Tyre, now under Amal supervision, Mehdi read about Mustafa's activities at that school and the organization of the students into militia groups.

Mehdi Chamran concluded his speech on this tour by pointing to "the importance of solidarity between the Islamic revolution and the Lebanese Shi'ite movements." For a moment, as he read these passages, Chamran implied that Iranian and Lebanese Shi'ites had been moving back and forth for centuries between their respective countries. However, although his reading of his brother's notes performatively evoked the events of the 1970s in 2002, Lebanese politics and Lebanese-Iranian relations have changed dramatically in the intervening years. This quasi-ritualistic commemoration was aimed at collapsing time and creating a sense of contemporaneity between events, downplaying the differences between the political context of the 1970s and the present.

The Iranian government claims Mustafa Chamran as part of a Shi'ite network linked to Khomeini and associates him with the current activities of the government in Lebanon. Cultural programs, such as the visit of Mehdi Chamran, propagate a narrative in which his brother's activities, such as fighting against the Israelis in South Lebanon prior to the Iranian revolution, are seen as a logical step in the creation of Hizbullah. In reality, however, postrevolutionary transnational ties between Iran and Lebanon are *not* simply a continuation of prerevolutionary Shi'ite ties, as I showed in chapter 3, according to the preferred official narrative of the Iranian government and the religious ruling elite in Iran. Scholars such as Houchang Chehabi privilege this official narrative in their analysis of postrevolutionary Iranian-Lebanese Shi'ite ties and frame the creation of Hizbullah as the latest episode in a long-standing relationship of mutual Shi'ite influences. Chehabi juxtaposes the sixteenth-century migration from Jabal 'Amil to Persia of scholars who assisted the Safavids in making their domain Shi'ite with the twentieth-century migration from Iran to Lebanon of Shi'ite activists and scholars who played key roles in the recent religious and political mobilization of Lebanese Shi'ites. He then concludes that "in a sense, history has come full circle."[30] Despite such a vision of deep continuities, the history of these interactions is deeply disputed and emerges in the tension between at least two contesting narratives about these Shi'ite ties, narratives that must be contextualized against the background of larger religious and political struggles. An account in which these relationships have "come full circle" is not a neutral description of the historical record, but indeed only one preferred reading of these ties, which by no means all participants in Lebanese-Iranian Shi'ite networks share.

Publications and Minimizing Boundaries

By supporting the publication and dissemination of large numbers of Shi'ite scholarly books in the Lebanese and larger Arab market the Iranian government believes it will strengthen its status as the official representative of Shi'ite Islam. The ICC finances publications in a number of fields. First, it edits the papers given at its conferences and seminars in books distributed by Dar al-Haqq, one of the leading Shi'ite-run publishing houses in Beirut.[31] In addition, the writings of a wide range of Shi'ite religious scholars, not surprisingly including a large selection of Khomeini's books, next to the works of 'Ali Khamenei and 'Abd al-Husayn Charafeddine, among others, have appeared in editions by the ICC. In his study of Hayderabadi Shi'ites, David Pinault reports different kinds of publication activities at the Iranian Culture House in Delhi, yet with seemingly similar goals, because in his view

> the Islamic Republic today seems to be courting Hayderabadi and other Indian Shiites in two ways: it seeks to consolidate a role for Iran as spiritual leader of the subcontinent's Shiites and it wishes to revive Iran's traditional role as source of inspiration and point of orientation for Indian Muslim culture. Thus, for example, the Iran Culture House in Delhi, under the aegis of the Iranian Consulate, is publishing a series of catalogues describing Arabic and Persian manuscripts in Indian libraries.[32]

By cataloging the Persian manuscripts in Indian libraries, the Iran Culture House in Delhi aims to remind Indians of the vital role of Persian in the Mughal empire. In this way, the Culture House hopes to construct a social memory of a past with intense interaction between Iran and India based on the important role of Persia in Indian Muslim courts since the fifteenth and sixteenth centuries and to deflect any suspicions that its activities in India are connected to establishing special relations with Indian Muslims.

On a subtle level, the activities of the Iran Culture House in Delhi also offer an alternative narrative of the history of India as directed against the project of powerful political forces in order to rewrite Indian history from a Hindu nationalist perspective. Despite the great differences between the political and historical contexts in which the Iran Culture House in Delhi and the ICC in Lebanon operate, one can nonetheless see some parallels between their aims and activities. Similar to the involvement of Iran Culture House in a struggle over the Indian past, ICC in Lebanon also offers a version of the history of Lebanon that is opposed to the Libanism narrative of some Maronites, who conceive of the country as part of an imagined Mediterranean civilization. Nevertheless, Indian Muslims as a whole are not in any position to politically and institutionally break the dominant Hindu national narrative in India. ICC activities in Lebanon, meanwhile, indirectly strengthen Lebanese Shi'ites' claims against the already politically weakened Maronite position by presenting Lebanon as part of an Islamic civilization, and ultimately as geographically and culturally closer to Iran.

From 1990 until 1997, the ICC was also involved in publishing its official monthly journal in Arabic, originally named *al-Rasid* (later known as *al-rasad al-thaqafi*, and finally as *al-rasad*), covering topics from the activities of the ICC in Beirut to news of Iranian cinema, and from the names of recent graduates at Lebanese universities to lists of books published in Iran and Lebanon. This journal best expresses the way the ICC—and ultimately the Iranian government—imagines and presents Iranian-Lebanese relations, and thus deserves a close study. If one were to pick up one of these journals and look at its cover, one might see the following selection of article titles: "The Lebanese National Museum," "The Cave of *'Ali-Sard*, an Example of Natural Beauty in Iran,"[33] "Kashan . . . Beauty of History and Present Radiance," and "The Development of Education in the Islamic Charity Foundation of al-'Amiliyya School."[34]

The content and layout of this journal suggest that the ICC aims at creating a shared Islamic and Shi'ite space characterized by multiple links between Iran and Lebanon. The editors seek to change the reader's experience of cultural and historical space between Iran and Lebanon. Events that took place in Lebanon are listed next to events in Iran. Articles discussing the linguistic mixing of Persian and Arabic, on Jabal 'Amilis' migration to Safavid Persia, thoughts and stories about Palestine, a list of the graduates at Lebanese universities and the topics of their theses, discussions about films in Iran, lists of Islamic books published in Persian and Arabic, reports on conferences with Shi'ite or broader Islamic relevance held in Tehran, Beirut, or Damascus all fill the pages of these journals.[35] In this way, the ICC seeks to downplay differences and underscores commonalities between the two nations. It succeeds— discursively and performatively on paper at least—in its project of obscuring differences and creating a sense of closeness between the Shi'ites of Lebanon and of Iran and between Arabs and Iranians in general.

But how successful has the ICC been in reconfiguring ideas about the interrelatedness of these two countries and of Lebanese and Iranian Shi'ites? Once I asked a Shi'ite shaykh in Beirut who used to be closely associated with official Iran about the audience for the ICC's publications, and he laughingly said that the number of editors of the ICC journals and books probably exceeds the number of its readers because nobody "listens to the stories Iran tells."

Though in undoubtedly exaggerated terms, the shaykh had raised a valid point, since at least the ICC's own journal ceased publication in 1997, and its attempt to reconfigure Iranian-Lebanese Shi'ite relations suggesting a closeness and lack of boundaries between the two communities and countries has so far largely been unsuccessful. This is certainly because many Lebanese Shi'ites resent and resist the ways the Iranian government presents itself at the center of a Shi'ite world and as the central contributor to Islamic civilization.

Visualizing a Modern Shi'ite Iran

The ICC offers a series of cultural events as part of its propagation programs (*barnameha-i tablighati*), with the goal of familiarizing Lebanese with the Iranian culture. For example, it introduces, although selectively, Iranian artists and films to the Lebanese public and, in the context of commemorating Khomeini, it annually sends a group of Lebanese to visit Iran. The goal of these activities is to highlight Iran's degree of modernity and civilization as exemplified by its diversity, the active role of women in the public sphere, and its commitment to pluralism, while emphasizing its preeminent position in Islamic civilization.

Iranian Films in Lebanon

The screening of Iranian films has proven to be one of the most successful ways for the ICC to establish contact with various communities in Lebanon and to convey a picture of Iran. The screening of *Bashu: The Little Stranger* moved Lebanese viewers to such an extent that for days the phone at the ICC was ringing with requests to order the film and for information about others.[36]

Produced by the well-known filmmaker Bahram Bayza'i in 1989, *Bashu* is the story of a young boy from southern Iran whose family is killed during the Iran-Iraq War. He hides in the back of a truck during the bombardment, only to wake up the next day to find himself in northern Iran. The contrast between the dry landscape of southern Iran and the lush green of the north, and the fact that neither Bashu nor his newfound northern family speak standard Persian, underscores the diversity of the Iranian population. As Bashu is dark-skinned and speaks Arabic, while many northerners are fair-skinned and speak a northern Persian dialect, the film points to ethnic and linguistic divisions within Iran but also to the possibilities of overcoming these differences.

Such films probably succeed with Lebanese audiences, as they have internationally, because of their artistic value and because many Lebanese clearly distinguish between the Iranian filmmaking industry and the Iranian government. The success of Iranian movies such as *Bashu* in Lebanon is also related to the familiarity of both societies with the devastation wrought by war, as Lebanese can certainly relate to the human suffering created as a result of a war regardless of its context. Through screening of these films, the ICC is able to create a sense of shared experience with the Lebanese, regardless of their religious identity.

The ICC, of course, prefers to regard the films' warm reception primarily as the result of the Lebanese audience's interest in the Islamic republic. It certainly does not call attention to the political differences between prominent Iranian filmmakers and those who speak for official Islam in Iran, or to the way many contemporary Iranian films have advanced subtle critiques of the strictures imposed by the government and the ruling religious establishment.

Gender, Art, and Modernity

Since the early 1990s, selected Iranian artists have been invited to exhibit their art in Beirut and to establish contacts with the Lebanese art scene. On the occasion of the birthday of Fatimah al-Zahra, the daughter of the Prophet Muhammad, an occasion declared the Day of the Woman in Iran after the revolution, three Iranian female artists exhibited their works at the ICC. The exhibition, which opened on September 4, 2002, was called The Scent of Jasmine (*'itr al-yasamin*).[37] Among the three Iranian artists who exhibited their works was Dr. Zahra Rahnavard, who is the head of the Iranian al-Zahra University, as well as an adviser to then-president Khatami and an advocate of women's rights within the government's defined gender roles.

This art exhibition, like other ICC cultural events, provided an opportunity for the Iranian religious elite to offer interpretations of what they considered Shi'ite piety, and especially the role of women in this vision of Shi'ite identity. At the opening session of the exhibition, Rahnavard gave a speech about the changes in the relationship between art, Islam, and female artists since the success of the revolution, emphasizing the importance of the presence of women in all public spheres and pointing to the necessity of cooperation between artists in Iran and Lebanon in the spirit of a dialogue between civilizations. Rahnavard is among the first Iranian women to address the growing discontent of secular Iranians with what they view as Islam's gender inequality. She offers a counter gender position through interpretations of the nature of Islam. In her view, Islam does not marginalize women because it does not exclusively confine them to the home.[38]

Mutran Khalil Abi Nadir, the Maronite bishop of Lebanon, attended the opening ceremony of the exhibition. In his speech he compared Fatimah to the Virgin Mary and spoke of the importance of coexistence and of positive Christian-Muslim dialogue in Lebanon. He proclaimed that both dialogue and coexistence are the messages of Lebanon to the world and wished the blessings of both Fatimah and Mary for both Lebanon and "our friend Iran" (*iran al-sadiqa*).[39]

The significance of this event generated debates among Shi'ites and gave rise to inter-Shi'ite differences. Among those who also visited the exhibition were Hizbullah members of parliament and other Hizbullah associates. The exhibited art included some sculptures of living beings, despite the widespread sense among many Muslims in Lebanon that creating and exhibiting sculptures is forbidden in Islam. One of the Hizbullah members present asked how Iran as an Islamic country could support the presentation of such art. Rahnavard replied by referring to the Shi'ite tradition of interpretation by rational inference (*bab al-ijtihad*). She said that certainly when the Prophet Muhammad forbade the creation of sculptures it was because people then began to worship these sculptures, but that creating such art now is clearly for artistic reasons, as no person with common sense would worship these sculptures today.[40] As specific Islamic or Shi'ite questions are raised, participants in the ICC expand their sphere of influence over aspects of civil society through what they rightly or wrongly depict as *ijtihad* (using rational methods for legal inference). Rahnavard, for example, though she lacked a theological-legal background, presented an interpretation of the authoritative record of the sayings and deeds of the Prophet Muhammad about making sculpture.

By offering gendered cultural programs, the ICC establishes itself at once as part of a modern Shi'ite nation that not only supports female participation in the public sphere but also allows them to practice *ijtihad* informally. However, the ICC indirectly offers authoritative interpretations of religious issues that matter to followers of the Lebanese Hizbullah (and potentially other Lebanese Shi'ites), although the ICC and the artists it invites and whose work it exhibits can certainly not claim a position equivalent to the *marja'* who usually decides such controversies.

In addition, these programs also provide the ICC with an avenue to participate in the gender debates that have intensified in public in postwar Lebanon, especially among the secular and pious intellectual members of the Lebanese Shi'ite community and which have resulted in an extensive production of literary and audio material, seminars, talk shows, and conventions.[41] For example, in 1995 Jamal al-Husayni, a liberal Lebanese Shi'ite woman, moderated a symposium on the occasion of the birthday of Fatimah al-Zahra. In her talk she criticized the slow progress of the Islamists in creating an Islamic public discourse to improve the plight of women, despite their claim that Islam is a religion that actually liberates women.[42] The participation of the Lebanese Shi'ite scholar Fadlallah in these debates "marks the beginning of a new trend toward reconceptualization of gender among the Shi'is in Lebanon . . . whereby the principle of 'Gender Equality' was adopted and rearticulated . . . to fit the context of Islamic discourse."[43] Through such programs the ICC competes with secular and pious Lebanese Shi'ites in defining proper gender roles among the Lebanese Shi'ite community while presenting itself as a role model that allows women's participation in its own society, thereby sidelining all the local Iranian debates over such questions and presenting just one favorable point of view, that of Rahnavard as she confirms the gender politics of the Islamic government. In debates over gender equality in Iran, however, the Iranian government actually seems most of the time to be the oppressor of women, while presenting itself as an advocate of women's rights in Lebanon.

"Iran Is Not al-Dahiyya"

Perhaps the most direct way for the ICC to introduce its version of Iran to the Lebanese has been to select a group of thirteen to fifteen people annually and to send them to Iran in the context of commemorating the death of Khomeini every year. These groups attend the commemoration ceremonies, travel throughout Iran, and visit cultural and research centers.

The ICC targets Lebanese intellectuals and scholars, as well as Shi'ite scholars and Shi'ite leaders from political parties. For instance, in 2002 the Lebanese group sent to Iran included two members of the Amal movement, two Sunnis associated with the Sunni party of *al-Tawhid al-Islami*, the Christian poet Joseph 'Aoun (who reads *zajal* poems at the ICC events discussed below), a journalist from the *al-Safir* newsletter, and a judge from the ministry of justice. Although most of the group is composed of Lebanese Muslims, every year a few Christians are included in the trip as well.

Hashemi pointed to the success of this project "as a way to correct the image of Iran in the mind of many Lebanese, as Iran had come to be associated wrongly with terrorism":[44]

> Many had imagined Tehran to be a larger version of *al-Dahiyya*; because of the connection they imagine exists between Iran and Hizbullah. They [the travelers] had thought Iran was like *al-Dahiyya al-janubiyya*, but once they visited the country, Wow! They realized, What a culture! What a civilization! Many of those who returned said, "Why take a vacation in Europe?" [They told us] "We'd rather go to Iran for vacation."

Hashemi is well aware of how many Lebanese envision al-Dahiyya as a poor, unsafe, dark, and dirty neighborhood whose residents seemingly all adhere to Hizbullah and he partially reproduces these stereotypes[45] by suggesting that Tehran cannot be compared to this place as those visitors compared Tehran to European cities, the ultimate compliment in the eyes of many Iranians, secular or religious. Several group members wrote a short travel report praising the country once they had returned from Iran. These were then published in their monthly journal.[46]

Staging Piety; or, Iran as Committed to Pluralism

In Lebanon, activities that express the importance of Muslim-Christian co-existence and symbolize interfaith dialogue date back to at least the 1960s. In July 1965, the first conference on Christian-Muslim dialogue in Lebanon took place at which eight participants, including Sadr, represented the various religious communities. The participants declared that Lebanon is the chosen land for Christian-Muslim dialogue and that "an exclusively

Christian or exclusively Muslim Lebanon would lose its raison d'être and would condemn itself, like Israel did."[47] Ever since 1965, conferences on interfaith dialogue in Lebanon have taken place regularly with international participants, arriving at official resolutions praising the value of coexistence. These conferences are supposed to make clear that both major religious groups acknowledge the existence of the other group, advocate tolerance and democracy, and reassure each other that despite the ongoing political power struggles they have no interest in eliminating each other. Both groups seek to present Lebanon as a successful example of Christian-Muslim coexistence. In this context of the importance of engaging in the discourse of interfaith dialogue as a means to be acknowledged as a member of the Lebanese nation, it comes as no surprise that Khatami's "dialogue of civilizations" finds resonance in Lebanon.

To Khatami, the first step to a more peaceful world is "to give up the will for power and instead appeal to the will for empathy and compassion."[48] He further points out that acknowledging and respecting the other, as an equal partner, is a necessary precondition for what he considers dialogue. Although Khatami's message is addressed to the world and proclaims a new direction for the Iranian government in the political world order, in the eyes of many Lebanese, Khatami is continuing the path of Sadr in advocating the importance of interfaith dialogue for a peaceful Lebanon. While many of the ICC's activities are not in line with Khatami's views on foreign policy, such as his desire to maintain only state-to-state relations with Lebanon, the ICC presents itself as a representative of Khatami's ideas and as a genuinely active participant in furthering interfaith dialogue in Lebanon,[49] because engaging in the discourse of interfaith and coexistence is key to any type of participation in Lebanese national affairs.

Coexistence with Christians

Fashionably dressed Christian Lebanese women, some with tight pants and colorful blouses and necklaces with crosses, are attending an East Beirut church to take part in a convocation in honor of a Lebanese Christian scholar who is presented with a prize for his academic achievements in 2003. The organizer of this event is none other than the ICC, which is honoring the scholarship of Sulayman Katani, a scholar of Shi'ite Islam. The festive gathering stands in stark contrast to the image of bearded Shi'ite men in military dress holding pictures of Khomeini and Kalashnikovs often circulated in the West, indicating the Iranian presence and their close ties to Shi'ites in Lebanon.

Born into a Christian family in 1912, Katani has written a series of books on the *ahl al-bayt,* such as his well-known work on Imam 'Ali published in 1967, his book on Fatimah al-Zahra published in 1968, one on Imam Hasan (1989), another on Imam Husayn (1990), and still another on Imam Jafar al-Sadiq (1997), among many. Katani has even written a book on Khomeini published in 1996. His books have been translated into Persian and some of them have been used as teaching materials at Iranian universities. At the event, various Lebanese public personalities, such as Ghassan Salamah, the Lebanese minister of culture, and Hani Fahs, a member of the Christian-Muslim Inter-Faith Dialogue Committee, gave speeches in praise of Katani, and the ICC honored him with a prize of five thousand dollars.[50]

Rapprochement with Sunnis

As part of its efforts to establish ties with non-Shi'ite communities in Lebanon, the ICC also organized an exhibition in Sidon in 2002 titled Echoes of Persian Art which put on display a series of Quran pages and covers, as well as contemporary art related to Quranic calligraphy in Iran. About 75 percent of the population of Sidon is Sunni and it is a stronghold of Hariri, so the ICC's exhibition of Quran-related art there comes as no surprise.[51] By organizing an exhibition on the Quran, believed to be a neutral subject removed from sectarian differences between Shi'ites and Sunnis, the ICC tried to emphasize the commonalities between its project and the interests of the Sunni establishment, presenting itself as working for the emergence of a united Muslim community in Lebanon. This became most obvious when Hashemi pointed out in his opening speech that "this exhibition that is now held in your city expresses the depth of the cultural relations between South Lebanon and Iran."

Sidon remains a contested place because Hariri's entire entourage's vision of the south and generally of the future of Lebanon is at odds with that of Hizbullah. Its conflict with Israel in the south certainly works against Hariri's economic interest and the economic growth of the Lebanon they envision. The city is part of the south, but the south has since the end of the war become largely identified with Shi'ites. With the growing importance and numbers of Shi'ite residents in Sidon since the civil war—they are now about 25 percent of the population—Hariri formed a local electoral alliance

with Amal.[52] Since the civil war, Amal has established itself as the main political force among Shi'ites in Sidon, especially in the neighborhood of Haret
Sayda, which it controlled during the civil war. Nevertheless, in recent years
Hizbullah seems to have had considerable success among the poor Shi'ite
inhabitants of Sidon, as its members have been ready to forge alliances with
old established Shi'ite *zu'ama* families of the city, such as the al-As'ad and
Osseyran, thereby limiting Amal's gains.[53]

This tense relationship between the Sunni political establishment led by
the Hariris and the growing Shi'ite political power in the region is the background against which the ICC has recently sought to cultivate relationships
with the Hariri camp. The ICC effectively demonstrated that Iranian government institutions do not need to rely only on Hizbullah in order to seek
influence in the Lebanese political scene. Thus sidelining the differences
between Hariri and Hizbullah, the ICC highlights a shared Muslim identity
in its attempt to establish good relationships with the Sunni leadership of
Sidon. Bahia Hariri, the sister of Hariri and the head of the Hariri Foundation as well as a parliamentary deputy and president of the parliamentary
commission for culture and education, spoke at the opening of the exhibition as well and expressed hope that the ICC and the Hariri Foundation
could cooperate on more such programs. Within days, the ICC held a similar exhibition of Quranic artifacts in Tripoli, which is yet another Sunni
stronghold in Lebanon.

BACKSTAGE ACTIVITIES: HIZBULLAH'S INSTITUTIONS AND NEGOTIATING AN IRAN-CENTERED *MARJA'IYYA*

Unlike activities in which the ICC emphasizes the public nature and sometimes non-Shi'ite character of its events, the set of activities discussed below
is directly related to promoting Hizbullah in Lebanon and of staging Iran as
the Vatican of Shi'ism. These activities are less visible to the larger Lebanese
public, as the ICC wants to avoid being associated exclusively with Lebanese Shi'ites. Perhaps it is hoping to establish itself one day as a cultural
center resembling the French Cultural Center in Lebanon, which successfully spreads its Francophone ideologies among many Christians and Muslims alike. Just like the French Cultural Center, which sometimes mediates
between Lebanese groups and French funding institutions on a variety of

projects, the ICC also functions as a mediator between Shiʻite groups and Iranian funding institutions.

The examples and debates introduced below tell a story of Hizbullah's institution-building and domestication of Iranian funds to advance its projects in the Lebanese context,[54] of Iranians' claim to a specifically *Iran*-centered *marjaʻiyya*, of Hizbullah's clear resistance to it; and finally of what the Iranian government expects in return for its support of Hizbullah. In short, this section gives an account of constant negotiations, apparent in practices, between the Iranian clerical establishment and Hizbullah, as mediated through the ICC, in shaping their ties and ultimately Hizbullah's identity.

Claiming Lebanon with Iranian Funds

The Iranian government-funded center of *al-majmaʻ al-ʻalami li ahl al-bayt*, the World Foundation of *ahl al-bayt*, was founded in 1990 by Khamenei with the goals of "the subordination of all Shiʻites under the political and religious leadership of Ayatollah Khomeini; the strengthening of relations between the Islamic Republic of Iran and Shiʻite communities outside of Iran's borders, as well as strengthening their politicization in accordance with the ideology of the Islamic revolution; and the creation of an institutional headquarters for Shiʻites in the world."[55]

The foundation aims at "successfully controlling and monitoring all activities of Islamic movements in the Islamic world in areas of culture, propaganda, economy, society, and politics."[56] Next to Khamenei and ʻAli Akbar Hashemi Rafsanjani, other prominent members of the foundation include Fadlallah and Muhammad ʻAli Taskhiri. Taskhiri (not to be confused with Mehdi Taskhiri, although they are relatives) was appointed general secretary in 1990.

In 1993 the foundation received a proposal from Lebanon asking for funding. A first draft project proposal was prepared by the Lebanese Shiʻite Islamist Muslim al-Rabiʻi for the previous Iranian cultural attaché to Beirut, Mehdi Taskhiri, to review and to forward to the Iran-based foundation.[57] This proposal is about opening eight cultural centers throughout Lebanon, with the ICC serving as an intermediary institution in helping establish contacts between groups seeking funding for such projects and appropriate funding institutions in Iran. The goal of the report is defined in terms of offering a "complete study of Lebanese Shi'ites." It was followed by his discussion of the "special features of Lebanese Shi'ites and of Lebanon" and explanations for the necessity of such cultural centers in Lebanon. The eight cultural centers are proposed to be located in Beirut, al-Dahiyya, Hermel, Ba'albak, Zahle, West al-Biqa', Sidon, and Tyre. The geographical borders of each region are defined in a way that clarifies for the reader that these cultural centers would sufficiently cover the needs of most parts of Lebanon. Furthermore, the local importance of each region for Lebanese Shi'ite politics is discussed with respect to how a Shi'ite cultural center would contribute to the empowerment of the Shi'ite community on a national level.

Rabi'i outlines the importance of opening a cultural center in Beirut, which would also serve the municipalities of al-Matn, Kisrawan, and Jubayl (Byblos), currently all heavily Christian-inhabited areas with a small Shi'ite population. After highlighting the history of Beirut as an exceptional intellectual and political center in the Middle East and as a place of the existence of the earliest educational centers and cultural life, the author points to the absence of Shi'ites from all aspects of this lively intellectual scene and introduces the three goals of creating a cultural center in Beirut that will enable Shi'ites to take a more active role in Lebanon.

First, he points to the necessity of the involvement of Shi'ites in this cultural movement in Beirut, and how the cultural center would enable Shi'ites to keep up with these developments in the capital. In this context he refers to other foundations with confessional affiliations, such as the Hariri Foundation, the most prosperous and influential Sunni foundation in Lebanon, which he believes is "one of the best equipped and most modern foundations in terms of its social, economic, administrative, media, and social activities." Second, the author notes the existence of Shi'ites in East Beirut and the municipalities of al-Matn and Kisrawan "who are unaware of their Islam and of their Shi'ite identity and who are only officially registered as Shi'ites on their identity cards." The activities of the cultural center in Beirut would then "cover the needs of these persons in form of cultural and ideological activities." Third, he points to the presence of all religious communities in Beirut, which makes Beirut suitable for projects concerning coexistence and dialogue. By initiating such activities or by taking part in these projects, the center can introduce to the public "the authentic Shi'ite Islamic thought (al-fikr al-islami al-shi'i al-asil)," and guide them to the "right path."

Rabi'i lists the geopolitical importance of Lebanon and the specificity of Lebanese Shi'ites to justify the urgent need for funds to create these cultural institutions. His main desire is to "preserve and to keep the community together so that it would maintain its roots and compete with other religious communities in the country." In his view the creation of the cultural centers and their planned activities achieve two goals at once. The first is to strengthen the Lebanese Shi'ite community vis-à-vis other communities in Lebanon. The second is to simultaneously influence the Lebanese Shi'ites in a way that would help the foundation achieve its desire of increasing the Iranian-centered *marja'iyya* position of Khomeini and Khamenei. After the author lays out the entire project, suggesting that Lebanon is a fertile ground for the propagation of Islamic ideology in the style of the ruling religious circles in Iran, he explains how a lack of funds has so far been the largest obstacle in the realization of this plan. He then concludes that the foundation has pioneered to take over the task to guide and defend the Shi'ites in the world.

Shi'ite Cultural Center Versus Hariri Foundation

Rafiq Hariri was a native of Sidon and a billionaire entrepreneur with strong ties to Saudi Arabia.[58] He was the prime minister of Lebanon for most of the postwar period from 1992 until his assassination in February 2005.[59] In chapter 1 I briefly discussed some of the features of Hariri's nationalism, such as promoting an urban-based, secular, upper-middle-class Lebanese identity with strong oligarchic tendencies. Advertisements in the Hariri-owned Future TV underline this vision. Scenes of fancy downtown reconstruction, of the graduation ceremonies of students, and of building new highways predominate. I also mentioned that his vision of Lebanon collides with that of Hizbullah, whose resistance activities stand in stark opposition to Hariri's vision of turning Lebanon into a merchant republic once again.

The Hariri Foundation, a nonprofit educational institution, was established in 1979. The main objective of the foundation is officially defined as facilitating the granting of loans to those seeking higher education regardless of their religious background.[60] But the foundation offers more services than just educational grants, such as providing books for public schools in areas with a Sunni majority, holding conferences on education, facilitating medical and social services, and reconstructing Sunni mosques.[61] It takes care of the needs of the Sunni community in Lebanon and marks their presence and strengthens their position vis-à-vis other communities.

It is in this context that Rabi'i argues for the importance of creating a Shi'ite cultural center with the support of the *ahl al-bayt* Foundation, comparing it with services the Hariri Foundation provides for Sunnis. Rabi'i suggests that through these cultural centers the *ahl al-bayt* Foundation can also successfully propagate the ideologies of the Islamic revolution and eventually realize the creation of an Islamic state in Lebanon.

In addition, he is aware of how an emphasis on difference, that is, on the public performance of Shi'ite identity, is the precondition to participation in the Lebanese nation as well as a successful strategy in breaking hegemony by claiming space. For Shi'ites to participate in the coexistence and dialogue projects they first need to develop fully and publicly perform their identity as a coherent and autonomous community vis-à-vis other religious communities. This becomes even more obvious when Rabi'i points to areas such as al-Matn and Kisrawan, heavily Christian populated, where in his view Shi'ites have not become aware of their Shi'ite identity.

This example shows quite clearly how transnational Shi'ite institution building can support Lebanese Shi'ites in claiming a more important political position and a more central role in the national imaginary of Lebanon while simultaneously propagating Khamenei's *marja'* position. Membership in such an obviously Iran-centered Shi'ite organization with transnational political goals should not necessarily be considered evidence of Hizbullah's (or Lebanese Islamists') lacking a commitment to Lebanon. Rather, such a *marja'*-funded transnational organization supports a Lebanese Shi'ite nationalist goal in claiming rights vis-à-vis the Lebanese state, and in remaking the Lebanese nation in line with its interests. Lebanese religious entrepreneurs often appropriate these transnational networks and the resources provided by them to enhance the power of their party or group in the local national context.

Providing an Alternative Voice to the State: A Hizbullah Research Center

The Consultative Center for Studies and Documentation (CCSD) (*al-markaz al-istishari lil-dirasat wa al-tawthiq*), established in 1988 in al-Dahiyya, is part of Hizbullah's institutions created with funds from Iran. CCSD members seek to accomplish the goals of "allocating, and guiding the social endeavors and civil activities" by preparing reports, studies, and consultations in areas of concern to the center as well as doing field surveys and statistical studies, building a data bank and press archive, publishing scientific and documenting periodicals and books, and organizing conferences, workshops, and panels.[62]

Large pictures of Khomeini and Khamenei hang in the hallways of CCSD, and all the employees are clearly Hizbullah members.[63] CCSD has been successful in providing research information on Lebanese Shi'ites and in publicizing its own views and interpretations of various aspects of Lebanon by publishing a series of books and holding conferences. For example, it published the papers of a conference it had organized on the economic crisis in Lebanon in 1999. These papers discussed the effects of the economic crisis on the daily lives of the Lebanese people and suggested to the government ways to "ameliorate the economic situation." Besides "documenting the entire resistance operations against Israeli occupation, and Israeli aggressions since 1982," and thus serving as a way to document claims to the nation, CCSD has directly interacted with the state by "accomplishing a survey of the political and electoral trends which included 400,000 voters, the night before the parliamentary elections in 1996." CCSD has been able to create a voice regarding three issues: making the presence of Shi'ites known, making public Hizbullah's readings of the political and economic events and maladies in Lebanon, and suggesting ways to improve them.

Their success in establishing themselves as a serious political and social voice in Lebanon is evident when foreign research institutions located in Lebanon establish contacts and organize joint programs with them. For example, the Orient Institute Beirut (OIB), a well-known German research institution, organized a joint conference with CCSD in February 2004 in Beirut called The Islamic World and Europe: From Dialogue Toward Understanding, at which members of Hizbullah such as Shaykh Na'im Qasim, its deputy secretary general, and 'Ali Fayyad, the head of CCSD, among others, gave papers.

Iran, the Vatican of Shi'ism?

But how has the Iranian ruling religious elite benefited from supporting Hizbullah if the party is involved in its own nationalist project? Through their ideological and economic support of Hizbullah in its fight against Israel, the ruling elite of Iran have been able to promote themselves as champions of the Palestinian cause. CCSD, for example, published an extensive volume titled *Iranian-Arab Relations* that contains a series of papers describing Iranian relations with several Arab countries, among them Lebanon, in October 2000. In this indirect way, the institute foregrounds the importance of Iranian-Arab relations and the strategic importance of Iran in the region, especially what it considers the positive aspects of Iranian government policies regarding the Palestinian cause.[64]

In addition, the ruling elite in Iran have been able to create an Islamic narrative of the struggle in Palestine that competes now with other more secular narratives of liberating Palestine. As discussed in chapter 3, prior to the Iranian revolution the support of the Palestinian cause had become an integral part of defining Shi'ite authenticity and legitimate rule for some anti-Shah opposition members. Support of Hizbullah by the ruling elites reflects their continuous strength in the government with regard to shaping Iran's regional role as well as in propagating their official Shi'ism. Why the Iranian ruling elite continues to support Hizbullah despite its orientation toward a Lebanese Arab audience then becomes a largely obsolete question, since official Iran's support of Hizbullah is to a considerable degree a matter of power struggles among political factions in Iran.

The Israeli-Lebanese war of summer 2006 only further hampered efforts for democracy in Iranian civil society. Events in Lebanon in 2006 strengthened the position of the ruling religious elite in the Iranian political landscape (although, as I discuss in the epilogue, it weakened their position in Lebanon), seemingly justifying its attacks on democratic movements in Iran by pointing to the Western—and immoral—origins of such movements, which are tied to the very same actors who supported the killing of Shi'ites in Lebanon and which delegitimize Hizbullah's defense of Lebanon. In addition, personal gains and economic and status rivalry among mid-ranking Iranian government and quasi-government foundation (*bunyads*) officials and militiamen also account for the continuation of Iranian ties to Lebanese Shi'ites, since an entire bureaucracy owes its status and existence to the maintenance of these ties. Finally, and on a more obvious level, the reputation of a *marja'*— in the case of Hizbullah, it is Khamenei—also depends on the number of his followers.[65] That Hizbullah's source of emulation is at the same time Iran's most powerful political leader strengthens the ability of the ruling religious elite in Iran to propagate their official Shi'ism outside Iran and sidelines their political opponents inside the country.

FIGURE 5.1. A postcard purchased at the Fatimah Gate in South Lebanon in 2000. Wearing a Palestinian scarf, Khamenei congratulates the Lebanese for their victory against Israel. But it appears that Khamenei is not looking directly at the Lebanese, but rather fixes his gaze on the viewer in greeting, as if to say, "we told you so." Khomeini is looking at Khamenei—his successor—smiling as if to give his approval of Khamenei's perpetuation and elaboration of his vision. Below are the Lebanese. The postcard clearly indicates to whom victory is owed. *Personal collection of the author.*

FIGURE 5.2. A sticker purchased at the Fatimah Gate in South Lebanon in 2000. A genealogy of Shi'ite authority, starting with Khomeini, then Khamenei, 'Abbas Musawi, and Sayyid Hassan Nasrallah. Another way of reading the sticker would be that the two deceased are on one side looking down at their successors, while the successors have their eyes fixed in the distance. The Iranian leaders are older, wiser, and more senior, as demonstrated by their white beards, larger heads, and their positioning at the top of the picture, while their Lebanese counterparts are younger and junior to them, as shown by their lower positioning and their black beards. *Personal collection of the author.*

Winning support among Arab Shi'ites by attracting followers (*muqallids*, lit. emulators) of Khamenei not only increases the power of the *vali*, as the number of his followers rises, but is also a way of reconfiguring Lebanese Shi'ite identities, so at least hopes the Iranian government.[66] The greater the number of Khamenei's *muqallids* in Lebanon, the stronger the claims of the Iranian government to leadership over Lebanese Shi'ites, potentially translating into greater political influence in Lebanon. In the view of Hashemi:

> As you probably know, Ayatollah Khamenei, our leader (*rahbar*), does not claim to be a *marja'* in Iran, as he said when he came to power that there are others in the country who are more qualified. But as for the Shi'ites outside of Iran, he said that "I cannot be indifferent toward the outside world. We cannot be indifferent to the requests of Shi'ites outside of Iran who are following Iran and the revolution, *who are emulating me (az man taqlid mikonand) and obeying us (az ma taba'iyyat mikonand)*." But let me clarify this for you, even those who are against us—and let me tell you that I cannot think of anyone really—cannot deny the prominent role of Iran as a Vatican for Shi'ites. They say Iran is our supporter, Iran is our Vatican . . . this is part of the culture and literature (*farhang va adabiyat*) of Shi'ites in various countries.[67]

Hashemi makes two interesting points in his explanation. First, and most important, he interchangeably uses the idea that those who follow Khamenei (i.e., emulate Khamenei) also "obey us" (i.e., obey the Iranian government). In Hashemi's view—and this probably reflects the unofficial view of many Iranians involved in maintaining Shi'ite transnational ties to Lebanon—there really is no difference between following the *marja'* Khamenei and obeying the Iranian government, as the two are figured as one and the same. Hashemi draws on a nationalist interpretation of *marja'iyya*, while ideally the *marja'iyya* is to be void of ethnic and national ideologies. The second point concerns his reference to the existence of a particular Shi'ite literary and cultural tradition, which acknowledges the position of Iran as the Vatican of all Shi'ites in the world. But which Shi'ite culture and literature in Lebanon did Hashemi refer to that praises Iran as a Vatican to Shi'ites? How is such a genre constructed and performed? One such production of literary genre is *zajal*, a popular oral poetry tradition in Lebanon and elsewhere in the Arab world, usually performed in spoken, nonstandard Arabic ('ammiyya). Groups of male poets challenge each other with improvised poetry recitations while someone plays the *daff*.[68]

Zajal *Meets* Vali

The ICC organizes yearly *zajal* poetry nights—Arabic poetry on honor, pride, and nationhood performed by a group of men—in various Shi'ite cities and towns in South Lebanon as part of its program to celebrate the success of the Iranian revolution in Lebanon. In February 2002, the program was held in Bint Jubayl, a town in South Lebanon released from Israeli occupation less than two years earlier.

Hashemi gave the opening speech, describing *zajal* literary traditions and the armed resistance as the two necessary elements to reach the goal of freeing the south from Zionist occupation. In his view, "*zajal* deserves the same praising as the resistance does, for it has fought Zionism on the same level." Three *zajal* poets[69] had been invited to perform. To a half-empty hall, they begin their performance in praise of the postrevolutionary Iranian government. A Christian poet, Joseph 'Aoun, read first:

> The dawn used to come this way and that
> But today it will come from Bint Jubayl
> As we have been invited to the most splendid occasion
> I carried my compassion and good intentions
> As I arrived, I greeted the crowd and held my breath
> And to bless it, I prayed upon the Prophet
> Tyranny and corruption
> That was the Shah's regime
> I wish that justice could be brought from exile
> And with God's command, Khomeini came back
> His country, its moonlight, the clouds of January
> And the cold of February greeted him
> And the long lasting darkness of suffering
> Was folded away by dawn's arrival
> Righteousness prevailed and people are cheering
> Evil before the Shah was forfeited
> And where the devil's embassy was
> Khomeini said that that is Palestine's

To hold its place and for its flag to fly
All the oppressed were praying for the Prophet.

Or consider this section of a poem by Nadim Shu'ayb:

Greetings to the Embassy on this day of victory
And to the Cultural Center as well
So that awareness in culture would fill all the places
And give the word its significance
We now need an attaché like Sayyid Hashemi for our corner
Worry not, O my dear country,
For your free rebels drove the worry away
They saddled their line to martyrdom long before their horses
Your eagles gather from everywhere
And from the West, from Paris, came the light
Carried aboard a flight
To the East he arrived filled with beautiful scent
He made the infidels wander in confusion
A moon and bright stars came with him
And from the heavens came nymphs
Was she watching her image on the sands of *Tabas*
Or was it a ship without sailors and sea
And when this light illuminated in Iran
All roles flipped and dawn came
Khomeini came, in the spirit of Muhammad's progeny,
In the strongest will and spirit.[70]

I suggest that the ICC is involved in the production of such literary genres
and that this serves as propaganda for and propagation (*tabligh*) of the position of Khomeini (and later Khamenei) as the leader and *marja'* who, as the
speech of Hashemi shows, also propagates the special position of Iran.

One of the ICC reports summarizing its activities on the ten-day celebrations of the success of the Iranian revolution in 2002 reads:

Every year at the anniversary of the success of the Islamic revolution in Iran,
the people of Lebanon remember the revolution with increasing love and af-
fection (*mardom-i lobnan ba 'ishq va shuri do-chandan be yad-i khaterehay-i an*

mishetaband.) . . . But ah, how difficult it is to celebrate the anniversary of the success of the revolution among these people, especially with such few facilities, where there is no match between their enthusiasm and their capacities, and between their love and the needs of this nation (*bayn-i chenin mardomi anham ba dastani tohi va emkanati andak ke hich movazeneh-i bayn-i an ba shur va 'ishq va niyaz-i in mellat barqarar nist*)!⁷¹

In other words, to a large extent (if not completely) the production of this type of culture and literature has been financed by the ICC itself, most probably because no initiative would have come from the Lebanese themselves. This is not because they are too poor to organize festivities, as the report suggests, but because the Iranian government simply does not have followers outside Hizbullah circles in Lebanon. Even Hizbullah's loyalty to the *marja'* is not expressed in celebrations of the success of the Iranian revolution without the financial involvement of the ICC or other Iranian funding sources.

These poems are reminiscent of those produced by companions of Khomeini during the first years after the success of the revolution in Iran. They describe it as being the result of his efforts. But just as there are fewer pictures of Khomeini on walls in the streets in Tehran today than there are in al-Dahiyya, resistance to the compulsory exposure to such poetic genres and visual representations has increased in Iran, while the ICC continues to cultivate and promote the performance of this literary genre through *zajal* in Lebanon. In 2003, during my stay in Beirut, a *zajal* poetry night was held in Tyre in which the poets overdid the praising of Khomeini to such an extent that the ICC decided to decrease their honorarium by half to avoid embarrassment. Part of what was felt to be an embarrassment was clearly the disjuncture between the lower esteem this genre enjoys in Iran today and the officially sponsored promotion of it in Lebanon.

Hizbullah: A Partner, Not a Puppet

While ideological support and appropriate funds from various sources in Iran have enabled Hizbullah to successfully express its vision of a moral society and to a certain degree put into practice its Lebanese national vision, Hizbullah has its own strategies for dealing with the Iranian ruling religious elite, who wish more obedience from Hizbullah members. These are not as blunt as those of Amal and Fadlallah, which often construct ethnic, linguistic, and gender differences to break Iran's hegemonic claims in Lebanon, but they are more nuanced and become apparent in the daily practices and in decision making of Hizbullah's various institutions and the popular responses to them. At this level, Hizbullah constantly negotiates with various Iranian formal and informal institutions to define their limits and its relation to Iran, and ultimately its own identity. As I tried to show throughout this book, analyzing speeches and ideological statements of Shi'ite leaders provides one window to study visions of Shi'ite Lebanon; nonetheless, it is often in the daily practices and debates of a large number of Shi'ites that these identities are negotiated and lived.

For example, in chapter 2, in providing a history of Persian language teaching in Shi'ite-run schools, I introduced one such instance of boundary making at the al-Shaahid School in Lebanon where attempts at introducing Farsi as a third foreign language failed. While the headmaster of this school was clearly supportive of teaching Persian, students and parents—all the most committed Hizbullah followers, as they are often the children of the resistance fighters—blocked this project successfully, arguing that the language does not benefit the students in the Lebanese national examination that is most important to their future academic success.

When Hizbullah Closes Its Doors to Iranian Mullahs

Annually, during the month of Muharram, a group of thirty or forty preachers selected by the Organization of Islamic Culture and Propaganda (*sazman-i farhang va irtebat-i islami*) are sent from Iran (mainly from Qom) to Lebanon to preach at various Hizbullah-dominated mosques and *husayniyyas*. The ICC serves as a coordination agency for these preachers and provides the logistics in Beirut, such as housing and airport transport.[72]

These preachers are mainly 'Ajamis—Iraqis of Iranian descent—whom Saddam Husayn expelled from Iraq starting in the 1970s and especially during the Iran-Iraq War. They are fluent in Arabic, more specifically in the Iraqi dialect, which is highly regarded among the Lebanese Shi'ites and considered the most authentic dialect for performing 'Ashura commemorations. The ICC also supervises the activities of approximately ten preachers from Iran who are permanently stationed in Lebanon. This group is also native Arabic speakers of Lebanese and Iraqi origin as well as two Iranians who are native Persian speakers. These preachers are themselves the followers (*muqallid*) of Khamenei, and as such preach and convey (*tabligh*) his messages.

As discussed in the previous chapter, 'Ashura commemorations are an arena where differences and solidarities between Amal and Hizbullah members are displayed and reproduced. These commemorative events are also important because different types of ritual performance indicate the type of networks each Lebanese Shi'ite group maintains with the Iranian religious ruling elite. ICC activities clearly reach beyond their self-defined domain of culture, since the work of these preachers, whose logistics and places of preaching are coordinated by the ICC with Hizbullah officials, is changing Shi'ite traditions in order to intensify Lebanese Shi'ite solidarities with official Iran.

However, in 2003, Hizbullah decided to send its own preachers to various mosques throughout the country and communicated to ICC that, from now on, it does not want so many Iranian preachers to come to its mosques during Muharram. This decision might have come in the context of Khatami's emphasis on strengthening official state-to-state relations between Iran and Lebanon and on creating more transparency in their ties with Hizbullah. Hizbullah members might have found Khatami's vision useful in limiting activities that put Hizbullah too obviously in a junior position. Iranian government officials, however, ignored this and sent the preachers anyway. On the first day of Muharram, they were dropped off at the various *husayni-yyas*, only to find out that they were barred from entering them. ICC members immediately complained to Hizbullah officials who began by claiming that the preachers had come too late and that they now had arranged for other preachers to take their position. ICC had to withdraw its preachers but managed to distribute some of them nonetheless in other less prestigious *husayniyyas*.

At the End of the Day, However, Everything Has a Price

Despite these incidents, the Iranian government nonetheless makes sure it receives its share of acknowledgment for its support of Hizbullah, especially in a way that allows it to present claims in South Lebanon. This is most obvious in a media agreement between the governments of Iran and Lebanon signed on September 21, 1998.

The Iranian government, represented by 'Ataallah Muhajirani, then head of the Ministry of Guidance and Culture under Khatami, signed the declaration in which both governments agree to produce TV programs important to both countries, while mentioning that one of the most obvious of these common interests could be documenting Israel's crimes committed in

South Lebanon and the reaction of the people of the south to such crimes. As the agreement states, "In this context the positive impact and cultural role (*naqsh-i shokufa konande va farhangi*) of the Iranian people and the Iranian government is very important and every effort should be made to use every possible means to point to this fact."[73] Almost all reports prepared by the ICC summarizing its own activities during the ten-day anniversary celebrations of the success of the Islamic revolution highlight how thankful the people of South Lebanon are for the support of the Iranian government in fighting the Zionist enemy and in rebuilding the south.

Whether in the *ahya* nights, in the Persian language classes, or in civil associations, the Iranian government has sought to disseminate and gain acceptance of its vision of Iranian-Lebanese relations in order to place Iran at the center of a Shi'ite and wider Islamic world. In this, the ICC has followed a double strategy. On one hand it downplays what are commonly perceived by followers of Amal as ethnic and national boundaries between Lebanon and Iran, and instead emphasizes shared religious identity as a central component of solidarity. On the other hand, it simultaneously emphasizes what it considers a pivotal position of Iran in Shi'ism and Islamic civilization at large. In so doing, it draws on mainstream Iranian nationalist ideologies regarding the splendor and importance of Persian cultural and intellectual traditions and the Persian language.

By creatively reworking temporal difference and spatial notions of center and periphery and rootedness, the ICC has been able to create a narrative of a modern, pious, Shi'ite Iran with deep historical ties to Lebanon—of which the postrevolutionary ties are but one episode. The nationalist reading of Jabal 'Amil-Safavid relations in the sixteenth century, inventing a tradition of Persian-language teaching as a sign of Shi'ite transnational ties and incorporating Chamran as part of the Khomeini circle are some of these strategies. Through the presentation of female artists and by taking part in debates about gender in Lebanon, sending visitors to Iran, and screening films, the ICC has aimed at presenting itself as deeply modern. Yet, while the Iranian government depoliticizes multiple voices in Iran with regard to piety and modernity and presents them as one official voice, it supports the further fragmentation of the Lebanese Shi'ite community exactly along those lines.

In addition, by facilitating the institution of *marja'iyya*, the ICC has tried to deterritorialize Lebanese Shi'ite identities by creating a sense of homogeneity in an imagined Shiʿite community transcending national borders while, at the same time, using the institution of *marjaʿiyya* as another avenue for an Iranian nationalist reading of the Shiʿite world. By creating Shiʿite institutions financed by the ruling elite in Iran, the Iranian government supports a specific project of Lebanese Shiʿite-centered nationalism, which draws lessons from both the Maronite and Hariri strategies of advancing their projects in Lebanon, and yet diverges from both in its vision of Lebanon.

The ICC and other Iranian government organizations envision that such a specifically Shiʿite imagination of a Lebanese nation is closely aligned with official Iran's perspective on its role in a Shiʿite world. Many Lebanese Shiʿites, however, including followers of Hizbullah, do not share this view. Instead, their nationalism is aimed at reformulating the position of Shiʿites in a specifically Lebanese context.

EPILOGUE

I began this book by suggesting that it will provide a background to understanding the current Lebanese crisis and that it would also create an analytical framework for assessing involvement by the Iranian government in post-Saddam Iraq. In the remaining pages I outline the main events in Lebanon since February 2005, offer my reading of current Iranian-Hizbullah relations, and conclude by proposing some alternative approaches to analyzing Iranian-Iraqi Shi'ite transnationalism.

Lebanon Since February 2005

Patriot or stooge? Nasrallah must decide.[1]

The assassination of Lebanon's former prime minister, Rafiq Hariri, on February 14, 2005, provoked a series of demonstrations and counterdemonstrations led by rival and dominant political parties and leaders. These power struggles were contested symbolically on Martyrs Square in downtown Beirut. Within weeks, pro-Hariri political figures had invented new memories of the past. In this new narrative they presented themselves as victims who have, through the tragic assassination of Hariri, suddenly found the courage to undertake an uprising. The assassination, which many of them described as a traumatic event, allowed these politicians to become finally and fully themselves: to be democratic and patriotic and to present, once more, Lebanese Shiʻites as antinational.

These struggles found expression in a discourse about representing the authentic voice of the Lebanese people, those true citizens of Lebanon who are interested in maintaining its sovereignty and independence. The main disagreements on the surface between the two camps seemed to revolve around the implementation of United Nations Security Council Resolution 1559, which demanded first the immediate withdrawal of Syrian troops from Lebanon, since the Syrian leadership had been the first suspects in the assassination of Hariri, and second the disarming of Hizbullah.

Demonstrations were led by the two Shiʻite parties beginning on March 8, 2005 (whence the name March 8 Alliance). They were pro-Syrian, expressing solidarity with the Syrian leader Bashir al-Asad, thanking him for his support of Lebanon in difficult times, condemning interference by the United States in Lebanese affairs, and signaling that Hizbullah will not give up its arms. Counterdemonstrations to respond to that of March 8 took place on March 14 (hence the March 14 Alliance). They consisted mainly of the followers and sympathizers of the Lebanese Forces led by a Maronite Christian, Samir Geaga, of the Progressive Socialist Party of Druze leader Walid Jumblat, of the Future Movement led by a Sunni, Saʻd Hariri, and of some members of the Christian coalition, Qurnat Shahwan. They called for the immediate withdrawal of Syrian forces from Lebanon and the creation of an international tribunal to investigate the Hariri case.

Numerous local and international observers blamed the Syrian government for Hariri's assassination; therefore, the positions of the respective parties toward the question of the Syrian presence in Lebanon became tightly connected to notions of Lebanese patriotism and good citizenship. Power struggles within the political elite became once more manifest in a discourse that pushed Lebanese toward one of two poles: loyal citizens or traitors, the latter being those who desired Syria's presence to continue.

Syria maintained a strong military presence in Lebanon from 1976 until its formal withdrawal in April 2005, and Lebanese state decisions could hardly be made without prior consultation with Damascus. In fact, a traffic lane was reserved at the border crossing from Lebanon to Syria for those Lebanese politicians visiting Damascus, the same lane used by the military (*khat ʻaskari*), where the usual border procedure was skipped. Syrian forces had initially entered Lebanon in 1976, during the first phase of the civil war, at the request of the Lebanese president, Sulayman Franjiyyah, under the pretext of protecting the government against growing PLO power. Various Lebanese communities have established closer ties with the Syrian leadership ever since. Many of those leading the March 14 Forces, such as Sa'd Hariri's father, Rafiq, and Jumblat, had maintained close links with the Syrian government and its chief of intelligence in Lebanon, Ghazi Kan'an.

While Syria certainly advanced its own political and economic interests in the country, it also often helped Lebanese politicians in the pursuit of their own interests. These Lebanese politicians, in other words, did exercise agency in dealing with the Syrian leadership. They were found across all religious communities and were not confined to Shi'ite leadership.

After the assassination, the March 14 Forces called for the pro-Syrian government to resign, and demanded new parliamentary elections. The government did resign under pressure of similar demonstrations and elections were held in June 2005. These elections, at first sight, seemed to blur the clear-cut divisions created since February 2005 between pro-Syrian and anti-Syrian forces, as the political parties and factions formed alliances. Members of the March 14 Forces have dominated the parliament ever since, and their government has become popularly known as the Sanyura government, with Fu'ad Sanyura being the newly appointed prime minister after the June 2005 parliamentary election. He is a close ally of the Hariri family and their Sunni Future Movement. The new government focused on two issues: internationalizing the investigation of the Hariri assassination by forming a UN-led investigation into the case and eventually establishing an international tribunal to try the murderers (the Netherlands has recently agreed to host the court), and the disarming of Hizbullah according to the U.S.-backed UN Resolution 1559. Hizbullah and Amal opposed both these plans as they had prior to the formation of the new government as well. In February 2006 the Maronite Christian leader of the Free Patriotic Movement, Michel 'Aoun, signed a memorandum with Hizbullah, supporting Hizbullah's and Amal's opposition to disarming Hizbullah. Since then, these two groups—the March 8 Alliance and the Free Patriotic Movement— have formed the opposition and have been presented as posing a threat to the so-called legitimate and democratically elected government of Sanyura.

In the wake of the assassination, many of the main leaders of the March 14 Forces created new narratives of the past. In this new vision, March 14 members were presented as having always been anti-Syrian, and the Syrian presence was viewed as enhancing only the position of the Shi'ites vis-à-vis other groups. They blamed, in the rhetoric that is common in the Lebanese political scene, an unspecified "those" who supported the Syrian presence and maintained their state-within-a-state status. No one had a doubt that they were referring to Hizbullah and, to some degree, to Amal. In addition, opposing the creation of an international investigation team to deal with the assassination case and favoring instead an investigation by Lebanese authorities as suggested by Amal and Hizbullah came as a sign of Amal and Hizbullah's antinational attitude because it was interpreted as a way to cover for what were believed to be their Syrian masters, the prime suspects in these investigations. Shi'ites were accused of being antipatriotic this time because they favored a *national* investigation instead of an international one. By now it was becoming clear that the struggle over power in Lebanon is not about a local Lebanese group against two Shi'ite parties with transnational ties. It is about limiting Shi'ite participation in the nation by creating and capitalizing on certain logics in which Shi'ites by default *always* remain outside.

The events since the assassination can also be read as the most striking moment since the end of the Lebanese civil war in 1990 for conflicting ideas about Lebanese nationhood to come to the fore again. Despite the fact that the anti-Syrian camp has also sought help from outside Lebanon, mainly from members of the European Union and the United States, in implementing UN Resolution 1559, it views Syria's relations with the Shi'ite parties as harming national unity and as an obstacle in the creation of democracy in Lebanon. The two Shi'ite parties criticized intervention by member states of the European Union and the United States in very similar terms, arguing that the Syrian presence in Lebanon had stabilized the country and that Hizbullah's armed resistance in the south protected the country from Israeli aggression.

Erstwhile Christian opposition groups, such as the Qurnat Shahwan Gathering (created in 2001) and, later on, the March 14 Forces, engaged in a political discourse in which the creation of an independent and democratic Lebanon depended on a Syrian military withdrawal from Lebanon, the end of Syrian interference in the Lebanese government and state institutions, and the resignation of what was then a pro-Syrian Lebanese government. However, the March 14 Forces did not view political sectarianism, the state structure that prevents the sort of Western democracy these members seem to have been advocating, as an obstacle. This is because democracy, as promoted by this group while rightly rejecting Syrian domination, does not refer to the creation of equal rights for *all* Lebanese citizens, but further enhances the position of a specific elite that does not see cooperation with Syria representing its interest anymore and fears the loss of power to those whom Syrian leadership favors more.

In the wake of the assassination, the March 14 Forces also presented themselves as true Lebanese patriots by referring to their resistance to the pro-Syrian government, which took the form of a series of demonstrations, as an Independence Uprising (*intifadat al-istiqlal*) and a Cedar Spring (*rabi' al-arz*). The number of Lebanese flags waved there and the slogans chanted during these demonstrations also reflected this self-image. Freedom, sovereignty, independence, national unity, and truth were all words variably combined in various slogans.

In fact, the extent to which the United States supported anti-Syrian demonstrations—certainly to weaken Syria in the context of the suspected Syrian support of some Sunni insurgents in Iraq—becomes clear in a term coined by Undersecretary of State for Global Affairs Paula Dobriansky, who referred to the demonstrations as a "Cedar Revolution." This term appropriates the official and popular emblem of Lebanon in accordance with how the March 14 Forces made use of the symbol during their demonstrations, while comparing these demonstrations with other democratic movements in the world, especially in the wake of the end of cold war and the collapse of the Soviet Union.

Amid this political turmoil in Lebanon, with both political camps accusing each other of a lack of patriotism and of dependence on foreign forces, two different visions of the Lebanese nation have emerged. Many observers viewed this period as a test for Hizbullah to prove its loyalty to Lebanon, because the March 14 Forces (and many independent Lebanese) and much of the Western media were arguing that patriotism is linked to the implementation of the 1559 resolution. In contrast, Hizbullah considers its own armed resistance in the south as the supreme act of patriotism. Yet again, in most Western media the networks of the March 14 Forces to Western governments are presented as contributing to a free and democratic Lebanon, while the transnational networks Shi'ites maintain have been portrayed as conflicting with their patriotism and their commitment to Lebanon.

Whether Nasrallah is a "patriot or stooge" is a question that evokes a particular ideology of the Lebanese nation, naturalizing one kind of foreign interference while condemning others, and that reproduces the discourse of anti-Hizbullah Lebanese groups, which marginalizes Shi'ites as full citizens in Lebanon. It also misses the larger point argued in this book that Shi'ite activism is precisely about breaking the mainly Christian and Sunni claims over the nation. In this recent Christian-Sunni national vision of the Sanyura cabinet, Hizbullah and Amal can be patriots only if they submit to the will of the current government, limit their political ambitions, and renounce their right to be more strongly represented in the parliament and in national decision making, according to the terms granted by the constitution. From such a perspective, only through acknowledging that they are politically and culturally marginal can Shi'ites be true Lebanese patriots. Their insistence on the terms of the constitution, i.e., representation in the cabinet, parliament, and civil service proportional to the numerical size of the communities, has drawn accusations of sectarianism and antinational attitudes.

The events since the assassination of Hariri have demonstrated the continuing importance of these center-periphery struggles and the importance of engaging in a certain type of nationalist discourse for maintaining political power and cultural hegemony. As suggested in the introduction, sectarianism is a label applied by various political groups to those whose political agenda is not in line with one's own. Sectarianism, in other words, is a set of activities aimed at breaking the hegemony of other groups in claiming the nation. Like all other ideologies, it has two goals: to denaturalize what others seek to make seem natural and to present its own visions as normative. To challenge the previously hegemonic image of the nation is a Shi'ite journey that started in the 1960s, and one which has brought Shi'ites so far as to create their own political parties that now pose a serious challenge to the Sanyura government. In the view of many Shi'ites, the Lebanese state can be legitimate only if it fully includes them in the nation-making process.

The War of July–August 2006

Hizbullah's kidnapping of two Israeli soldiers on July 12, 2006, triggered thirty-four days of heavy Israeli air and ground attacks on Lebanon, to which Hizbullah, although admittedly surprised, responded by fighting the Israeli army in Lebanon and by firing a large number of missiles on northern Israel. About a million Lebanese, mainly Shi'ites from the south, were displaced. Israel destroyed much of Lebanon's infrastructure and flattened large parts of al-Dahiyya, and the war has caused billions of dollars in damage to

Lebanon. Tourists, one of the main sources of income for Lebanese, fled, and few returned in the following year.

Hizbullah's nationalism manifests itself in the unconditional fight against Zionism and an acceptance that suffering and loss are part of upholding this notion of social justice. This war has greatly reemphasized the divergence of Hizbullah's nationalism from the Maronite or Sunni bourgeoisie visions of Lebanon. Hizbullah positions Lebanon as part of an Islamic and Arab nation in which it wants Lebanon and its party to take an exemplary role. The vision of a tranquil Christian village in Mount Lebanon, or that of a Monte Carlo of the Middle East, is farthest from how Hizbullah hopes to shape this nation. Neither are Hizbullah's ideologues, unlike Hariri, enthralled by a nationalism that imagines Lebanon as an investment haven and an upper-middle-class society with neoliberal economics. To Hariri's nationalism, tourists in the summer season were a visible sign of Lebanon's economic potential and its stable political prospect and future that in turn enhanced his *own* economic projects. Conversely, UN Resolution 1559 demanded the disarming of Hizbullah.

Notwithstanding the fact that Hizbullah did not expect such heavy Israeli retaliations and hoped to exchange those soldiers for their own who were captives in Israel, a practice that had been established a few years earlier, the timing of the kidnapping of the Israeli soldiers in July 2006, the high point of tourism in Lebanon, has shown how Hizbullah's vision of Lebanon diverges from that of Hariri, for example.

The Iranian government's support of Hizbullah has again helped it to win over Arab public opinion (some have even compared Nasrallah to Nasser), while the governments of some Arab states, especially those with close ties to the United States, such as Jordan, Egypt, and Saudi Arabia, have become even more suspicious of Iran's role in the Arab world.

The war between Israel and Lebanon ended on August 14, 2006, with UN Security Council Resolution 1701. The resolution called for a ceasefire between Israel and Lebanon, for Israeli withdrawal of its forces from Lebanese territories (excluding Shaba'a' Farms) while UN forces should be deployed throughout the south and along the borders, and for Hizbullah's disarming and the full control by the Lebanese government and its legitimate army over Lebanese territories.

Hizbullah, with financial backing from the Iranian ruling elite, engaged immediately in massive reconstruction and provided some compensation for many of those war victims. The Lebanese government, on the other hand, was slow to act (some say on purpose) and engaged only halfheartedly in reconstruction efforts. Other Arab states seek to compete with the massive reconstruction effort by Hizbullah, which enhances Hizbullah's prestige as they acknowledge its existence and power as deserving of competition.

The summer war brought Hizbullah-Iranian relations into the limelight again. Many argued that Hizbullah was fighting Iran's war against the United States on Lebanese territory and that its methods of resistance against the Israeli forces gave a taste of what a United States war against Iran would look like. It was an opportunity for some to again present Hizbullah as a puppet of the Iranian government that was willing to scarify Lebanese lives to please its leaders in Iran. Hizbullah leaders, as they themselves admit, had not anticipated such a reaction from Israel after the kidnapping, but they said that they were well aware that Israel had planned a war against Hizbullah whether or not the kidnapping had taken place. The timing simply had not yet been clear. Israel had hoped to finish off Hizbullah by destroying the neighborhoods in which it is strongly represented, understanding or preferring to believe that what Hizbullah members referred to as resistance was simply a relatively small militia. In fact, the resistance was part of the culture of a large section of the Shi'ite community, even among those Shi'ites who did not sympathize directly with Hizbullah. They were not neatly separable entities, as Israel had hoped they were, and this posed the biggest challenge to Israel during the war and will remain a puzzle for it and for the United States. As mentioned in chapter 3, for example, when Iranian volunteers moved to al-Biqa' in 1982, they wanted to propagate and, most important, to popularize the idea that Israel is defeatable. To fight Hizbullah the way Israel did only enhanced its position and made it a global example for fighting imperialism among many in the Muslim world.

But how can one define Hizbullah-Iranian relations in a way that is neither dismissive of these ties nor gives them too much importance? In other words, what makes Hizbullah Lebanese? I ask this question to frame a discussion of the way production of any type of national identity takes place in an increasingly dense transnational world and not as a way to reproduce and engage in the discourse of those anti-Hizbullah Lebanese groups who marginalize Hizbullah and other Shi'ites by presenting them as outside the mainstream of Lebanese nationalism.

Hizbullah, as is well known, shares with the Iranian ruling elite, especially Khamenei and his circle, common notions of piety: the belief that "guardianship by the Jurist-Theologian is imperative for the preservation and implementation of Islam."[2] However, sharing common notions of piety does *not* necessarily mean that both ends in this transnational network have a fixed definition of what this Islam is composed of. In other words, the boundary between Islam and non-Islam is constantly negotiated and is a source of disagreement and debate.

Based on my own ethnographic observations, some of which are reflected in chapter 2 when I discuss the failed attempts at teaching Persian in the Lebanese Martyr's School and in chapter 5 when I tell the story of how Hizbullah barred Iranian preachers from entering their *husayniyyas* during Muharram in 2003, I suggest that it is exactly in these transnational debates with the Iranian government over what falls under authentic Islam and the nature of this *marja'* network that part of Hizbullah's *Lebanese* identity is constructed.

While Hizbullah's relation to Khamenei is ideally structured through *vilayat-i faqih*, which obliges Hizbullah to obey the fatwas of Khamenei and structure all aspects of life according to his rulings, the story is obviously more complicated than this. The Iranian government and Hizbullah are involved with each other through a whole set of institutions, bureaucracies, and economies (shareholding in Hizbullah's supermarket chains is one example). Although Hizbullah is in charge of its own institutions, it inevitably works with other Iranian institutions who claim in some way or other to be representatives of the *marja'* network. That is because, as shown in chapter 5, many of those Iranian officials do not distinguish between the *marja'* network and the Iranian government. As I argued previously, the distinction is in fact an artificial one as the Iranian government is pursuing its religious nationalist agenda in Lebanon partially through the *marja'* network.

I suggest that Hizbullah members selectively choose from the flow of the network those elements that prove useful for their agenda in Lebanon. I argue that Hizbullah members consider some activities to be authentic Islam, while rejecting other Iranian *marja'* and government activities and labeling them as Iranian rather than authentically Islamic. In fact, many Hizbullah members made a distinction between two categories of activities when speaking about their relation to the Iranian government and explaining the nature of their transnational ties. They referred to one as Iranian, meaning those activities of Iranian institutions and officials which they did not believe supported their project in Lebanon and which were thus labeled as nationalist, the goal of which was to subjugate Hizbullah to a specifically ethnic and linguistic nationalism that had nothing to do with what they argued to be part of this ideal-typical Islam.

Hizbullah members referred to activities with which they agreed and which they believed supported their own projects in Lebanon as being based on the *marja'* network, thus seemingly void of Iranian nationalist ideologies and representing authentic Islam and appropriate to these networks. Hizbullah members did not view such flows in these networks as attempts to create Iranian hegemony over Lebanese Shi'ites but as defining the relation between a *marja'* and his followers. Most often, Iranian officials in Lebanon argued that *all* their activities are part of the *marja'* network, which led to the kind of tensions between Hizbullah followers and Iranian officials discussed in previous chapters. In this common Islamic space, what is Iranian, what is Lebanese, what is authentic Islam, what is inauthentic Islam, and what falls under those aspects is negotiated daily and changes over time as well. I do not want to portray Hizbullah as cynical and opportunistic but merely want to point to its agency and to the fact that where they draw the boundary between authentic and inauthentic Islam is how they position themselves as specifically Lebanese. Further research is needed in this direction instead of solely focusing on the more intellectual writings and speeches of representatives of Hizbullah and the Iranian ruling elite, or describing Hizbullah's institutions and their formal functions. Important as they are, such scholarly works do not show us clearly the tensions between Hizbullah and the Iranian ruling elite; as a result, an important part of the making of Hizbullah's nationalism goes missing.

With its resistance activities backed by the Iranian ruling religious elite, Hizbullah has been able to establish itself as a champion of *Arab* nationalism, and as a religious group worthy of emulation among both Sunnis and Shi'ites in the Arab world and beyond. Through its daily practices, Hizbullah has also shown that it is not a puppet of the Iranian ruling religious elite but a partner, even if a junior one, that must be taken seriously and negotiated with. The *vali* in Iran, also, does not issue rulings that Hizbullah is likely to be unable or unwilling to follow, as he is well aware of its particular position in Lebanon and the importance of its engaging in discourses and performances that emphasize the party's independence from Iran. One can even go so far as to say that Khamenei's rulings and fatwas are issued in light of negotiations and are a product of dialogic, multilevel conversations taking place behind the scenes with Hizbullah that are *not* expressed in the form of theological and legal debates. The fatwas, after all, are not created in an empty space but are issued to address a specific sociopolitical and historical context. As such, Hizbullah, while junior in position compared to the *vali*, exercises its agency. The fatwas, although pronounced by a single authority, Khamenei in this case, are much more a product of dialogue than anyone involved (or for that matter most decision makers in the West) would like to admit. While Hizbullah derives meaning from *vilayat-i faqih*, it also takes part in the shaping of rulings by the *vali*.

The summer war in Lebanon, in fact, created an obstacle in the Iranian government's project in Lebanon, since it was slowly building its networks beyond the Lebanese Shi'ite community and establishing relations with Jumblat and Hariri. After the end of the war, it seems the Iranian government is again at a position comparable to 1990 when the Lebanese civil war ended and when Hizbullah was viewed as a representative of the Iranians. It is in the interest of the Iranian government to emphasize Hizbullah's independence from Iran (no matter how much in fact it desires the reverse) because the ruling elite has realized that to safeguard their long-term interest in Lebanon they need to establish ties beyond Hizbullah and beyond the Shi'ite community and to support Hizbullah's project of embedding itself in the Lebanese political scene as much as possible.

But what did the war mean to other Shi'ite groups such as Amal? For its part, Amal has become a mediator between Hizbullah and the Lebanese state. Amal sent some of its militia forces to the south to fight alongside Hizbullah against the Israeli invasion. Berri, the leader of Amal and the speaker of the Lebanese parliament, had his own calculations for this show of solidarity. By sending its militia to the south, Amal presented itself as a party as much concerned about defending the nation as was Hizbullah, while at the same time reaping the benefits among Shi'ites by presenting itself as fighting Zionism. In the Lebanese Shi'ite context, this solidarity among competitors shows the interdependence of each of these Shi'ite nationalisms and how, through a politics of solidarity and boundary making among these Shi'ite groups, each strengthens its own vision of Lebanon and wins legitimacy among Lebanese Shi'ites. To Amal, Hizbullah's 2006 kidnapping of Israeli soldiers has been perhaps its best chance to win support among Lebanese Shi'ites and the wider Shi'ite world and to enhance its position among non-Shi'ite Lebanese as the only Shi'ite party capable of some negotiation. In an interesting way then, Amal's support of Hizbullah cannot be viewed outside the context of their competition.

My argument has been that, in an era of transnationalism, religious identities cannot be studied outside their national context. What makes studies of the triangle of transnationalism, nationalism, and religion interesting and worthwhile is the way in which such religious nationalisms are produced in a transnational era. In other words, the task is to analyze how religious groups with transnational ties position themselves within the nation against the backdrop of a widely held view that national identifications and religious solidarities with transnational dimensions are separate and irreconcilable forces.

The Presidential Elections of 2007

Since December 2006, supporters of the opposition—Amal, Hizbullah, and 'Aounists—have turned Martyrs Square into a tent city, where it is demanded that the government resign. As a protest against details of UN Resolution 1559, Shi'ite members of the government resigned and Berri, the Speaker of the parliament, does not convene the parliament. As a result, government decisions cannot be passed as all require a two-thirds majority vote and the members of the March 14 Forces have only sixty-eight seats of 128 seats in the parliament now. In other words, the government is in a deadlock.

Of the Lebanese loyalist politicians currently in the majority in the parliament, Sanyura, Sa'd Hariri, and Jumblat have each taken trips to Saudi Arabia, the United States, and France (and have maintained close ties to the current U.S. ambassador, David Feltman) to rally support for keeping their power in the government. They have engaged in a discourse of maintaining the sovereignty and independence of Lebanon. They have portrayed the opposition as fanatics who want to destroy Lebanese democracy and freedom and to turn Lebanon into a satellite state of Iran and Syria. In effect, the rhetoric of the political marginalization of Lebanese Shi'ites since the success of the Iranian revolution has changed little: its core has been always to portray Shi'ites as stooges of foreigners, especially of Iran and its ally Syria. To government supporters, the opposition is still the puppet of the Iranians and Syrians, while they are defenders of pluralism and democracy.

When Lebanon was created, Shi'ites made up that large but invisible population conveniently situated in the al-Biqa' and South Lebanon away from Beirut. They were a largely unwanted population forcefully brought into the map of so-called real Lebanon. In the 1960s, Shi'ites became more politically visible, slowly challenging the Maronite-Sunni dominated state.

The civil war brought these marginalized citizens to the center of attention, not just in Lebanon but to a wider international public. Their opponents sought to politically and culturally marginalize Shi'ites by portraying them as backward and antimodern, but then the discourse that they were anti-national did not yet exist, as they were hardly viewed as part of that nation. Then were added to the list of negative labels their supposedly excessive religiosity and their transnational, rather than national, identity. Now they are presented as antinational *and* antidemocratic and as having a pathological desire for martyrdom. These tend to be negative labels that resonate more globally than does the traditional image of Shi'ites as unfit for full citizenship because of their assumed lack of education and status as a predominantly rural underclass. To appeal for support to a Western global audience, supporters of the current government seek to present Shi'ites (and their Christian 'Aounist allies) as undermining democratic values in order to justify their relative exclusion. The Sanyura government is well aware of U.S. interests in Lebanon and willingly cooperates with them. It envisions a close relation among Saudi Arabia, Lebanon, and the United States, creating an alliance against what is perceived to be the growing power of Iran. This cooperation in turn should ideally ensure the Sanyura government's relative dominance.

With the November 2007 deadline for the presidential elections approaching, the two camps have initially insisted on their own candidates. The opposition proposed 'Aoun, while the government loyalists rejected this candidate, proposing instead those with close ties to the United States (such as Nassib Lahoud, a former Lebanese ambassador to the United States) and deep ties to the world of industry and financing. Finally in September 2007, Berri, playing the role of broker between feuding camps, suggested that the involved parties agree on a consensus candidate. This would effectively mean that both camps agree on a president ahead of the elections. In the beginning, the March 14 Forces rejected this proposal, as it would go against their plans for electing the future president, but because of the intervention of Maronite patriarch Boutros Sfeir, negotiations are under way at this time to elect a president who would not be affiliated with either camp but would supposedly represent the interest of all the citizens in Lebanon.

However, the possible election of a neutral president will change little in the overall dynamics of Lebanese politics. As long as political sectarianism is not abolished, decisions in politics will take the form of consensus, not because of democratic values, but because the other option would be a civil war, for which none of the parties involved is fully prepared. Consensus in this case is likely to mean a lack of movement and the maintenance of the status quo, and a delay in dealing with major disagreements between the opposing parties. But, even now, the alignment of the Maronite 'Aoun with two rivaling Shi'ite parties shows the potential for a democratic political landscape for Lebanon, where there will be no certainty that Amal and Hizbullah will form an alliance against other political (sectarian) groups and seek to form a Shi'ite-dominated government. As this book has made clear, the differences between Amal and Hizbullah are considerable. This is not to say that they will always remain so, but their visions of Lebanon do differ greatly. If they are allied now, it is because of political sectarianism that makes their followers expect such a display of solidarity and forces them as members of the same community to unite to achieve their goals. If twenty years ago, when in September 1988 'Aoun formed a government in East Beirut, and in 1989 declared a war to liberate Lebanon from the Syrian presence, someone had predicted that 'Aoun will ally itself with Hizbullah and Amal—those two Shi'ite parties now accused of being stooges of Syrian and Iranian interests—it would have seemed like an extremely unlikely prediction. If in twenty years from now political sectarianism is abolished, the Lebanese and the wider international public will be astonished about the political pluralism that might be possible in Lebanon. Then, perhaps, the Lebanese could with some justification feel that their democracy is superior to that of their neighboring countries.

Iraq Since 2003: History and Memory

Concerns about the shifting, context-dependent, and constructed nature of ethnic, linguistic, religious, and cultural differences between Lebanese Arab and Iranian Shi'ites—and the political tactics of the Lebanese state to marginalize Shi'ites by presenting them as sectarian and as stooges of foreign powers, particularly of Iran, which I have placed at the center of my analysis—are equally applicable to the Iraqi context. Although the historical context of Shi'ite politics in Iraq is quite different from that of Lebanon, nonetheless similar to Hizbullah's portrayal by its opponents as agents of the Iranian government, many in the United States administration and many Sunnis in the Middle East have accused Iraqi Shi'ites as serving the interests of Iran in Iraq after Saddam. And, similar to Shi'ites in Lebanon, Iraqi

Shi'ites have represented the largest religious community among the Iraqi population—about 60 percent—without adequate political representation in the government until recently. So one can draw some parallels between the identity politics of the Iraqi and Lebanese Shi'ites without ignoring the historical and political uniqueness of each country and each community.

Historically, Shi'ite ties between the territories of modern Iraq and Iran have been dense, with few interruptions, and have also been characterized by many political tensions. Iraqi-Iranian transnational networks represent an interesting and complex web of economic, political, and marital relationships, wars, and religious exchanges, memories of which both sides can draw on to build solidarities and shared identifications or to construct differences and draw boundaries. To understand current Iranian relations with various Iraqi Shi'ite factions and parties, one needs to study exactly how the complex memories of these relations are produced. There are no transnational ties that reproduce simply based on mere arms supply, secret negotiations between leaders, and a notion of a common enemy. To create solidarity, shared memories are of central importance. It is in moments of agreement over narratives of the past that ethnic and linguistic barriers, those components of identity that seem so natural and fixed for many, are weakened.

For example, to understand the nuances of the relationship between the Supreme Islamic Iraqi Council (SIIC), until recently known as the Supreme Council of the Islamic Revolution in Iraq (SCIRI), an Iraqi Shi'ite political party formed in Tehran in November 1982 where many of its members had taken refuge from the Ba'ath regime, and the Iranian government, it is not enough to point out that they both envision an Islamic government according to the rule of the jurisprudent. Neither can one understand their relationship by pointing out that SIIC's military wing, the Badr organization, spent years in Iran and established ties with Iranian paramilitaries. As seductive as this narrative seems, nuances of SIIC identity politics, and ultimately their vision of Iraq, get lost. To reflect the complexity of these ties and do justice to their agency, the voices of these members have to be heard. How would SIIC's members describe their relation to Iran? Do they position this episode of their lives spent in Iran within a larger framework of transnational Shi'ite ties, and, if so, on what memories do they draw to create such narratives of solidarity? What does Shi'ite transnationalism mean to them, and how do they imagine its hierarchies? It is only when we have answers to these types of questions that a more complete picture of Iranian-Iraqi Shi'ite ties can emerge. Below, I give one example of the complexity, but also the flexibility, of Shi'ite identities: that of the currently most important political figure in Iraq, Ayatollah 'Ali Husayni Sistani.

Sistani or al-Sistani? Iranian or Iraqi?

The severely anti-Shi'ite politics of Saddam and the Iran-Iraq War resulted in the decline of Najaf as a center of religious learning. As the newly established Shi'ite government in Iran promoted Qom as a prestigious center of religious learning (as a way to propagate its own version of Shi'ism), Shi'ite religious students from all over the world moved to Qom. Although Qom became a center of learning under the guidance and supervision of the Iranian government, many religious scholars, both Iranian and non-Iranian, resisted the government's attempted control over religious affairs and disagreed with Khomeini's reading of the principle of the rule of the jurisprudent (*vilayat-i faqih*) which gave Khomeini, and then Khamenei, the position of the highest *marja'* and power over both the spiritual and temporal worlds.

One of the most well known of these religious scholars has been Sayyid 'Ali Husayni Sistani. Born in Mashhad in 1930, Sistani completed the first part of his theological education there and then moved to Qom to study with Ayatollah Borujerdi in 1949. After three years of study in the theological school in Qom, Sistani moved back to Mashhad to complete his education with Ayatollah Kho'i, becoming the grand-*marja'* following Kho'i's death in 1992 in Najaf. Currently, Sistani is considered the most important Shi'ite power broker on the Iraqi political scene.

The Iranian origin of Sistani and his supposedly thick Persian accent have forced Sistani to take a position and to explain his motives in Iraq. Many Sunnis in Iraq automatically assumed that Sistani, as an Iranian religious scholar, would favor an Islamic government for Iraq oriented toward the political concept of *vilayat-i faqih*. This became most obvious when a delegation of Sunni tribal chiefs, among them Ibrahim al-Shawi, the leader of the Sunni al-Shawi tribe from central Iraq, visited Sistani in February 2004. These leaders wanted to know for themselves what Sistani's position was on the political future of Iraq and the role of Shi'ites in it. Al-Shawi's first impression about Sistani was: "He had a heavy (and I mean really heavy) Persian accent which he didn't (and couldn't) hide. He used classical Arabic, but the structure of his sentence was not perfect." But then, after he listened to Sistani's views on the future of Iraq, and found out that Sistani was against the concept of the *vilayat-i faqih*, al-Shawi concluded: "[Sistani] mentioned the Arab Nation so many times! He evidently viewed himself as an Arab. Being born Persian did not affect the fact that he was a Sayyid [a descendant of the Prophet Muhammad]. He made that perfectly clear."[3]

In other words, Sistani had to position himself as an Arab within an Iraqi national narrative, and capitalize on his Sayyid origins, according to which his genealogy can be traced back to the *Arab* family of the Prophet Muhammad, in order to carry out his activities as a Shi'ite *marja'* and to be influential in the politics of Iraq. Al-Shawi and the other Sunni leaders were content with Sistani's views, and thus it seems that his Persian accent, just like the accent of Musa Sadr, then appeared as a mere coincidence, not a marker of his "foreign" identity that linked him to the imposition of an Islamic state as in Iran. These Sunni leaders, just like Amal members, drew on a discourse of distant genealogical origin to position Sistani within the Iraqi national narrative, as they had found Sistani's vision of the future of Iraq more favorable compared with that of Muqtada al-Sadr and other Shi'ite leaders.

Many view Muqtada al-Sadr, the son of the late Iraqi Shi'ite leader Muhammad Sadiq al-Sadr (d. 1999), as an agent of Iranian interests in Iraq. Muhammad Sadiq al-Sadr had organized the poor Iraqi Shi'ites in a manner recalling the activities of *harakat al-mahrumin* led by Musa Sadr in Lebanon. The connection between Muqtada al-Sadr and official Iran is made because Muqtada al-Sadr desires to establish an Islamic government in Iraq and because his anti-U.S. polemic echoes Iran's official line. Yet, in reality, Muqtada al-Sadr was until recently a follower of Ayatollah Kazim al-Ha'iri (b. 1938 in Karbala), a former student of Muqtada al-Sadr's father and currently living in Qom, who is against the doctrine of *vilayat-i faqih* and competes with 'Ali Khamenei in winning followers. Both Muqtada al-Sadr and Sistani also compete to win support among Iraqi Shi'ites, while both promote different versions of Iraqi religious nationalism. Muqtada al-Sadr points to the Iranian origins of Sistani and presents himself as the only true Arab Iraqi Shi'ite leader as a way to exclude him from Iraqi national politics. Because of Muqtada al-Sadr's junior position in religious education and because many Iraqi Shi'ites disagree with the activities of his militia, however, he does not pose a serious threat to the established authority of Sistani in Iraq.

Saddam made use of a very similar discourse and logic when he expelled thousands of so-called 'Ajamis from Iraq beginning in the mid-1970s, guided by the rationale that no matter how long one lives in another country, bonds of origin and ancestry are stronger; thus, 'Ajami Shi'ites represent a threat to the Iraqi nation. Yet, in the case of Iraqi Shi'ites, Saddam's policy of systematically excluding Shi'ites from the Iraqi nation and national narrative has had the effect of artificially separating religious identity from national identity. This Arab national identity as promoted by Saddam, which in reality reflected an unmarked Sunni-dominated ideology, came to be viewed as promoting secular nationalism. Thus, by envisioning two neatly separable identities, Saddam had been able to accuse Iraqi and 'Ajami Shi'ites of loyalty to the enemy nation, Iran, and of sectarianism.

A Shi'ite Crescent?

It should by now have become obvious that a putative Shi'ite crescent in the Middle East, as unlikely as its formation is, will be as divided as the Sunni-dominated Arab states. There is a cacophony of Shi'ite voices, each of which claims to represent the best path to more social justice; to more economic security and political independence; and to provide just the right blend between religion and politics. To achieve these visions and to marginalize their Shi'ite competitors, these Shi'ite groups will ally with Sunni, Christian, Kurdish, or other like-minded Shi'ite groups.

There is competition over political power and dominance over state resources, and so far for the previously Sunni leadership in Iraq and now the Sunni insurgents there, as well as for the present government in Lebanon, the preferred strategy to sideline these new, emerging Shi'ite forces has been to return to the old rhetoric used by the Ottoman sultans and their officials. There supposedly was a Shi'ite problem, as one presumably could not rely on their allegiance to the Sunni sultan, who presented itself as the guardian of authentic Islam. Specifically, Shi'ites posed a threat to the Ottoman empire because of their religious affinity with the rival Safavid and Qajar powers. But the late Ottomans, especially under Sultan Abdülhamid, sought to solve that so-called problem precisely because they were interested in maintaining their dominance. Activities of Shi'ite religious leaders among the Iraqi tribes and their mass conversions to Shi'ism in the last quarter of the nineteenth century worried the Ottoman officials increasingly who saw this as strengthening the position of their Persian rival in Ottoman territories.[4] In the Ottoman *vilayets* of Baghdad and Basra, for example, the late Ottoman government first attempted to integrate Shi'ites through educational and other policies and guide them to the right path, that is, to eventually persuade them to convert to Sunnism. When this project failed, and once the Ottomans acknowledged that considerable differences existed between Shi'ite religious groups in Ottoman Iraq and Qajar Persia, the Ottoman sultan encouraged pan-Islamic unity and rapprochement between Sunnis and Shi'ites to weaken the power of their rivals in Persia and to strengthen the empire against the encroaching Western interests. However, British colonial interests prevented that project and, soon after, World War I began.

Currently, the Sanyura government in Lebanon as well as some other Arab states (mainly Jordan, Egypt, and Saudi Arabia) are engaged in the old sectarian rhetoric with its Ottoman genealogy. The Iranian government is advocating pan-Islamic unity precisely to combat the marginalization of Shi'ites and to promote its own policies in the Middle East as a powerful broker in the region. If, as Vali Nasr suggests, current political struggles in the Middle East are framed in sectarian rhetoric,[5] Shi'ite and Sunni leaders in Iraq should engage in Sunni–Shi'ite rapprochement and appeal to Islamic unity, which would allow the formation of a pluralistic government in Iraq. They could counter both U.S. and Iranian hegemonic plans, if that is what they desire at all. There is no way to establish total Sunni dominance over Shi'ites anymore. That is a fact.

The question now in these mixed sectarian countries, but specifically in Iraq, remains one of power sharing. Given the political differences among Shi'ites, in the long run the best way for (secular and Islamist) Sunnis to preserve some of their power is to agree to and to fully participate in democratic elections. This at first sight seems to mean the end of Sunni power (if one can speak of such a homogeneous bloc at all), but Shi'ite parties tend to unite only when they attempt to break a hegemony, and once that does not exist anymore, their differences provide possibilities for pluralism and alliances across sectarian and ethnic lines.

In the current context of the Middle East, unequal access to political power and state resources have the potential to promote sectarian readings of tensions. As the latter can take on a reality of their own, so that Sunnis and Shi'ites view themselves as naturally in opposition to the other, so can they be deconstructed in ways that are not defined through antagonism, while differences are acknowledged.

For many reasons, this is the era of Islamism in the Middle East, but Islam has the capacity to incorporate many of the notions that secularists advocate, above all democracy and pluralism, and to advance many of the political causes secularists in the Middle East have wished for (one cannot argue for the reverse). After all, it should be recalled that the boundary between religion and secularism leaks. A willingness to share power across sectarian lines should be followed by acknowledging the diversity among Shi'ites and accepting that there is *no* inherent logic that Iran is the center of Shi'ism and that Shi'ites from other parts of the world coordinate their activities with Iran. Every appeal for transnational religious solidarity and for postnationalism is rooted somewhere in a nationalist agenda. The future power struggles in the Middle East might then not be cast in the familiar tensions between secularists and Islamists or Sunnis versus Shi'ites, but defined in new, unexpected alliances across these lines.

NOTES

Preface

1. Rula Jurdi Abisaab, "Shi'ite Beginnings and Scholastic Tradition in Jabal 'Amil in Lebanon," *Muslim World* 89 (January 1999): 1–21.

2. Theodor Hanf, *Coexistence in Wartime Lebanon: Decline of a State and Rise of a Nation* (London: I. B. Tauris, 1993), 72.

Introduction

1. *Daily Star*, 18 November 2003.

2. *Daily Star*, 8 November 2004.

3. For a discussion of how Michel Chiha, one of the main ideologues of Lebanese Christian nationalism, constructed a Lebanese national narrative based on Christian hegemony, see Michelle Hartman and Alessandro Olsaretti, "The First Boat and the First Oar," *Radical History Review* 86 (2003): 37–65.

4. Anderson, *Imagined Communities: Reflections on the Origin and Spread of Nationalism* (London: Verso, 1991); Gellner, *Nations and Nationalism* (Ithaca: Cornell University Press, 1983).

5. "Britishness and Otherness: An Argument," *Journal of British Studies* 31 (October 1992): 309–29.

6. *Religious Nationalism: Hindus and Muslims in India* (Berkeley: University of California Press, 1994).

7. Van der Veer and Hartmut Lehmann, eds., *Nation and Religion: Perspectives on Europe and Asia* (Princeton: Princeton University Press, 1999); Van der Veer, *Imperial Encounters: Religion and Modernity in India and Britain* (Princeton: Princeton University Press, 2001).

8. An exception is Hartman and Olsaretti, "The First Boat."

9. Talal Asad, *Genealogies of Religion: Discipline and Reasons of Power in Christianity and Islam* (Baltimore: Johns Hopkins University Press, 1993).

10. Amal Saad-Ghorayeb, *Hizbullah: Politics and Religion* (London: Pluto, 2002), 190; Sami Ofeish, "Lebanon's Second Republic: Secular Talk, Sectarian Application," *Arab Studies Quarterly* (Winter 1999): 97–116.

11. Saad-Ghorayeb, *Hizbullah*, 191.

12. Talal Asad, *Formations of the Secular: Christianity, Islam, Modernity* (Stanford: Stanford University Press, 2003).

13. "When Ethnic Identity Is a Social Stigma," in Fredrik Barth, ed., *Ethnic Groups and Boundaries: The Social Organization of Cultural Difference* (Boston: Little Brown, 1969).

14. Ussama Makdisi, *The Culture of Sectarianism* (Berkeley: University of California Press, 2000).

15. Samir Khalaf, *Cultural Resistance: Global and Local Encounters in the Middle East* (Beirut: Saqi, 2002), ch. 9.

16. Sami Ofeisch, "Lebanon's Second Republic."

17. For a detailed discussion of Mahdi 'Amil's views on sectarianism see Kais Firro, *Inventing Lebanon* (London: I. B. Tauris, 2003), 62.

18. Makdisi, *The Culture of Sectarianism*, 174.

19. Ibid., 166.

20. Brubaker and Cooper, "Beyond 'Identity.'"

21. Ibid., 4–5.

22. See, for example, Aida Kanafani-Zahar, "The Religion of the 'Other' as Bond: The Interreligious in Lebanon," in Thomas Scheffler, ed., *Religion between Violence and Reconciliation* (Würzburg: Ergon Verlag, 2002), 401–18; Theodor Hanf, *Coexistence in Wartime Lebanon: Decline of a State and Rise of a Nation* (London: I. B. Tauris, 1993).

23. Makdisi, *The Culture of Sectarianism*, 166, 174.

24. Among many other scholars, see Waddah Sharara, *Dawlat Hizb Allah: Lubnan mujtama'an islamiyyan* (Beirut: Dar al-Nahar, 1996).

25. "The Politics of Identity in the Middle East International Relations" in Louise Fawcett, ed., *International Relations of the Middle East* (Oxford: Oxford University Press, 2005), 171.

26. *The Arab Shi'a: The Forgotten Muslims* (New York: St. Martin's Press, 1999), 72, 77.

27. "The Nature of Shi'ism in Iraq," in Faleh Abdul-Jabar, ed., *Ayatollahs, Sufis and Ideologues: State, Religion, and Social Movements in Iraq* (London: Saqi, 2002), 23–35.

28. *Sacred Space and Holy War: The Politics, Culture and History of Shi'ite Islam* (London: I. B. Tauris, 2002), 1.

29. *The Renewal of Islamic Law: Muhammad Baqer as-Sadr, Najaf and the Shi'i International* (Cambridge: Cambridge University Press, 1993), 45–46.

30. Shimon Shapira, *Hizbullah Between Iran and Lebanon* (Tel Aviv: Hakibbutz Hameuchad, 2000) [in Hebrew]; Roger Shanahan, *The Shi'a of Lebanon: Clans, Parties and Clerics* (London: I. B. Tauris, 2005), 139.

31. 'Abbas William Samii, "The Shah's Lebanon Policy: The Role of SAVAK," *Middle Eastern Studies* 33, no. 1 (1997): 66–91.

1. Two Nations and One State

1. *Tadhkirati* can mean "my identity card" or "my ticket," but in this context she is clearly referring to an identity card.

2. *Da'at mini al-huwiyya.* The word *huwiyya* means identity. She is referring to an identity card as *huwiyya* using an idiomatic shorthand, but she is also playing on the word to actually mean that her identity was lost.

3. *Ajyal al-Mustafa* 18 (2001): 55. The poem was written by Marwa Harb, a student at al-Mustafa School in Nabatiyya, a Shi'ite-run school closely associated with Hizbullah and the Iranian ruling elite.

4. Kais Firro, *Inventing Lebanon* (London: I. B. Tauris, 2003), 11.

5. For a discussion of Lebanese Maronite nationalism, see Walid Phares, *Lebanese Christian Nationalism: The Rise and Fall of an Ethnic Resistance* (Boulder, CO: Lynne Rienner, 1995); Asher Kaufman, "Reviving Phoenicia: The Search for an Identity in Lebanon," Ph.D. diss., Brandeis University, 2000. For scholarship that takes Lebanese nationalism as a Maronite project see, among many other scholars, Meir Zamir, *The Formation of Modern Lebanon* (Ithaca, NY: Cornell University Press, 1985).

6. Raghid el-Solh, *Lebanon and Arabism: National Identity and State Formation* (London: I. B. Tauris, 2004).

7. Michael Johnson, *Class and Client in Beirut: The Sunni Muslim Community and the Lebanese State 1840–1985* (London: Ithaca, 1986), 78.

8. The Lebanese TV channel *al-Mustaqbal* (Future TV) owned by Hariri provides yet another avenue to study his type of nationalism and his vision of Lebanon. Hariri's own Web site, in which he laid out his vision of Lebanon, is congruent with the ads on Future TV. Pictures of downtown reconstruction, graduation ceremonies of students, the Lebanese flag, and scenes of building new highways were a common feature of his futuristic and optimistic presentation of Lebanon and his eminent role in realizing this vision. He promoted himself for the parliamentary elections in 2000 on his Web site, *www.hariri.com*. His slogan was "Toward a new vision for a new Lebanon." An analysis of his speeches delivered between November 1992 and April 1993 also throws light on how he imagined Lebanon; that is, by his discussing local and international concerns. See Joseph Samaha's article in *al-Nahar*, 20 July 1993, for such an analysis.

9. For a discussion of Solidere's activities, see Heiko Wimmen, "Beirut: Visionen einer Nation," *Beiruter Blätter* 3 (1995): 9–20. For discussions on the politics of reconstructing Beirut, see Peter G. Rowe and Hashim Sarkis, eds., *Projecting Beirut: Episodes in the Construction and Reconstruction of a Modern City* (New York: Prestel, 1998).

10. In his discussion on the reconstruction of downtown Beirut, Saree Makdisi speaks of a discourse of Harirism, comparing it to Reaganism and Thatcherism. In his view, "Harirism offers the public a vastly improved infrastructure—the new cellular phone lines, the new roadways, the new cable television (also owned by Hariri), the new airport and newly expanded air services—whether or not they [the Lebanese] need or can afford to use them . . . indeed to the broad mass of the Lebanese population Harirism has little or nothing to offer." Saree Makdisi, "Laying Claim to Beirut: Urban Narrative and Spatial Identity in the Age of Solidere," *Critical Inquiry* 23 (Spring 1997): 661–705.

11. Hizbullah, for example, forbade its followers from buying shares in Solidere to boycott Hariri's project.

12. Tamara Chalabi, *The Shi'is of Jabal 'Amil and the New Lebanon: Community and Nation-State, 1918–1943* (New York: Palgrave Macmillan, 2006).

13. See chapter 4 in this book for a discussion of why asking whether Musa Sadr was Iranian or Lebanese is problematic.

14. For genealogy and biography of the al-Sadr family, see Sabrina Mervin, *Un Réformisme chiite: Ulémas et lettrés du Gabal 'Amil (actuel Liban-Sud) de la fin de l'empire Ottoman à l'indépendance du Liban* (Paris: Karthala, 2000).

15. For biography and important writings of Baqir al-Sadr, see Chibli Mallat, *The Renewal of Islamic Law: Muhammad Baqer as-Sadr, Najaf and the Shi'i International* (Cambridge: Cambridge University Press, 1993).

16. For more biographical details of Musa Sadr, see Fouad Ajami, *The Vanished Imam: Musa al Sadr and the Shia of Lebanon* (Ithaca: Cornell University Press, 1986). For details on the creation of Amal and its goals, see Richard Augustus Norton, *Amal and the Shi'a: Struggle for the Soul of Lebanon* (Austin: University of Texas Press, 1987).

17. See Hayat Nabeel Osseyran, "The Shi'ite Leadership of South Lebanon: A Reconsideration," M.A. thesis, American University of Beirut, 1997, 123ff.

18. For a contrary argument on the role of the *zu'ama* families and their treatment of Shi'ite masses, see Osseyran, "Shi'ite Leadership of South Lebanon." Note that Hayat Nabeel Osseyran is a member of the family of the Osseyran *zu'ama*; to a certain extent, her M.A. thesis reads as a personal defense of *zu'ama* structures.

19. "Al-Harakat al-wataniyya al-lubnaniyya," *Documents of the Lebanese National Movement 1975–1981* (Beirut, 1981), 7–9. See also Nizah Richani, *Dilemmas of Democracy and Political Parties in Sectarian Societies: The Case of the Progressive Socialist Party of Lebanon, 1949–1996* (New York: St. Martin's, 1998).

20. *Al-Nahar*, 6 August 1969.

21. To mention only a few scholars: Fouad Ajami, *Vanished Imam*; Norton, *Amal and the Shi'a*; Andreas Rieck, *Die Schiiten und der Kampf um den Libanon* (Hamburg: Deutsches Orient-Institut, 1989); Majid Halawi, *A Lebanon Defied: Musa al-Sadr and the Shi'a Community* (Boulder: Westview, 1992); Stefan Rosiny, *Islamismus bei den Shiiten im Libanon: Religion im Übergang von Tradition zur Moderne* (Berlin: Das Arabische Buch, 1996).

22. Sandria Freitag introduces nine common strategies utilized among religious leaders to mobilize communities. "Contesting in Public: Colonial Legacies and Contemporary Communalism," in David Ludden, ed., *Contesting the Nation: Religion, Community, and the Politics of Democracy in India* (Philadelphia: University of Pennsylvania Press, 1996), 220–23.

23. It is worth noting that Mufti Khalid, Lebanon's late Sunni leader, stood firmly against both secularization and political sectarianism as acceptable political structures for Lebanon. His views are in line with Musa Sadr's. See Hasan Khalid, *Al-Muslimun fi Lubnan wa-harb al-sanatayn* (Beirut: Dar al-Kindi, 1978), 24, 84, 299. This book contains interviews as well as speeches by Mufti Khalid.

24. *Kul Shay'*, 14 February 1976 (emphasis added).

25. *Al-Dabbur*, 23 July 1971.

26. A parallel can be drawn between colonial practices in Lebanon and India, in that official colonial divisions into communities and sects created a homogenized image of a large group of people as a religious political community and as a numeric

force sidelining the importance of class, regional, and political divisions. See Mushirul Hasan, "The Myth of Unity," in *Contesting the Nation*, 193.

27. *La Croix* newspaper, 30 August 1970. The following story provides an example of the constructedness of such moral discourses: The late Hasan al-Amin, a well-
known Shi'ite scholar and the son of Muhsin al-Amin, one of the strong promoters
of the concept of *taqrib*, which is Sunni-Shi'ite rapprochement, had been opposed to
Sadr's activities and viewed them as promoting sectarianism and *fitna* among Muslims by insisting on creating specific Shi'ite institutions. (Hasan al-Amin, personal
interview, Beirut, 2 September 2000). Just as Sadr did, al-Amin emphasized the importance of coexistence in Lebanon. See al-Amin views also in *al-Safir*, 1 April 1993.

28. Michel Chiha, quoted in Michelle Hartman and Alessandro Olsaretti, "The
First Boat and the First Oar," *Radical History Review* 86 (2003): 7.

29. Ibid.

30. *Sawt al-Mahrumin*, 1 December 1976 (emphasis added).

31. *Al-Hawadith*, 24 December 1976 (emphasis added).

32. Sandria Freitag, "Contesting in Public," 221.

33. It is interesting to note that piety and grounding in authentic religious tradition has also been identified with good citizenship and successful coexistence in
other nation-states such as India and Mauritius, where the citizenry is officially classified as belonging to separate religious communities. See Patrick Eisenlohr, "The
Politics of Diaspora and the Morality of Secularism: Muslim Identities and Islamic
Authority in Mauritius," *Journal of the Royal Anthropological Institute (new series)* 12
(2006): 395–412; Ashis Nandy, "The Politics of Secularism and the Recovery of Religious Tolerance," in Veena Das, ed., *Mirrors of Violence* (Delhi: Oxford University
Press, 1990), 69–93.

34. See the illuminating article of Mona Fawaz, "Contradicting Urban Regulations and State Practices: The Informal Settlements of Beirut," in Mona Harb, ed.,
The Lebanese National Master Plan (Beirut: American University of Beirut, 2003),
23–33. She shows successfully that state agencies and actors often act in contradiction to legal regulations.

35. Bassim al-Jisr, *Fu'ad Shihab* (Beirut, 2000), 53.

36. For a discussion of the Lebanese civil war of 1975–1990 and Shi'ite involvement, see Robert Fisk, *Pity the Nation: Lebanon at War* (London: Deutsch, 1990); Judith Harik, "The Public and Social Services of the Lebanese Militias," *Papers on Lebanon* 14 (Oxford: Centre for Lebanese Studies, 1994). On the Syrian intervention in
Lebanon and its support for Amal members, see Anoushiravan Ehteshami and Raymond A. Hinnebusch, *Syria and Iran: Middle Powers in a Penetrated Regional System*
(London: Routledge, 1997).

37. *Al-Janub: Dhakirat watan* (Beirut: Majlis al-Janub, 1998), 53.

38. Ibid., 75.

39. *Al-Janub: Dhakirat watan* (Beirut: Majlis al-Janub, 2001), 80.

40. For a study of this party see Joyce Wiley, *The Islamic Movement of Iraqi Shi'as* (Boulder: Rienner, 1992).

41. For a discussion of the deteriorating relation between Berri and Shamseddine, see Rieck, *Die Schiiten*, 315, 617ff.

42. Rosiny, *Islamismus bei den Shiiten im Libanon*, 149.

43. Ibid., 52–53.

44. Interview with Shamseddine, in *al-Diyyar*, 6 May 1985.

45. Ghassan Tueni, ed., *al-Wasaya* (Beirut: Dar al-Nahar, 2001).

46. Ibid., 27.

47. Ibid., 28.

48. Ibid., 83–84.

49. Ibid., 87.

50. Ibid., 30–31.

51. Ibid., 29, 55–58, 68.

52. Ibid., 55. He wrote, "*Iran hiya dawla qa'ima bi-nafsiha*," which translates literally as "Iran is an independent country," but from the context it becomes clear that he makes a distinction between the Iranian situation and that of the Arab Shi'ites.

53. Naim Qassem, *Hizbullah: The Story from Within* (London: Saqi, 2005), 211.

54. Ibid., 210.

55. Ibid.

56. For the names of other Hizbullah members in the parliament, see Rosiny, *Islamismus bei den Shiiten im Libanon*, 160.

57. *Al-Kifah al-'Arabi*, 14 April 2001. Muslim leaders, especially Shi'ites, favored sectarian representation in Lebanon during the French Mandate since it gave them political power at last. For example, Yusuf al-Zayn, deputy of the south, wondered what the share of his sect would be if political sectarianism was abolished. See, Yusuf Q. Khoury, *al-Ta'ifiyya fi Lubnan min khilal munaqashat majlis al-nuwwab, 1923–1987* (Beirut: Dar al-Hamra, 1989), 8. See also *al-Nahar*, 28 January 1995, for a similar argument. For the Lebanese Christians, the abolition would mean a clear loss of political power once the demographic reality became undeniable. For their views on opposing this concept, see Nabil Khalifa in *al-Nahar*, 2 March 1993.

58. Mona Harb and Reinoud Leenders, "Know the Enemy: Hizbullah, 'Terrorism' and the Politics of Perception," *Third World Quarterly* 26 (1): 173–97.

59. See Harb, "Know the Enemy," for an illuminating discussion of how Hizbullah propagates its vision of a resistance society.

60. Ahmad Nizar Hamzeh, *In the Path of Hizbullah* (New York: Syracuse University Press, 2004), 74–76.

61. Naim Qassem, *Hizbullah*, 32–33.

62. Ussama Makdisi, *Culture of Sectarianism* (Berkeley: University of California Press, 2000); Max Weiss, *Institutionalizing Sectarianism: Law, Religious Culture, and the Remaking of Shiʻi Lebanon 1920–1947*, Ph.D. diss., Stanford University, 2007.

63. Lara Deeb shows how, in fact, Shiʻite Islamists in Lebanon imagine themselves as deeply modern and cosmopolitan but pious, while rejecting notions of secularism. See, *An Enchanted Modern: Gender and Public Piety in Shiʻi Lebanon* (Princeton: Princeton University Press, 2006).

64. I am aware that this politics of peripheralization that attempts at breaking the hegemony of other sectarian groups also takes place among other communities in Lebanon, but my focus in this section has been on how Lebanese Shiʻites are presented and how they negotiate a place for themselves in the Lebanese nation.

65. For a discussion of the word *metwali*, see Rula Jurdi, "Migration and Social Change: The ʻUlema of Ottoman Jabal ʻAmil in Safavid Iran, 1501–1736," Ph.D. diss., Yale University, 1998, ch. 1; Sabrina Mervin, *Un Réformisme chiite: Ulémas et lettrés du Gabal ʻAmil (actuel Liban-Sud) de la fin de l'empire Ottoman à l'indépendance du Liban* (Paris: Karthala, 2000). I am not sure when the term began to be used in its derogatory form, but because the Shiʻites formed the main population in the rural areas and they were economically poor and uneducated compared with the urban population, the application of the term in modern Lebanon might be no surprise. Perhaps it was even used in premodern Lebanon in its derogatory form to push Shiʻites to the margins in the Sunni-dominated Ottoman period; now it is used in a new context. But more research needs to be done to determine when the term came to be used in this fashion.

66. Pierre Bourdieu, *Distinction: A Social Critique of the Judgment of Taste* (Cambridge: Harvard University Press, 1984).

67. Elise Salem, *Constructing Lebanon: A Century of Literary Narratives* (Gainesville: University Press of Florida, 2003), esp. ch. 5, 145–51.

2. Schooling and the Creation of Lebanese Shiʻite Public Identity

1. Fawwaz Traboulsi, *A History of Modern Lebanon* (London: Pluto, 2007), 109.

2. Public schools in al-Dahiyya serve only 10 percent of students there. For the number of students and of public schools according to gender and education level in al-Dahiyya, see *al-Safir*, 6 October 1997.

3. "Lebanon," *UNDP Report 2001*: 27, 82. Statistics are based on a survey conducted during the 1995–1996 academic year.

4. Ibid., 66.

5. Outside Beirut, the cities of Ba'albak and Nabatiyya have a mainly Shi'ite population, and the majority of Shi'ite foundations maintain branches there. In Ba'albak the public schools are only 50.2 percent of the schools in the district. In the entire region of al-Biqa', 34.3 percent of students go to public schools and 42.8 percent go to fee-charging private schools. Of all the schools in the region, 55 percent are public and 27 percent are private ("Ba'albak," *UNDP Report 2001*: 15, 97). These statistics are based on a survey conducted during the academic year 1998–1999. In the district of Nabatiyya the grand total of operational schools is eighty-three, of which only about 56 percent are public, accommodating 48.2 percent of the students, whereas the fee-paying private schools receive 38.2 percent. In short, in Ba'albak and Nabatiyya, between one-third to half of the students attend fee-paying private schools ("al-Nabatiyya," *UNDP Report 2001*: 22, 42). Statistics are based on a survey conducted in 1996.

6. Etienne Balibar, "The Nation Form: History and Ideology," in Etienne Balibar and Immanuel Wallerstein, eds., *Race, Nation, Class: Ambiguous Identities* (London: Verso, 1991).

7. Besides the schools discussed in this chapter, there are many other Shi'ite-run schools in Beirut. Two of them are technical schools *(mihaniyya)*, such as *al-Ma'had al-'Arabi*, under the supervision of Dr. Husayn Yatim, and *al-Ma'had al-Fanni al-Islami*, belonging to the larger foundation of *al-Jam'iyya al-Khayriyya al-Thaqafiyya* and supervised by Ibrahim Shamseddine, the son of the late Shaykh Muhammad Mahdi Shamseddine. *Mu'assasat al-Imam al-Sadr* also offers training and technical education to Shi'ite students in Beirut. They are rather small in terms of numbers of students and the political weight of their current school directors, as compared with schools run by the Amal or JTDI. Since these schools provide mainly technical education to older students, they are outside the frame of my discussion of the production of Shi'ite citizens in Shi'ite-run schools.

8. Tamara Chalabi, *The Shi'is of Jabal 'Amil and the New Lebanon: Community and Nation-State, 1918–1943* (New York: Palgrave Macmillan, 2006), ch. 6.

9. Boutros Labaki, *Education et mobilité sociale dans la société multicommunautaire du Liban: Approche socio-historique* (n.p., 1988).

10. Annabelle Böttcher, "Ayatollah Fadlallah und seine Wohltätigkeitsorganisation al-Mabarrat," in Rainer Brunner and Monika Gronke, eds., *Islamstudien ohne Ende* (Würzburg: Ergon Verlag, 2002), 41–47; Maria Holt, "Lebanese Shi'i Women and Islamism: A Response to War," in Lamia Rustum Shehadeh, ed., *Women and War in Lebanon* (Gainesville: University of Florida Press, 1999), 180; Hayat Nabeel

Osseyran, "The Shi'ite Leadership of South Lebanon: A Reconsideration," M.A. thesis, American University of Beirut, 1997, 135ff.

11. Evelyn Aleene Early, "The Amiliyya Society of Beirut: A Case Study of an Emerging Urban Za'im," M.A. thesis, American University of Beirut, 1971; Aman Atiyya, "Development of Shi'ite Education in Lebanon," M.A. thesis, American University of Beirut, 1972.

12. Hayat Nabeel Osseyran, "The Shi'ite Leadership of South Lebanon"; Hala Jaber, *Hezbollah: Born with a Vengeance* (New York: Columbia University Press, 1997).

13. Identity production among Shi'ite secularists and Communists is not discussed here, as my discussion in this chapter centers on faith-based institutions.

14. See interview with Muhammad Samaha, the general director of al-Mustafa schools, in *al-Safir*, 1 October 1994. Also note that the first school was opened in 1983, just a year after the intensification of Iranian influence among Shi'ites in Lebanon.

15. Among many other scholars, see, for example, Daoud L. Khairallah, "Secular Democracy: A Viable Alternative to the Confessional System," in Deirdre Collings, ed., *Peace for Lebanon? From War to Reconstruction* (Boulder: Rienner, 1994).

16. 'Adnan al-Amin, *al-Ta'lim fi Lubnan: Zawaya wa mashahid* (Beirut: Dar al-Jadid, 1994), esp. ch. 2.

17. For a useful discussion of the central maladies of the education system in Lebanon set in a historical timeframe, see "Tis' qadaya li-islah al-ta'lim fi Lubnan," *al-Nahar*, 26 February 1994.

18. For a discussion of how the debate on unifying the national education system is divided along sectarian lines, see "Pluralism versus National Cohesion," in Leila Shahine Saleeby, "State Policy Toward Private Education in Lebanon," M.A. thesis, American University of Beirut, 1987, 178ff. Also, for a history of development of a wide range of missionary, foreign nonmissionary, Ottoman, and Muslim schools in Lebanon prior to independence, see J. A. Babikian, "Education and Civilization in Syria and Lebanon: A Historical, Comparative, and Critical Survey of the Syrian and Lebanese Education and Civilization," M.A. thesis, American University of Beirut, 1933, 132ff.

19. I researched the discussions from 1982 to 2002 on Lebanese education and on Lebanese Shi'ite education in *al-Nahar, al-Safir, al-Liwa'*, and some other newsletters. Sunni and Christian religious leaders argue, as Shi'ite religious scholars do, in favor of the importance of teaching religion in schools, and ultimately its continued importance in public life. See, for example, the views of the Sunni Mufti of Lebanon,

al-Shaykh Muhammad ʿAli al-Juzu, in *al-Liwaʾ*, 16 August 1998, or of the Maronite Patriarch Khalil Abi Nadir, in *al-Liwaʾ*, 23 September 1998.

20. For a historical background of the Lebanese (lack of) national educational policy and the role of the state, as well as for the emergence of civil society organizations to compensate for the state's failure to define a clear policy for education in Lebanon, see "al-Siyasa al-tarbawiyya fi Lubnan mundhu thalathin sana," special issue, *al-Jarida* 53 (January 1982).

21. For a detailed discussion of the type of civics books, and the interpretation of certain words such as *confessionalism* in civics books, see Fadia El Mourtada, "Les Manuels d'instruction civique et la formation du citoyen au Liban," Ph.D. diss., University of Paris, 1991.

22. See Jean Obeid's statement regarding the necessity of keeping religious education in public schools, which was made only after pressure from various religious leaders. See *al-Nahar*, 12 September 1998.

23. For an overview of the post-Taʾif debates regarding education policies in Lebanon, see Munir Bashshur, "The Deepening Cleavage in the Education System," in Theodor Hanf and Nawaf Salam, eds., *Lebanon in Limbo: Postwar Society and State in an Uncertain Regional Environment* (Baden-Baden: Nomos Verlagsgesellschaft, 2003), 159–81.

24. Salibi's *House of Many Mansions* is perhaps the best-known scholarly book on this issue and is widely read beyond academic circles in Lebanon. Kamal Salibi, *A House of Many Mansions: The History of Lebanon Reconsidered* (Berkeley: University of California Press, 1988).

25. In 1993, a group of scholars (ranging from the Shiʿite intellectual Ahmad Baydun to the Maronite academic Farid el-Khazen) and social activists from various communities published the first civic education textbook as a model for later textbooks, which was called *al-Muwatin wa al-tarbiyya al-madaniyya fi Lubnan* (Beirut: al-Markaz al-Lubnani lil Dirasat, 1993). Some of the topics discussed are democracy, human rights, civil duties, and the United Nations. A unified civic education textbook has existed in schools since 1997, and every school, regardless of its status, has to teach civic education for one hour per week. See also Fadia El Mourtada, "Manuels d'instruction civique."

26. Debates over civil marriage in Lebanon follow a similar path. One cannot but point to the hegemonic interest of religious leaders in keeping religion in public institutions. For a discussion of civil marriage in Lebanon, see Ahmad Baydun, *Tisʿ ʿashar firqa najiha: al-Lubnaniyun fi maʿarakat al-zawaj al-madani* (Beirut: Dar al-Nahar, 1999).

27. See Dr. Saud al-Mawla's response to dealing with whether religious education should become an optional subject in public schools: *al-Liwa'*, 18 September 1998. He states that not only religious education but also the actual practice of religion protects generations from moral decay. Dr. Saud al-Mawla was the attaché (*mustashar*) of the late Shaykh Muhammad Mahdi Shamseddine and is a member of the Committee on Muslim-Christian Dialogue.

28. International schools operating in Lebanon would count as a fourth category, but as the language of instruction in these schools is not Arabic, I have omitted them from this discussion.

29. For narratives of the experiences of early Shi'ite migrants to Beirut, see Atiyya, "Development of Shi'ite Education," 145ff.

30. For his biography and details on Rashid Baydun's activities, see Husayn Makki, *Qawl wa fi'l* (Beirut: Matba' al-Musri, 1967).

31. See Atiyya, "Development of Shi'ite Education," 168.

32. Ibid., 151ff.

33. Madrasat al-Banat al-'Amiliyya, a primary school for girls, opened in 1954 (ibid., 157ff). See also the three-part article in *al-Shira'* for the history of the al-'Amiliyya school, and for information regarding its girls' schools, see *al-Shira'*, 15 February 1988, 29 February 1988, 14 March 1988.

34. Atiyya, "Development of Shi'ite Education," 160.

35. Two excellent M.A. theses cover the activities of this secondary school of al-'Amiliyya. See Early, "Amiliyya Society of Beirut"; Atiyya, "Development of Shi'ite Education."

36. Makki, *Qawl wa fi'l*, 23.

37. I am, of course, aware that Lebanese Shi'ite ties to diaspora Shi'ites in Africa were not only related to securing funding but represent a set of identity production that deserves a separate study.

38. Makki, *Qawl wa fi'l*, 35, 132.

39. Ibid., 176.

40. See, for example, the sports festivities in 1950 and 1963, which the president of Lebanon attended (ibid., 86, 163).

41. For a discussion of Egyptian-Lebanese relations, see Nasser M. Kalawoun, *The Struggle for Lebanon: A Modern History of Lebanese-Egyptian Relations* (London: I. B. Tauris, 2000). Kalawoun mentions Nasser's monetary support of Sunni schools in Lebanon, but not his support for the al-'Amiliyya school.

42. *Report of al-'Amiliyya of 1958–1962*, 32, 52, 209. Note that the year 1959 marks the arrival of Musa Sadr in Lebanon. According to Dr. Husayn Yatim, this

timing and the heavy Persian accent in Sadr's Arabic made many Lebanese Shi'ite leaders suspicious of the motifs of Sadr, and for a long time he was believed to be connected to the Iranian secret service Savak, which was active outside of Iran through the Iranian embassies. This made Sadr's entrance into the circle of Shi'ite ethnic leaders difficult in the beginning (interview with Dr. Husayn Yatim, Beirut, 22 May 2003).

43. Dr. Yatim recalls that in the three years of the training schedule none of the teachers ever made serious attempts to learn Farsi and attended classes only because the school received funds from Iran.

44. Makki, *Qawl wa fi'l*, 151, 156.

45. Farsi was also taught in the same period at the al-Ja'fariyya school in Tyre.

46. Makki, *Qawl wa fi'l*, 156.

47. For a history of Iranian-Israeli relations, see Sohrab Sobhani, *The Pragmatic Entente: Israeli-Iranian Relations, 1948–1988* (New York: Praeger, 1989).

48. The 1970s opened a new page in the relation of al-'Amiliyya and Pahlavi Iran. Members of al-'Amiliyya were in touch with the Iranian embassy in the 1970s. Musa Sadr commemorated the fortieth-day anniversary of the death of 'Ali Shari'ati at al-'Amiliyya as well. Muhammad Baydun and Husayn Makki, then the head of the al-'Amiliyya school, visited the Iranian embassy in Beirut on 18 August 1977 and expressed their regret for the anti-Shah activities at al-'Amiliyya that day. According to Savak files, the conversation between Mansur Qadar, the Iranian ambassador to Lebanon at that time, and Baydun and Makki went as follows: "These two persons added that Musa Sadr had betrayed them and had not told them whose commemoration it was, that we did not know that Shari'ati was a leftist *(chap-gara)*[sic], and that Arafat and other armed leftists would attend and talk about such [anti-Shah] issues." The summary of the conversation continues with an account of how Qadar responded to Baydun by stating that "the lies of Musa Sadr and an Iranian anarchist [probably referring to Mustafa Chamran] are not worth taking the time of the Iranian embassy, but now that these two people have come here and want to know the opinion of the Iranian embassy regarding this issue, we believe that it is necessary for Muhammad Baydun to announce his opinion in the media . . . otherwise what would be the use of him coming here and privately apologizing while there would be no public resonance from it?" *Shari'ati be ravayat-i asnad-i savak* (Tehran: Markaz-i Asnad-i Inqilab-i Islami, 2000), 272, 273.

49. The al-Shahid Charity Foundation began operating in 1982 after the Israeli invasion of Lebanon to provide various social services to the families of those killed fighting the Israelis. The foundation launched its educational institutions under the

slogan: "We want to bring forth religious scholars out of the houses of the martyrs (*nuridu an nukhrija al-'ulama min buyut al-shuhada*)," *al-Safir*, 18 October 1999. Estimates of the number of martyrs affiliated with Hizbullah range between 1,375 (*Time*, 10 April 2000) and 1,281 (*al-Safir*, 15 November 2000).

50. *Time*, 10 April 2000.

51. *Shabab al-Ghad*, October 2000.

52. Interview with Muna Mu'ayyad, Beirut, 21 February 2003.

53 Roschanack Shaery-Eisenlohr, "Die Rolle der persischen Sprache in der Legitimierung des iranischen Nationalismus: Eine ethnohistorische Analyse," M.A. thesis, University of Heidelberg, 1998.

54. *Ajyal al-Mustafa* 11/12 (1999): 5ff.

55. Musa Sadr, *al-Islam: Din wa Hayat* (Beirut: al-Kitab al-Lubnani, 1961).

56. Rida Ahmad, *Hidayat al-Muta'allimin* (Sidon: Matba'at al-'Irfan, 1957).

57. Atiyya, "Development of Shi'ite Education," 134–35.

58. See *al-Liwa'*, 18 September 1998.

59. *Ajyal al-Mustafa* 11/12 (1999): 3.

60. Interview with Khudur al-Musawi, Beirut, 11 October 2002.

61. *Ajyal al-Mustafa* 11/12 (1999): 7.

62. Ibid., 9.

63. Ibid., 7.

64. Iraqi Shi'ite shaykhs have played an important role in Lebanon in performing 'Ashura rituals as well. In fact, some of these Iraqi teachers also performed rituals in houses and in *husayniyyas* in that period.

65. I suggest that there are two reasons for the popular idea that Iraqi Shi'ism is the most authentic form among many Lebanese and Iraqi (and Iraqi 'Ajami) Shi'ites. First, the sacred land of Najaf and Karbala legitimizes such hierarchical ordering by virtue of the relative authenticity of the different regional traditions of Shi'ism. A second reason is that the Iraqi dialect of Arabic is believed to be the variety in which the Imams conversed. Thus, land and language become two central justifications for Shi'ite authenticity and seniority.

66. Speaking of the construction of a Shi'ite person is clearly avoided, although all extracurricular activities are Shi'ite-related. Birthdays and commemorations of the *ahl al-bayt* are some of the most obvious of them, but there is also constant reference to Karbala in poems, texts, and images. Commemorating the death of Imam 'Ali and of the child of 'Abbas al-Musawi, the former leader of Hizbullah who was killed with his family by the Israelis, are part of this Islamic education. These are two among many examples indicating that by Islamic education they actually mean

Shi'ite Islamic education. The difference between theory and practice on this point is an important part of understanding Shi'ite national rhetoric in Lebanon.

67. *Ajyal al-Mustafa* 8 (1998): 9.

68. Robert W. Hefner and Muhammad Qasim Zaman, eds., *Schooling Islam: The Culture and Politics of Modern Muslim Education* (Princeton: Princeton University Press, 2007), 33. The term *objectifying Islam* is used in a different context here, but I have found it useful in comparing Amal and JTDI's approach to teaching religion, although neither group really represents the state.

69. *Ajyal al-Mustafa* 8 (1998): 9.

70. *Jam'iyyat al-ta'lim al-dini al-islami*, 2001–2002.

71. *Ajyal al-Mustafa* 8 (1998): 9.

72. *Jam'iyyat al-ta'lim al-dini al-islami*, 2001–2002. To view more details on these activities, see "al-Tarbiyya al-islamiyya," *Ajyal al-Mustafa* 5 (1997): 13.

73. See the article by Muhammad Samaha, the general director of JTDI, in *Ajyal al-Mustafa* 5 (1997): 2. See also Shaykh Naim Qassem, *Hizbullah: The Story from Within* (London: Saqi, 2005), 211.

74. *Ajyal al-Mustafa* 5 (1997): 6.

75. *Ajyal al-Mustafa* 8 (1998): 48.

76. *An Enchanted Modern: Gender and Public Piety in Shi'i Lebanon* (Princeton, NJ: Princeton University Press, 2006).

77. Poem written in English by Zainab Kandil, a student at the Batul High School; *Ajyal al-Mustafa* 2 (1996): 31.

78. Poem written in Arabic by Zahra Basma from the al-Mustapha secondary school in Tyre; *Ajyal al-Mustafa* 11/12 (1999): 54.

79. Front cover of *Ajyal al-Mustafa* 15 (2000).

80. *Ajyal al-Mustafa* 20 (2002): 72.

81. *Ajyal al-Mustafa* 15 (2000): 6–8; 18 (2001): 42.

82. *Ajyal al-Mustafa* 14 (2000): 56.

83. *Ajyal al-Mustafa* 8 (1998): 49.

84. *Ajyal al-Mustafa* 14 (2000): 10.

85. *Ajyal al-Mustafa* 20 (2002): 60.

86. Personal conversation with Khudur al-Musawi, JTDI employee in Beirut.

87. For a detailed description of *mabarrat* and their sources of funding, see Annabelle Böttcher, "Die Dollars der Ayatollahs: Finanzströme islamischer Netzwerke," *Neue Züricher Zeitung*, 14 October 2002, 5; and "Im Schatten des Ayatollahs: Shiitische feministische Theologie in Libanon am Anfang," *Neue Züricher Zeitung*, 7 March 2001, 5.

88. For a more detailed biography of Fadlallah and his activities and institutions, see Anabelle Böttcher, "Sunni and Shi'i Networking in the Middle East," *Mediterranean Politics* 7, no. 3 (2002): 42–63 (special issue: *Shaping the Current Islamic Reformation*).

89. *Al-Mu'assasat al-marja'iyya: Injazat waamal*, 2002.

90. "Al-Madaris al-mabarrat: Nahj islah wamasar al-taqrir," paper presented at *Mu'tamar al-islah al-tarbawi lil-madrasa fi al-buldan al-'arabiyya*, American University of Beirut, 2000.

91. "Al-Madaris al-mabarrat."

92. See interview with Rana Isma'il, executive director of al-Kawthar school, in the *Daily Star*, 28 December 2002.

93. Personal interview with Rana Isma'il, Beirut, 16 October 2002 (emphasis added).

94. The number of students at the Beirut branch reached 917 in 2002; the school operated from kindergarten up to the eighth grade. See the brochure *Mu'assasat al-Shahid Hasan Qasir* (Beirut). This chapter provides information mainly on Amal's Martyr Bilal Fahs School, located in Tul, a city in South Lebanon. Shahid Hasan Qasir School, located in Beirut, only began operating in the academic year 2001–2002, and their yearbook had not yet appeared during my stay in Beirut.

95. *Mu'assasat Amal al-tarbawiyya*, 2002/2003.

96. Osseyran, "Shi'ite Leadership of South Lebanon," 135ff.

97. *Mu'assasat Amal al-tarbawiyya*, 2002/2003.

98. Personal interview with Muhammad Nasrallah, Beirut, 4 September 2002.

99. Shaking a woman's hand is another such field. Few Amal men shook hands when meeting with me; those who did referred to the others as the "Hizbullah among Amal" and wondered about their "fanaticism." To many Amal men who knew that I was engaged in research that also involved meeting non-Amal Shi'ites (such as Hizbullah members), the emphasis on their own religiosity became important. They pointed to the fact that Nabih Berri prays regularly and that he never shakes hands with women, but they also stressed that, as they put it, he is also not a "fanatic" like other non-Amal Shi'ite groups. To them, fanaticism was Hizbullah's "unwillingness" to soften its religious fervor, while they themselves sought to convey the impression of having found a moderate path between religious fervor in public and secularism, which they believed was the only means for coexistence in Lebanon.

100. I spent several days at this school, observed English, religion, and history classes and spoke to various employees. One striking moment came in a third-grade English class where the students were reading a story in *A Thousand and One Arabian Nights* that mentioned a Persian carpet. The teacher turned to me and told the

students that I am from Persia, the land where the carpet comes from, and explained that Persia is the same country as Iran. To the students, this made no sense, as they seemed to have never heard of the word Iran, and they insisted that I was either Syrian or Egyptian. None showed any reaction to the word Iran. To me this underlined the fact that Iran has not been relevant to them so far, either as part of their activities or in any other context. In contrast, when one looks at the activities of JTDI, young children already take part in programs in which the names of Khamenei and Iran occur repeatedly.

101. I reviewed both series of religion textbooks and could not find any noteworthy differences between them. In fact, Amal still uses JTDI books for the final three years in high school, since, according to Muhammad Nasrallah, so far no appropriate religion textbooks have been produced by SISC.

102. In a conversation with one of the Amal members on the relationship between Amal and SISC, I was told to bring my ear close to his mouth. He said something in my ear, then pulled back, saying, "Now say it loud." Laughingly, he turned to me and explained, "That's the relation between our leaders" (referring to Berri and Shaykh Qabalan). The little game was meant to express that Shaykh Qabalan, who presently leads SISC, is a powerless figure who obeys whatever political orders Berri suggests. Berri and Shaykh Qabalan are indeed close: the brother of Shaykh Qabalan is the director of the Council of the South, which is under Berri's supervision.

103. For a discussion of how various social and political entrepreneurs view the idea of a unified religion textbook, and the problems with creating a unified book that according to the author contains religion and does not become a history of civilizations, see "I'adat al-ta'lim al-dini bi-kitab muwahhad hal yuhassin al-mina'a al-wataniyya wa-yasil al-fawariq?" *al-Nahar*, 13 November 1999.

104. For a discussion of their goals, see *Mu'assasat Amal al-tarbawiyya: al-Iqtat; al-Kitab al-madrasi lil-'am al-dirasi 2001–2002; Thanawiyyat al-Shahid Bilal Fahs, Tul,* 100–2.

105. *Sada al-Risala* 46 (2000): 14.

106. I took part in two of these commemorations, on 31 August, 2000, in Tyre, and on 31 August, 2002, in Beirut. Young students marched with Lebanese and Amal flags and pictures of Musa Sadr through the crowd. For a report of the commemoration and the scout activities on that day, see also *al-'Awasif*, 6 September 2002.

107. See the periodical journal *Sada al-Risala*, a publication of Amal's scouts, for extensive description of their activities all over Lebanon.

108. *Mu'assasat Amal al-tarbawiyya: al-Iqtat; al-Kitab al-madrasi lil-'am al-dirasi 2001–2002; Thanawiyyat al-Shahid Bilal Fahs, Tul,* 86ff.

109. David R. Jones, "Forerunners of the Komsomol: Scouting in Imperial

Russia," in Schimmelpenninck van der Oye and Bruce W. Menning, eds., *Reforming the Tsar's Army: Military Innovation in Imperial Russia from Peter the Great to the Revolution* (Cambridge: Cambridge University Press, 2004), 58.

110. Ronald Hyam, *Britain's Imperial Century, 1815–1914: A Study of Empire and Expansion* (New York: Harper and Row, 1976), 129–34.

111. Jones, "Forerunners of the Komsomol," 66.

112. Traboulsi, *A History of Modern Lebanon*, 102.

113. Information based on a conversation with Muhammad Nasrallah.

3. Shi'ite Piety and the Palestinian Cause

1. For details on the Lebanese-Egyptian relations in this period, see Nasser M. Kalawoun, *The Struggle for Lebanon: A Modern History of Lebanese-Egyptian Relations* (London: I. B. Tauris, 2000), ch. 3.

2. The Shah's aid to Chamoun consisted of small arms and munitions delivered through Savak. See "Shah Promotes Security in Lebanon," *Christian Science Monitor*, 19 April 1978, p. 7. See also *Bozorgdasht-i Doktor 'Ali Shari'ati dar Beirut* (n.p., n.d.), 70. According to this source, the Shah purchased six thousand rifles from France to be given to the Lebanese right-wing Maronite al-Ahrar Party.

3. 'Abbas W. Samii, "The Shah's Lebanon Policy: The Role of SAVAK," *Middle Eastern Studies* 33, no. 1 (1997): 69.

4. In the 1970s and against the background of increasing Israeli attacks to South Lebanon, Musa Sadr turned to Iranian religious scholars for two reasons. First, he wanted them to use their influence in persuading the Shah to stop supporting Israel. Second, he hoped for donations for Lebanese Shi'ites. In October 1973 Sadr wrote from Lebanon to Ayatollah Shari'atmadani and Ayatollah Golpayegani in Qom that "Muslims are burning in the fire of the war of the Israelis. Israel has occupied the territories. . . . Muslims have expectations from Iran and want you to pressure the government to stop this war and bloodshed and the support America gives to Israel." *Savak va ruhaniyyat* (Tehran: Shaqaeq, 1992), 1:95. Ayatollah Kho'i sent a message from Iraq at the end of 1974 to Ayatollah Milani in Mashhad, reporting on the situation of the Shi'ites throughout the world. On the Shi'ites of Lebanon, he wrote, "Palestinians who live in the south of Lebanon, a Shi'ite region, are constantly bombed by the Israelis. This results also in the death of many Shi'ites there." *Savak va ruhaniyyat*, 1:115. Another entry in the Savak files reports on Golpayegani organizing a public prayer session in Qom in January 1976 in order to demonstrate solidarity with the Shi'ites of Lebanon. According to the Savak files, at the beginning of the prayer ses-

sion a Lebanese man gave a speech in Arabic about the situation of the Shi'ites in Lebanon, attacking the Lebanese Christians and the Israeli government. They then prayed for the success of the Lebanese Muslim community in the conflict. Golpayegani asked for donations for the Lebanese Muslims to be paid into an account at the Saderat bank in Qom (*Savak va ruhaniyyat*, 1:140). In other cities of Iran, the religious scholars spread Golpayegani's call for donations, and only one month later, on 22 February 1976, more than three million riyals had been collected. Musa Sadr's brother, Reza Sadr, and Golpayegani's son were to travel to Lebanon to give the money to Shi'ite representatives. Savak also records that Reza Sadr left Iran on 15 March 1976 for Lebanon.

5. See Samii for an account of Sadr's relationship with the Iranian embassy in Beirut, "The Shah's Lebanon Policy."

6. From April 1969 until July 1971, diplomatic relations between Iran and Lebanon were broken off because the head of Savak operations in Lebanon, General Taymur Bakhtiyar, was arrested for illegal gunrunning in Lebanon, apparently for personal profit. Once the Iranian government was able to bring Bakhtiyar back to Iran, and following Chamoun's visit to Iran in early 1971, diplomatic relations resumed. For details on Bakhtiyar's involvement in Lebanon, see *Sepahbod Taymur Bakhtiyar be ravayat-i asnad-i savak* (Tehran: Markaz-i Barressi-i Asnad-i Tarikhi-i Vizarat-i Itila'at, 2000), vol. 2. All the reports in the second volume are concerned with Bakhtiyar's arrest in Lebanon and the Iranian embassy's strategies to persuade the Lebanese government to extradite Bakhtiyar. Once all attempts failed, the Iranian government withdrew its embassy members from Lebanon and broke diplomatic contacts with it for almost two years.

7. This material was published, although selectively, in the context of the policy of the postrevolutionary Iranian government to provide documentation of what it saw as the crimes of the Shah regime. It is interesting not only as a historical document but also because it shows how little the Savak knew about the actual activities of the anti-Shah members in Lebanon and how its interpretations and narratives about the events differed from how the opposition members viewed their own activities and intentions. One of the most obvious mistakes throughout the documents was that the party of Amal (which means hope) was referred to as 'Amal (meaning work); both words are pronounced the same way in Persian. But the latter word can give the sense that Amal had leftist leanings. In addition, Chamran was labeled as *chap-gara* (a leftist), though he obviously was not.

8. Two large volumes are dedicated to the monitoring of Musa Sadr's activities and two to Mustafa Chamran's. In the files on 'Ali Shari'ati, another member of the opposition movement, one finds constant references to Lebanon as well. See *Imam*

Musa Sadr: Yaran-i imam be ravayat-i asnad-i savak (Tehran: Markaz-i Barressi-i Asnad-i Tarikhi-i Vizarat-i Itila'at, 2001), vols. 1 and 2; *Shahid-i sarafraz Doctor Mustafa Chamran: Yaran-i imam be ravayat-i asnad-i savak* (Tehran: Markaz-i Barressi-i Asnad-i Tarikhi-i Vizarat-i Itila'at, 2000), vols. 1 and 2; *Shari'ati be ravayat-i asnad-i savak* (Tehran: Markaz-i Barressi-i Asnad-i Tarikhi-i Vizarat-i Itila'at, 2000), vols. 1, 2, and especially 3, which describes in detail Savak's view on Shari'ati's commemoration in Beirut.

9. The Savak files contain a series of written exchanges between the Lebanese and the Iranian foreign ministries, in which the Lebanese authorities apologized for the anti-Shah activities that took place during the fortieth anniversary of Shari'ati's death and distanced themselves from the Shi'ite anti-Shah activities in Lebanon. *Shari'ati be ravayat-i asnad-i savak* (Tehran: Markaz-i Barressi-i Asnad-i Tarikhi-i Vizarat-i Itila'at, 2000), 57, 266, 271, 278, 316, 319.

10. Ibid., 277–78.

11. Ibid., 283–84.

12. Ibid., 284.

13. Besides this network, two others between Iran and Lebanon centered on links between Palestinian organizations and Iranian opposition groups. First there was the connection between the Iranian Mojahedin-i Khalq and Fatah, the dominant movement in the PLO, in Lebanon. The People's Mojahedin of Iran, a movement that split off from the LMI in the early 1960s, was characterized by an outlook combining Islam and Marxism. For information on the history of establishing these networks with Fatah, see *Sharh-i ta'sis va tarikhcheha-i vaqaye-'i Sazman-i Mojahedin-i Khalq-i Iran 1344–1350* (Long Beach, CA: Sazman-i Mojahedin-i Khalq-i Iran, 1980). The second link was the network between the Popular Front for the Liberation of Palestine (PFLP), a Palestinian Marxist faction, led by Dr. George Habash, and the Marxist Iranian Cherikha-i Fadai-i Khalq, who received military training by the PFLP. For detailed information on how they established contacts to PFLP, see Iraj Sepehri, *Az jebhe' nabard-i Felestin: Khaterat-i rafiq kargar-i fada'i Shahid Iraj Sepehri* (Tehran: n.p., 1977).

14. For details on the members of the National Resistance Movement and their activities, see H. E. Chehabi, *Iranian Politics and Religious Modernism: The Liberation Movement of Iran under the Shah and Khomeini* (Ithaca: Cornell University Press, 1990), 128–39.

15. Nehzat-i Azadi-i Iran, *Zendeginameh-i sardar-i rashid-i Islam Shahid Doktor Mostafa Chamran* (Tehran, 1983); *Zendeginameh: Shahid Doctor Chamran* (Tehran: Bonyad-i Shahid Chamran, n.d.).

16. Mustafa Chamran, *Lobnan* (Tehran: Bonyad-i Shahid Chamran, 1983). This was published after his death.

17. Ibid., 20. See also Roschanack Shaery-Eisenlohr, "Post-revolutionary Iran and Shi'i Lebanon: Contested Histories of Shi'i Transnationalism," *International Journal of Middle East Studies* 39 (2): 271–89 for more details on Chamran's activities in Lebanon and how he is commemorated in Iran and in Lebanon.

18. For information on Muhammad Montazeri's activities after the success of the revolution, see Wilfried Buchta, *Die iranische Schia und die islamische Einheit, 1979–1996* (Hamburg: Deutsches Orient-Institut, 1997), 119–20.

19. Jalal al-Din Farsi, *Zavaya-i tarik* (Tehran: Hawze-i Andishe va Honar-i Islami, 1994). Farsi intended to run for president, but rumors about his Afghani origin prevented him from doing so. As a result, Abul-Hasan Bani Sadr became president of Iran, and Farsi became his archenemy.

20. 'Ali Akbar Mohtashami, *Khaterat-i siyasi* (Tehran: Daftar-i Adabiyyat-i Jomhuri-i Islami, 2000), vol. 2. Mohtashami was a close relation of Khomeini and was his personal secretary in Paris. In 1982 he became the Iranian ambassador to Syria.

21. This becomes most obvious in Murtada Elwiri's memoirs when he mentions his meeting with Qutbzadeh, a leading member of LMI(a) in Paris. Murtada Elwiri, *Khatirat-i Murtada Elwiri* (Tehran: Daftar-i Adabiyyat-i Jomhuri-i Islami, 1997), 59.

22. *Tahlili az awza'-i janub-i Lubnan. Sazman-i Amal va Doctor Chamran* (n.p., n.d.), 47. For a similar argument, see Sayyid Hamid Rawhani, *Nihzat-i Imam Khomeini* (Tehran: Sazman-i Asnad-i Inqilab-i Islami, 1995), 3:821–22.

23. Rawhani, *Nihzat-i Imam*, 832.

24. The Shah of Iran can be considered a third Shi'ite transnational politician, as he did at times give money to Lebanese Shi'ites and invested in the renovation of holy tombs, such as that of Sayyida Zaynab in Damascus. However, this section is concerned with how the memory of the Shi'ite network between Iranian opposition leaders and the party of Amal in the 1970s frames postrevolutionary relations between the two groups. For the relation between Musa Sadr and the Iranian embassy in Beirut and for the Shah's charitable support of Lebanese Shi'ites, see 'Abbas William Samii, "The Security Relationship between Lebanon and Pre-Revolutionary Iran," in Houchang Chehabi, ed., *Distant Relations: Five Hundred Years of Iranian-Lebanese Relations*. (London: I. B. Tauris, 2006), 162–79.

25. *Imam Musa Sadr: Yaran-i imam be ravayat-i asnad-i savak* (Tehran: Markaz-i Barressi-i Asnad-i Tarikhi-i Vizarat-i Itila'at, 2001), 481.

26. *Asnad-i faj'i-ye Lubnan* (n.p., n.d.), 21.

27. See Chamran's Savak files, *Shahid-i sarafraz Doctor Mustafa Chamran: Yaran-i imam be ravayat-i asnad-i savak* (Tehran: Markaz-i Barressi-i Asnad-i Tarikhi-i Vizarat-i Itila'at, 2000), 289, 327.

28. *Tahlili az awza'-i janub-i Lubnan*, 62.

. SHI'ITE PIETY AND THE PALESTINIAN CAUSE

29. During his exile in Iraq, Khomeini approached Iraqi religious scholars to support his political activism against the Shah of Iran, but scholars such as Ayatollah al-Hakim did not agree to support him as he wished. Iraqi scholars worked within the logic of the Iraqi state and were more interested in gradual change in the early 1970s. See Joyce Wiley, *The Islamic Movement of Iraqi Shi'as* (Boulder: Rienner, 1992).

30. Ervand Abrahamian, *Iran Between Two Revolutions* (Princeton: Princeton University Press, 1982), 473.

31. Devin Stewart, "The Portrayal of an Academic Rivalry: Najaf and Qum in the Writings and Speeches of Khomeini, 1964–78," in Linda S. Walbridge, ed., *The Most Learned of the Shi'a. The Institution of the Marja' Taqlid* (Oxford: Oxford University Press, 2001), 216–29.

32. *Az Shah ta Chamoun* (n.p., 1978), 93. See for example how they accused Sadr for derailing from authentic Islam by inviting a non-Muslim to lead the Friday prayer.

33. Mohtashami, *Khaterat-i siyasi*, 143.

34. Ibid. See also Farsi's memoirs when Farsi expresses similar comments and opinions about Musa Sadr in a more indirect way. He emphasizes the "good relations" between Sadr and the Shah, for example, which was equal to labeling Sadr as traitorous in the eyes of anti-Shah opposition activists Farsi. *Zavaya-i tarik*, 252–53, 256–57, 261.

35. Chamran, *Lobnan*, 92, 98, 122.

36. As'ad AbuKhalil, "Syria and the Shiites: Al-Asad's Policy in Lebanon," *Third World Quarterly* 12 (2): 1–20; As'ad AbuKhalil, "Shiites and the Palestinians: Underlying Causes of the Amal-Palestinian Conflict," in Elaine C. Hagopian, ed., *Amal and the Palestinians: Understanding the Battle of the Camps*. Arab World Issues: Occasional Papers no. 9 (1985), 12.

37. See Richard Norton, *Amal and the Shi'a: Struggle for the Soul of Lebanon* (Austin: University of Texas Press, 1987), 42–48.

38. Chamran, *Lobnan*, 129–30.

39. Rawhani, *Nihzat-i Imam*, 821.

40. *Tahlili az awza'-i janub-i Lubnan*, 62.

41. *Az Shah ta Chamoun*, 93.

42. Navab Safavi formed the party of Fada'iyan-i Islam in 1945 and assassinated, among others, Ahmad Kasravi, a leading Iranian secular intellectual in 1948. The Shah regime executed Safavi in 1955. Khalkhali revived the party after the success of the revolution, as the ruling religious elite in Iran connected its ideologies to the Fada'iyan, whose goal was to combat the secularization efforts of the Pahlavi regime.

43. *Amal*, 16 May 1980; *Amal*, 28 May 1980.

44. The Iranian government put the total at seventy-two in order to construct a resemblance to what Shi'ites believe was the number of Imam Husayn's followers present at Karbala.

45. *Amal*, 10 July 1981. A commemoration of Ayatollah Muhammad Husayn Beheshti's death was organized by Amal members in Ba'albak. The death of Chamran was commemorated in Tyre where Mufti Qabalan gave a speech. Commemorations took place in Beirut (al-Burj) as well; *Amal*, 3 July 1981. The Shi'ite community in Abidjan, Ivory Coast, also organized a commemoration for Chamran; *Amal*, 10 July 1981.

46. *Amal*, 27 September 1980.

47. For a biography of Bint al-Huda and her importance to the Iraqi Da'wa Party see Joyce Wiley, "Alima Bint al-Huda, Women's Advocate," in Linda S. Walbridge, ed., *The Most Learned of the Shi'a: The Institution of the Marja' Taqlid* (Oxford: Oxford University Press, 2001), 149–60.

48. 'Ali 'Abbas, a young Shi'ite Amal member, was martyred in Susangard, Iran, in June 1981 at the front, and his death is commemorated by Amal members annually. Another Lebanese Shi'ite Amal member martyred at the front in Susangard was 'Abd al-Rida al-Musawi.

49. Interview with Hasan Shaqra, Nabatiyya, 23 November 2002.

50. Interview with Abu Kharif, Beirut, 12 November 2002.

51. Depending on the political stance of who is telling the story, various arguments are advanced as to why Qaddafi was interested in killing Musa Sadr. To many Amal members, Arafat and Khomeini cooperated with Qaddafi to get rid of Sadr because he stood in the way of their leadership. In the view of some Shi'ite *zu'ama*, Qaddafi supported Sadr financially in Lebanon during the civil war but felt that he was working with the Maronite forces and Syria against the Palestinians especially after the fall of Nab'a and thus took revenge for what Qaddafi considered Sadr's betrayal and had him killed.

52. The pages of *Amal*, the official weekly newspaper of the Amal Party between 1980 and 1982, are full of descriptions of the visit of Amal members Muhammad Mahdi Shamseddine' and Rababa Sadr to Iran to ask about Musa Sadr's whereabouts. A few examples of such reports of the delegations' visit to Iran and the telegrams sent can be found in *Amal*, 18 January 1980; *Amal*, 15 February 1980; and *Amal*, 23 May 1980. In addition, Amal leaders sent a telegram to Bani Sadr and Khomeini, requesting a delegation be sent to Libya to investigate and not to put the task off any longer; *Amal*, 18 April 1980.

53. *Amal*, 4 April 1980.

54. Khalkhali's visit to Libya outraged Amal members who demanded an explanation from the Iranian government, whereupon the Iranian embassy in Beirut publicly stated that Khalkhali's visit was for "personal reasons" and not part of the official policy of the Iranian government; *Amal*, 4 April 1980.

55. Ibid., 14 January 1980.

56. Ibid., 14 January 1980.

57. Ibid., 27 June 1980.

58. Andreas Rieck, *Die Schiiten und der Kampf um den Libanon: Politische Chronik, 1958–1988* (Hamburg: Deutsches Orient-Institut, 1989), 415. This view is prevalent not only among scholars. In my view, public discourse in Lebanon reflected the presumed pan-Islamic and less nationalist ideologies of Hizbullah even after the liberation of the south in May 2000. According to this perspective, pan-Islamic and nationalist orientations are opposed to each other. One of the earliest nonscholarly writings on Hizbullah's ideologies is that of the Maronite Lebanese journalist and independent researcher Nabil Khalifa, who published a series of booklets on various Lebanese political parties and their ideologies in the 1980s. In 1984 he dedicated one of these booklets to the study of the Shi'ites in Lebanon. He clearly distinguished between the identity of the Amal Party as a Lebanese national political party (*huwiyya siyasiyya wataniyya lubnaniyya*) as opposed to the "identity of the Khomeini revolution" and its supporters, who split with Amal in 1982 and eventually formed Hizbullah. The author described the orientation of the newly founded party as based on an internationalist pan-Islamic religious identity (*huwiyya diniyya umamiyya islamiyya*). This clear-cut division still prevails in the minds of many Lebanese, as I discovered through their discussions of the book by Amal Saad-Ghorayeb on the Lebanese Hizbullah (translated into Arabic), in which she is convinced of the nationalist sentiments of Hizbullah. Many dismissed the book, pointing to the fact that her father has good relations with Hizbullah. They also maintained that her writing was more propagandistic than scholarly. For the booklet on Shi'ites see Nabil Khalifa, *al-Shi'a fi Lubnan: Thawra dimughrafiyya waal-hirman* (Beirut, 1984), 22–25.

59. Stefan Rosiny, *Islamismus bei den Schiiten im Libanon: Religion im Übergang von Tradition zur Moderne* (Berlin: Das Arabische Buch, 1996), 121.

60. In a speech Berri delivered on the seventh annual commemoration of the disappearance of Musa Sadr in August 1985 in Ba'albak, he made a similar statement that Iran treats Amal members as if they were *kuffar*. He expressed his surprise at this behavior, as in his view many of the leaders of the Iranian revolution were closely associated with Amal prior to the success of the revolution; *al-Nahar*, 1 September 1985.

61. Farsi, *Zavaya-i tarik*, 480.

62. See Amal Saad-Ghorayeb, *Hizbullah: Politics and Religion* (London: Pluto Press, 2002); Mona Harb and Reinoud Leenders, "Know the Enemy: Hizbullah, 'Terrorism' and the Politics of Perception," *Third World Quarterly* 26 (1): 173–97.

63. Actually, the volunteers were stationed only in the al-Biqa' region and never made it to the south.

64. *Omid-i Inqilab* 36 (3 July 1982): 16ff.

65. Ibid., 36.

66. Ibid., 41.

67. Ibid., 49.

68. *Omid-i Inqilab* 38 (31 July 1982): 73.

69. *Omid-i Inqilab* 36 (3 July 1982): 45.

70. Ibid., 77.

71. See for example the words he uses in this writing in 1980. Muhammad Husayn Fadlallah, "al- Thawra al-islamiyya fi Iran bayna al-takhtit al-maddi wa al-isnad al-ilahi," *al-Muntalaq* 10 (1980): 12.

72. *Omid-i Inqilab* 39 (14 August 1982): 18–19. Sayyid 'Abbas Musawi was born in 1952 in Nabisheet in the al-Biqa'. During his short period serving as Hizbullah's general secretary, he made efforts to integrate Hizbullah as a political party in Lebanon. He was killed by the Israelis in February 1992 and has become an icon of martyrdom for Hizbullah followers ever since.

73. Sayyid Sadiq Musavi is an Iranian cleric and was a member of Hizbullah's *shura*. He lives mainly in Lebanon.

74. *Omid-i Inqilab* 38 (31 July 1982): 68ff.

75. *Daily Star*, 14 May 2003.

76. Both Lebanese Shi'ite political parties, Amal and Hizbullah, had organized a large rally for Khatami at the Beirut sports stadium where Khatami delivered a speech in Arabic to the Shi'ite audience. In my conversations with some Shi'ite intellectuals and Amal members, they revealed their surprise at Khatami's move. They viewed it as a contradiction of his claimed desire to maintain relations with all Lebanese.

4. The Politics of Shi'ite Authenticity Since 1982

1. Personal conversation, Beirut, August 2000.

2. Magnus Ranstorp, *Hizb'Allah in Lebanon: The Politics of the Western Hostage Crisis* (New York: St. Martin's, 1997), 26.

3. *Daily Star*, 10 September 2004.

4. Kathryn A. Woolard and Bambi Schieffelin, "Language Ideology," *Annual Review of Anthropology* 23 (1994): 55–82.

5. In describing how my interlocutors animate the voices of absent others, I draw on Erving Goffman's treatment of microlevel interaction as strategic stage-play in which participants engage in impression management through mobilizing available social roles and characters. Erving Goffman, *Frame Analysis: An Essay on the Organization of Experience* (New York: Harper and Row, 1974).

6. For a discussion of the meaning of *tarof* and the choice of words used "marking *tarof*" in Iranian society, see William O. Beeman, *Language, Status, and Power in Iran* (Bloomington: Indiana University Press, 1986), ch. 6.

7. English translation from Rula Jurdi Abisaab, *Converting Persia: Religion and Power in the Safavid Empire* (London: I. B. Tauris, 2004), 41.

8. Rula Jurdi Abisaab, "Shi'ite Beginnings and the Scholastic Tradition in Jabal 'Amil in Lebanon," *Muslim World* 89 (January 1999), 1:4.

9. All the information in this section has been taken from Rula Jurdi Abisaab, "Shi'ite Beginnings."

10. Jurdi Abisaab, *Converting Persia*, 95 and 102.

11. For a discussion of how these 'Amili scholars set out to prove the Arab origins of Jabal 'Amili Shi'ites, see Rula Jurdi, "Migration and Social Change: The 'Ulema of Ottoman Jabal 'Amil in Safavid Iran, 1501–1736," Ph.D. diss., Yale University, 1998, 3. For the existence of such ideologies in the public discourse among Lebanese Shi'ites and the ways the author, 'Ali Rafiq al-Musawi, constructs differences between Lebanese and Iranian Shi'ism, see "al-Shi'a waal-'uruba fi Lubnan: Khalfiyat wamaqasid tansib al-Shi'a lil Furs," *al-Safir*, 23 August 1985.

12. During my stay in Lebanon I took a two-week trip to Iran. As it was the first anniversary of the death of my grandfather, our house in Tehran was filled with relatives from Yazd and the north of Iran, many from Tehran and Shahrud. As they had not seen me in many years, they were curious about what I was doing with my life. When I told them about Lebanon, many either wondered whether it was part of Palestine or were not sure where Lebanon was at all. Some of my relatives who had satellite television in their homes had watched LBC, a Christian-owned television station in Lebanon known for its sexy and trendy women. They thought of Lebanon as a Christian country. Many repeatedly affirmed the cliché that Beirut was the Paris of the Middle East, but they thought the civil war was still going on. During my visit I frequently took taxis on shopping trips within Tehran and made a point of mentioning that I lived in Lebanon so that I could see the reaction. Most taxi drivers were surprised and couldn't really place Lebanon on the map, as it is not a destination for Iranian immigrants; they knew nothing about Lebanon. As a result of these observations and

my conversations with many educated Iranians in the Western diaspora, I hold the view that the average Iranian, no matter whether she or he is from Tehran or from the provinces, has no idea about Lebanon nor about the Lebanese Shiʿites, nor about Iran's politics in the region. For many, Hizbullah is simply a Palestinian group, as these two are most often connected in the news on television and on radio in Iran. But unless Iranians are connected in some way to the Shiʿite transnational network or are educated in the humanities or social sciences, they are unlikely to have ever heard of Jabal ʿAmil or to know anything about Lebanon. This ignorance serves as an interesting counterpoint to the Lebanese Shiʿite stereotypes of Iranians.

13. Jurdi Abisaab argues that most of the Jabal ʿAmili scholars in Persia "were not a monolithic group acting on the basis of a projected ethnic solidarity, but rather divided along professional and political lines" (*Converting Persia*, 51). She further argues that, by the seventeenth century, Persianization on the class and state level had occurred, because "a complete eclipse of ʿAmilism as a scholastic-ethnic phenomenon" became evident in the Safavid court (*Converting Persia*, 5).

14. *Al-Hayat*, 22 December 1961.

15. *Al-Hawadith*, 7 October 1966 (emphasis added).

16. Yet, Musa Sadr's brother in-law, Husayn Charafeddine, is free from such politics because his family is rooted in South Lebanon. Thus he can proudly acclaim the transnational background of his family: "In this family you will not find two generations having lived in the same country. We are truly a religious family (*ʿaaʾila diniyya*)." He clearly did not mean religious family as a way to define oneself as more or less religious, as religion in his view is not bound to national boundaries (conversation with Husayn Charafeddine, Beirut, January 2003).

17. Unlike the relatively small number of studies conducted on Muharram rituals in Lebanon, there is a vast literature on them and on their transformation after the success of the Iranian revolution in Iran. Among many other works on them in the Iranian context, see Peter J. Chelkowski, ed., *Taʿziyeh: Ritual and Drama in Iran* (New York: New York University Press, 1979); Michael Fisher, *Iran: From Religious Dispute to Revolution* (Cambridge: Harvard University Press, 1980), chs. 5, 6, and epilogue; Mary Hegland, "Two Images of Husain: Accommodation and Revolution in an Iranian Village," in Nikki Keddie, ed., *Religion and Politics in Iran: Shiʿism from Quietism to Revolution* (New Haven: Yale University Press, 1983), 218–35; Kamran Scot Aghaie, *The Martyrs of Karbala: Shiʿi Symbols and Rituals in Modern Iran* (Seattle: University of Washington Press, 2004).

18. Karen M. Kern, "The Prohibition of Sunni-Shiʿite Marriages in the Ottoman Empire: A Study of Ideologies," Ph.D. diss., Columbia University, 1999, 112–15. For descriptions of the rituals see also Erika Glassen, "Muharram Ceremonies (ʿ*Azadari*)

in Istanbul at the End of the Nineteenth and the Beginning of the Twentieth Century," in Th. Zarcone and F. Zarinebaf, eds., *Les Iraniens d'Istanbul* (Paris: IFDRI, 1993), 113–29.

19. For a discussion of the reasons to advocate or to oppose the practice of *haydar* among Lebanese Shi'ite scholars, see *al-Nahar*, 21 March 2002.

20. For a discussion of the Muharram rituals and the practice of *haydar* in Nabatiyya in the 1970s, see Bärbel Reuter, *Ashura-Feiern im Libanon: Zum politischen Potential eines religiösen Festes* (Hamburg: LIT Verlag, 1993), ch. 5. She describes how in 1970 the reenacting of the battle of Karbala (*shabih*) became more organized in Nabatiyya as a stage was specifically erected for this performance and new masks and clothes were designed. Then, three years later, in 1973 a commission was appointed to improve the quality of the performance. While in the 1960s thirty thousand to forty thousand people attended Muharram ceremonies in Nabatiyya, in the early 1970s about sixty thousand took part, and about five hundred people took part in the processions on 'Ashura. In 1976, a year after the civil war began in Lebanon, the number of self-flagellants doubled to about a thousand. For a detailed description of the various performances that took place during 'Ashura in Nabatiyya and in Beirut in 1975, see also Ibrahim Haidari, "Taziyya in Libanon," *Zeitschrift der Deutschen Morgenländischen Gesellschaft*, suppl. 3 (1977): 430–37.

21. See the yearly reports during Muharram in *al-Hayat* from 1974 to 1983 for a description of the practice and the debates revolving around this issue.

22. *L'Orient le Jour*, 5 September 1987.

23. For a discussion of how Khamenei's fatwa in 1994 influenced Shi'ites in India, see David Pinault, *Horse of Karbala: Muslim Devotional Life in India* (New York: Palgrave, 2001), ch. 9.

24. For a discussion of Hizbullah-style 'Ashura commemorations, see Lara Deeb, *An Enchanted Modern: Gender and Public Piety in Shi'i Lebanon* (Princeton: Princeton University Press, 2006), ch. 5.

25. Ibid. See Deeb, *An Enchanted Modern*, for how discussions on proper conduct of 'Ashura rituals form part of everyday conversations of Shi'ite Islamists in Beirut.

26. Although in another context, it is worth noting an episode related to interpretations of 'Ashura commemorations in Lebanon. At a conference held in 1993, shortly after the end of the Lebanese civil war, there was a session titled "Lebanese Folk Traditions." Its goal was to overcome differences among communities and strengthen the so-called common cultural aspects. One of the scholars suggested viewing 'Ashura as a *masrahiyya*, that is, a theater performance that should be viewed as part of the Lebanese popular culture heritage. He thus positions 'Ashura commemorations in the Lebanese context and puts Shi'ites in the context of the Leba-

nese nation and not outside it, since Lebanese folklore is about the nation. Zaka al-Hurr, "al-Khatib: al-Turath al-sha'bi al-dini ('Ashura)," in *Al-Thaqafa al-sha'biyya min muqawamat wahdat al-sha'b wa al-watan* (Beirut, 1993), 339–51.

27. The Islamic Health Committee, a Hizbullah-run NGO, collects blood donations during 'Ashura and forwards the donated blood to various hospitals throughout Lebanon.

28. Blood donation is also viewed as preferable by many Shi'ites.

29. I observed the 'Ashura rituals in Nabatiyya in 2003 and was amazed at the relaxed atmosphere. Many young women were dressed in fashionable black dresses and exchanged glances with the young men who were "hitting *haydar*" and were all bloody as a result. After the end of the procession, many young men and young women were talking to each other and laughing, despite blood on their faces and the smell of blood in the entire city. When I returned the next day to my office in the German Orient Institute, I found that two of my colleagues had observed the processions in Nabatiyya as well. Both turned to me and said, "It reminded us of carnival in Germany, it wasn't sad at all." On the other hand, two Lebanese colleagues who were used to seeing clips of the processions on television were looking at us in wonder. They couldn't believe we had attended the processions. Here I do not intend to deemphasize the importance of 'Ashura processions, but would like to point out that "hitting *haydar*" has multiple functions; one certainly is the construction of masculinity, so as to perhaps be as fearless as Imam Husayn.

30. While it has condemned American actions in Iraq in speeches given at 'Ashura or on Yawm al-Quds (the Day of Jerusalem), the most recent attack on Israeli posts in the occupied Shaba'a Farms on 22 March, 2004 to "retaliate for the murder of Shaykh Ahmad Yassin [Hamas leader in Gaza] at the hand of the Zionists" is one of the clearest signals of Hizbullah's interpretation of the Lebanese nation. It should not be seen so much as one of its moves against the idea of the nation, but as a clear sign of its active involvement in the creation of nationalism as modeled after Hizbullah's ideologies.

31. "Al-Tuqus al-'unfiyya 'ala masrah 'Ashura," *al-Nahar*, 21 March 2002.

32. Since 1994 the style and meaning of both—*ta'ziyya* and the content of the speeches held during the mourning ceremonies—have also changed among Hizbullah members, but this is beyond the focus of this work. See Deeb, *An Enchanted Modern* for a discussion of these changes.

33. See, for example, a collection of Nasrallah's speeches given during 'Ashura over the past several years. The importance of martyrdom is directly connected to fighting the Zionist occupation of Lebanon. His speeches are often lectures on the meaning (interpretations) of certain words, which he then puts in the Lebanese

context. For example, in one of his speeches on the first night of Muharram 1998, referring to the activism of Imam Husayn in standing up for his rights, he points that "if our land continues to be occupied, that is because we are the problem and the cause for their occupation. It is possible that when one of you says, 'They always say America and Israel are the problem,' I would say yes, the two are the problem and the reason for it but we also are the problem and the reason [for this situation] because America and Israel continue to have hegemony over us. So if we stand in the face of our enemy . . . they will not be our problem any more." Religious interpretations that justify the freedom of the land and the independence of the nation are one of the most obvious examples of the promotion of religious nationalisms. Hasan Nasrallah, *Khitab 'Ashura* (Beirut: Dar al-Safwa, 2000), 112–13.

34. Deeb, *An Enchanted Modern*, ch. 4.

35. Mikhail Bakhtin, *The Dialogic Imagination* (Austin: University of Texas Press, 1981).

36. Ibid.

37. Jane Hill, "The Refiguration of the Anthropology of Language," *Cultural Anthropology* 1 (1986): 89–102.

38. Linda S. Walbridge, ed., *The Most Learned of the Shi'a: The Institution of the Marja' Taqlid* (Oxford: Oxford University Press, 2001), 4.

39. *Al-Majallah,* 21 March 1998, 36.

40. *L'Orient le Jour,* 25 January 2003.

41. *Al-Shira',* 16 November 1998.

42. Jafar Fadlallah, ed., *Hadith 'Ashura* (Beirut: Dar al-Malik, 1997), 76.

43. For Fadlallah's view of the relation between Islam and Arab nationalism, see also Martin Kramer, "The Oracle of Hizbullah," in R. Scott Appleby, ed., *Spokesmen for the Despised: Fundamentalist Leaders of the Middle East* (Chicago: University of Chicago Press, 1997), 83–181. Although I certainly disagree with Kramer's labeling Fadlallah as a fundamentalist Shi'ite leader, the article nonetheless provides a useful summary of some of Fadlallah's ideas as well as his biography. See also Ibrahim M. Abu-Rabi', "Toward an Islamic Liberation Theology: Muhammad Husayn Fadlallah and the Principles of Shi'i Resurgence," *Intellectual Origins of Islamic Resurgence in the Modern Arab World* (Albany, NY: SUNY Press, 1996), ch. 7. Abu Rabi' discusses the various dimensions of Fadlallah's theory of Islamic liberation—a new interpretation of traditional Islamic principles to save the Muslims from their current state of decline—calling him a "post-Qutbian thinker."

44. For a detailed discussion of how the word "Arab" is used in speeches of Arab Islamists and how Islamists view Arab nationalism, see Emmanuel Sivan, "Arab Nationalism in the Age of the Islamic Resurgence," in James Jankowski and Israel Ger-

shoni, eds., *Rethinking Nationalism in the Arab Middle East* (New York: Columbia University Press, 1997), 207–29.

45. For a discussion of the problems with using modern national and categories such as Arab and Persians to discuss early and medieval Islamic history to interpret the events in the past, see Fred M. Donner, "Modern Nationalism and Medieval Islamic History," *Al-'Usur al-Wusta: The Bulletin of Middle East Medievalists* 13, no. 1 (April 2001): 21–22.

46. For a convincing discussion of this point, see Fred M. Donner, "From Believers to Muslims: Confessional Self-Identity in the Early Islamic Community," *al-Abhath* 50–51 (2002–2003): 9–53.

47. Personal interview, Jibsheet, 26 October 2002.

48. Yitzhak Nakash, "The Nature of Shi'ism in Iraq," in Faleh Abdul-Jabar, ed., *Ayatollahs, Sufis and Ideologues* (London: Saqi, 2002), 27.

49. This view originated in writings of Orientalists such as those of James Darmesteter, who connected the mental and cultural attitude of the Aryan race to Shi'ite practices and opposed them to Semitic mental attitudes, which he believed were the reason for a Sunni tradition among Arabs. See, for example, James Darmesteter, "Persia: A Historical and Literary Sketch," in C. P. Tiele, ed., *The Religion of Iranian Peoples* (Bombay: Parsi, 1912). For a critical study of theories of Aryan-Semitic differences related to the construction of Shi'ism as a less monotheistic religion, see Holly A. Shissler, *Between Two Empires: Ahmet Ağaoğlu and the New Turkey* (London: I. B. Tauris, 2003), ch. 3. For a discussion of how the theories of these Orientalists were taken up selectively by the first generation of Persian nationalists who helped construct Persian nationalism based on Aryan race ideologies and the purity of the Persian language and which resulted in the exclusion of Islam from nationalism, see Roschanack Shaery-Eisenlohr, "Die Rolle der persischen Sprache in der Legitimierung des iranischen Nationalismus: Eine ethnohistorische Analyse," M.A. thesis, University of Heidelberg, 1998.

50. Frank J. Korom, *Hosay Trinidad: Muharram Performances in an Indo-Caribbean Diaspora* (Philadelphia: University of Pennsylvania Press, 2003), 34.

51. Ibid., 35.

52. Ibid.

53. See, for example, Talib Aziz's article on Fadlallah for a similar line of argument, portraying Fadlallah in a positive light as *the* religious scholar who aims to renew Shi'ite tradition. Talib Aziz, "Fadlallah and the Remaking of the Marja'iyya," in Linda S. Walbridge, ed., *The Most Learned of the Shi'a* (Oxford: Oxford University Press, 2001), 205–15. For more examples of how Fadlallah is viewed in Lebanon see Deeb, *An Enchanted Modern*, 92–95.

54. Ibid., ch. 5.

55. *Al-Mu'assasat al-marja'iyya: Injazat wa amal* (Beirut, 2002), 9, 15.

56. Fadlallah, *Hadith 'Ashura*, 154.

57. Stefan Rosiny, "The Tragedy of Fatima al-Zahra in the Debate of Two Shiite Theologians in Lebanon," in Rainer Brunner and Werner Ende, eds., *The Twelver Shia in Modern Times: Religious Culture and Political History* (Leiden: Brill, 2001), 216.

58. Deeb, *An Enchanted Modern*, 4.

59. For more details on this story see Rosiny, "The Tragedy of Fatima al-Zahra."

60. Sayyid Ja'far Murtada 'Amili, *Ranjha-i hazrat-i Zahra* (Tehran: Daftar-i Tablighat-i Islami, 2001). The book has been translated from Arabic into Persian, which is indicative of the political importance of this debate. In the foreword the translator states how the name of the person against whom this study is directed will not be revealed to avoid the creation of hostile feelings between the two parties. Instead, he claims that this study is aimed to provide evidence and should be viewed as fulfilling the religious duty (*taklif-i shar'i*) of the author. Yet, throughout the book, while the name of Fadlallah is not mentioned, the tone of harsh criticism prevails. See, for example, pp. 47, 121–24.

61. Rosiny, "The Tragedy of Fatima al-Zahra," 214 (emphasis added). See also www.yahosein.net for an interview with Sayyid Muhammad Sadiq Rawhani, an Iranian *marja'*, on Fadlallah's interpretation of the event. The article is titled "Difa'an 'an al-shahida 'alayha al-salam." He refers to Fadlallah as the "lost one (*dall*) and the deceiver (*mudill*) . . . whom perhaps God will guide so that he will recover from his blindness."

62. Rosiny, "The Tragedy of Fatima al-Zahra," 210 (emphasis added).

63. Ibid., 208 (emphasis added).

64. For a similar conviction that a rational and objective approach to texts—understood as an index of modernity—helps Muslims overcome some of their current problems, helping them find their way back to an authentic and original form of Islam, see Laith Kubba, "Towards an Objective, Relative and Rational Islamic Discourse," in Roel Meijer, ed., *Cosmopolitanism, Identity and Authenticity in the Middle East* (Surrey: Curzon, 1999), 129–42.

65. Rosiny, "The Tragedy of Fatima al-Zahra," 218 (emphasis added).

66. Ibid.

67. Fadlallah, *Hadith 'Ashura*, 222.

68. Ibid., 238–39. For the strategies of Islamists in claiming to be part of the modern world, see Ahmad S. Moussalli, "Islamism: Modernisation of Islam or Islamisation of Knowledge," in Roel Meijer, ed., *Cosmopolitanism, Identity and Authenticity* (Surrey: Curzon, 1999), 87–101. Fadlallah's line of argumentation fits into

Moussalli's description of how these Islamists use ideas about philosophy, knowledge, and modern science, to present themselves as possessing a more modern understanding of the religious and historical texts.

69. Fadlallah, *Hadith 'Ashura*, 154.

70. Max Weiss, "The Cultural Politics of Shi'i Modernism: Morality and Gender in Early 20th-Century Lebanon," *International Journal of Middle East Studies* 39 (2): 249–70.

71. Tamara Chalabi, "Community and Nation-State: The Shiis of Jabal Amil and the New Lebanon 1918–1943," Ph.D. diss., Harvard University, 2003, 282.

72. Rosiny, cited in Deeb, *An Enchanted Modern*, 94.

73. Weiss, "The Cultural Politics of Shi'i Modernism," and Deeb, *An Enchanted Modern*.

74. Aghaie, *The Martyrs of Karbala*, ch. 7.

5. Iranian Cultural Politics in Lebanon

1. *Ajyal al-Mustafa* 21 (June 2002): 17.

2. *Salnameh* (Beirut, 1968).

3. See a series of articles on Iranian cultural sites and cities in *al-'Irfan* 50, files 6–7 (1963).

4. Ibid., p. 547.

5. Information in this section is mainly based on interviews conducted with Sayyid Muhammad Husayn Hashemi, the Iranian cultural attaché, in Beirut on 28 January 2003 and 8 April 2003, as well as on an interview with Ms. Fatimah Charafeddine, one of the first employees at ICC since its establishment, on 27 February 2003 in Beirut.

6. *Ajyal al-Mustafa* 21 (June 2002): 16.

7. Ibid.

8. He is a cousin of Sayyid Husayn Charafeddine, the brother-in-law of Musa Sadr. Born into a Lebanese religious family with an Iranian mother and a Lebanese father, Dr. Charafeddine spent part of his life in Iran and earned his PhD in laboratory sciences at Tehran University before returning to Lebanon to work. "Ravabet-i tarikhi va farhangi bayn-i Iran va Lubnan," unpublished manuscript, Beirut, 1998.

9. Charafeddine, *"Ravabet-i tarikhi"* (emphasis added).

10. *Ajyal al-Mustafa* 21 (June 2002): 16–18.

11. See, for example, Roger Shanahan, *The Shi'a of Lebanon: Clans, Parties and Clerics* (London: I. B. Tauris, 2005), 139.

12. The contents of the boxes at the LU's Center for Persian Language and Its Civilization revealed much about the sudden interruption of the program and the closing down of the center. It was clear that one person had just cleared everything off the desks of all the employees and professors of the center and put it hastily into boxes, since personal notes, letters, secretaries' reminder notes of personal and faculty appointments, the files of the students, and some books, could all be found in these boxes. I researched only what was left of the students' files, but certainly the contents of the boxes and the way they were packed could be studied as material objects that can function as narratives of the war.

13. In the academic year 1970–1971, a minimum of thirty-two Sunnis and thirty-two Shiʻites, fifty Maronites, twenty-three Greek Orthodox, and seven Druze registered for Persian. In other academic years the number of Christian students was also very high. In the 1960s and 1970s Shiʻites did not have as much access to education as other religious communities; here I want to point out solely that, prior to the Islamic revolution, Persian was not in any way connected to Shiʻism. This is true even though (see chapter 2) some Shiʻites viewed the Shah's policy of providing financial support for the al-ʻAmiliyya school and forcing al-ʻAmiliyya staff to accept the teaching of Persian in the school as an effort to further connect to the Shiʻite population in Lebanon. But the Persian employees at LU prior to the revolution did not make such a claim, at least not in any official discourse. Thus the presence of high numbers of non-Shiʻite students at these classes supports my argument, even if proportionately more Muslims (many students only stated their Muslim and not their sectarian identity) took Persian.

14. *Al-Dirasat al-Adabiyya* 1–2 (Spring 2000): 354.

15. Interview with Hashemi, Beirut, 8 April 2003.

16. *Al-Dirasat al-Adabiyya* 1 (Spring 1959): 14.

17. Prior to the revolution, there were Iranian cultural centers outside the control of the Iranian embassies in some other countries. Pakistan and India were among the countries in which these cultural centers operated independently from the Iranian embassy. For a detailed account of the activities of the Iranian Cultural Center in Pakistan prior to the revolution and the clashes between these cultural centers and the Iranian embassy, see, for example, the autobiographical account of the Iranian cultural attaché to Lahore in the 1960s, Mariam Behnam, *Zelzelah: A Woman Before Her Time* (Dubai: Motivate, 1994). For an analysis of how the Iranian revolution and the consequent shift in the activities of the Iranian Cultural Center were perceived among non-Shiʻite Pakistanis, see Muhammad Qasim Zaman, *The Ulama in Contemporary Islam: Custodians of Change* (Princeton: Princeton University Press, 2002), ch. 5, esp. p. 123. Viewing the publications and activities of the Iranian Cultural Center in Lahore as at-

tempts to strengthen Pakistani Shi'ites, and consequently as a threat to Sunni dominance in Pakistan, led a member of a radical Pakistani Sunni group to assassinate the head of the Iranian Cultural Center in Lahore in December 1990.

18. *Al-Dirasat al-Adabiyya* 1 (Spring 1959): 13–14.

19. *Al-Dirasat al-Adabiyya* 1–2 (Spring 2000): 356–57.

20. *Al-Dirasat al-Adabiyya* 1 (Spring 1959): 13–14.

21. Both articles can be found in *al-Dirasat al-Adabiyya* 3–4 (Fall/Winter 2001).

22. See, for example, interviews conducted with three Lebanese professors of Persian at LU, where the question of the mutual influence of the languages comes up again and again. It is important to note that the interviews were specifically conducted for publication in ICC's own journal. For one such example, see *al-Rasad* 56 (1996): 131–37.

23. Henri Lammens, *Les "Perses" du Liban et l'origine des Métoualis* (Beyrouth, 1929).

24. Kathryn Woolard and Bambi Schieffelin, "Language Ideology," *Annual Review of Anthropology* 23 (1994): 55–82.

25. *Al-Kifah al-'Arabi*, 9 October 2002.

26. It is clear that Hashemi is referring to members of the *ahl al-bayt*, who are mainly relevant to Shi'ites, but he emphasizes their importance to all Islamic sects. The nationalist interpretation of the identity of the scholars and the members of the *ahl al-bayt* expresses the type of religious nationalism current in Iran and the ways in which Iran maneuvers for more acknowledgment of its contributions to Islamic civilization.

27. *Al-Kifah al-'Arabi*, 9 October 2002.

28. Interview with Muna Mu'ayyad, a Persian language teacher at ICC, Beirut, 21 February 2003. Mu'ayyad was also a lecturer in Persian at LU's branch in Zahle for the academic year 2002–2003.

29. Mustafa Chamran, *Lobnan* (Tehran: Bonyad-i Shahid Chamran, 1983).

30. Houchang Chehabi, ed., *Distant Relations: Five Hundred Years of Iranian-Lebanese Relations* (London: I. B. Tauris, 2006), 45.

31. For a history of the activities of Lebanese Shi'ite book distributors and an extensive list of Lebanese Shi'ite-run publishing houses, see Stefan Rosiny, *Shia's Publishing in Lebanon: With Special Reference to Islamic and Islamist Publications* (Berlin: Das Arabische Buch, 1999). Dar al-Haqq is one of the leading Lebanese Shi'ite book distributors connected to various religious institutions in Iran. According to my own data, besides distributing ICC books in Beirut and Damascus, Dar al-Haqq distributes the books of *al-Mujtama' al-'alami li ahl al-bayt*, a Shi'ite organization based in Iran promoting Shi'ite knowledge in the world. Dar al-Haqq also distributes the

books of the two Iranian-based Shi'ite organizations called *al-Rabita al-thaqafiyya wa al-'alaqat al-islamiyya* and *Sazman-i tablighat-i islami*. In 2002 Dar al-Haqq distributed over 212 Shi'ite-related books in Arabic in cooperation with these Iranian organizations in Lebanon. These estimates are based on unpublished booklists.

32. David Pinault, *The Shiites: Ritual and Popular Piety in a Muslim Community* (New York: St. Martin's, 1992), 95.

33. *Al-Rasad al-Thaqafi* 39 (January 1994).

34. *Al-Rasad al-Thaqafi* 36 (October 1993).

35. For my analysis I randomly chose fifteen volumes of the above-mentioned journal published between 1990 and 1997.

36. Conversation with Fatimah Charafeddine, a senior employee at the ICC, who recalled how shortly before the end of the civil war, the ICC began showing a series of Iranian movies in Beirut Theater and told me about the positive reaction of Lebanese to these movies.

37. For details on this exhibition, see *al-Kifah al-'Arabi*, 9 September 2002. For a summary of the speeches and questions asked at the discussion table held at the opening of the exhibition, see *al-Anwar*, 6 September 2002; *al-Bayraq*, 7 September 2002. The specific case I discuss here is not reflected in the press and was told to me during a conversation with Hashemi.

38. Moulouk Berry, "Radical Transitions: Shifting Gender Discourses in Lebanese Muslim Shi'i Jurisprudence and Ideology, 1960–1979 and 1990–1999," PhD diss., University of Michigan, 2002, 3.

39. For a full text of Mutran Khalil Abi Nadir's speech, see *al-Diyyar*, 6 September 2002.

40. For the entire text of the interview with Dr. Rahnavard, see *al-Safir*, 7 September 2002.

41. Moulouk Berry, "Gender Debates in Lebanon: Muslim Shi'i Jurisprudence in Relation to Women's Marital Sexual Rights," *HAWWA: Journal of Women of the Middle East and the Islamic World* 4 (2006): 131–58; see also Berry, "*Radical Transitions,*" 39.

42. Berry, "Gender Debates in Lebanon," 134–35.

43. Ibid., 140.

44. Interview with Hashemi, Beirut, 8 April 2003.

45. Ibid. For a discussion of the existing stereotypes regarding the southern suburbs of Beirut as a ghetto, see Mona Harb el-Kak, "Transforming the Site of Dereliction into the Urban Culture of Modernity: Beirut's Southern Suburb and Elisar Project," in Peter G. Rowe and Hashim Sarkis, eds., *Projecting Beirut: Episodes in the Construction and Reconstruction of a Modern City* (New York: Prestel, 1998), 173–81.

46. For such travel reports see *al-Rasid* 18 (April 1992): 36–41.

47. Cited in Carole H. Dagher, *Bring Down the Walls: Lebanon's Post-War Challenge* (New York: Palgrave, 2000), 51.

48. For the entire speech of Khatami in a roundtable discussion titled "Dialogue among Civilizations" in September 2000 at the United Nations, see www.unesco. org/dialogue2001/en/khatami.htm.

49. Even within the Shi'ite community of Lebanon, ideas about interfaith dialogue and the degree of concession to other religious groups differ to a considerable extent. For example, in the view of many Lebanese Shi'ites, the late Muhammad Mahdi Shamseddine, who was a prominent figure in interfaith dialogue activities, made far too many concessions to Lebanese Christians by not wanting to push for the abolishment of political sectarianism, which is at the top of the political agenda of Amal and Hizbullah.

50. For more details on this program, see *al-Liwa'*, 20 January 2003; *al-Bayraq*, 20 January 2003.

51. Sidon is clearly identified as a Sunni city, and the Hariri Foundation has accomplished much to transform the public space in the city and to turn it into a Sunni domain. The gigantic Sunni mosque, designed and built by the late Hariri in commemoration of his father at the entrance of the city, is just one example.

52. Emmanuel Bonne, *Vie publique, patronage et clientèle: Rafic Hariri à Saïda* (Beirut: CERMOC, 1995), 85–86.

53. Ibid., 32.

54. For example, Mona Fawaz has discussed convincingly how two Iranian Islamic NGOs active in al-Dahiyya, *Jihad al-bina'* (Struggle for Construction) and *al-Imdad* (Support) have evolved over the years from complete dependence on Iran to being de facto independent organizations. Even though each of these two NGOs still has close relations to their Iranian founding organizations, and despite the fact that a portion of their funding still comes from various sources in Iran under the control of Khamenei, they have succeeded in generating most of their support locally and have adapted the discourse of poverty and dispossession prevalent in these NGOs to the specific needs of the Lebanese Shi'ites so that they can voice their needs to the state. Mona Fawaz, "Islam, Resistance and Community Development: The Case of the Southern Suburb of Beirut City," M.A. thesis, Massachusetts Institute of Technology, 1998.

55. Information in this section on the *ahl al-bayt* Foundation has been taken from Wilfried Buchta, *Die iranische Schia und die islamische Einheit, 1979–1996* (Hamburg: Deutsches Orient-Institut, 1997), 275–92.

56. *Kayhan*, 26 May 1990, in Buchta, *Die iranische Schia*, 278.

57. Muslim al-Rabi'i, "Mashru': al-Marakiz al-thaqafiyya fi Lubnan," unpublished manuscript, Beirut, December 1993.

58. René Naba, *Rafic Hariri: Un homme d'affaires premier ministre* (Paris: L'Harmattan, 1999). Naba describes in detail the growing influence of Hariri in Lebanon and how through his successful investments he had been able to buy newspapers and other media outlets in Lebanon to influence public opinion. In Naba's opinion, Hariri believed that he was the state and did not distinguish between state investments and his private entrepreneurial activities.

59. For a biography of Rafiq Hariri, see Andreas Rieck, "Rafiq Hariri," *Orient* 34, no. 2 (1993): 179–83.

60. While I heard from some Shi'ites that they had received grants from the Hariri Foundation at the beginning of its establishment, they also said that the foundation changed its policy over the years and now focuses on funding Sunni students only.

61. For more information on the activities of the Hariri Foundation, see www. hariri-foundation.org.lb. For Hariri's activities in Sidon specifically, see Bonne, *Vie publique, patronage et clientèle*. He analyzes the activities of Hariri in Sidon and some of the difficulties he and his sister Bahia faced in establishing themselves as a *zu'ama* family in Sidon. He also describes the city reconstruction plans of the Hariri Foundation there, and the way this reconstruction has changed the public space of Sidon.

62. All the information in this section is taken from a CCSD booklet that contains a list of their activities and publications since 1988, as well as information on the history of CCSD and the names of its presidents and members of its scientific committee.

63. For a description of the overall Islamic mood expressed through dress code, types of greeting, and pictures on the walls of Hizbullah's NGOs in al-Dahiyya, see also Fawaz, "Islam, Resistance and Community Development," 66–71. CCSD's atmosphere is very similar to that in other NGOs in al-Dahiyya.

64. Two other research institutions also associated with Hizbullah are often concerned with Arab-Iranian relations. The first is the *Markaz al-abhath al-'ilmiyya wa al-dirasat al-istratijiyya lil sharq al-awsat* created in 1988 in Tehran under the supervision of the Ministry of Guidance. It has a branch in Beirut. In spring 2002 the center launched its first quarterly journal in Arabic, *Iran al-'Arab*, dealing with various economic, political, and social aspects of Iranian-Arab relations. In addition, articles are published that discuss solely Iranian topics, such as interviews with the former Iranian president 'Ali Akbar Hashemi Rafsanjani, or topics related to the Arab world, such as discussions on the future of the Arab culture in the twenty-first century. Board members for this journal are mainly a mix of Iranians and Lebanese Shi'ites,

all associated with Hizbullah and the Iranian embassy in Beirut. For example, 'Ali Fayyad, the head of the CCSD, is on the editorial board; see *Iran waal-'Arab* (Spring 2002). There are other research institutions, such as the Center for Strategic Studies: Research and Documentation. Created in 1990 in Beirut, the center wants to "take part in developing a new strategic awareness," by focusing on four main fields: "The Arab-Israeli struggle, the Arab order, the neighboring Islamic countries, especially Turkey and Iran, the international strategies and politics that have an impact on the Middle East." The academic consulting board of their journal, called *Shu'un al-awsat*, is more diverse. Some Western scholars, such as Volker Perthes, and some non-Shi'ite Lebanese, such as the well-known Sunni scholar Ridwan al-Sayyid, sit on the board. Some of the issues of the *Shu'un al-awsat* are dedicated to issues concerning Iran's strategic role in the Middle East as well as to discussions about social and political currents, such as the relation between civil society, religion, and politics; see, for example, *Shu'un al-awsat* 103 (Summer 2001). Sayyid Husayn al-Musawi, the head of the Arab-Iranian Friendship Society (*anjoman-i dusti-i iran va arab*), is the general supervisor (*al-mushrif al-'amm*) of both journals mentioned here. That the persons involved in production also supervise these journals is indicative of their overall policy and similar orientation.

65. Ideally, the power of a *marja'* increases with the number of his followers, as they contribute religious taxes and donations. In other words, the economic power of the *marja'* can attract even more followers. But this was not the case with Khamenei's followers in Lebanon because Khamenei has access to Iranian state funds. Both he and Khomeini before him used these funds to finance projects which increase their own power, such as the support of Hizbullah in Lebanon. So there is no need for Khamenei to expect any serious economic support from his followers, though at the same time the followers do benefit greatly from this situation.

66. The result of the 2004 municipal elections in Lebanon is the best illustration of Hizbullah's increasing power in al-Dahiyya, al-Biqa', and South Lebanon.

67. Interview with Hashemi, Beirut, 28 January 2003 (emphasis added).

68. At ICC-organized *zajal* poetry nights, there is no music; the poets also prepare their poems in advance, which avoids the dialogic and improvisational character of the folk event, where the poets recite without a written text.

69. The three Lebanese poets were Talil Hamdan, Nadim Shu'ayb, and Joseph 'Aoun. When I mentioned their names to other Lebanese, they shook their heads in disapproval. While Talil Hamdan is a well-known poet in the *zajal* tradition, his performance at ICC for an honorarium seems to have disappointed many Lebanese. At a 2003 Tyre poetry night, the poets were George Wakim, Joseph 'Aoun, Husayn 'Isa, and Nadim Shu'ayb. It is worth mentioning that not all the poets were Shi'ites.

Listening to a non-Shi'ite Lebanese praise ICC seems to underscore the popularity of the Iranian government among Lebanese from the ICC's perspective, even though the poets do receive an honorarium for their performance.

70. I thank Mr. Louay Charafeddine for translating both Arabic poems into English for use in this chapter.

71. "Dahe-ye mobarak-i fajr dar Lobnan," *Fa'aliyatha-i raizani-i farhangi-i jomhuri-i islami-i Iran-Beirut,* unpublished manuscript, Beirut, February 2002, 6–7.

72. Almost a week after 'Ashura in March 2003, an event which almost coincided with the Persian New Year (*nowruz*) on March 21, I flew from Beirut to Tehran on Iran Air and saw a group of almost forty preachers in their cloaks on their way back to Tehran. The passengers on our plane consisted entirely of these male preachers except for me and another Iranian woman. At that time I realized how postrevolutionary Iranian-Lebanese spaces are dominated by Shi'ite religious networks, as the Lebanese person in charge of passport control gazed at my German passport (my picture without a headscarf), looked at me wearing the *hijab* at the airport in disbelief, and asked me twice to assure himself that I had not confused my actual destination with Iran. Two weeks later, on my return to Beirut, I realized that the Lebanese passport control officials were unfriendly to the Iranian passengers in a way I had never observed before, almost throwing the passports back at people after stamping them. When my turn came, they looked at my German passport and asked me where I had come from. I responded in Arabic that I had come from Iran. Two other persons standing there came to me and asked me again, and I explained to them that I held both Iranian and German passports and was conducting research in Lebanon. A series of questions in a friendly tone were directed toward me regarding what I was doing in Lebanon and why my *hijab* was not worn in the way that other women who commute between Iran and Lebanon wear it. All these questions and others clarified for me that postrevolutionary Iranian-Lebanese relations are dominated not only by Shi'ite religious groups but by a certain type of Shi'ite religious group, the network between Hizbullah and Khamenei in Iran.

73. "Tafahom-nameh'-i hamkariha-i tablighati-resaneh-i bayn-i jomhuri-i islami-i Iran va jomhuri-i Lobnan," unpublished manuscript, 1998.

Epilogue

1. *Daily Star,* 15 March 2005.

2. Naim Qassem, *Hizbullah: The Story from Within* (London: Dar al-Saqi, 2005), 52.

3. http://www.occupationwatch.org/article.php?id=3252, retrieved on 14 February 2004.

4. Gökhan Çentinsaya, *Ottoman Administration of Iraq, 1890–1908* (London: Routledge, 2005), ch. 5. All information on Ottoman Iraq in this section is taken from this book.

5. Vali Nasr, *The Shia Revival: How Conflicts within Islam Will Shape the Future* (New York: Norton, 2006).

References

Primary Sources

Interviews

Abu Kharif. Beirut, 12 November 2002

al-Amin, Hasan. Beirut, 2 September 2000

Charafeddine, Fatimah. Beirut, 27 February 2003

Fahs, Hani. Beirut, 11 August 2000; 14 August 2000; several interviews and written exchanges between 2002 and 2003

Hashemi, Muhammad Husayn. Beirut, 28 January 2003 and 8 April 2003

Isma'il, Rana. Beirut, 16 October 2002

Mu'ayyad, Muna. Beirut, 21 February 2003

al-Musawi, Khudur. Beirut, 11 October 2002

Nasrallah, Muhammad. Beirut, 4 September 2002

Shaqra, Hasan. Nabatiyya, 23 November 2002

A Shi'ite shaykh. Jibsheet, 26 October 2002

Yatim, Husayn. Beirut, 22 May 2003

Manuscripts

Charafeddine, Muhammad. *Ravabet-i tarikhi va farhangi bayn-i Iran va Lobnan*. Unpublished manuscript, Beirut, 1998.

———. "Dahe-ye mobarak-i fajr dar Lobnan." *Fa'aliyatha-i raizani-i farhangi-i jomhuri-i islami-i Iran-Beirut*. Unpublished manuscript, Beirut, February 2002.

"Al-Madaris al-mabarrat: Nahj islah wa masar al-taqrir." Paper presented at Mu'tamar al-islah al-tarbawi lil madrasa fi al-buldan al-'arabiyya, American University of Beirut, 2000.

Al-Rabi'i, Muslim. *Mashru': al-Marakiz al-thaqafiyya fi Lubnan*. Unpublished manuscript, Beirut, December 1993.

Tafahom-nameh'-i hamkariha-i tablighati-resaneh-i bayn-i jomhuri-i islami-i Iran va jomhuri-i Lobnan. Unpublished manuscript, ICC, 1998.

Newspapers and Periodicals

Ajyal al-Mustafa 2–21 (1996–June 2002)

Amal, 1980–1982

Al-Anwar, 6 September 2002

Al-'Awasif, 9 February 2002–6 September 2002

Al-Bayraq, 7 September 2002–20 January 2003

Christian Science Monitor, 19 April 1978

Al-Dabbur, 23 July 1971

Daily Star, 28 December 2002–15 March 2005

Al-Dirasat al-Adabiyya 1 (Spring 1959)

Al-Dirasat al-Adabiyya 1–4 (Spring 2000–Winter 2001)

Al-Diyyar, 6 May 1985–6 September 2002

Al-Hawadith, 7 October 1966–24 December 1976

Al-Hayat, 1961–1983

Iran wa al-'Arab, Spring 2002

Al-'Irfan, 1962–1963

Al-Jarida 53 (January 1982)

Al-Kifah al-'Arabi, 14 April 2001–9 October 2002

Kul Shay', 14 February 1976

Al-Liwa', 16 August 1998–20 January 2003

Al-Majallah, 21 March 1998

Al-Mustaqbal, 10 June 2002

Al-Nahar, 6 August 1969–10 June 2002

Neue Züricher Zeitung, 7 March 2001–14 October 2002

Nida' al-Watan, 27 February 1998

Omid-i Inqilab 36–39 (3 July 1982–14 August 1982)

L'Orient le Jour, 5 September 1987–25 January 2003

Al-Rasad 56–57 (1996–April 1996)

Al-Rasad al-Thaqafi 28–45 (February 1993–July 1994)

Al-Rasid 18–24 (April 1992–October 1992)

Report of al-'Amiliyya of 1958–1962

Sada al-Risala 46 (2000)

Al-Safir, 23 August 1985–7 September 2002

Salnameh (Beirut), 1968

Sawt al-Mahrumin, 1 December 1976

Shabab al-Ghad, October 2000

Al-Shira', 15 February 1988–16 November 1998

Shu'un al-Awsat 103 (Summer 2001)

UNDP Report 2001

Books and Articles

'Amili, Sayyid Ja'far Murtada. *Ranjha-i hazrat-i Zahra*. Tehran: Daftar-i Tablighat-i Islami, 2001.

Asnad-i faj'i-ye Lubnan. N.p., n.d.

Az Shah ta Chamoun. N.p., 1978.

Bonyad-i Shahid Chamran. *Zendeginameh: Shahid Doctor Chamran*. Tehran: Bonyad-i Shahid Chamran, n.d.

Bozorgdasht-i Doktor 'Ali Shari'ati dar Beirut. N.p., n.d.

Chamran, Mustafa. *Lobnan*. Tehran: Bonyad-i Shahid Chamran, 1983.

Elwiri, Murtada. *Khatirat-i Murtada Elwiri*. Tehran: Daftar-i Adabiyyat-i Jomhuri-i Islami, 1997.

Fadlallah, Jafar, ed. *Hadith 'Ashura*. Beirut: Dar al-Malik, 1997.

Fadlallah, Muhammad Husayn. "Al-Thawra al-islamiyya fi Iran bayn al-takhtit al-maddi wa al-isnad al-ilahi." *Al-Muntalaq* 10 (1980): 12.

Farsi, Jalal al-Din. *Zavaya-i tarik*. Tehran: Hawze-i Andishe va Honar-i Islami, 1994.

Imam Musa Sadr: Yaran-i imam be ravayat-i asnad-i savak. Tehran: Markaz-i Barressi-i Asnad-i Tarikhi-i Vizarat-i Itila'at, 2001.

Al-Janub: Dhakirat watan. Beirut: Majlis al-Janub, 1998 and 2001.

Makki, Husayn. *Qawl wa fi'l*. Beirut: Matba' al-Musri, 1967.

Mohtashami, 'Ali Akbar. *Khaterat-i siyasi*. Tehran: Daftar-i Adabiyyat-i Jomhuri-i Islami, 2000.

———. *Al-Muwatin wa al-tarbiyya al-madaniyya fi Lubnan*. Beirut: Al-Markaz al-Lubnani lil Dirasat, 1993.

Nasrallah, Hassan. *Khitab 'Ashura*. Beirut: Dar al-Safwa, 2000.

Nehzat-i Azadi-i Iran. *Zendeginameh-i sardar-i rashid-i Islam Shahid Doktor Mostafa Chamran*. Tehran, 1983.

Rawhani, Sayyid Hamid. *Nihzat-i Imam Khomeini*, 3:821–22. Tehran: Sazman-i Asnad-i Inqilab-i Islami, 1995.

Savak va ruhaniyyat. Tehran: Shaqaeq, 1992.

Sepahbod Taymur Bakhtiyar be ravayat-i asnad-i savak. Tehran: Markaz-i Barressi-i Asnad-i Tarikhi-i Vizarat-i Itila'at, 2000.

Sepehri, Iraj. *Az jebhe'-i nabard-i Felestin: Khaterat-i rafiq kargar-i fada'i Shahid Iraj Sepehri*. Tehran: n.p., 1977.

Shahid-i sarafraz Doctor Mustafa Chamran: Yaran-i imam be ravayat-i asnad-i savak. Tehran: Markaz-i Barressi-i Asnad-i Tarikhi-i Vizarat-i Itila'at, 2000.

Sharh-i ta'sis va tarikhcheha-i vaqaye'-i Sazman-i Mojahedin-i Khalq-i Iran 1344–1350. Long Beach, CA: Sazman-i Mojahedin-i Khalq-i Iran, 1980.

Shari'ati be ravayat-i asnad-i savak. Tehran: Markaz-i Asnad-i Inqilab-i Islami, 2000.

Tahlili az awza'-i janub-i Lubnan. Sazman-i Amal va Doctor Chamran (n.p, n.d.).

Tueni, Ghassan, ed. *al-Wasaya*. Beirut: Dar al-Nahar, 2001.

Pamphlets

Jam'iyyat al-ta'lim al-dini al-islami, 2001–2002

Al-Kitab al-madrasi lil 'am al-dirasi, 2001–2002

Al-Mu'assasat al-marja'iyya: Injazat wa aamaal, Beirut, 2002

Mu'assasat al-Shahid Hasan Qasir, Beirut, n.d.

Mu'assasat Amal al-tarbawiyya, 2002–2003

Websites

http://www.bayynat.org

http://www.hariri.com

http://www.hariri-foundation.org.lb

http://www.occupationwatch.org/article.php?id = 3252

http://www.unesco.org/dialogue2001/en/khatami.htm
http://www.yahosein.net

Secondary Sources

Theses and Dissertations

Atiyya, Aman. "Development of Shiʻite Education in Lebanon." M.A. thesis, American University of Beirut, 1972.

Babikian, J. A. "Education and Civilization in Syria and Lebanon: A Historical, Comparative and Critical Survey of the Syrian and Lebanese Education and Civilization." M.A. thesis, American University of Beirut, 1933.

Berry, Moulouk. "Radical Transitions: Shifting Gender Discourses in Lebanese Muslim Shiʻi Jurisprudence and Ideology, 1960–1979 and 1990–1999." Ph.D. diss., University of Michigan, 2002.

Chalabi, Tamara. "Community and Nation-State: The Shiʻis of Jabal ʻAmil and the New Lebanon 1918–1943." Ph.D. diss., Harvard University, 2003.

Early, Evelyn Aleene. "The Amiliyya Society of Beirut: A Case Study of an Emerging Urban Zaʻim." M.A. thesis, American University of Beirut, 1971.

Fawaz, Mona. "Islam, Resistance and Community Development: The Case of the Southern Suburb of Beirut City." M.A. thesis, Massachusetts Institute of Technology, 1998.

Jurdi, Rula. "Migration and Social Change: The ʻUlema of Ottoman Jabal ʻAmil in Safavid Iran, 1501–1736." Ph.D. diss., Yale University, 1998.

Kaufman, Asher. "Reviving Phoenicia: The Search for an Identity in Lebanon." Ph.D. diss., Brandeis University, 2000.

Kern, Karen M. "The Prohibition of Sunni-Shiʻite Marriages in the Ottoman Empire: A Study of Ideologies." Ph.D. diss., Columbia University, 1999.

Mourtada, Fadia El. "Les Manuels d' instruction civique et la formation du citoyen au Liban." Ph.D. diss., Université de Paris, 1991.

Osseyran, Hayat Nabeel. "The Shiʻite Leadership of South Lebanon: A Reconsideration." M.A. thesis, American University in Beirut, 1997.

Saleeby, Leila Shahine. "State Policy Towards Private Education in Lebanon." M.A. thesis, American University of Beirut, 1987.

Shaery-Eisenlohr, Roschanack. "Die Rolle der persischen Sprache in der Legitimierung des iranischen Nationalismus: Eine ethnohistorische Analyse." M.A. thesis, University of Heidelberg, 1998.

Weiss, Max. "Institutionalizing Sectarianism. Law, Religious Culture, and the Re-making of Shi'i Lebanon. 1920–1947." Ph.D. diss., Stanford University, 2007.

Articles and Books

Abrahamian, Ervand. *Iran Between Two Revolutions*. Princeton: Princeton University Press, 1982.

Abukhalil, As'ad. "Shiites and the Palestinians: Underlying Causes of the Amal-Palestinian Conflict." In Elaine C. Hagopian, ed., *Amal and the Palestinians: Understanding the Battle of the Camps*. Arab World Issues, Occasional Papers no. 9 (1985), 12.

———. "Syria and the Shiites: Al-Asad's Policy in Lebanon." *Third World Quarterly* 12 (2): 1–20.

Abu-Rabi', Ibrahim M. "Toward an Islamic Liberation Theology: Muhammad Husayn Fadlallah and the Principles of Shi'i Resurgence." In *Intellectual Origins of Islamic Resurgence in the Modern Arab World*. Albany: SUNY Press, 1996.

Aghaie, Kamran Scot. *The Martyrs of Karbala: Shi'i Symbols and Rituals in Modern Iran*. Seattle: University of Washington Press, 2004.

Ahmad, Rida. *Hidayat al-muta'allimin*. Sidon: Matba'at al-'Irfan, 1957.

Ajami, Fouad. *The Vanished Imam: Musa al Sadr and the Shia of Lebanon*. Ithaca: Cornell University Press, 1986.

———. "Imam Musa Sadr." In Seyyed Hossein Nasr, Hamid Dabashi, and Seyyed Vali Reza Nasr, eds., *Expectation of the Millennium: Shi'ism in History*. Albany: SUNY Press, 1989.

Al-Amin, 'Adnan. *al-Ta'lim fi Lubnan: Zawaya wa mashahid*. Beirut: Dar al-Jadid, 1994.

Anderson, Benedict. *Imagined Communities: Reflections on the Origin and Spread of Nationalism*. London: Verso, 1991.

Asad, Talal. *Formations of the Secular: Christianity, Islam, Modernity*. Stanford: Stanford University Press, 2003.

———. *Genealogies of Religion: Discipline and Reasons of Power in Christianity and Islam*. Baltimore: Johns Hopkins University Press, 1993.

Aziz, Talib. "Fadlallah and the Remaking of the Marja'iyya." In Linda S. Walbridge, ed., *The Most Learned of the Shi'a: The Institution of the Marja' Taqlid*. Oxford: Oxford University Press, 2001.

Bakhtin, Mikhail. *The Dialogic Imagination*. Austin: University of Texas Press, 1981.

Balibar, Etienne. "The Nation Form: History and Ideology." In Etienne Balibar and Immanuel Wallerstein, eds., *Race, Nation, Class: Ambiguous Identities*. London: Verso, 1991.

Barth, Fredrik. "When Ethnic Identity Is a Social Stigma." In Fredrik Barth, ed., *Ethnic Groups and Boundaries: The Social Organization of Cultural Difference*. Boston: Little, Brown, 1969.

Bashshur, Munir. "The Deepening Cleavage in the Education System." In Theodor Hanf and Nawaf Salam, eds., *Lebanon in Limbo: Postwar Society and State in an Uncertain Regional Environment*. Baden-Baden: Nomos Verlagsgesellschaft, 2003.

Baydun, Ahmad. *Tis' 'ashar firqa najiha: al-Lubnaniyun fi ma'arakat al-zawaj al-madani*. Beirut: Dar al-Nahar, 1999.

Beeman, William O. *Language, Status, and Power in Iran*. Bloomington: Indiana University Press, 1986.

Behnam, Mariam. *Zelzelah: A Woman Before Her Time*. Dubai: Motivate, 1994.

Berry, Moulouk. "Gender Debates in Lebanon: Muslim Shi'i Jurisprudence in Relation to Women's Marital Sexual Rights." *HAWWA: Journal of Women of the Middle East and the Islamic World* 4 (2006): 131–58.

Bonne, Emmanuel. *Vie publique, patronage et clientèle: Rafic Hariri à Saïda*. Beirut: CERMOC, 1995.

Böttcher, Annabelle. "Ayatollah Fadlallah und seine Wohltätigkeitsorganisation al-Mabarrat." In Rainer Brunner and Monika Gronke, eds., *Islamstudien ohne Ende*. Würzburg: Ergon Verlag, 2002.

——. "Sunni and Shi'i Networking in the Middle East," *Mediterranean Politics* 7, no. 3. Special issue: *Shaping the Current Islamic Reformation* (2002): 42–63.

Bourdieu, Pierre. *Distinction: A Social Critique of the Judgment of Taste*. Cambridge: Harvard University Press, 1984.

Brubaker, Rogers, and Frederick Cooper. "Beyond 'Identity,'" *Theory and Society* 29 (2000): 1–47.

Buchta, Wilfried. *Die iranische Schia und die islamische Einheit, 1979–1996*. Hamburg: Deutsches Orient-Institut, 1997.

Çentinsaya, Gökhan. *Ottoman Administration of Iraq, 1890–1908*. London: Routledge, 2005, ch. 5.

Chalabi, Tamara. *The Shi'is of Jabal 'Amil and the New Lebanon: Community and Nation-State, 1918–1943*. New York: Palgrave Macmillan, 2006.

Chehabi, Houchang. *Iranian Politics and Religious Modernism: The Liberation Movement of Iran under the Shah and Khomeini*. Ithaca: Cornell University Press, 1990.

———— ed. *Distant Relations: Five Hundred Years of Iranian–Lebanese Relations.* London: I. B. Tauris, 2006.

Chelkowski, Peter J., ed. *Ta'ziyeh: Ritual and Drama in Iran.* New York: New York University Press, 1979.

Cole, Juan. *Sacred Space and Holy War: The Politics, Culture and History of Shi'ite Islam.* London: I. B. Tauris, 2002.

Colley, Linda. "Britishness and Otherness: An Argument," *Journal of British Studies* 31 (October 1992): 309–29.

Dagher, Carole H. *Bring Down the Walls: Lebanon's Post-War Challenge.* New York: Palgrave, 2000.

Darmesteter, James. "Persia: A Historical and Literary Sketch." In C. P. Tiele, ed., *The Religion of Iranian Peoples.* Bombay: Parsi, 1912.

Deeb, Lara. *An Enchanted Modern: Gender and Public Piety in Shi'i Lebanon.* Princeton: Princeton University Press, 2006.

Donner, Fred M. "From Believers to Muslims: Confessional Self-Identity in the Early Islamic Community," *al-Abhath* 50–51 (2002–2003): 9–53.

————. "Modern Nationalism and Medieval Islamic History," *al-'Usur al-Wusta: The Bulletin of Middle East Medievalists* 13, no. 1 (April 2001): 21–22.

Ehteshami, Anoushiravan, and Raymond A. Hinnebusch, *Syria and Iran: Middle Powers in a Penetrated Regional System.* London: Routledge, 1997.

Eisenlohr, Patrick. "The Politics of Diaspora and the Morality of Secularism: Muslim Identities and Islamic Authority in Mauritius," *Journal of the Royal Anthropological Institute* (n.s.) 12 (2006): 395–412.

Ende, Werner. "The Flagellations of Muharram and the Shi'ite 'Ulama," *Der Islam* 55, no. 1 (1978): 19–36.

Fawaz, Mona. "Contradicting Urban Regulations and State Practices: The Informal Settlements of Beirut." In Mona Harb, ed., *The Lebanese National Master Plan.* Beirut: American University of Beirut, 2003.

Fisher, Michael. *Iran: From Religious Dispute to Revolution.* Cambridge: Harvard University Press, 1980,

Firro, Kais. *Inventing Lebanon.* London: I. B. Tauris, 2003.

Fisk, Robert. *Pity the Nation: Lebanon at War.* London: Deutsch, 1990.

Freitag, Sandria. "Contesting in Public: Colonial Legacies and Contemporary Communalism." In David Ludden, ed., *Contesting the Nation: Religion, Community, and the Politics of Democracy in India.* Philadelphia: University of Pennsylvania Press, 1996.

Fuller, Graham, and Rend Rahim Francke. *The Arab Shi'a: The Forgotten Muslims.* New York: St. Martin's, 1999.

Gellner, Ernest. *Nations and Nationalism*. Ithaca: Cornell University Press, 1983.

Glassen, Erika. "Muharram-Ceremonies (*'Azadari*) in Istanbul at the End of the Nineteenth and the Beginning of the Twentieth Century." In Th. Zarcone and F. Zarinebaf, eds., *Les Iraniens d'Istanbul*. Paris: IFDRI, 1993.

Goffman, Erving. *Frame Analysis: An Essay on the Organization of Experience*. New York: Harper and Row, 1974.

Hagopian, Elaine, ed. *Amal and the Palestinians: Understanding the Battle of the Camps; Viewpoints*. Arab World Issues, Occasional Papers 9. Belmont, MA: Association of Arab-American University Graduates, 1985.

Haidari, Ibrahim. "Taziyya in Libanon," *Zeitschrift der Deutschen Morgenländischen Gesellschaft*, suppl. 3 (1977): 430–37.

Halawi, Majid. *A Lebanon Defied: Musa al-Sadr and the Shi'a Community*. Boulder, CO: Westview, 1992.

Hamzeh, Nizar Ahmad. *In the Path of Hizbullah*. Syracuse: Syracuse University Press, 2004.

Hanf, Theodor. *Coexistence in Wartime Lebanon: Decline of a State and Rise of a Nation*. London: I. B. Tauris, 1993.

"Al-Harakat al-wataniyya al-lubnaniyya." *Documents of the Lebanese National Movement 1975–1981*. Beirut, 1981.

Harb, Mona, and Reinoud Leenders. "Know the Enemy: Hizbullah, 'Terrorism' and the Politics of Perception," *Third World Quarterly* 26 (1): 173–97.

Harik, Judith Palmer. *Hezbollah: The Changing Face of Terrorism*. London: I. B. Tauris, 2004.

———. "The Public and Social Services of the Lebanese Militias." Papers on Lebanon 14 Oxford: Centre for Lebanese Studies, 1994.

Hartman, Michelle, and Alessandro Olsaretti. "The First Boat and the First Oar," *Radical History Review* 86 (2003): 37–65.

Hasan, Mushirul. "The Myth of Unity." In David Ludden, ed., *Contesting the Nation: Religion, Community, and the Politics of Democracy in India*. Philadelphia: University of Pennsylvania Press, 1996.

Hefner, Robert W., and Muhammad Qasim Zaman, eds. *Schooling Islam. The Culture and Politics of Modern Muslim Education*. Princeton: Princeton University Press, 2007.

Hegland, Mary. "Two Images of Husain: Accommodation and Revolution in an Iranian Village." In Nikki Keddie, ed., *Religion and Politics in Iran: Shi'ism from Quitism to Revolution*. New Haven: Yale University Press, 1983.

Hill, Jane. "The Refiguration of the Anthropology of Language," *Cultural Anthropology* 1, no. 1 (1986): 89–102.

269

Hinnebusch, Raymond. "The Politics of Identity in Middle East International Relations." In Louise Fawcett, ed., *International Relations of the Middle East*. Oxford: Oxford University Press, 2005.

Holt, Maria. "Lebanese Shi'i Women and Islamism: A Response to War." In Lamia Rustum Shehadeh, ed., *Women and War in Lebanon*. Gainesville: University of Florida Press, 1999.

Al-Hurr, Zaka. "Al-Khatib: al-Turath al-sha'abi al-dini ('Ashura)." In *al-Thaqafa al-sha'abiyya min muqawamat wahdat al-sha'ab wa al-watan*. Beirut, 1993.

Hyam, Ronald. *Britain's Imperial Century, 1815–1914: A Study of Empire and Expansion*. New York: Harper and Row, 1976.

Irvine, Judith, and Susan Gal. "Language Ideology and Linguistic Differentiation." In Paul V. Kroskrity, ed., *Regimes of Language: Ideologies, Polities and Identities*. Santa Fe: School of American Research Press, 2000.

Jaber, Hala. *Hezbollah: Born with a Vengeance*. New York: Columbia University Press, 1997.

al-Jisr, Bassim. *Fu'ad Shihab*. Beirut, 2000.

Johnson, Michael. *Class and Client in Beirut: The Sunni Muslim Community and the Lebanese State 1840–1985*. London: Ithaca, 1986.

Jones, David R. "Forerunners of the Komsomol: Scouting in Imperial Russia." In Schimmelpenninck van der Oye and Bruce W. Menning, eds., *Reforming the Tsar's Army: Military Innovation in Imperial Russia from Peter the Great to the Revolution*. Cambridge: Cambridge University Press, 2004.

Jurdi Abisaab, Rula. *Converting Persia: Religion and Power in the Safavid Empire*. London: I. B. Tauris, 2004.

———. "Shi'ite Beginnings and Scholastic Tradition in Jabal 'Amil in Lebanon," *The Muslim World* 89 (January 1999): 1–21.

el-Kak, Mona Harb. "Transforming the Site of Dereliction into the Urban Culture of Modernity: Beirut's Southern Suburb and Elisar Project." In Peter G. Rowe and Hashim Sarkis, eds., *Projecting Beirut: Episodes in the Construction and Reconstruction of a Modern City*. New York: Prestel, 1998.

Kalawoun, Nasser M. *The Struggle for Lebanon: A Modern History of Lebanese-Egyptian Relations*. London: I. B. Tauris, 2000.

Kanafani-Zahar, Aida. "The Religion of the 'Other' as Bond: The Interreligious in Lebanon." In Thomas Scheffler, ed., *Religion between Violence and Reconciliation*. Würzburg: Ergon, 2002, 401–18.

Khairallah, Daoud L. "Secular Democracy: A Viable Alternative to the Confessional System." In Deirdre Collings, ed., *Peace for Lebanon? From War to Reconstruction*. Boulder: Rienner, 1994.

Khalaf, Samir. *Cultural Resistance: Global and Local Encounters in the Middle East*. Beirut: Saqi, 2002.

Khalid, Hasan. *Al-Muslimun fi Lubnan wa harb al-sanatayn*. Beirut: Dar al-Kindi, 1978.

Khoury, Yusuf Q. *Al-Ta'ifiyya fi Lubnan min khilal munaqashat majlis al-nuwwab, 1923–1987*. Beirut: Dar al-Hamra, 1989.

Korom, Frank J. *Hosay Trinidad: Muharram Performances in an Indo-Caribbean Diaspora*. Philadelphia: University of Pennsylvania Press, 2003.

Kramer, Martin. "The Oracle of Hizbullah." In R. Scott Appleby, ed., *Spokesmen for the Despised: Fundamentalist Leaders of the Middle East*. Chicago: University of Chicago Press, 1997.

———. "Muhammad Hussein Fadlallah," *Orient* 26, no. 2 (1985): 147–49.

Kubba, Laith. "Towards an Objective, Relative and Rational Islamic Discourse." In Roel Meijer, ed., *Cosmopolitanism, Identity and Authenticity in the Middle East*. Surrey: Curzon, 1999.

Labaki, Boutros. *Education et mobilité sociale dans la société multicommunautaire du Liban: Approche socio-historique*. n.p., 1988.

Lammens, Henri. *Les "Perses" du Liban et l'origine des Métoualis*. Beyrouth, 1929.

Makdisi, Saree. "Laying Claim to Beirut: Urban Narrative and Spatial Identity in the Age of Solidere," *Critical Inquiry* 23 (Spring 1997): 661–705.

Makdisi, Ussama. *The Culture of Sectarianism*. Berkeley: University of California Press, 2000.

Mallat, Chibli. *The Renewal of Islamic Law: Muhammad Baqer as-Sadr, Najaf and the Shi'i International*. Cambridge: Cambridge University Press, 1993.

Mervin, Sabrina. *Un Réformisme chiite: Ulémas et lettrés du Gabal 'Amil (actuel Liban-Sud) de la fin de l'empire Ottoman à l'indépendance du Liban*. Paris: Karthala, 2000.

Moussalli, Ahmad S. "Islamism: Modernisation of Islam or Islamisation of Knowledge." In Roel Meijer, ed., *Cosmopolitanism, Identity and Authenticity*. Surrey: Curzon, 1999.

Al-Muhajir, Ja'far. *Al-Hijra al-'amiliyya ila Iran fi al-'asr al-safavi*. Beirut, 1989.

Naba, René. *Rafic Hariri: Un homme d'affaires premier ministre*. Paris: L'Harmattan, 1999.

Nakash, Yitzhak. "The Nature of Shi'ism in Iraq." In Faleh Abdul-Jabar, ed., *Ayatollahs, Sufis and Ideologues: State, Religion, and Social Movements in Iraq*. London: Saqi, 2002, 23–35.

Nandy, Ashis. "The Politics of Secularism and the Recovery of Religious Tolerance." In Veena Das, ed., *Mirrors of Violence*. Delhi: Oxford University Press, 1990.

Nasr, Vali. *The Shia Revival. How Conflicts within Islam Will Shape the Future.* New York: Norton, 2006.

Norton, Richard Augustus. *Amal and the Shi'a: Struggle for the Soul of Lebanon.* Austin: University of Texas Press, 1987.

Norton, Richard Augustus, and 'Ali Safa. "'Ashura in Nabatiyya," *Middle East Insight* 15 (2000): 21–28.

Ofeisch, Sami. "Lebanon's Second Republic: Secular Talk, Sectarian Application," *Arab Studies Quarterly* (Winter 1999): 97–116.

Phares, Walid. *Lebanese Christian Nationalism: The Rise and Fall of an Ethnic Resistance.* Boulder: Rienner, 1995.

Pinault, David. *Horse of Karbala: Muslim Devotional Life in India.* New York: Palgrave, 2001.

———. *The Shiites: Ritual and Popular Piety in a Muslim Community.* New York: St. Martin's, 1992.

Qassem, Naim. *Hizbullah. The Story from Within.* London: Saqi, 2005.

Rahnema, Ali. *An Islamic Utopian: A Political Biography of 'Ali Shari'ati.* London: I. B. Tauris, 1998.

Ranstorp, Magnus. *Hizb'Allah in Lebanon: The Politics of the Western Hostage Crisis.* New York: St. Martin's, 1997.

Reuter, Bärbel. *Ashura-Feiern im Libanon: Zum politischen Potential eines religiösen Festes.* Hamburg: LIT, 1993.

Richani, Nizah. *Dilemmas of Democracy and Political Parties in Sectarian Societies: The Case of the Progressive Socialist Party of Lebanon, 1949–1996.* New York: St. Martin's Press, 1998.

Rieck, Andreas. "Rafiq Hariri," *Orient* 34, no. 2 (1993): 179–83.

———. *Die Schiiten und der Kampf um den Libanon: Politische Chronik, 1958–1988.* Hamburg: Deutsches Orient-Institut, 1989.

Rosiny, Stefan. "The Tragedy of Fatima al-Zahra in the Debate of Two Shiite Theologians in Lebanon." In Rainer Brunner and Werner Ende, eds., *The Twelver Shia in Modern Times: Religious Culture and Political History.* Boston: Brill, 2001.

———. *Shia's Publishing in Lebanon: With Special Reference to Islamic and Islamist Publications.* Berlin: Das Arabische Buch, 1999.

———. *Islamismus bei den Shiiten im Libanon: Religion im Übergang von Tradition zur Moderne.* Berlin: Das Arabische Buch, 1996.

Rowe, Peter G., and Hashim Sarkis, eds. *Projecting Beirut: Episodes in the Construction and Reconstruction of a Modern City.* Munich, New York: Prestel, 1998.

Saad-Ghorayeb, Amal. *Hizbullah: Politics and Religion.* London: Pluto, 2002.

Sadr, Musa. *Al-Islam: Din wa Hayat.* Beirut: al-Kitab al-Lubnani, 1961.

Salem, Elise. *Constructing Lebanon: A Century of Literary Narratives.* Gainesville: University Press of Florida, 2003.

Salibi, Kamal. *A House of Many Mansions: The History of Lebanon Reconsidered.* Berkeley: University of California Press, 1988.

Samii, Abbas William. "The Security Relationship between Lebanon and Pre-Revolutionary Iran." In Houchang Chehabi, ed., *Distant Relations: Five Hundred Years of Iranian-Lebanese Relations.* London: I. B. Tauris, 2006.

———. "The Shah's Lebanon Policy: The Role of SAVAK," *Middle Eastern Studies* 33, no. 1 (1997): 66–91.

Shaery-Eisenlohr, Roschanack. "Imagining Shiʻite Iran: Transnationalism and Religious Authenticity in the Muslim World," *Iranian Studies* 40(1): 17–35.

———. "Post-revolutionary Iran and Shiʻi Lebanon: Contested Histories of Shiʻi Transnationalism," *International Journal of Middle East Studies* 39(2): 271–89.

Shanahan, Roger. *The Shiʻa of Lebanon: Clans, Parties and Clerics.* London: I. B. Tauris, 2005.

Shapira, Shimon. *Hizbullah between Iran and Lebanon* [in Hebrew]. Tel Aviv: Hakibbutz Hameuchad, 2000.

Sharara, Waddah. *Dawlat Hizb Allah: Lubnan mujtamaʻan islamiyyan.* Beirut: Dar al-Nahar, 1996.

Shissler, A. Holly. *Between Two Empires: Ahmet Ağaoğlu and the New Turkey.* London: I. B. Tauris, 2003.

Sivan, Emmanuel. "Arab Nationalism in the Age of the Islamic Resurgence." In James Jankowski and Israel Gershoni, eds., *Rethinking Nationalism in the Arab Middle East.* New York: Columbia University Press, 1997.

———. "Islamic Radicalism: Sunni and Shiʻite." In Emanual Sivan and Menachem Friedman, eds., *Religious Radicalism and Politics in the Middle East.* Albany: SUNY Press, 1990.

Sobhani, Sohrab. *The Pragmatic Entente: Israeli-Iranian Relations, 1948–1988.* New York: Praeger, 1989.

el-Solh, Raghid. *Lebanon and Arabism: National Identity and State Formation.* London: I. B. Tauris, 2004.

Stewart, Devin. "The Portrayal of an Academic Rivalry: Najaf and Qum in the Writings and Speeches of Khomeini, 1964–1978." In Linda S. Walbridge, ed., *The Most Learned of the Shiʻa. The Institution of the Marjaʻ Taqlid.* Oxford: Oxford University Press, 2001.

Traboulsi, Fawwaz. *A History of Modern Lebanon.* London: Pluto, 2007.

Van der Veer, Peter. *Religious Nationalism: Hindus and Muslims in India*. Berkeley: University of California Press, 1994.

———. *Imperial Encounters: Religion and Modernity in India and Britain*. Princeton: Princeton University Press, 2001.

Van der Veer, Peter, and Hartmut Lehmann, eds. *Nation and Religion: Perspectives on Europe and Asia*. Princeton: Princeton University Press, 1999.

Walbridge, Linda S., ed. *The Most Learned of the Shiʻa: The Institution of the Marjaʻ Taqlid*. Oxford: Oxford University Press, 2001.

Weiss, Max. "The Cultural Politics of Shiʻi Modernism. Morality and Gender in Early 20th-Century Lebanon," *International Journal of Middle East Studies* 39 (2): 249–70.

Wiley, Joyce. "Alima Bint al-Huda, Women's Advocate." In Linda S. Walbridge, ed., *The Most Learned of the Shiʻa: The Institution of the Marjaʻ Taqlid*. Oxford: Oxford University Press, 2001.

———. *The Islamic Movement of Iraqi Shiʻas*. Boulder: Rienner, 1992.

Wimmen, Heiko. "Beirut: Visionen einer Nation," *Beiruter Blätter* 3 (1995): 9–20.

Woolard, Kathryn A., and Bambi Schieffelin. "Language Ideology," *Annual Review of Anthropology* 23 (1994): 55–82.

Zaman, Muhammad Qasim. *The Ulama in Contemporary Islam: Custodians of Change*. Princeton: Princeton University Press, 2002.

Zamir, Meir. *The Formation of Modern Lebanon*. Ithaca: Cornell University Press, 1985.

Zonis, Marvin, and Daniel Brumberg. *Khomeini, the Islamic Republic of Iran, and the Arab World*. Harvard Middle East Papers 5. Cambridge: Center for Middle Eastern Studies, Harvard University, 1987.

Index

71; Islamic school competition with, 63; -Muslim coexistence, 179–80; Persian language study by Muslims and, 165–66, 252n13; poem by, 192; Sunnis and, merchants as, 20–22; Syrian presence opposition from, 202; West Beirut, 47–48

Christianity, 38, 63, 85; dominance of, 2, 91–94; merchants of Sunni-ism and, 20–22; Sunnis and, West Beirut's, 47–48

Citizenship, xii; Amal v. Hizbullah, 38; Hizbullah shaping of, 39–40; loyal, transnationalism and, 10–13; piety and, 40, 224n33

Civil war, 94, 158–59, 200–1; Amal party during/after, 32–34

Class, 41–42, 43–45, 155; 'Ashura com-memorations and, 153; *haydar* and, 134–35; *metwali* as low, 46; under-, 43–45; West Beirut stereotyped, 47–48

Coexistence: Beirut, 184; politics of, 28–30, 149–50

Coexistence, religious (ta'ayush), 21, 23, 28; Maronites and, 23; Muslim-Christian, 179–80

Cole, Juan, 10–11

Colley, Linda, 4

Color, taste and, 46

Commemoration(s): 'Ashura, 31, 57–58, 65, 120, 130–36, 131, 153–55, 156–57, 195, 232n64, 246n26; Chamran, 2002, 117–18; Khomeini, death of, 72; new forms of, 153–55

Communities: membership in, impor-tance of, xii; merchant, Christian/

Sunni, 20–22; religious, xi, 28–29; religious, names of, xi

Competition, 216; Amal-Hizbullah, 76–77, 86; Amal-Iranian ruling elite, 118; identity, 22; nationalism, 22, 86; political, 22; school, Chris-tian/Islamic, 63

Confessional system, 27

Consensus, 212

The Consultative Center for Studies and Documentation (CCSD), 186–87

Council of the South (majlis al-janub), 32–34

Crying, 153–55

Cultural centers, funding proposal for, 183–85

Culture, 159; Amal party's Lebanese, 123–24; ICC monitoring/controlling, 161–63, 164–65; Iranian politics and, 158–97; language and, 62; new policy of, 161–62; Shi'ites lacking, 40–41

Curriculum, hidden, 75

Da'wa Party, 34–35, 74

Al-Dahiyya, xix, 15, 31, 40–41; Iran v., 178–79; Israeli-Lebanese summer war influence on, 204–5; public schools in, 54, 226n2, 255n54

Damascus, 200

Day of the Woman, 176–78

Deeb, Lara, 66, 150, 226n63. 246n25, 247n32

Democracy, 202–3, 212, 217

Dialect: 'Ashura commemoration, 195; Lebanese Arabic, 21

Dialogue (hiwar), 21

278

Headscarf, *see* Hijab

Hegemony: Christian ideological, 6; Hariri strategy for breaking, 185–86; Maronite, 49, 83–84, 91–94

Hidden curriculum, 75

Hijab (headscarf), 79, 139, 258n72; as school uniform, 75

Hinnebusch, Raymond, 10

Historian(s): nationalism perspective of, 10–11; al-Zahra perspective of, 152

History: of India, 173; Iran/*haydar*, 137–38; Iranian cultural activities in Lebanon, 159–61; Iran/Lebanon, ICC using, 162–64; Islamic, Arabism connected to, 145–46; Jabal 'Amil/Shi'ite, 126–28, 169; Maronite version of, 173; *see also* Memory

Hiwar, *see* Dialogue

Hizbullah party, xiii–xiv, 3, 7, 114–15, 194–97; Amal split into, 37, 108, 115–17; 'Ashura commemorations taken over by, 135–36; citizens shaped by, 39–40; creation of, 12, 90–91, 172; disarming of, 2005 issue of, 201; general secretary of, 113–14, 138; Hariri and, 182; *haydar* not practiced by, 137–38; ideologue of, 66; institutions of, 182–97; Iranian government support of, 182–83, 196–97, 205–7; -Iran ties, 14, 72; Islam viewed by, 38, 72, 205, 206–9; Israeli soldiers kidnapping by, 204–10; JTDI and, 85; leadership competition between Amal and, 76–77; nationalism/vision of, 66–72, 86; poor Shi'ites alliance with, 181–82; representatives of, 39; research center for, 186–87; resis-

tance/resistance society and, 7, 70, 71; rhetoric of, unofficial use of, 112, *112*; schools run by, 52; transnationalism ties of, 37–39, 72; *vilayat-i faqih* for, 209

Holiday: official weekly/Christian dominance through changing, 2; Ramadan, 65

Husayn, Saddam, ix, 214, 216

ICC, *see* Islamic Republic of Iran

Identity card, Amal member, *103*

Identity, Shi'ite: competition over, 22; de-/reterritorializing, 158–82; as disadvantaged (mahrum), 36–37; Iranian revolution altering Shi'ite, xiv; production of, x, 206; transnationalism and, 74

Ideologues, of Hizbullah party, 66

Ideology(ies), 11–12; Hizbullah, 37–39; Iranian government, Lebanese presence need for, 12; linguistic, 125–26

Image: Council of the South portrayal of, 32–34; Iran's, 160; Karbala, 49; mainstream/legitimate, 141; piety, 120; secular, 107; South Lebanon, 33–34; subaltern, 36–37, 71; Tehran's, 179

Image/imagery: Hizbullah's religious, 66; Karbala, 49

Imam: Shi'ite, third, 5; twelfth, absence of, 142–43

Imam Husayn, 135, 153–55, 180–81

Imam Khomeini, 105–6

India, 4, 147, 173, 223n26; history of, 173

Infrastructure, school/public, weak, 50–51

Lebanese University (LU), 165; Persian language taught at, 169, 170

Lebanon: as Christian/Sunni nation of merchants, 20–22; citizenship of, xii; cultural politics in, 158–97; fieldwork/research in, 13–16; Greater, xi; India and, 223n26; Iranian cultural activities in, history of, 159–61; Iranian films in, 175–76; Iranians' knowledge of, 244n12; Mount, 21, 23; opposed visions of/dichotomy within, 20; presidents of, 22, 59; prime minister of, postwar, 185; religious communities in, xi, 28–29; since February 2005, 199–204; Syrian forces in, 200–4; *see also* Israeli-Lebanese summer war; South Lebanon

Lehmann, Hartmut, 4

Libanism, 21, 173; Arabism and, dichotomy between, 20

Liberation Movement of Iran (LMI), 93, 94–99, 109–13; founding members of, 93

LMI, *see* Liberation Movement of Iran

LNM, *see* Lebanese National Movement

LNM-PLO coalition, 100

Loan-words, Arabic, 124

Lobnan (Chamran), 95

Local authenticity, 130–38; foreign tradition from, 136–38

Loyalty, 35–36; Hizbullah, 37–39

LU, *see* Lebanese University

Mabarrat Charity Foundation (jam'iyyat al-mabarrat al-khayriyya), 74–76

Madaris al-haraka (Amal schools), 52–53

Madaris al-Mahdi (Hizbullah-run schools), 52

Mahrum (disadvantaged), 155

Mahrumin, bourgeois: Amal party as, 32–34; Shi'ite marginalization and, 40–43

Majlis al-janub (Council of the South), 32–34

Makdisi, Ussama, 8, 9–10, 41

Manners, system of *(Tarof)*, 139

March 8 alliance, 200

March 14 alliance, 200

Marginalization, Shi'ite, xiv, 23; class/coexistence, 155; continuing, 201–2, 211; *Mahrumin* and, 40–43; Shah support of, 91; struggle against, 23

Marja', 97–98; Fadlallah as, 144; Khomeini as, 143; network, 208

Marja'iyya, 142–44, 182–97

Marja'iyya (religious establishments), xv

Maronite(s): French importance to, 21; hegemony, 49, 83–84, 91–94; home of, 21; Libanism of, 173; nationalism, 23; Sadr and, 30–32, 93–94

Martyrdom, 146, 154, 156

Martyrs Foundation, 60

Marxism, sectarianism viewed by, 8

Mediterranean civilization, Maronite history and, 173

Membership training, Hizbullah, 40

Memory, x, xiii, 11, 23, 32, 115, 116, 127, 164, 239n24; Chamran, M., and, 117–18; haydar and, 137; ICC and, 162; India's, Persian influence in, 173; Iranian revolution/production of, 113–15; Iraq and, 212–14

Merchants, Christian/Sunni, 20–22

Metwali, 46

modernization and, 5–6; nationalism and, 27; public expression of, 6; Sadr's view of, 26, 27–30, 31, 32; schools taken over by, 50–51; schools teaching, 55; South Lebanon and, 52; state-based, Iran's, 152; teaching of, 64–66; use of term, 4; *see also* Religious education

Religion-politics divide, 7, 143

Religious coexistence, (ta'ayush), 21, 23, 28

Religious communities, Lebanon, xi, 28–29

Religious education, 62–66; divisions in, three, 65; extracurricular activities in, 65–66, 81; textbooks for, 62–64, 75, 79–81, 229n25

Religious institutions (marja'iyya), xv

Religious nationalism: Sadr's, 26, 27–30, 31, 32

Religious performance, 30; class and, 153; public, 42

Religious practices: class and, 134–35; *Haydar*, 132, *133*, 134–35, 136, 137–38, 246n20; mourning ceremonies as, 138–42, 156–57; Muharram, 46–49; pre-Islamic, 159–60; ta'ziyya, 147

Research institutions, Hizbullah party, 186–87, 256n64

Research, methodology, 13

Resistance: to Fadlallah as *marja'*, 144; Hizbullah, 7, 70, 71; to Israel, 73, 105, 196, 236n4; Israeli occupation aid, 119–20; to Sadr, 25–26, 30–32, 97

Resistance society, Hizbullah/Fadlallah as part of, 7, 71

Revolution, Cedar, 203

Revolution, Iranian: Amal and, 105–6; credit for success of, 167; cultural politics from, 161; Hizbullah and, 71; language prior to, 126; memories of, production of, 113–15; rhetoric before/after, 167–69; scholarship focus on pre/post, 14; Shi'ite identity politics altered by, xiv; victory celebration of, 72

Revolution, Islamic, 183; language of, 169–71

Rieck, Andreas, 108, 242n58

Rule of jurisprudent *(vilayat-i faqih)*, 104, 105, 106, 107–8, 109–10, 143–44, 207–9, 214–15

Ruling elite, Iran's, 205–7; competition between Amal and, 118; establishment of, 89–90; Hizbullah strategies for dealing with, 194–97; Palestinian cause supported by, 89–90, 187–88; Shi'ite ties to, 72–74, 76

Saad-Ghorayeb, Amal, 5, 242n58

Al-Sadr, Muhammad Sadiq, 215

Al-Sadr, Muqtada, 215

Sadr, Musa, xiii–xiv, 14–15, 24–27, 101, 106–7, 180; accent v. genealogy of, 128–30, 230n42; activism prior to, Shi'ite, 24–25; Amal party influenced by Shamseddine and, 36; birthplace of, 129; contemporary of, 74; disappearance of, 103–4, 241n52; Fadlallah allusion to, 113; family/educational background of, 24; Hizbullah general secretary portrayal of, 114–15; Hizbullah party and, xiv; interview with, 29, 129; Maronites and, 30–32, 93–94;